DATE DUE

NO 24 '93		
MR 10 '95		
AP 28 '95		
MY 3 '96		
OC 1 '96		
FE 8 '01		
NO 23 '02		
DE 14 '02		

DEMCO 38-296

Modernity and Tradition

"Presented with the compliments of
the Ministry of Information
in order to enhance understanding of
the history, objectives and achievements of
the Kingdom of Saudi Arabia"

In the Name of Allah,
the Compassionate,
the Merciful

DEDICATION

To King Fahd bin Abdul Aziz Al Sa'ud, the patron of the Saudi revival and leader of the Kingdom's progress and development.

If a man (whether he be a national leader, a military commander, a social reformer, or a scientific researcher) performed a single act in the national interest which secured the defense of his homeland, or assured for his country a prominent place amongst the nations of the world, or improved living conditions for the citizens, or ensured the prosperity of his people, or established security, stability and social justice, then such a man would, from the national viewpoint, deserve for this single act the highest degree of admiration and respect.

What then would history say of a man who has achieved all this for his country, many times over!

Any attempt to comprehend the scope and scale of the achievements of King Fahd bin Abdul Aziz can be only partially successful, for his unique personality and outstanding abilities are not limited to the material benefits he has brought to the Kingdom of Saudi Arabia, but extend to issues of morality and humanity in the world at large. King Fahd has been recognized as a "powerful statesman; skilful, talented and experienced politician; leader of his country's march to development; a powerful voice for Arab and Islamic solidarity; and a moderate international politician who works tirelessly to achieve peace based upon justice for all nations."

This book is dedicated with the deepest respect, appreciation and gratitude to the Custodian of the two Holy Mosques, King Fahd bin Abdul Aziz. His acceptance of this dedication will do me the greatest honor, for this modest book is but one of the fruits of his flourishing and auspicious reign.

Fouad Al-Farsy

MODERNITY AND TRADITION

The Saudi Equation

FOUAD AL-FARSY

KEGAN PAUL INTERNATIONAL

London and New York

PO Box 256, London WC1B 3SW, England

Distributed by
John Wiley & Sons Ltd
Southern Cross Trading Estate
1 Oldlands Way, Bognor Regis,
West Sussex, PO22 9SA, England

Routledge, Chapman & Hall Inc
29 West 35th Street
New York, NY 10001, USA

The Canterbury Press Pty Ltd
Unit 2, 71 Rushdale Street
Scoresby, Victoria 3179, Australia

© Fouad Al-Farsy 1990

Set in Palatino 11/13pt
by Columns Design & Production Services Ltd, Reading

Printed in Great Britain

ISBN 0 7103 0395 5

British Library Cataloguing in Publication Data
al – Farsy, Fouad, 1946–
   Modernity and tradition: The Saudi equation.
   1. Saudi Arabia, 1964
   I. Title
   953.8053

   ISBN 0–7103–0395–5

US Library of Congress Cataloging in Publication Data
Applied for

Contents

DS
204

Foreword

More than thirteen years ago, when I began preparing my first book in English (entitled *Saudi Arabia: A Case Study in Development*), I based my study of the subject on a purely academic foundation. At that time, there was an urgent need in the West for reference books with well-documented information on the Kingdom of Saudi Arabia. As a result, *Saudi Arabia: A Case Study in Development* has become a standard reference source in many universities, schools and other centers of learning, particularly in the United States of America and Great Britain.

A country's development does not take place in a vacuum and it was therefore essential in this earlier work that the main subject (the Kingdom's development) should be set into an historical, political and social context. I therefore devoted much of the text to a summary of this background information, starting with the Kingdom's geographical location and proceeding with a brief account of its history, its political importance and its role in the world economy. Within this context, I described the development and progress the Kingdom had achieved, outlining the country's governmental structure, its administrative divisions, its available investment potential, its prevailing legal and commercial regulations, and its future plans and ambitions.

Collating all these data in a book of 264 pages revealed the difficulty of balancing such an equation. One of the difficulties was (and still is) that development is not an historical event which can be recorded once and for all, but a continuing process which demands permanent follow-up, lest the information supplied should become out of date. As a result, for every new edition of *Saudi Arabia: A Case Study in Development*, (of which there have been four), I had to revise substantial sections of the book.

I have now reached the conclusion that it is no longer sensible to continue simply altering the data, since the new information on the Kingdom's development, which now extends to many areas not originally covered in the earlier work, imposes an insupportable strain on that book's structure.

I have therefore decided to publish this new book, *Modernity and Tradition: The Saudi Equation*, as a natural extension of my earlier researches. This new book, which has been structured to encompass all aspects of the Kingdom's development, contains the latest statistical data on the Kingdom's progress, together with the newly revised background information of the former book. Thus each of the books complements the other, for each records the relevant information at a particular stage in the Kingdom of Saudi Arabia's continuing developmental process.

F.A.-F.

Preface

This book greatly extends the scope of the author's original work (*Saudi Arabia: A Case Study in Development*) to cover all major aspects of development in the Kingdom of Saudi Arabia. In its new form it has three main aims:

- to give a succinct account of the historical development of the Kingdom
- to provide a useful reference book for any specialist reader (be he academic, businessman, journalist or politician) who seeks detailed and up-to-date statistical information on the Kingdom's progress
- to provide the lay public with an overview of what must surely rank as the most ambitious development program ever undertaken

In attempting to fulfil these objectives, the author confesses that he hopes to modify the stereotype of the Kingdom and of its citizens so often projected by the Western media.

The sources on which the author has drawn are many. References to direct quotations in the text and the bibliography give some indication of the author's debt to others. Most of the statistical information in the book has been drawn from Saudi Arabian Government sources and the author's debt to the ministries and Government officers who have been so generous with their time and patience is here acknowledged.

In a book which attempts to cover so large a subject, some errors are inevitable despite all efforts to eliminate them. Responsibility for those that remain rests with the author.

Fouad Al-Farsy

Tables

Charts

Maps and Illustrations

MAPS

ILLUSTRATIONS

(Section following page 200)

1   King Abdul Aziz Al Saud, the founder of the Kingdom of Saudi Arabia
2   King Fahd bin Abdul Aziz, Custodian of the Two Holy Mosques
3   HRH Crown Prince Abdullah bin Abdul Aziz,
    Deputy Prime Minister and Head of the National Guard
4   HRH Crown Prince Sultan bin Abdul Aziz, Second Deputy Prime
    Minister, Minister of Defence and Aviation, and the Inspector General
5   View of Jeddah today
6   The Holy Mosque in Makkah
7   King Khalid International Airport in Riyadh (internal view)
8   Traditional architecture in Riyadh City
9   King Fahd bin Abdul Aziz, laying the foundation stone for one of the
    major developmental projects in the Kingdom: to the right
    of the King stands HRH Prince Abdullah bin Abdul Aziz,
    and to the left HRH Prince Sultan bin Abdul Aziz

All the photographs in this book have been supplied by
the Saudi photographer Khaled Kadr

Introduction

For a variety of reasons, few would deny the vital importance of the Kingdom of Saudi Arabia. First, it is a bridge between the Western world and Asia. With Africa on one side and Iran and South Asia on the other, it is in the middle of the strategically important Indian Ocean area which is a zone of concentration between the communist and non-communist centers of power. Secondly, Saudi Arabia's unique form of government suggests its significance to comparative politics and to development studies generally. The only nation to use a sacred scripture, namely the *Quran*, as a Constitution, it is adjusting well to the conditions of the twentieth century while sustaining its distinctive Islamic identity. The fact that Islam appears not to be an obstacle or a hindrance towards progress and development suggests that a secular system is not necessarily a prerequisite for progress. King Faisal, on a State visit to Malaysia, stated that he felt

> sorry for those who think Islam . . . impedes progress or stands as an obstacle in the way of advanced development. Those who think so must have not understood [the] essential principles of Islam. The opposite is the truth. The most important requirements Islam calls for are to maintain progress, to carry out justice, to create equality, and to breed in people good behavior and in nations moral conduct.

A third reason for the importance of Saudi Arabia is the crucial significance of its vast petroleum deposits, which add more political and economic weight to the Kingdom's position. Petroleum production creates a condition of development in the context of wealth rather than poverty. Such developmental affluence is shared only by Kuwait, the United Arab Emirates, Bahrain and Qatar. But these are small states compared with Saudi Arabia which, geographically and economically, is a major state in the Middle East.

Fourthly, and most important, is the fact that Saudi Arabia is the religious site for more than 1,000 million Muslims all over the world. This cannot be overlooked, especially when it is realized that Islam is a way of life closely intertwined with daily living. Religion plays a very important role in a Muslim's life. The significance of religion is starting to fade away in at least two major religions of the world: Christianity and Judaism. In brief, Saudi Arabia's political and religious impact is tremendous and should be accounted for when dealing with the status of the Kingdom domestically, regionally, and internationally.

Fifthly, Saudi Arabia is a unique model of nation building in which a country has been able to transform its polity from the conditions of the eighteenth century to those of the twentieth century within three decades. Modernization and development have occurred and are still occurring at a slower but forceful pace and in a manner which will enable the Kingdom to maintain and preserve its culture, heritage, and distinctive identity. Most developing countries risk the loss of their cultural identity while modern transformation takes place. Alien societal norms and values, not in harmony with these nations' heritages and cultures, seem to overwhelm indigenous values.

The author unequivocally agrees with Ralph Braibanti's profound appraisal of the significance of Saudi Arabia's unique political system among the developing nations. Braibanti has stated that

> It has long been a theoretical ideal that transnationally induced change should be carefully articulated to the cultural context of the recipient nation. . . . A prerequisite of this is that the recipient nation identify and evaluate its own values and control both the quality and the rate of introduction of outside ideas which will modify these values.
>
> There are only three political systems in the world in which a conscious effort is made to control the admission of transnationally induced values in this way . . . Saudi Arabia [is one of these three political systems]
>
> *Source*: *Saudi Arabia: Contextual Considerations*, a report submitted to the Ford Foundation
> (Beirut, 1972)

A final and no less important reason for treating Saudi Arabia as a unique case is the fact that the Kingdom has strongly maintained an equilibrium in the process of establishing its political system *vis-à-vis* the various sequences and stages of development.

> Ideally a strong institutional base should be constructed before demands (inputs) escalate to a point at which they cannot easily be converted into effective governmental responses (output). This has not happened in most developing systems simply because the rapid expansion of mass participation and the idiosyncratic influences of foreign assistance which stimulate escalation of demands have made this impossible.
>
> *Source: Ibid*

Fortunately, Saudi Arabia's control over external influences on its own values and its ability to sponsor and finance the foreign assistance it needs has made it possible to control – to a great extent – the process of its development. The freedom thus provided by enormous wealth is a condition not enjoyed by most developing countries.

The uniqueness of the Kingdom is manifested in its political developmental process, which can be characterized by the relatively even development of institutions which have been selected as targets either by design or default. Braibanti characterizes it thus: ". . . [the] building of Saudi Arabian institutions start[ed] almost *de novo* [largely in the early 1950s]. The institutions which exist are of relatively equal organizational strength and viability". (*Ibid*) In a sense there exist two separate spheres of legal validity in Saudi Arabia: The judicial system based on *Shari'ah* (Islamic law) and the administrative, commercial, labor, and military institutions based on Western norms, each capable of coping with current needs, and each in its own sphere of influence.

The primary objective of this work is to deal as comprehensively as possible with the development of Saudi Arabia as a political, economic and social system. The need for such a study is suggested, in part, by the inadequacy of critical material dealing with Saudi Arabia.

Chapter 1

The geography of the Kingdom

This chapter offers a brief account of the main geographical characteristics of the Kingdom of Saudi Arabia. It includes sections on the Kingdom's size and population; on the natural resources with which the Kingdom is so generously endowed; on the climate; on the flora and fauna which, for a "desert kingdom", are surprisingly rich; and on the Kingdom's main regions and major cities.

Of necessity, the treatment of these subjects here is cursory. Those who seek more detailed information are referred to the sources mentioned in this chapter and to the Bibliography.

1.1   Saudi Arabia and its neighbors

The Kingdom of Saudi Arabia encompasses about four-fifths of the Arabian Peninsula, a land mass constituting a distinct geographical entity bordered on the west by the Red Sea, on the south by the Indian Ocean and on the east by the Arabian Gulf.

The Kingdom itself is bounded on the north by Jordan, Iraq and Kuwait; on the east by the Gulf, Bahrain, Qatar and the United Arab Emirates (consisting of Abu-Dhabi, Dubai, Sharjah, Ras Al-Khaimah, Fujairah, Umm Al-Qawain and Ajman); on the south by the Sultanate of Oman and the two Yemeni Republics (North and South), and on the west by the Red Sea.

Between Saudi Arabia and Kuwait there are two adjacent areas of neutral territory (the Neutral Zone) which, since 1966, have been divided between the two countries, with each administering its own portion. Another Neutral Zone, between the Kingdom and Iraq, existed until 1975 when it was agreed that the zone should be equally divided between the two parties.

Aside from the country's religious and economic significance,

> the potential importance of Saudi Arabia's geographical position is quickly apparent: it is strategically located between Africa and mainland

Asia, lies close to the Suez Canal and has frontiers on both the Red Sea and the Arabian Gulf.

Source: Saudi Arabia, Its People, Its Society, Its Culture by George Lipsky (New Haven, CT: HRAF Press, 1959, page 19)

1.2 Characteristics of the Kingdom of Saudi Arabia

1.2.1 SIZE AND POPULATION

Saudi Arabia occupies 2,240,000 square kilometers (865,000 square miles).

According to the 1974 census (the last available), the Kingdom's population was just over 7 million. But, since then, by all accounts the population has grown dramatically. More recent estimates (by, for example, the World Bank, 1987) give a figure of above 11 million. The official estimate in 1987 was 13.6 million. Currently, according to a reference from the Agency of Public Statistics in Riyadh, the population is estimated at 14,435,000.

The estimated population density in 1986 was 5.4 people per square kilometer, a figure roughly comparable to the population density of the United States in 1790.

As an indication of the growth of urbanization, we quote the population figures for the city of Riyadh, capital of the Kingdom of Saudi Arabia. In 1862, the population (as estimated by W Palgrave) was 7,500. One hundred years later it was 169,000 (Riyadh City Planning Office). By 1982, the estimate was 1.5 million.

1.2.2 NATURAL RESOURCES

Oil
Any survey of Saudi Arabia's natural resources must begin with oil.

According to the latest estimate of the Kingdom's recoverable crude oil, issued by Aramco in January 1989 at the end of a six-year study, reserves now stand at 252,380 million barrels. This figure represents an increase of 85,000 million barrels on the previous estimate and means that Saudi Arabia has roughly 25% of the world's proven oil reserves. Using the latest estimate as a base, we can calculate that, on its current OPEC production quota of 4.5 million barrels a day, the oil reserves of the Kingdom of Saudi Arabia will last for more than 150 years.

Gas
The same Aramco study put the Kingdom's proven gas reserves at 177.3 trillion cubic feet, an increase of 25% over the last estimate.

Minerals
In addition to its vast oil and gas reserves, the Kingdom is rich in mineral deposits. According to the Fourth Five Year Development Plan, gold has been discovered at

some 600 sites around the Kingdom and a total of 29 prospects have been drilled. The Mahad al Dhabab gold mine has been re-opened by Petromin with the intention of developing a high-grade underground goldmine with a capacity of 400 tons of ore per day. This venture has encouraged further exploration for gold elsewhere in the Kingdom.

Silver and base metal deposits (bauxite, copper, iron, lead, tin and zinc), as well as non-metallic minerals (bentonite, diatomite, fluorite, potash and high-purity silica sand) have all been discovered, attesting to the wealth that remains, still largely unexploited, beneath the Kingdom's soil.

Water

In a country with the geography and climate of the Kingdom, water is a natural resource which must be highly valued and conserved. The Kingdom draws its water from four main sources:

- surface water, which is to be found predominantly in the west and south-west of the country. In 1985, surface water provided 10% of the Kingdom's supply.
- ground water, held in aquifers, some of which are naturally replenished, while others are non-renewable. In 1985, ground water provided 84% of the Kingdom's supply, but it is noteworthy that most of this water came from non-renewable aquifers.
- desalinated seawater, a source of water production in which the Kingdom is now a world leader. Desalination technology, which also produces electricity, has reached an advanced stage of technology in the Kingdom and, in 1985, this source provided 5% of the Kingdom's supply. (Saudi daily production of desalinated water is currently running at about 5.5 million gallons, a quantity unequalled anywhere else in the world.)
- reclaimed wastewater, a source of water which is still in its early stages but which offers scope for considerable expansion. In 1985, the reclamation of wastewater provided 1% of the Kingdom's supply.

Source: Fourth Development Plan

1.2.3   PHYSICAL FEATURES AND CLIMATE

Structurally, the whole of Arabia is a vast platform of ancient rocks, once continuous with north-east Africa. In relatively recent geological time a series of great fissures opened, as the result of which a large trough, or rift valley, was formed and later occupied by the sea, to produce the Red Sea and the Gulf of Aden. The Arabian platform is tilted, with its highest part in the extreme west, along the Red Sea, and it slopes gradually down from the west to the east. Thus the Red Sea coast is often bold and mountainous, whereas the Arabian Gulf coast is flat, low-lying and fringed with extensive coral reefs which make it difficult to approach the shore in many places.

Source: Middle East and North Africa (Europa Publications, 1989)

Geographically, Saudi Arabia is divided into four (and if the *Rub'al-Khali* is included, five) major regions. The first is Najd, a high country in the heart of the Kingdom; secondly, Hijaz, the region along which lies the Red Sea coast. The region of Asir, in the southern Red Sea–Yemen border area, constitutes the third region. Fourthly, there is Al-Hasa, the sandy and stormy eastern part of Saudi Arabia, the richest of all the regions in petroleum (see map on page 11).

The Najd region, considered the heartland of Saudi Arabia both physically and culturally, is a vast eroded plateau, consisting of areas of uplands, broad valleys and dry rivers. The area also contains a number of marshes. These are thought to be the remnants of inland seas which existed in ancient geological times, but most of the Najd region is arid, with some oases in the north around Buraydah and Unaizah. At the centre of the Najd is the royal capital of Riyadh. The area around Kharj which lies south of Riyadh, has now become a major source of wheat, part of the Kingdom's burgeoning agricultural industry; while 300 miles to the north of Riyadh lies the province of Qasim, an even larger farming area which has contributed on a massive scale to the Kingdom's self-sufficiency in wheat and poultry. The climate of the region is hot and dry in summer and cold in winter. Summer temperatures sometimes exceed 45 °C, while in winter the temperature falls to 5 °C or lower.

The Hijaz includes the rest of the west coast region, along with the mountain chain (with peaks rising to 3,000 meters) decreasing gradually in elevation as it moves northward, and the coastal plain bordering the Red Sea. In this region is the busy seaport of Jeddah, known as the Islamic Port of Jeddah, a thriving commercial center. Of greatest note is that the Hijaz region contains the holiest cities of Islam – Makkah and Medina – which are visited by well over a million Muslims annually. The coastal region of the Hijaz is renowned for its humidity, with summer temperatures rising to above 50 °C.

The Asir region is the relatively fertile area of coastal mountains in the extreme south-west (near North Yemen). Mountain peaks rise to 3,000 meters and with ample rainfall to support cultivation, Asir has always been relatively densely populated. With the implementation of Government irrigation schemes, the agricultural potential of the region is being increasingly exploited.

The Al-Hasa region, also called the Eastern Province, is the country's wealthiest area, containing its massive petroleum resources. The headquarters of the Arabian-American Oil Company (Aramco) is located in this region at Dhahran, a few miles from the administrative capital and port of Dammam. Ras Tanura, the world's largest petroleum port, is located to the north of Dhahran. Up the coast is the site of the Kingdom's new industrial complex at Jubail. The fertile oasis-cities of Qatif and Hofof are also located here. A special weather phenomenon affecting chiefly the Eastern Province is the dust-storm with strong north-westerly winds, called the *Shamal*. These are prevalent during late spring and early summer, reaching their greatest frequency in June.

In the south of the Kingdom is the famous *Rub'al-Khali* (the Empty Quarter), a massive, trackless expanse of shifting sand dunes – one of the largest sand deserts in the world – which covers an area of more than 500,000 square kilometers and extends to 1,200 by 500 kilometers.

1.2.4   FLORA AND FAUNA

The stereotype of the Kingdom as a dry, barren desert devoid of almost all flora and fauna, a view which an airflight across much of the Kingdom tends to confirm, is far from correct. Of course, both plants and animals have had to adapt to the rigors of the climate but, for those who look, there is a wealth of wildlife to be discovered, even in the desert regions – and, as we have already noted, there are parts of the Kingdom, notably the Asir region, which enjoy ample rainfall and support a wide variety of crops as well as plants and animals.

Flora
In recent years, the Kingdom's flora has attracted increasing interest, resulting in the publication of several books on the subject. *Wild Flowers of Central Arabia* by Betty A Lipscombe Vincett lists more than 80 wild flowers growing in a region often thought to be entirely barren. Desert regions also support Acacias and desert shrubs, salt bushes and tussock grass, as well as cacti. More fertile regions boast date palms and, in the shade of these desert trees, apricot, lime and quince trees thrive, together with grape vines and vegetables.

With the Kingdom's determined effort to irrigate and cultivate the desert, we must not omit those vast areas of the Kingdom devoted to the production of cereal crops (barley, millet and wheat).

Fauna
A wide variety of fauna have their habitat in the Arabian peninsula, despite the often harsh physical conditions.

Source: *Arabian Fauna* by John and Patricia Gasperetti (Middle East Economic Digest 1981)

There are some ten species of birds indigenous to the Kingdom of Saudi Arabia and literally hundreds more are passing migrants. In the winter birds of prey, including falcons, arrive in the Kingdom. Other seasonal visitors include doves, ducks, geese, the houbara, kingfishers, martins, owls, pipits, quail, swallows, vultures of various types and warblers.

Crows, black kites and, above all, sparrows, encouraged by more plentiful sources of water, have thrived within the Kingdom.

Asir has the richest bird population of any region within the Kingdom. Bustards, eagles, goshawks, linnets, magpies, partridges, thrushes and wood-peckers are amongst the species to be found there at some time of the year.

Mammalian life is equally rich. Antelopes, baboons, honey badgers, bats, camels, cats, dormice, foxes, gazelles, gerbils, goats, hamsters, hedgehogs, hyenas, jackals, jerboas, leopards, mongooses, porcupines, rats, sheep, shrews, voles and wolves are amongst those mammals still to be found in some part of the Kingdom, though unhappily hunting has brought some of the more vulnerable species close to extinction.

The oryx was one such endangered species, saved by the determined efforts of the Fauna Preservation Society and the worldwide support the Society's efforts engendered. Oryx, captured in Saudi Arabia, were bred in captivity in the United States of America. Although still limited in number, there are now sufficient for some to be returned to the wild.

To this list must be added a wide variety of lizards (some 100 species) and snakes (53 species, including some highly venomous sea-snakes).

This account of the flora and fauna of the Kingdom of Saudi Arabia, though obviously brief and far from complete, at least serves to correct the widely held impression that the Kingdom is a desert devoid of wildlife.

The National Commission for Wildlife Conservation and Development (NCWCD)
As evidence of the Kingdom's commitment to the conservation, protection and development of the wildlife population (including both marine and terrestrial life), we should note the functions of the National Commission for Wildlife Conservation and Development:

1   To encourage and carry out scientific research in different fields of biology, with special emphasis on the plant and animal life of Saudi Arabia.
2   To promote public interest in the environmental issues related to the wildlife of Saudi Arabia, and to seek proper solutions to problems through organizing meetings, symposia and conferences.
3   To develop and implement plans and projects drawn up to preserve wildlife in its natural environment and to propose the establishment of protected areas and reserves for wildlife in the Kingdom, and execute relevant laws and regulations.

The Commission has a Board of Directors, consisting of the following:

1 His Royal Highness Prince Sultan bin Abdul Aziz, Second Deputy Prime Minister, Minister of Defense and Aviation, Inspector General, and Head of the Co-ordination Committee of Environment Protection: President
2 His Royal Highness Prince Naif bin Abdul Aziz, Minister of the Interior: Member
3 His Royal Highness Prince Sa'ud Al-Faisal, Minister of Foreign Affairs: Managing Director
4 His Royal Highness Prince Khalid Al-Faisal, Governor of the Asir region: Member
5 His Excellency Dr Abdul Rahman Abdulaziz Al-Sheikh, Minister of Agriculture and Water: Member
6 His Excellency Dr Professor Salih Al-Azil, President of King Abdulaziz City for Sciences and Technology: Member
7 His Excellency Dr Abdulbarr Al-Gain, President of Meteorology and Environment Protection: Member
8 His Excellency Professor Dr Abdulaziz Abuzinada, Secretary General of the Commission: Member

1.3 Major regions of the Kingdom

For administrative purposes, the Kingdom of Saudi Arabia is divided into five regions:

- Central Region (national center and capital city, Riyadh)
- Western Region (national centers, Jeddah and the Holy Cities of Makkah and Medina)
- Eastern Region (national centers, Dammam, Al Khobar)
- Northern Region (including Ha'il and Tabuk)
- Southern/South-Western Region (national centers, Abha, Khamis Mushayt)

1.4 Major cities of the Kingdom

1.4.1 RIYADH

Riyadh, which lies in the Najd region (central province), is the capital city of the Kingdom of Saudi Arabia and now rivals any modern city in the world for the splendor of its architecture. Broad highways sweep through the city, passing over or under each other in an impressive and still growing road network. Trees now bedeck the broad streets and avenues, giving pleasure to passers-by and shade to those who loiter beneath them.

Of all the Kingdom's developmental achievements, Riyadh is perhaps the most obvious and accessible to the foreign visitor. From the moment he lands at the King Khalid International Airport, itself a marvel of design wedding the traditional Arab style to the best of modern architecture in a happy marriage of spacious practicality, the traveller is aware that he has reached a city that must be counted one of the wonders of the twentieth century.

The history of Riyadh and its growth from a relatively small settlement into a great modern city is inextricably involved with the rise of the House of Sa'ud (see Chapter 2). With Riyadh as the capital of the Saudi Arabian Kingdom which Ibn Saud founded, it was inevitable that the city would grow. By 1375 AH (1955 AD), all ministries and government offices had been moved to or established in Riyadh. In the same year, a Royal Decree was issued raising the status of the municipality of Riyadh to that of mayoralty. Its scope of responsibility was greatly enlarged and its resources increased to enable it to cope with its growing size and population.

Today, apart from its importance as a seat of government and as a thriving commercial center, Riyadh is also a center of Arab diplomacy. It is the venue for many international Arab meetings and is the site of the Diplomatic Quarter, an area built specifically to accommodate all embassies and their staff.

In the midst of the city's extraordinary growth, history has not been forgotten. Preservation orders now ensure the survival of the Musmak fort which King Abdul Aziz scaled in 1902, a fitting reminder of a turning point in the history of the city and, indeed of the Arabian peninsula.

1.4.2 TAIF

Taif (which lies south-east of Jeddah and the Holy City of Makkah) stands 1,800 meters above sea-level. Its cooler temperatures have made it a traditional summer resort for both these cities and, in the summer months, the seat of government is moved from the dry heat of Riyadh to the more equable climate of Taif.

1.4.3 THE HOLY CITY OF MAKKAH

The Holy City of Makkah, which lies inland 73 kilometers east of Jeddah, was the birthplace of the Prophet Muhammad (peace be upon him) and was the city to which he returned after the migration to Medina in 622 AD. Makkah is the holiest city on earth to Muslims. Five times each day, the world's 1,000 million Muslims, wherever they may be, turn to the Holy City of Makkah to pray. And at least once in their lives, all Muslims who are not prevented by personal circumstance, perform the *Hajj*, the pilgrimage to Makkah. Thus each year, the Holy City of Makkah is host to some 2 million *hajjis* (pilgrims) from all over the world.

The Holy Mosque in Makkah houses the *Ka'aba*, in the corner of which is set the Black Stone which marks the starting point for the seven circuits of the Holy Mosque which every *hajji* must complete.

1.4.4   THE HOLY CITY OF MEDINA

Medina, which lies 447 kilometers north of the Holy City of Makkah, is the second holiest city in Islam. It was to Medina that the Prophet Muhammad (peace be upon him) and his followers, faced by the hostility and persecution of the Makkan merchants, departed in 622 AD – and, when the citizens of Medina asked the Prophet to live amongst them and to arbitrate in their affairs (an invitation taken to mean rejection of polytheism and submission to the will of the one God, Allah), it was in Medina that the Islamic era began.

1.4.5   JEDDAH

The Red Sea port of Jeddah is a bustling, thriving city. Its location on the ancient trade routes and its status as the seaport and airport for *hajjis* visiting the Holy City of Makkah have ensured that Jeddah is the most cosmopolitan of all Saudi Arabia's cities.

By the end of the 1970s, the population of Jeddah was estimated to be close to 1 million. Today, it is probably closer to 1.5 million.

The extraordinary growth of Jeddah, demanded by the Kingdom's development programs, has been achieved in a remarkably short period. (The expansion of the seaport's capacity is a case study of what can be achieved if the will, the management and the resources are available.) At the same time, aesthetic considerations have not been ignored. Jeddah now boasts some of the most beautiful examples of modern architecture in the world. Tree-lined avenues and the generous distribution of bronze sculptures attest to the success of the city's beautification program.

1.4.6   JUBAIL AND YANBU

The industrial complexes built at Jubail on the Arabian Gulf and Yanbu on the Red Sea by the Royal Commission for Jubail and Yanbu are the key to the Kingdom's national industrialization plans. These two industrial cities provide the basis for the Kingdom's program to develop hydrocarbon-based and energy intensive industries. The massive investment in these industrial cities has as its major objective a reduction in the Kingdom's dependence on oil revenues by gaining access to the world's petrochemical markets. This route to industrialization takes advantage of the Kingdom's natural advantages, in terms of cheap energy and cheap raw materials for petrochemical manufacture.

The following statistics from the fourth Development Plan are a good indication of the scale of investment in these two major industrialization projects:

Employment at Jubail and Yanbu, 1400–10 AH (1980–90)

Area/type of employment	1400 (1980) No. of Employees	1405 (1985) No. of Employees	1410 (1990) No. of Employees
Jubail			
Industrial	1,000	13,000	22,000
Services	2,000	4,000	14,000
Construction	14,000	28,000	16,000
Total	17,000	45,000	52,000
Yanbu			
Industrial	1,000	10,000	9,000
Services	2,000	7,000	15,000
Construction	14,000	10,000	11,000
Total	17,000	27,000	35,000

KINGDOM OF SAUDI ARABIA

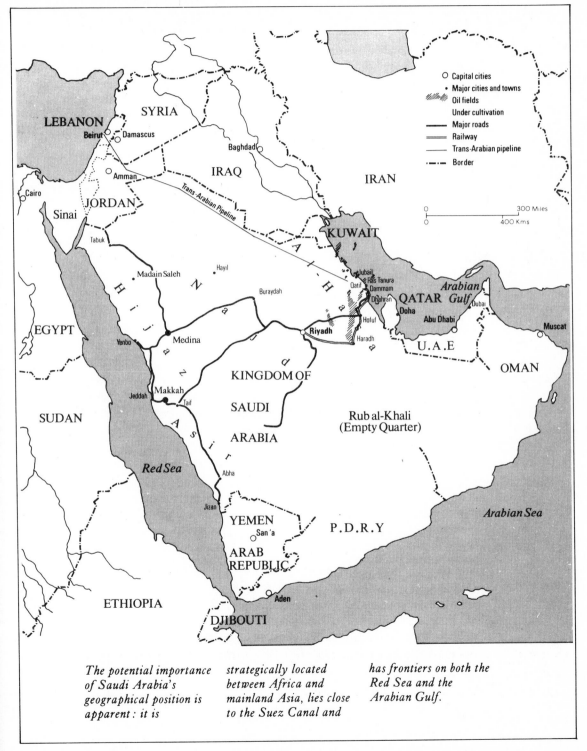

The potential importance of Saudi Arabia's geographical position is apparent: it is strategically located between Africa and mainland Asia, lies close to the Suez Canal and has frontiers on both the Red Sea and the Arabian Gulf.

Source: *Saudi Arabia: A Case Study in Development*, Kegan Paul International, 1986

Chapter **2**

Historical and Cultural Background

Some knowledge of the history leading to the formation of the Kingdom of Saudi Arabia and, in particular, of the cultural background, is essential to an understanding of the principles which have guided the Kingdom's development. This chapter tells the story of the Saudi royal family, of its triumphs and setbacks, and how, through the political and military genius of King Abdul Aziz bin Sa'ud, the tribes of most of the Arabian peninsula were eventually welded together to form a single nation within a Kingdom founded upon Islam.

2.1 A brief history of the Saudi Royal Family

The history of the House of Sa'ud, the Royal Family of the Kingdom of Saudi Arabia, goes back over two centuries. As part of this chapter three charts have been designed dealing with the royal family's structure and political leadership. The first chart (IIa) covers the period starting with the first ruler of the Saudi dynasty from 1744 through 1818. The second chart (IIb) deals with the continued succession of the Saudi house from 1824 through 1891. The final chart (IIc) traces the third ascendancy of the royal family, the period starting in 1902 and continuing through the current era.

The name of "Al-Sa'ud", which means "Family of Sa'ud" or "House of Sa'ud", comes from Sa'ud bin Muhammad bin Mugrin, who lived in the early eighteenth century.

The first ruler of the First House of Sa'ud was Muhammad bin Sa'ud (forbear of the present rulers). He started as ruler of Ad-Dir'iyah where he was to join forces with Sheikh Muhammad bin Abdul Wahhab, the eminent religious leader, in what could be called the first alliance.

Imam Muhammad bin Abdul Wahhab was born in the town of Uyaina in Najd of a highly respected and religious family. Showing a keen interest in religion and dismayed by contemporary deviations from Islamic teachings, the Sheikh started "preaching [the] . . . revival of Islam. . . He ripped away the heresies and abuses which had grown up around Islam and he preached the Faith in its original

Chart IIa   *The first house of Al Sa'ud*

Sa'ud bin Muhammad bin Mugrin

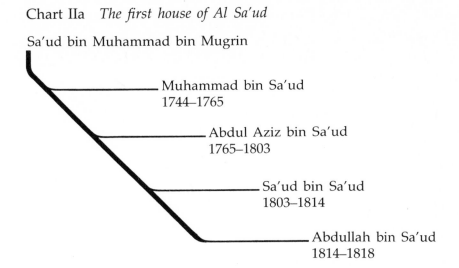

Muhammad bin Sa'ud
1744–1765

Abdul Aziz bin Sa'ud
1765–1803

Sa'ud bin Sa'ud
1803–1814

Abdullah bin Sa'ud
1814–1818

simplicity" (*Source: Lord of Arabia: Ibn Saud* by H C Armstrong: Arthur Barker Ltd, 1934). For that he was prosecuted and forced to leave his town. He took refuge at Ad-Dir'iyah, the home of Al Sa'ud, under the protection of Amir Muhammad bin Sa'ud.

Perceiving the value of Imam Muhammad bin Adbul Wahhab, Muhammad bin Sa'ud concluded an agreement with him that together they would bring the Arabs of the peninsula back to the true faith of the Islamic religion. They confirmed this agreement with an oath in 1157 AH (1744). They were successful.

Muhammad bin Sa'ud's son, Abdul Aziz bin Muhammad bin Sa'ud, ruled from 1765 through 1803, retaining the association with Imam Muhammad bin Abdul Wahhab in the same capacity as his father and continuing to reform Islam in the peninsula. Abdul Aziz successfully captured the city of Riyadh in 1773. The combination of a deeply held theological conviction and military success proved irresistible to many. As a result, the Saudi state began to spread rapidly and within fifteen years had extended its authority all over Najd.

After the death of Abdul Aziz, his son, Sa'ud, ruled from 1803 through 1814. In 1803, Sa'ud, provoked by the Sharif of the Holy City of Makkah, marched on the Holy City and took it. There he and his men performed *Hajj*. The Saudi Kingdom now stretched from Najd to Hasa in the west and south towards Najran.

Such an increase in authority was not to pass unchallenged. The Turkish Empire concluded that action must be taken and invited Muhammad Ali, the Viceroy of Egypt (which at that time came within the Ottoman sphere of influence), to dismantle the work of Muhammad bin Sa'ud, his son and grandson, and to put an end to the emerging nation. Before Sa'ud died in 1814, Muhammad Ali retook the Hijaz.

Sa'ud's successor, his son Abdullah (who ruled until 1818), was unable to halt the Egyptian advance. Ad Dir'iyah was taken and Abdullah removed to Istanbul where his captors executed him. Riyadh was captured in 1818. From 1818 through 1824, the Ottoman Empire maintained a few garrisons in Najd, as a gesture of their dominance. Thus, the first temporary decline in the House of Sa'ud occurred.

Within a few years, however, the fortunes of the House of Sa'ud were to revive. In 1824, Turki bin Sa'ud, a cousin of Sa'ud bin Sa'ud, assumed the Amirship of Najd. In the course of his rule (1824 through 1834), Turki bin Sa'ud retook Riyadh. While continuing the Saudi drive for consolidation of the area, he recognized the symbolic suzerainty of the Viceroy of Egypt, Muhammad Ali.

In 1834, Turki was assassinated. Turki's eldest son, Faisal, defeated the assassin and became Imam. Faisal bin Sa'ud refused to acknowledge the Viceroy of Egypt. Muhammad Ali was not prepared to see his earlier victories so quickly reversed, and in 1838, Egyptian forces defeated Faisal, retaking the Najd. Faisal was taken captive and sent to Cairo. Later, when Muhammad Ali declared Egypt's independence from the Ottoman Empire and was forced to withdraw his troops stationed in Najd in order to support his own position in Egypt, Faisal bin Sa'ud escaped from Cairo (after five years of captivity) returning home and resuming his reign, which lasted till 1865. By then, the House of Sa'ud once more controlled most of Najd and Hasa.

On Faisal's death, however, Saudi fortunes declined once more (see *Arabian Days* by Sheikh Hafiz Wahba, published by Arthur Barker Ltd, 1964). Disagreements between the sons of Faisal weakened the House of Sa'ud. At the same time, a tribal leader of the Shammar, Muhammad bin Raschid, based in Hail, created a strong political body which rapidly covered the greater part of Najd, and by 1871, after concluding a pact with Turkey, captured Al-Hasa. In 1889, the third son of Faisal, Abdul-Rahman bin Faisal, managed to confirm the rule of the Saudi dynasty by assuming the leadership of the family. At that time, the authority of the Saudi

Chart IIb   *The second house of Al Sa'ud*

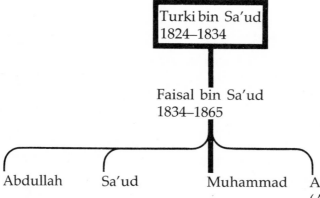

Turki bin Sa'ud
1824–1834

Faisal bin Sa'ud
1834–1865

Abdullah   Sa'ud   Muhammad   Abdul Rahman bin Faisal
(Amir of Riyadh 1889–189
forced into exile in Bahra\
in 1981 by the Raschid: the
settled in Kuwait)

family centred on Riyadh but, in 1891, the House of Sa'ud faced a further setback. Muhammad ibn Raschid completed his control of Najd by capturing Riyadh, the citadel of the House of Sa'ud. Adbul Rahman was forced to leave the city. He settled for months with the Murra tribes at the Great Waste, in the outskirts of the *Rub'al-Khali*, the Empty Quarter, accompanied by his son, Abdul Aziz, the future King of Arabia. Eventually he left for Bahrain, to gather his family, and then went to Kuwait to live there in exile.

Abdul Aziz, son of Abdul Rahman, was deeply concerned with thoughts of his home territory, Najd, the land of his ancestors. He anticipated that he would some day go back again and regain control of that part of Arabia.

Section 2.2 gives an account of how Abdul Aziz and his successors consolidated the Kingdom of Saudi Arabia. Here we will simply outline the main historical events, to bring this account up to date.

In 1902 King Abdul Aziz Al Sa'ud recaptured the city of Riyadh and established his rule over that area. From 1902 through 1926, King Abdul Aziz vigorously and brilliantly extended his authority over most of the Arabian Peninsula. In September 1932, the Kingdom of Saudi Arabia officially acquired its present name.

Chart IIc traces the third rise of the House of Sa'ud, from 1902 onward, and the eventual establishment of the Kingdom of Saudi Arabia.

Chart IIc   *The third house of Al Sa'ud*

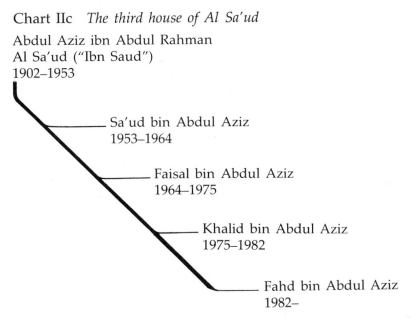

Abdul Aziz ibn Abdul Rahman
Al Sa'ud ("Ibn Saud")
1902–1953

Sa'ud bin Abdul Aziz
1953–1964

Faisal bin Abdul Aziz
1964–1975

Khalid bin Abdul Aziz
1975–1982

Fahd bin Abdul Aziz
1982–

From Chart IIc one can deduce a basic political phenomenon in the structure of the Royal Family; that is, in the dynamics of succession to the leadership of the Kingdom. Since the first Saudi rule in 1744 by Muhammad bin Sa'ud, through 1902, the succession process was from father to son and, on the death of King Abdul

Aziz, in 1953, his son, Sa'ud, assumed the leadership. But, in 1964, King Sa'ud was succeeded by his brother, Faisal, and, since then the father–son succession has ended. In 1975 King Khalid succeeded his brother, King Faisal; and in 1982, King Fahd succeeded his brother King Khalid. Thus a new process of succession to the leadership of the Kingdom has been established – succession among the sons of King Abdul Aziz Al Sa'ud in order of their ages. There are over 35 sons of Ibn Saud.

Another new political factor, equally important, is the majestic size of the Kingdom founded by Ibn Saud. Currently, members of the Royal Family hold positions in the government at all levels throughout the Kingdom.

2.2   The consolidation of the Kingdom

The consolidation of the Arabian Peninsula by King Abdul Aziz bin Sa'ud within a period of little more than twenty years is an outstanding example of nation building.

When he reached the age of seventeen, Abdul Aziz realized that

> he had had enough of idling. For six years he had sat in Kuwait, eating out his heart, listening to the hopeless grumbles of the exiles. That was no life for a man. It might do for shopmen and clerks, but not for a Saud. He was a fighting man . . . He wanted action . . . [and] with God's help he [knew that he] would win. He was sure of himself and of the people of Najd. If he gave them the lead they would rise and join him and throw out the Raschid.
>
> *Source: Lord of Arabia* by H C Armstrong (London: Arthur Barker Ltd, 1934)

When he was 21, he decided to move on Riyadh with 30 of his devoted friends. Having departed from Kuwait in December 1901, Ibn Saud reached Riyadh in January. Of all the stories of modern Arabia, there is none more dramatic than the account of Abdul Aziz bin Sa'ud's assault on the Musmak fort and his recapture of Riyadh from the Raschid in 1902. The following extracts are taken from *Arabia Unified* by Mohammed Almana, (Hutchinson Benham, 1980):

> So hopeless did the Prince's quest seem to his men that only a handful volunteered to enter the town with him, one of them being his cousin, Abdullah Ibn Jelawi. The Prince led his tiny force to a part of the wall which he knew would suit his purpose, and by using grappling irons and ropes the small party climbed into the town undetected.

After eliciting useful information on "Ajlan, the Amir of Riyadh" from the wife of a man who had served Ibn Saud's father when the Sa'uds had held Riyadh,

> Abdul Aziz (Ibn Saud) and his men crept unobserved along the silent streets and entered an empty house near the one occupied by the Amir's wife.

There, they waited.

> At dawn after prayers, Ajlan emerged as expected through the postern door in the roadway outside. Abdul Aziz watched his progress through the slits in the door of the house. . . . Abdul Aziz had planned to deal with Ajlan after he had entered the house, but the sight of his enemy only a few feet away was too much for the Prince to bear; with a violent war-cry he threw open the door and burst upon the unsuspecting Amir. Although taken completely by surprise, Ajlan managed to defend himself long enough to retreat to the gate and attempt to fling himself through the postern door. Inside the mosque, he was cut down by the sword of the Prince's cousin, Abdullah Ibn Jelawi.

Thus, the Saudi dynasty became once more the rulers of Riyadh.

> The population of Riad [sic] rose. They were tired of the Raschid and his injustices. They wiped out the other posts of Raschid soldiers in the town, and welcomed Ibn Saud with open arms. . . . Ibn Saud was master of Riad.
>
> (*Source*: *Lord of Arabia* by H C Armstrong (London: Arthur Barker Ltd, 1934)

Naturally, this was not the end of the journey for Abdul Aziz bin Sa'ud. It was merely the beginning. His father, Abdul Rahman, who was the legal and rightful ruler of Najd, was recalled from Kuwait, and in a council formed of the *Ulama* (religious leaders) and the notables, he abdicated his rights and declared Abdul Aziz his successor. From 1902 through 1904, through a sequence of military campaigns, Abdul Aziz bin Sa'ud extended his authority all over the Najd. He was now, however, faced with a much greater task – unifying the various tribes in Arabia. Aside from marriage alliances, Abdul Aziz employed his unique personality in persuading the tribes to unite.

> Ibn Saud talked much and eloquently, but when he appeared to be giving most he was in reality giving little. As he talked he concentrated on the man [to] whom he spoke as if he were his one interest in life. He had a smile, irresistible, all-absorbing, which swept his listeners up with

him, blinding their judgement so that each one went away satisfied and only later found that he had come away empty handed, and even then did not resent the fact.

Source: Ibid

Consequently, his drive for consolidation was quite successful to the extent that by the end of 1904, Abdul Aziz had managed to break the stranglehold of the Raschid and push them into the area at Jabal Shammar in northern Najd. The Raschid, desperately, appealed to the Turks who sent them reinforcements. Nevertheless, Ibn Saud's desert fighters kept control of the situation in Najd. Through diplomatic negotiations at one time, and guerrilla warfare at another, Abdul Aziz forced the Ottoman Empire to recall its troops from Najd. Thus on the death of Al Raschid in 1906, Ibn Saud won complete control over Najd. Having accomplished this objective, he turned his attention to Al-Hasa and the area of the Arabian Gulf which was still under Turkish rule. Calculating on the Ottoman Empire's preoccupation with uprisings in Europe, and on his belief that Britain, considering the situation a domestic affair, would remain neutral, Ibn Saud launched a successful assault, and by 1913 his sovereignty was extended to both Najd and Al-Hasa.

Having reached this goal, he once more confronted the perennial problem of the Bedouins and their practice of raiding and moving from place to place at will. This continual practice spelled insecurity and instability which Ibn Saud was determined to put an end to. Realizing "that any attempt to establish a stable, large-scale political organization in the conquered territories was impeded by the difficulty of creating loyalties beyond those of the local units, whether it was tribe or village" (*Source: Area Handbook for Saudi Arabia*), he conceived a brilliant two-stage plan. First, he sent preachers to various tribes, teaching them the essence of Islam and encouraging them to engage in agricultural labor. Secondly, he settled the Bedouins in agricultural settlements established according to the Wahhabi teachings, in Najd. The first of these projects was a success, and was followed by many others (sixty) so that by 1916 the tribes constituted a formidable political-military force which enabled Ibn Saud further to consolidate his rule over Najd and Al-Hasa. These settlers, known as the *Ikhwan* (meaning "brethren" in Arabic), became such a powerful force that Ibn Saud assumed personal command of them.

In 1916, he concluded another treaty with Britain, recognizing him as the sole ruler of Najd and Al-Hasa. This agreement gave Abdul Aziz the tacit right to eliminate the remaining members of the Raschid family. He did so, and by 1918 his authority was extended to reach the outskirts of Ha'il, the capital of the Raschid. During the next year clashes occurred between the forces of Sherif Hussein of Makkah and a force of the *Ikhwan*. Nevertheless, Abdul Aziz withheld his troops from attacking the Hijaz. In 1920, he moved further south and consolidated Asir. The following year, he completed his campaign against the Raschid in Ha'il, which fell under his control. Restraining himself time and time again from proceeding to

Hijaz because of his word to Britain, Abdul Aziz "Ibn Saud" adopted a policy of sitting and waiting.

During the following three years, relations between the Sherif of Makkah and Britain began to deteriorate. The Sherif's maladministration of the holy cities further isolated him from other Arab countries. When, in March 1924, the Sherif proclaimed himself King of Arabia and Caliph of Islam, Ibn Saud's patience was exhausted, and in September of that year an army of the *Ikhwan* captured the city of Taif. With little delay and only minor resistance, Makkah, Medina and the whole area of Hijaz came under the sovereignty of Ibn Saud. This final consolidation of the Arabian Kingdom was accomplished by the end of 1925. In the following year, Ibn Saud, responding to a popular demand from the people of Makkah, became the King of Hijaz and the Sultan of Najd and its Dependencies. Thus,

> with the exception of the Yemen and the territory far to the south beyond the Great Waste on the coast of the Indian Ocean, Ibn Saud . . . ruled all Arabia from the Red Sea to the [Arabian] Gulf and from the Great Waste to the edges of Syria. He was Guardian of the Sacred Cities of Islam and Imam of the Wahhabis. He was Lord of Arabia.
>
> *Source*: *Lord of Arabia* by H C Armstrong (London: Arthur Barker Ltd, 1934)

The formal foundation of the Kingdom of Saudi Arabia took place on 23rd September 1932, when a majority of the world powers recognized the sovereignty of the new nation.

In 1933, a discovery to prove of the greatest political and economic significance was made. A survey of the new Kingdom's natural resources, commissioned by the King, confirmed the existence of oil in the Eastern Province. By 1938, the exploitation of these oil fields, which contain approximately 25% of the world's proven oil resources, had begun.

In the course of his long reign, King Abdul Aziz gave studious attention to the development of international relations. In 1945, on board the USS *Quincy*, the Saudi king met the US President Franklin D Roosevelt. (It was at that famous meeting that the American President gave his undertaking to the Saudi king that Arab interests in Palestine would not be sacrificed to Jewish aspirations for nationhood. See Chapter 18, Section 3.) Also in 1945, King Abdul Aziz met the British Prime Minister, Winston Churchill.

The economic and technical co-operation which exploitation of the Kingdom's oil demanded and a community of political interest in many areas ensured that the friendship between the Kingdom of Saudi Arabia and the United States of America, initiated by King Abdul Aziz, was to grow in succeeding decades. Despite political differences in some areas, notably on the issue of Palestinian rights, that special relationship still survives and flourishes today.

On his death in 1953, King Abdul Aziz was succeeded by his son, Sa'ud, who, after a reign of eleven years, was succeeded by his brother Faisal. King Faisal had been carefully groomed for leadership from an early age and it was during his reign that the Kingdom's industrial development began in earnest. King Faisal brought stability to the economy and then utilized the Kingdom's vast oil wealth to finance the country's ambitious development program. The last five years of his rule saw the implementation of the first of the Kingdom's Development Plans.

On the death of King Faisal in 1975, he was succeeded by his brother, Khaled. King Khaled oversaw the implementation of the second Five Year Plan (1975–1980) and the preparation of the third. During this period, great progress was made in the building of the Kingdom's infrastructure and the policy of industrialization was pursued with vigour under the leadership of the then Crown Prince Fahd.

In 1982, on the death of King Khaled, Fahd, brother to Khaled and Crown Prince throughout his reign, became king. King Fahd has presided over the implementation of the third Five Year Plan (1980–1985) and, at the time of writing, most of the fourth Five Year Plan (1985–1990). Both he and Crown Prince Abdullah have shown an unquestionable commitment to the educational, industrial and agricultural development of the Kingdom, providing the greatest possible opportunities for self-fulfilment to all Saudi citizens within a stable political framework, firmly based on Islamic precepts.

2.3   The Wahhabi movement

At this point, it is perhaps appropriate to make reference to the Wahhabi movement in Saudi Arabia. A brief examination of Wahhabism will be sufficient to inform the reader of the doctrinal essence of the movement, which has sometimes been misunderstood. (Since Wahhabism is concomitant to the events which led to the formation of Saudi Arabia by King Abdul Aziz Al Sa'ud, the historical significance of the Wahhabi movement emerges from the account of the consolidation of the Kingdom by King Abdul Aziz at the beginning of this century.)

Muhammad bin Abdul Wahab did not found a new sect. His travels through the Arab lands which then formed part of the Ottoman Empire revealed to him diverse deviations from the true Islamic faith. His purpose was to strip away those deviations and to re-establish Islam in its pure form.

A survey of various books, both in English and in Arabic, that have dealt with Wahhabism demonstrates that no one could be better qualified than King Abdul Aziz Al Sa'ud to explain the true significance and meaning of Wahhabism. In a speech delivered by His Majesty King Abdul Aziz Al Sa'ud in Makkah, at the Royal Palace on 11th May 1929, the King said that

> They call us the "Wahhabis" and they call our creed a "Wahhabi" one as if it were a special one . . . and this is an extremely erroneous allegation

that has arisen from the false propaganda launched by those who had ill feelings as well as ill intentions towards the movement. We are not proclaiming a new creed or a new dogma. Muhammad ibn Abdul Wahhab did not come with anything new. Our creed is the creed of those good people who preceded us and which came in the Book of God (the *Quran*) as well as that of his Messenger (the prophet Muhammad, prayer and peace be upon him).

And we respect the four Imams. We hold no preference between Malike and al Shafie, Ahmad and Abu-Hanifa; in our view they are all to be respected by us.

This is the creed which Sheikh al-Islam Muhammad ibn Abdul Wahhab is calling for, and it is our creed. It is a creed built on the oneness of the Almighty God, totally for His sake, and it is divorced from any ills or false innovation. The Unitarian creed is the creed or dogma which we are calling for, and it is the one which will save us from calamity and catastrophe.

2.4   The importance of Islam as a unifying force

Throughout any account of the development of the Kingdom of Saudi Arabia, there must be a thread that binds all the parts together. That thread is Islam.

Throughout the history of the Arabian peninsula, from the time of the Prophet Muhammad, peace be upon him, the history of the region has been largely determined by Islam.

Indeed, it was Islam that had led to the emergence of the Arabian Empire, and unified the Arabs not only in the Arabian Peninsula, but also from Asia to the Atlantic Ocean during the seventh and eighth centuries. Again in the early years of the twentieth century King Abdul Aziz Al Sa'ud, "by the name of God and the force of his right hand", consolidated his control over the major parts of the Arabian Peninsula until Saudi Arabia was officially proclaimed fully sovereign on 22nd September 22 1932.

In unifying the Arab States into one cohesive nation it was Islam, which, like a spinning wheel, wove the various Arab peoples together in one strong fabric. It was the tie of faith rather than anything else which enabled King Abdul Aziz to found his Kingdom; and if Arabs are ever destined to unite again in one nation or in a federation of nations it will be through their religion.

Something similar, though not identical, happened in the United States. In its early years, almost everybody had one thing in common: their religion. Moreover, in many colonies a religious perspective was a significant part of the culture. One could say that, in terms of their overall cultural philosophy and orientation, Americans were originally religious people, though not necessarily in terms of the practice of religion. Early leaders did not always practise religion or attend church regularly, but they thought of themselves as Christians. Briefly, a general belief in Christianity was and is the American consensus over religion. The American people's adherence to Judaeo-Christian ethics was influential in forming and solidifying the American nation of today.

It is worth emphasizing that, amidst all the accounts of the Kingdom's achievements, behind all the remarkable statistics which indicate the extraordinary development and growth of the Kingdom in all areas, the spirit that drives and pervades all and the guidance which has ensured that the available resources have been so wisely utilized is Islam.

2.5   Archaeology

Moves to explore and preserve the Kingdom of Saudi Arabia's archaeological remains are a relatively recent phenomenon. The investigation and the safe-keeping of the Kingdom's archaeological finds are in the hands of the Department of Antiquities and Museums. A complete survey of the Kingdom's archaeological resources was undertaken between 1976 and 1980.

As a guide to the main sites of archaeological interest in Riyadh and as a clear expression of the Kingdom's respect for its past, we quote from *Riyadh – City of the Future*: (Riyadh: King Saud University Press, date unknown):

> The cultural and historical sites in any city are an indication of its roots. Protecting these landmarks is a sign of respect to traditions and heritage and also of pride. Riyadh is one of the cities which is rich in historical and cultural landmarks. Riyadh Municipality is deeply committed to the preservation of its heritage.

> *Sites of major interest*

> Old Historical Gates of Riyadh

> The Thumaira Gate – located in the east wall
> The Al-Suwailem Gate – located in the north wall
> The Dukhna Gate – located in the south wall
> The Al-Madhbah Gate – located in the west wall
> The Shumaisi Gate – located in the south-west

> Historic Palaces

> The Musmak Palace
> The Palace of King Abdul Aziz (the Al-Murabba Palace)
> The Palace of Prince Mohammad bin Abdulrahman
> The Shamsiya Palace

The Eastern Province, not surprisingly in view of its position as a crossroads for trade and cultural exchange in the ancient world, is a rich region for archaeological exploration. The survey of archaeological resources revealed some 300 sites of interest, from the Stone Age to the late Islamic period.

As for the Western Province, with Jeddah as a key trading city both for seafarers and for the caravans following the old trade routes along the Red Sea coast, the riches of the archaeological treasures are immense.

The Department of Antiquities and Museums is responsible for the Museum of Archaeology and Ethnography (founded in 1978) which contains exhibits from the Stone Age, through the "Age of Trade", to "After the Revelation" (the rise and spread of Islam).

2.6   King Abdul Aziz Research Center

We should not leave this section on the Kingdom without mention of the King Abdul Aziz Research Center which was established by Royal Decree in 1392 AH (1972).

The Center, which includes a Library and a National Archive and Manuscripts Center was set up as a focal point for the study of the Kingdom's history, geography and literature, with particular reference to the history of King Abdul Aziz.

Chapter 3

Islam, the faith on which the Kingdom is founded

Throughout this book, the reader will find references to Islam. The reason is simple. To understand the history of the Kingdom and its political, economic and social development, it is necessary to realize that Islam, which permeates every aspect of a Muslim's life, also permeates every aspect of the Saudi Arabian state.

It is not the function of this book to attempt to describe or explain Islam. It is nevertheless true that some grasp of the spirit of Islam will help the reader to see, in the correct context, the policies of the Kingdom, both in terms of its efforts to benefit its own citizens and in terms of the aid it has given to other countries. This chapter therefore offers brief notes on the origins of Islam and an account of the five Pillars of Islam which represent the essential duties of all Muslims.

3.1   The origins of Islam

> Moslem Arabs, heirs of the Semitic tradition . . . held aloft the torch of enlightenment throughout a large portion of the civilized world. From their Syrian capital Damascus, they ruled an empire extending from the Atlantic to central Asia. From their subsequent capital Baghdad, they spread their translations and renditions of Greek, Persian and Indian philosophy, science and literature throughout the vast domain. From Moslem Spain, Sicily and crusading Syria, some of these intellectual treasures passed on to Europe to become a vital force in its modern renaissance.
>
> *Source*: *A Short History of the Near East* by Philip K Hitti (Princeton, NJ: D Van Nostrand Co, 1966)

The history of the Arabs since the *Hijrah* (the year in which the Prophet was forced to flee from Makkah to Medina, the first year of the Islamic calendar – 622 AD) reveals the salient fact that only under Islam did Muslims unite, thus becoming more powerful. Once united, they ruled an empire for more than 200 years. Before the rise of Islam in the seventh century, the Arabian Peninsula was under diverse and various external influences.

During the fifth and sixth centuries AD the north-west of Arabia was held by the Ghassanids,

> who claimed descent from one of the South Arabian tribes, and were under Byzantine influence; in the north-east the Lakhmids of the Kingdom of Hira were under the protection of the Sassanid Persians. In the south the remains of the Himyarite Kingdom was controlled first by the Christian Abyssinians and later by the Persians.
>
> Source: *Area Handbook for Saudi Arabia*, (Washington DC: US Government Printing Office, 1971)

It was only during the fourth century AD that towns began to take shape in South Arabia, due to the proximity of major trade routes, especially along the west and east coasts. Among these towns was Makkah, which was an aggregation of tribal groups, the most important of which was the Quraysh tribe. It was from the Quraysh that the Prophet Muhammad Alayhi al-Salah wa Salam (peace and prayer be upon him) was descended.

Before the rise of Islam in Arabia

> the primitive religion of the desert was restricted to the worship of trees and streams and stones in which the deity was supposed to reside . . . Nomads had naturally no temples or priesthoods, they usually carried their gods with them in a tent or tabernacle, and consulted them by casting lots with arrows, while their Kahins (high priests) or soothsayers delivered oracles in short rhymed sentences.
>
> Source: *A History of Medieval Islam* by J J Saunders (New York: Barnes and Noble, 1965)

Within Makkah itself tribes worshipped idols placed around and over the *Ka'aba*. In such a heterodox religious atmosphere, Muhammad was born in 570 AD, in Makkah, of the Quraysh, the keepers and protectors of the *Ka'aba*.

At the age of 40, Muhammad received his call to become a prophet. He received the word of God through the Archangel Gabriel and the divine message was recorded in the Holy *Qur'an*.

The God that spoke to Muhammad was the God of Abraham. Islam is thus essentially part of the great monotheistic movement that emerged and developed in the Near East. In Muhammad, regarded as the "seal of the prophets", the message of God for man was finally comprehended and Islam (submission to the will of Allah) is seen by Muslims as the apotheosis of the Judaeo-Christian tradition.

The purpose of this brief section has been simply to provide the reader with a brief account of the origins of Islam, not to provide a detailed historical chronology of the religion.

The essence of Islam lies in the five Pillars of Islam and the following pages offer an explanation of these five central tenets.

3.2   The five tenets of Islam

Islam is a religion that informs every part of daily life. The five Pillars of Islam constitute the basic religious duties which every Muslim must perform.

3.2.1   AL-SHAHADAH (OR TESTIMONY)

The first of the five tenets of Islam is the testimony and the pronouncing of the words that "There is no God but Allah and Muhammad is His Prophet." This *Shahadah*, or testimony, when recited by a person of sincerity, sound capacity and without any mental reservations, constitutes the first major requirement for being a Muslim. Of parallel importance and in accordance with the *Shahadah* is the solemn belief in a general resurrection, in the final day of judgement, in all the prophets of God and in the Scriptures of God – that is, the *Quran* (widely referred to by Muslims as *Al-Quran Al-Karim*), the Pentateuch and the Christian Gospels.

3.2.2   AL-SALAH (PRAYER)

Prayers are of such great significance that some leading scholars of the religion describe them as the backbone of Islam. Each Muslim is required to pray five times daily, in a prescribed manner. The first prayer is at dawn; the next is at high noon; then in the afternoon; after sunset; and finally at night. The formalized prayer consists of a sequence of obeisances made first from a standing position and then from a kneeling one. Muslims may pray in any place, alone or in the company of others. When praying, the Muslim faces in the direction of the Holy City of Makkah.

Inseparable from prayers in Islam is the *Tahara*, that is, the complete cleanliness of clothes, body and place. Without the *Tahara*, a Muslim's prayers will be rendered null. It is the Muslim's obligation, therefore, to be clean at the time of each prayer before facing his Creator. Emphasizing the importance of bodily cleanliness, Allah is quoted in the *Quran*:

> O ye who believe! When ye prepare for prayer, wash your faces, and your hands [and arms] to the elbows; rub your heads [with water]; and [wash] your feet to the ankles. If ye are in a state of ceremonial impurity, bathe your whole body. But if ye are ill, or on a journey, or one of you

cometh from offices of nature, or ye have been in contact with women, and ye find no water, then take for yourselves clean sand or earth, and rub there with your faces and hands. God doth not wish to place you in a difficulty, but to make you clean.

Source: *Al-Quran Al-Karim*, Surat Al Ma'ida, verse 7, pp 242–3

Indeed, these verses of the *Quran* are but a small manifestation of the tremendous emphasis Islam places on cleanliness and its demand for purification.

It should be noted here, before moving to the third tenet of Islam, that the most important thing in prayer is total devotion and solemnity before God.

3.2.3 AL-SIYAM (FASTING)

The imposition of fasting, which means complete abstention from food and drink from sunrise until sunset during the month of Ramadan, is the third basic tenet of the Islamic religion. Ramadan is the ninth month of the Arabian calendar, which consists of twelve lunar months. Therefore, the Arabian lunar month is either 29 or 30 days long, but never 31 days. Fasting in Ramadan, besides being a religious duty, is no doubt of great benefit as it trains one to be patient, wise, well disciplined and to share the feelings of others. In Surat Al Baqara of the *Quran*, in speaking of fasting the Almighty Allah says

O ye who believe! Fasting is prescribed to you as it was prescribed to those before you, that ye may [learn] Self-restraint, . . . [Fasting] for a fixed number of days; but if any of you is ill, or on a journey, the prescribed number [should be made up] from days later. For those who can do it [with hardship], is a ransom, the feeding of one that is indigent. But he that will give more, of his own free will, . . . it is better for him. And it is better for you that ye fast, if ye only knew.

Source: *Al-Quran Al-Karim*, Surat al Baqara, page 72

Ramadan, traditionally held to be the month in which the Prophet Muhammad (peace be upon him) received his first revelation and the month in which the *Quran* was revealed to the Prophet, is considered particularly holy by Muslims.

3.2.4 AL-ZAKAT (ALMSGIVING)

In various parts of the *Quran* great stress is laid on the *Zakat*, that is almsgiving to those who deserve it. Each able Muslim should give a certain percentage of his annual income, either in money or kind, to the poor and the indigent. In Saudi Arabia, the religious obligation of *Al-Zakat* has been officially recognized by the establishment of the Department of *Zakat* under the auspices of the Ministry of

Finance. *Al-Zakat* on the individual's annual income from any legal source amounts to almost two and a half per cent.

It is believed that one of the reasons for the imposition of *Al-Zakat* is the fact that Islam calls for the purity of both the soul and the body. (*Zakat* means purification, and the payment of *Zakat* is regarded primarily as an act of worship of God.) Since it is required from the rich to satisfy the needs of the poor, the paying of *Al-Zakat* no doubt enhances amity and caring within society and strengthens the relationship between the wealthy and the indigent. It reflects fulfilment of an early concept of social justice, as it is taken from each person according to his capacity. The Book of God, the *Quran*, says "Take of their wealth a portion (as charity) to purify them by it", and who better qualified than God Almighty to stress the significance of *Al-Zakat* as a humanitarian source in Islam?

3.2.5   AL HAJJ (PILGRIMAGE)

The fifth and last Pillar of Islam is the *Hajj*. It is explicitly stated in the Holy *Quran* that every physically and financially able Muslim should make the *Hajj* to the Holy City of Makkah once in his or her lifetime. The *Hajj* is considered the final culmination of each Muslim's religious duties and aspiration. Statistics obtained from the Saudi Ministry of Interior, Annual Reports of Passport Affairs, reveal the intensity of Islamic devotion amongst the world's Muslim population:

Pilgrims arriving from foreign countries by mode of arrival

Year		By air	By sea	By land	Total
1402	(1982)	623,425	55,735	174,395	853,555
1403	(1983)	724,002	61,371	218,539	1,003,911
1404	(1984)	698,233	52,928	168,520	919,671
1405	(1985)	645,303	48,800	157,658	851,761
1406	(1986)	657,387	41,380	157,951	856,718
1407	(1987)	694,286	41,585	224,515	960,386

Table 3.1, from the same source, gives a detailed breakdown of the country of origin of foreign pilgrims for the year 1407 (1987).

In 1409 AH (1989), the pilgrimage statistics showed that the number of pilgrims visiting the Kingdom during the pilgrimage season was 774,560, of which 460,250 were male and 314,310 female. Their mode of arrival was:

- by air: 534,662
- by land: 195,950
- by sea: 43,948

Table 3.1 *Pilgrims arriving from foreign countries by nationality and mode of arrival, 1407 AH (1987)*

Nationality	By land	By sea	By air	Total
		Mode of Arrival		
Arab Countries				
U.A.E.	1,687	–	4,574	6,261
Jordan	20,156	–	1,592	21,748
Bahrain	2,851	–	1,556	4,407
Tunisia	547	–	6,450	6,997
Algeria	1,547	7	28,121	29,675
Sudan	522	2,461	25,801	28,784
Syria	980	2	13,990	14,972
Somalia	150	5	4,731	4,886
Iraq	27,016	–	2,506	29,522
Oman Sultanate	11,350	–	764	12,114
Palestine	1,221	2	1,344	2,567
Qatar	657	–	544	1,201
Kuwait	3,877	–	3,086	6,963
Lebanon	2,601	–	2,196	4,797
Libya	–	1,624	27,240	28,864
Egypt	3,370	24,802	69,044	97,216
Morocco	992	1	28,341	29,334
Mauritania	15	–	1,618	1,633
North Yemen	41,620	1	19,795	61,416
South Yemen	187	–	7,038	7,225
Djibouti	–	–	497	497
Total Arab Countries	**121,346**	**28,905**	**250,828**	**410,079**
Asian Non-Arab Countries				
Afghanistan	155	3	5,272	5,430
Indonesia	7	49	57,463	57,519
Iran	876	–	156,519	157,395
Pakistan	13,197	7,758	72,058	93,013
Bangladesh	987	1	16,656	17,644
Brunei	–	–	3,253	3,253
Thailand	5	11	2,389	2,405
Turkey	84,834	–	11,877	96,711
Singapore	1	–	3,089	3,090
Sri Lanka	54	–	1,603	1,657
China (Formosa)	–	–	160	160
Philippines	52	–	1,372	1,424
Burma	–	1	116	117
Maldives Republic	–	–	757	757

Table 3.1–contd.

Nationality	Mode of Arrival			Total
	By land	By sea	By air	
Peoples Rep. of China	28	–	1,390	1,418
Cambodia	–	–	3	3
Japan	–	–	1	1
South Korea	3	–	2	5
North Korea	–	–	4	4
Nepal	–	–	26	26
Malaysia	1	21	25,456	25,478
India	2,159	4,685	34,010	40,854
Hong Kong	–	–	4	4
Total Asian Non-Arab Countries	**102,359**	**12,529**	**393,480**	**508,368**
African Non-Arab Countries				
Ethiopia	2	3	896	901
Uganda	15	–	329	344
Botswanaland	13	–	8	21
Chad	–	5	1,305	1,310
Tanzania	32	–	755	787
Togo	–	–	222	222
Gambia	1	–	796	797
Gabon	1	–	141	142
Comoro Island	1	–	386	387
South Africa	–	–	2,329	2,329
Congo Brazaville	–	–	10	10
Burundi	1	–	3	4
Zaïre	–	1	13	14
Zambia	–	–	50	50
Ivory Coast	1	14	686	701
Senegal	16	18	3,105	3,139
Sierra Leone	2	–	145	147
Rwanda	–	1	9	10
Ghana	3	–	1,063	1,066
Guinea	1	1	1,092	1,094
Benin	7	–	424	431
Zimbabwe	–	–	32	32
Cameroon	–	–	1,259	1,259
Kenya	7	–	966	973
Liberia	1	–	74	75
Mali	11	2	2,154	2,167
Malagasy	–	–	8	8
Mauritius	2	–	383	385

Table 3.1–contd.

Nationality	Mode of Arrival			Total
	By land	By sea	By air	
Mozambique	–	–	7	7
Nigeria	8	106	20,623	20,737
Niger	–	–	868	868
Central Africa	–	–	391	391
Burkina Faso	2	–	974	976
Other African Countries	–	–	327	327
Total African Non-Arab Countries	**127**	**151**	**41,833**	**42,111**
European Countries				
Spain	–	–	10	10
West Germany	14	–	69	83
Ireland	–	–	7	7
U.K.	80	–	3,979	4,059
Portugal	–	–	14	14
Belgium	1	–	18	19
France	178	–	629	807
Cyprus	–	–	–	–
Holland	13	–	201	214
Yugoslavia	266	–	648	914
Greece	120	–	44	164
Italy	1	–	6	7
Denmark	–	–	41	41
Sweden	–	–	31	31
Switzerland	–	–	12	12
Finland	–	–	4	4
Soviet Union	1	–	16	17
Norway	–	–	36	36
Austria	–	–	13	13
Romania	–	–	–	–
Bulgaria	1	–	–	1
Poland	–	–	–	–
Other Non-Arab Countries	–	–	1	1
Total European Countries	**675**	**–**	**5,779**	**6,454**
American Countries				
U.S.A.	3	–	1,247	1,250
Canada	–	–	477	477
Colombia	–	–	2	2
Brazil	–	–	21	21
Trinidad	–	–	129	129

Table 3.1–contd.

Nationality	Mode of Arrival			Total
	By land	By sea	By air	
Paraguay	–	–	1	1
Jamaica	–	–	3	3
Guyana	–	–	23	23
Grenada	–	–	1	1
Venezuela	–	–	6	6
Surinam	–	–	53	53
Barbados	–	–	12	12
Panama	–	–	2	2
Dominican Rep.	–	–	–	–
Mexico	–	–	2	2
Argentina	–	–	4	4
Total American Countries	**–**	**–**	**4**	**4**
Australia & Neighbouring Islands				
Australia	–	–	347	347
Fiji Islands	5	–	25	30
New Zealand	–	–	7	7
Total Australia & Neighbouring Islands	**5**	**–**	**379**	**384**

Source: Deputy Ministry of the Interior for Passport and Civil Status

These figures give some indication of the religious devotion of Muslims of the different countries. But it must be noted that, due to monetary and financial constraints prevalent in some of the countries, not everyone wishing to make the *Hajj* is able to do so. In some of these countries, Muslims wishing to make the *Hajj* are required to submit an application to the local authorities. The authority in charge of the *Hajj* applications then selects at random up to a total for the year which the government concerned will authorize. Even so, the *Hajj* attracts almost a million foreign pilgrims each year. If we add to these figures the hundreds of thousands of Saudi citizens who perform *Hajj* each year, it will be clear that *Hajj* represents a truly unique gathering of peoples from around the world, bound together in their submission to the will of God.

When dealing with the *Hajj*, the fifth pillar of Islam, one must pause and give special attention to its meaning and implications. The fulfilment of this corner of the Islamic religion is mandatory, providing that it is not financially or physically impossible. Perhaps more should be said about this principle. Muslims from all over the world seek to make the *Hajj* to the Holy City of Makkah, which occurs between the eighth and thirteenth days of the last month of the Islamic calendar – Dhu al-Hijjah – each year. Muslims travel thousands of miles to reach the Holy City of Makkah for the *Hajj* and perform the rituals in the same manner as the Prophet Muhammad (*Alayhi al-Salah wa Salam*) almost fourteen centuries ago.

3.2.6   HOW THE PILLARS OF ISLAM ARE PRACTISED

In Islam, the *Salah* (prayers) five times a day is considered the backbone of religion. It can be individually practised, although it is strongly urged that Muslims perform the *Salah* in groups whenever possible. Thus a delicate equilibrium between the importance of worshipping God in solitude and of individual worship in the company of others has been established.

Equally, *Al-Shahadah*, the first tenet of the religion, may be considered an individual practice which is performed upon accepting the Islamic religion. The Faith does not require any rigid rules at certain times for its fulfilment. *Al-Zakat* (almsgiving), similarly, may be implemented by individuals and by the government; and in the former case, it is done at the person's own recognizance without any outside control. Therefore, this principle of Islam also is a self-practised duty. *Al-Siyam* (fasting) must be observed during Ramadan each year. This pillar of the religion can be maintained in any part of the world with no difficulty at all. Consequently, *Al-Siyam* is also a self-practised religious duty which is fulfilled on an individual basis.

Chapter 4

The Judicial System

This chapter examines the origins of the Kingdom's judicial system and describes the various courts which the Kingdom has set in place to meet the demands of a rapidly developing society with expanding industrial and commercial sectors.

4.1 Origins

The administration and application of the judicial system of Saudi Arabia illustrates the importance of the *Ulama* (religious leaders). When King Abdul Aziz extended his rule over the western part of the Kingdom, the Hijaz, he was faced with the existence of three separate judicial systems.

The first was that of the Hijaz, with an Ottoman orientation. The second was that of the small town of Najd. Under this system, an Amir (similar to a regional governor), with the assistance of one judge, represented the law. The Amir would try to solve the disputes submitted to him or refer them to the judge for a final ruling. The implementation of the judge's decisions was the Amir's duty. The third, more primitive and indigenous, was the tribal law. Here, the conflicting parties would refer their disputes to the individual tribe's law, and its own lawyers would give a final decision according to precedent.

4.2 *Shari'ah* and other courts

While recommending temporary measures to cope with the current situation, King Abdul Aziz did not allow the persistence of such perplexing and impeding judicial systems. A Royal Decree was issued in 1927 with the aim of unifying the judicial system of the nation. Its institutions were classified into three hierarchical categories: "expeditious courts, *Shari'ah* courts, and the Commission on Judicial Supervision" (*Source: Kingdom of Saudi Arabia, Majmo'at al-Nuzum* – "Collections of Regulations" – Makkah: Umm al-Qura Press, 1958). The first courts handled the more simple criminal and civil cases and were divided into first expeditious courts and second expeditious courts. The latter dealt with cases involving nomads. All other cases were within the jurisdiction of the *Shari'ah* courts. In addition to inspecting and supervising the courts, the commission had the function of judicial review.

> *Source*: *Saudi Arabia's Judicial System* by Solaim (Unpublished Ph.D. dissertation, 1970)

This classification of courts in the Kingdom of Saudi Arabia is basically the same today, and the latest important legislation on the subject, the Attributions of Shari'ah Jurisprudence Responsibilities of 1952, though more detailed, and covering such subjects as the Notaries Public, the Property Departments and Summoning Officers, has not signified any radical departure.

The organizational framework remained as shown in Chart IVa.

Chart IVa   *Judicial framework of the Kingdom*

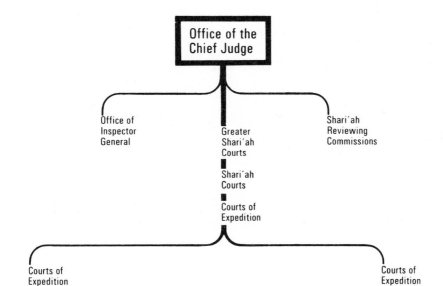

Source: *Ibid*

4.3 The role of the *Ulama* (religious leaders)

The role of the *Ulama* in Saudi Arabia has a long history and great significance. A brief summary will have to suffice.

The first alliance between Muhammad bin Sa'ud and Imam Muhammad bin Abdul Wahhab, and its continued success through the years, reflect the important role played by the *Ulama* in Saudi Arabia. That first alliance was both political and religious in nature and clearly emphasized the true notion of the state in Islam; that is, state and religion are inseparable. The Kingdom of Saudi Arabia is an example of an Islamic state governed by the Holy *Quran*. It is therefore inevitable that the *Ulama* should play a key role within the Kingdom. They play an influential part in the following fields of government:

1 The judicial system of Saudi Arabia
2 The implementation of the rules of the Islamic *Shari'ah*
3 Religious Guidance Group with affiliated offices all over the Kingdom
4 Religious education, that is, Islamic legal education and theology at all levels in Saudi Arabia
5 Religious jurisprudence
6 Preaching and guidance throughout the nation
7 Supervision of girls' education
8 Religious supervision of all Mosques in the Kingdom
9 Preaching of Islam abroad
10 Continuous scientific and Islamic research
11 Notaries public
12 The handling of legal cases in courts according to Islamic law

Undoubtedly the Saudi Arabian *Ulama* enjoyed a unique status while developing, reforming and unifying the judicial system of the country. The Ulama were never handicapped by a situation which confronted various Muslim countries; they

> were not faced with an imposed foreign law as the country was never under any colonial rule which would confront them with the dilemma of either calling for its repeal and thus creating a vacuum, or producing an instant Islamic alternative, something beyond their human reach.

Source: *Saudi Arabia's Judicial System* by Solaim

The *Ulama* of Saudi Arabia were not imitators "picking isolated fragments of opinions from the early centuries of Islamic law, arranging them into a kind of arbitrary mosaic, and concealing behind this screen an essentially different structure of ideas borrowed from the West" (*Source: Problems of Modern Islamic Legislation*, by Joseph Schacht, quoted in *The Modern Middle East*, New York: Atherton Press, 1963). Rather, they were faithful, broad-minded followers of the teachings of the Holy *Quran* and the *Sunnah* (tradition), and implemented Islamic laws according to one of the accepted trends of law in Islam, the *Hanbali* school of thought.

4.4   Schools of Islamic law

Underlying the judicial structure are the four schools of thought in Islamic law. They are: the *Hanbali* school; the *Shafii* school; the *Hanafi* school; and, finally, the *Ma'liki* school.

Before the unification of the Saudi judicial system, the courts, as well as individual judges, used to derive their legal judgments from these various schools. That is to say, in Hijaz there were two dominant schools of thought – the *Hanafi*, and the *Shafii*, whereas in Najd, the *Hanbali* school had been the only major source of legal guidance.

After 1927, all the courts of Saudi Arabia were instructed to use six *Hanbali* books for their legal decisions in an effort to establish one sound judicial system. Judges have recourse to the other three schools of legal thought, as well as to their personal discretion, in cases for which no provision is available in the six *Hanbali* books. This has added more flexibility to the judicial system. As the author concluded from his study of the *Shari'ah* at the law schools of Beirut Arab University "the diversity of the four Imams for whom these four schools of thought were named is a god-send for the Islamic nation", reflecting as it does the inherent flexibility of Islamic law in general.

4.5   Other judicial bodies

In order to keep pace with twentieth-century developments, it became evident that the Kingdom's judicial system needed more workable subsidiary organs to cope with the inevitable increase in litigation.

As a result, various judicial organs were created. The following are the most important:

1 The Grievance Board
2 The Committee on Cases of Forgery
3 The Commission on Cases of Bribery
4 The Commission on the Impeachment of Ministers
5 The Commission on the Settlement of Commercial Disputes
6 The Central Committee on Cases of Adulteration
7 The Supreme Commission on Labor Disputes

 8 The Disciplinary Councils for Civil Servants
 9 The Disciplinary Councils for Military Personnel

While some of these organs, such as the Grievance Board, function on a continuous basis, others, such as the various Disciplinary Councils, are *ad hoc* in character (see *Saudi Arabia's Judicial System* by Solaim).

4.6   Religious and Judicial Affairs Agencies

The Religious and Judicial Affairs Agencies play a crucial role in the protection and promulgation of the Islamic faith. The fourth Development Plan (1405–10 AH: 1985–90) provided a brief summary of their responsibilities:

> The Kingdom of Saudi Arabia has, since its inception, followed the *Shari'ah* as its governing code. As the Protector of the Holy Places, it has a particular duty to Islam and the Islamic States to preserve Islamic values and to defend the Religion through the Religious and Judicial Affairs Agencies. The Religious Affairs Agencies are responsible for the Holy Mosque in Makkah and the Prophet's Mosque in Medina. They receive Muslim students from all over the world and train them to be *Ulama* in their own countries. Other activities include religious guidance to enforce public morality, and the propagation of the Faith.
>
> They also translate, print and distribute religious books. Religious Affairs Agencies have further responsibilities for pilgrims providing services and facilities at the borders, on roads leading to Makkah during the *Hajj* period, and at the Holy Places. The Agencies build and maintain mosques, manage public and private philanthropic endowments, and residences for the destitute (*Al Arbatah*). These residences consist of buildings and homes which have been donated by private citizens as charity housing for the poor. Private citizens also donate funds for other religious activities and build mosques. Supervision is provided for endowed libraries which contain rare manuscripts and books, and for a large centre for printing the Holy *Quran*.
>
> The Judicial Services administer the *Shari'ah*, the basis for the legal system. They provide the necessary legal services for civil and criminal cases through the courts. The Notaries Public provide the legal certification required in major personal and commercial transactions such as contracts, registration, and judicial affidavits needed for house mortgages and social security benefits.
>
> The Religious and Judicial Affairs Agencies have specific roles in safeguarding Islamic values and maintaining social stability.

Chapter 5

The Political System

This chapter describes the unique constitution of the Kingdom of Saudi Arabia and provides an account of the formation and role of the Council of Ministers (*Majlis Al-Wuzara*) in the government of the Kingdom.

5.1 The Holy *Quran* as the Constitution

> Prudence, indeed, will dictate that governments long established, should not be changed for light and transient causes; and, accordingly, all experience hath shown, that mankind are more disposed to suffer, while evils are sufferable, than to right themselves by abolishing the forms to which they are accustomed.
>
> *Source*: Declaration of Independence of the United States of America

The purpose of this section is to analyze how the Holy *Quran*, as the Constitution* of Saudi Arabia, provides an effective flexible ground for a governmental system, despite allegations from both East and West that after almost fourteen centuries, the Holy *Quran* may not be adaptable to modern conditions and that, consequently, it would be best to resort to an organic secular constitution.

It is the fundamental assumption of the polity of Saudi Arabia that the Holy *Quran*, correctly implemented, is more suitable for Saudi Muslims than any secular constitution. This assumption must be viewed in the context of a nation which is completely Islamic. Hence, no churches, synagogues, temples or shrines of other religions exist. No proselytizing by other faiths is allowed. The entire Saudi population is Muslim; the only non-Muslims in the country are foreigners engaged

---

* The capitalized version of "Constitution" refers to the fundamental document of Saudi Arabia's polity, ie the Holy *Quran*. This should not be confused with the lower case version, "constitution", which is the official term used to refer to the constitutive terms of reference establishing and governing the Council of Ministers.

in diplomacy, technical assistance or international commerce. If they are non-Muslims, they may practise the rituals of their religion only in the privacy of their homes. So there is no problem of ethnic, religious or linguistic pluralism or (to use Braibanti's term) polycommunality, such as is found in virtually all other developing countries.

It may, however, be worth considering the commonly advanced argument that, since the Holy *Quran* is almost fourteen centuries old, it does not meet current circumstances, is out of date and should be replaced by an organic constitution which presumably would suit these needs and conditions. The author considers that the Holy *Quran*, which Muslims believe is the divine word of God, does suffice to cope with the events and matters of all times if it is rightly followed. Let us look, nevertheless, at the argument that the Holy *Quran* should be replaced by an organic constitution to fit modern times.

To begin with, Islam is a distinctive religion in that according to Islamic doctrine

> the very text and wording of the Holy Book, the *Quran*, has remained unchanged, being neither reworded nor interpolated, for God has undertaken to safeguard it. Other [sacred scriptures], on the other hand, have undergone many influences that have led to discrepancies between their texts as well as division among their followers. In spite of the changed wording which these [scriptures] have undergone, they often fit with similar doctrines adopted by the various nations of the world. These are ascribed to reformers belonging to these people. For the basis of these doctrines is that they fit with the fundamental human nature with which Allah has created mankind.
>
> *Source*: A speech entitled "How the Free World Should Look at the Religion of Islam" by Al Sa'yed Hassan Kutbi (former Minister of Pilgrimage and Endowments), delivered by the Minister in South Korea in his official capacity in 1975

It must also be noted that the Holy *Quran* was written originally in Arabic and that this same Arabic is a living language among over 700 million Muslims. The *Quran* has been translated, but only the Arabic version is used in religious ceremonies and education throughout the world. This is in marked contrast to the scriptural languages of other religions – Pali for Buddhism, Sanskrit for Hinduism, Aramaic and ancient Greek for Christianity – which are no longer spoken by the multitudes. Even Hebrew, the language of Judaism, is regarded as a scriptural language and orthodox Jews view its everyday colloquial (as opposed to liturgical) use as sacrilege.

Islam governed by the Holy *Quran* is not just another religious doctrine; rather, it is unique among other religions as it penetrates into the whole spirit of its adherents through the Holy *Quran* whether individually or collectively, for it has put together authority in the form of the political state. It has been protected against division between religious affairs and state affairs. Religion has been given the authority for legislation and jurisprudence.

Source: *Ibid*

In response to a request to the Saudi Embassy in Paris, the Saudi Ministry of Justice sponsored a seminar dealing with the Islamic *Shari'ah* (law) and human rights in Islam in March 1972 (7 Safar 1392 AH). Among the major interests of the group of Western jurists who participated was a desire to study further the Kingdom's total reliance on the Holy *Quran* for all matters of state.* Examining this crucial issue, a member of the Saudi group replied that, in order to answer this question, we must first realize the basic difference between the two groups – Muslims and Christians – in their understanding of the essence of religion. He noted that the article on religion in the French *Grande Encyclopédie des Sciences, des Lettres et des Arts* included a hundred definitions of religion, and said that, in a similar conference at Paris sponsored by the French government in 1951, 98 definitions out of the existing hundred had been excluded by the participants as being incoherent. They had agreed to discuss only the following two definitions of religion:

1 Religion is the way by which mankind achieves its relations with the supernatural forces
2 Religion is that which includes everything known and a power not coincident with science

As for the first definition, the same member stated that the Muslim delegation to the 1951 conference disagreed with their Western counterparts since Islam simultaneously deals with everything known regarding men's relations with one another as well as with God. Muslims would also disagree with the second definition, because Islam, based on the Holy *Quran*, is compatible with science and intellect. So it does not seem strange that Muslims believe all their affairs should be derived from the Holy *Quran*. One of the prominent *Ulama* of the Islamic *Shari'ah* said, "whenever there is common interest, there exists the *Shari'ah* of God" – even when there are no divine revelations or the Prophet's tradition (*Sunnah*). According to this view, Islamic laws are compatible with science, and, therefore, should be able to cope with civil, criminal and personal affairs in the light of existing conditions.

* The seminar dealing with the Islamic *Shari'ah* and Human Rights in Islam, attended by a group of highly regarded *Ulama* of Saudi Arabia and a group of prominent Western jurists, sponsored by the Ministry of Justice of Saudi Arabia at Riyadh, 1972.

When dealing with the Islamic *Shari'ah*, a distinction should be made between those general rules which are unamendable and unchangeable and those which are interpretive applications of the general rules. The latter may be modified according to changing times and circumstances. As for the general rules, embodied in the Holy *Quran*, they are the Constitution and major system of the Islamic *Shari'ah*, from which are derived the explanatory and detailed rules.* There exist a few man-made constitutions, such as that of the United States of America, which are expected to continue indefinitely as the supreme law of the land; *a fortiori*, the divine Constitution of Islam, the Holy *Quran*, is held in Saudi Arabia to be capable of governing the affairs of Muslims all over the world suitably, relevantly and for all time.

5.2   The Council of Ministers (*Majlis Al-Wuzara*)

> Of all the agencies and organized bodies of the government of Saudi Arabia, the Council of Ministers is the most potent. It derives the power directly from the King. It can examine almost any matters in the Kingdom.(6)
>
> *Source*: *The Saudi Arabian Council of Ministers*, by Charles W Harrington, (*Middle East Journal*, Vol 12, 1958)

Despite its relatively recent origin, the Saudi Council of Ministers emerged in 1953 as the natural political outcome of Abdul Aziz bin Sa'ud's final consolidation of power and unity over the young Kingdom.

After the establishment of Saudi Arabia, King Abdul Aziz divided the administration. He took personal and direct charge of the affairs of both the Central and Eastern Provinces while appointing his second son, Faisal, later to be King, as Viceroy of the Western Province. It was in that Western Province that the grassroots of the present Council of Ministers originated. King Abdul Aziz established two major bodies to govern the affairs of the Hijaz, the Western Province. The first body, which still exists, was the Consultative Council (*Majlis Al-Shura*). A second body, created later, was the Council of Deputies (*Majlis Al-Wukala*) which, in 1953, evolved into the Council of Ministers.

The more important of these two governing bodies was the Council of Deputies (*Majlis Al-Wukala*), established by Royal Decree in December 1931. This decree authorized the establishment of a four member council consisting of a president, the Viceroy of Hijaz (then Prince Faisal), a deputy for foreign affairs, a deputy for finance, and the vice-president of the consultative council. In retrospect, the Council of Deputies was a stronger governing body than the Council of Ministers.

---

* Seminar dealing with the Islamic *Shari'ah* and Human Rights in Islam

According to the decree establishing it, the Council of Deputies derived its authority directly from the King and was able to issue direct instructions originated in the Council to various government departments and agencies.

The Council, upon reaching a decision which concerned a government department, would transmit its policy directly to that body rather than to the King for approval, as the Council of Ministers under its 1954 constitution had to do. It is believed that the need for a decisive and centralized governmental body to deal directly with the affairs of the Hijaz, which was then being gradually but firmly incorporated to the Kingdom, was the reason behind such a move. In fact, the basic difference between the Council of Deputies and its successor was that while the former confined its authority to the Hijaz, the latter became the central administration for the whole Kingdom.

In the early 1940s, having achieved its immediate objective, namely the elimination of the dual administration, the Council of Deputies began to decline, while the central Government began to exercise more comprehensive authority over the whole country, as well as provide more services at the national and local levels. With expansion of the area centrally administered and of services provided by the central Government, new ministries and departments had to be established. Ministries of Foreign Affairs and Finance had already existed since 1930 and 1932 respectively. In 1944, the Ministry of Defense was established, replacing the previous defense agency. In 1951, the jurisdiction of the Ministry of the Interior was extended to the whole of the nation; previously it had been limited to Hijaz Province, functioning as an agency of the interior rather than as a ministry. In 1953, the Ministries of Communications, Education and Agriculture were established, and the Ministry of Commerce was inaugurated in 1954. In the same year, the Ministry of Health was detached from the Ministry of Interior and given separate status.

The successful integration of the Hijaz within the Kingdom enhanced the efforts of King Abdul Aziz to establish the country's first central administrative body, the Saudi Council of Ministers. It was the last stage in the national consolidation of the Kingdom. And since "functions were being assembled under new ministries, it remained for the ministries to be assembled into a co-ordinating body" (Charles W Harrington, *Ibid*). A Royal Decree (dated 9th October 1953: 1 Safar 1373 AH) issued by King Abdul Aziz established the first Saudi Council of Ministers. The Royal Decree dealt with five issues:

1 organization of the Council
2 jurisdiction of the Council
3 the Council's procedures
4 jurisdiction of the President of the Council
5 divisions of the Council of Ministers, council cabinet (staff facilities).

Articles 1 and 2 of Part 1, Article 7 of Part II and Article 8 of Part III of the constitution of the Council of Ministers delineated the Council's main provisions.

Article 1

A council of ministers shall be created under our presidency and, in our absence, under the presidency of our viceroy and Crown Prince.

Article 2

The Council of Ministers shall consist of:

A   His Majesty's active Ministers who are appointed by a Royal Order.

B   The King's Advisers who are appointed by a Royal Order as active members in the Council of Ministers as Ministers of His Majesty.

C   Those whose attendance at the Council of Ministers is desired by His Majesty, the King.

Article 7

State policy within the country and abroad shall be under the surveillance of the Council of Ministers.

Article 8

However, the decisions of the Council of Ministers shall not come into effect until they have been sanctioned by His Majesty the King

> *Source*: "Constitution of the Council of Ministers and Constitution of the Divisions of the Council of Ministers", published in *Umm al-Qura* (Government Official Gazette), No 1508, 26th March 1954 (21 Rajab 1373 AH)

Article 8 reflected a very important aspect of the overall authority of the Council of Ministers. Although the Council of Deputies' competence had been limited to the Hijaz, it exercised more authority than the Council of Ministers, as its decisions were not subject to a Royal sanction. This can be attributed to the events and circumstances that surrounded the creation of the Council of Deputies. First, its authority was geographically limited; secondly, it existed at a time when the need was great for a direct and prompt decision-making process. Also, the fact that King Abdul Aziz used to spend most of his time governing the Central and Eastern provinces while his son, Prince Faisal, was his viceroy in Hijaz, justified the extra measure of authority granted to the Council of Deputies. On the other hand, the establishment of the Council of Ministers came at a time when the central Government had completed the administrative consolidation of the Kingdom. *Mutatis mutandis*, the King's final approval of the Council of Ministers' resolutions paralleled that of the President of the United States' final signature on bills to become law. But this analogy is valid only when restricted to the final signature as the last phase of the decision-making process. Article 18 of Part IV of the constitution of the Council (1954), in describing the mechanism of the Council of Ministers, enumerated the President of the Council's (the King's) functions:

Article 18
The President of the Council of Ministers shall:

First: Supervise the Council of Ministers, the Ministries, and
the Public Departments;
Second: Supervise the execution of Royal Orders and Decrees, and the
laws and decisions issued by the Council of Ministers;
Third: Supervise the carrying out of the budget, through the Office of the
Comptroller of State Accounts;
Fourth: Issue the regulating decisions, instructions, and rules required to
execute Royal Orders and Decrees and laws and decisions approved by
the Council of Ministers and sanctioned by His Majesty the King.

Source: *Ibid*

In essence, the King, as the President of the Council of Ministers, can veto the Council's resolutions. In addition, both the First Deputy and the Second Deputy are responsible to the President of the Council (1958 constitution of the Council of Ministers). As for the member ministers, they are also responsible to the Council of Ministers and its President. Both the resignation and dismissal of ministers are subject to the approval of the President of the Council through a Royal Order.

Article 7 of Part III of the Council's constitution enumerated its spheres of authority. These duties and functions are:

1   The annual budget, the approval of the year-end balance sheet of the State . . ., and the making of new appropriations;
2   international treaties and agreements, and authorizing the Minister of Foreign Affairs to sign them;
3   concession and monopoly contracts granted to individual companies;
4   any contract, measure . . . or obligation for which there is an appropriation in the provisions of the public budget and which involves thirty thousand Saudi Riyals or more if the Ministry concerned deems it necessary, in executing it, to go beyond the established laws of the State. Any appropriation provided for in the authorized budget, however, shall be executed by the Ministry concerned in accordance with the established regulations of the State without reference to the Council of Ministers.
5   The formation of stock companies and the authorization of foreign companies to operate in the Kingdom.
6   Conciliation in disputes to which the State is a party, when such conciliation involves a charge to the State Treasury or a waiver of amounts payable to the State in excess of fifty thousand Saudi Riyals regardless of the origin of the obligation.

7   The appointment and dismissal of directors of Departments and of officials of grade four and above.

8   The creation of new positions, jobs, or grades not included in the budget.

9   All contracts for the employment of foreigners. The employment of foreigners, however, shall be permissible only in case of necessity and when no Saudi national can be found to fill the position or perform the work stipulated in the contract.

10   Agreement to conditional donations. Ministries or Departments may not dispose of State funds, whether by way of donation, sale, exchange, or otherwise, or grant a lease for a period exceeding one year, under the terms of the contract or by way of renewal, unless permission has been requested from the Council of Ministers and its consent to the said contracts has been obtained before they are signed.

The Council of Ministers shall consider those matters which the president of the Council or the Council itself decides to ask (to have referred to it) by the source concerned for discussion and settlement, and it shall also consider the regulations enacted by the Consultative Council or the Department concerned, in order to approve, amend, or reject them.

Source: *Ibid*

These wide and comprehensive functions enabled the Council to achieve a great deal in the administration of the Kingdom.

To a considerable extent, the Saudi Council of Ministers is analogous to the presidential cabinet of the United States as it

does not have independent authority any more than the presidential cabinet has. The Council derives its powers from The King. He has delegated to the Council authority to examine, decide and recommend on almost any phase of Saudi government administration.

Source: *The Saudi Arabian Council of Ministers* by Charles W Harrington

As to procedures followed by the Council of Ministers, the tendency has been towards greater flexibility. Fixed rules regulating procedures at meetings are thus not found in Part III of the Council's constitution. Article 8 of the 1954 Constitution of the Council of Ministers specified that two-thirds of the members should constitute a quorum for a meeting and that its decisions were to be voted on by the majority of members present. An affirmative vote of a majority of those present is essential to ratify a decision. These decisions are not final until sanctioned by the

King, the Council's president. Article 10 of the 1954 constitution stated that the Council's meetings were to be conducted monthly, but the King could call for an extraordinary meeting whenever he deemed it necessary. At present, it is customary for the Council to meet weekly. The Council's deliberations are not made public as a rule. However, its decisions are usually announced except when the Council, in accordance with Article 11 of its constitution, decides otherwise. Articles 12 and 13 discussed the Council's agenda and it was decided by the Council that the agenda should be submitted to the Council's members for study a week prior to a meeting. However, in practice, this requirement of a week's advance notice was not always met. The agenda, due to its urgency or the intensive nature of the Council's work, was sometimes only distributed three days prior to a meeting. Very important or urgent items could be handed out to the Council's members at the opening of the meeting.

According to practice and the new 1958 constitution of the Council of Ministers, the President of the Council and (since the era of King Faisal) his deputy may preside over the Council, regulate debate, conduct voting, announce the Council's decisions and adjourn its meetings. In the 1970s it became customary for the First Deputy of the President's Council to preside over the Council in its weekly meetings by authority of the King. The King himself presided only over extraordinary sessions, such as those for the approval of the country's annual budget and the inauguration of the Kingdom's development plans. The President of the Council may preside over all its meetings at the discretion of the King.

The final part of the constitution deals with the Council of Ministers' four divisions: the Secretariat General, the Office of the Comptroller of the State Accounts, Technical Experts and the Board of Grievance.

The differences between the 1954 and 1958 constitutions of the Council of Ministers are as follows:

1   While the constitution of the Council of Ministers of 1958 abrogated that of 1954, it maintained the four divisions of the Council.
2   In the new constitution, the post of Vice President (now First Deputy President) was made permanent. The Crown Prince, according to previous and present practice, is the First Deputy of the Council of Ministers.
3   The 1958 constitution does not specify the number of sessions of the Council. The constitution of 1954, Article 10, Part III, explicitly required monthly sessions.
4   A significant new rule on voting was introduced in the 1958 constitution: the President of the Council casts the decisive vote in the event of a tie.
5   A new rule for making the Council's decisions final was also introduced in the 1958 constitution. The Kingdom's statutes, treaties, international agreements, concessions and contracts for government

loans are subject to royal approval and the approval of the President of the Council. Such approval is announced by Royal Decree. Aside from these affairs, the Council's approval of other resolutions suffices to render its decisions final.

6   The Council's authority was enlarged by Article 48 of the 1958 constitution. This article authorized the Council to promulgate regulations for internal rules for the Council of Ministers, as well as internal rules for each of the ministries, for the State's municipalities, regulations for impeachment of ministers, regulations for selling and leasing state property and, finally, regulations for provincial administration.

7   The new constitution is composed of 50 articles, while that of 1954 consisted of 21 articles.

5.3   The Cabinet

The phenomenal expansion in the government's activities, along with continued effort to enhance the development of the Kingdom and the wide-ranging program for providing better and expanded services to its citizens, has resulted in the establishment of more ministries, departments and governmental agencies.

Until 1975 (1395 AH), the Saudi cabinet consisted of fourteen ministries represented in the Council of Ministers. But the cabinet formed by Royal Order No A/236 on 13th October 1975 (8 Sh'awal 1395 AH) increased the number of ministries from fourteen to twenty.

This was the largest cabinet in the Kingdom's history. The decision to include new, well-trained, young ministers in the Council further enhanced its performance and quality, and yielded dividends for the country. The Royal Decree appointed three more ministers of state without portfolio as members of the Council of Ministers. It has long been a practice of the King to appoint by Royal Decree ministers of state who are not members of the Council of the Ministers. In appointing a minister of state, the Royal Decree must explicitly indicate that the appointed minister is a member of the Council of the Ministers; otherwise he is automatically excluded.

The fourteen ministries which existed before the expansion of the cabinet were as follows:

Defense
Foreign Affairs
Labor and Social Affairs
Interior
Education
Communications

Chart Va   *The Saudi Council of Ministers*

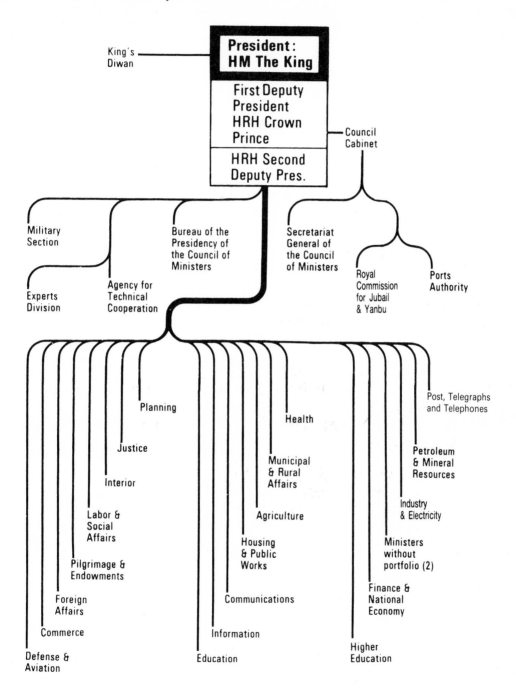

Agriculture
Finance and National Economy
Petroleum and Mineral Resources
Health
Commerce
Pilgrimage and Endowments
Justice
Information

The cabinet of October 1975 established six new ministries for the first time:

Public Works and Housing
Municipal and Rural Affairs
Higher Education
Industry and Electricity
Post, Telegraphs and Telephones
Planning

With the Minister of Planning and the three ministers of state without portfolio, the number of ministers in the Council of Ministers became 23.

By 1987, the Council of Ministers consisted of:

1   the Prime Minister, the King
2   the First Deputy Prime Minister, who is the Commander of the National Guard
3   the Second Deputy Prime Minister, who is Minister of Defense and Aviation

Minister of Agriculture and Water
Minister of Commerce
Minister of Communications
Minister of Education
Minister of Finance and National Economy
Minister of Foreign Affairs
Minister of Health
Minister of Higher Education
Minister of Industry and Electricity
Minister of Information
Minister of Interior, and the Deputy Minister of the Interior
Minister of Justice
Minister of Labor and Social Affairs
Minister of Municipal and Rural Affairs
Minister of Petroleum and Mineral Resources

Minister of Pilgrimage and Endowments
Minister of Planning
Minister of Post, Telegraphs and Telephones (PTT)
Minister of Public Works and Housing
Ministers of State (three)
Minister without portfolio

In 1988, by Royal Decree, the President of the Saudi Ports Authority, the President of the Central Auditing Bureau and the President of the Investigation and Control Board also became members of the Council of Ministers.

5.4   Regional government

The government of the Kingdom's regions is the direct responsibility of the Regional Governors.

With the basic infrastructure of the Kingdom in place, increasing attention is being given to regional development, to ensure that all parts of the Kingdom benefit from the country's continuing progress.

The relevant Strategic Principle of the Fifth Development Plan (1410–15 AH: 1990–95) sets out this objective thus:

> to realize a balanced development between the different regions of the Kingdom, through:
> – considering the development centers as a basis for regional development, according to the defined standards
> – complete utilization of the services and utilities in the different regions of the Kingdom.

Chapter 6

Description and organizational structure of the Kingdom's ministries

This chapter provides the reader with a unique overview of the function and structure of the Kingdom's government at ministerial level. Included at the end of this chapter is the General Presidency of Youth Welfare.

In each case there is a brief introduction, explaining the main responsibilities of the organization and, in many cases, brief background notes on the development, goals and achievements of the ministry are given.

For ease of reference, the ministries have been dealt with in alphabetical order, as follows:

1   Agriculture and Water
2   Commerce
3   Communications
4   Defense and Aviation
5   Education
6   Finance and National Economy
7   Foreign Affairs
8   Health
9   Higher Education
10   Industry and Electricity
11   Information
12   Interior
13   Justice
14   Labor and Social Affairs
15   Municipal and Rural Affairs
16   Petroleum and Mineral Resources
17   Pilgrimage and Endowments
18   Planning
19   Post, Telegraphs and Telephones
20   Public Works and Housing
21   Youth Welfare

Chart VIa   *Ministry of Agriculture and Water*

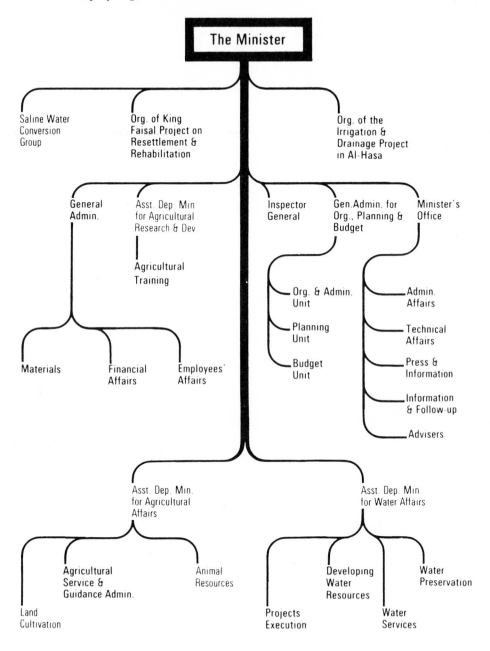

Source: Obtained by the author from the Ministry of Agriculture, Riyadh. Author's translation.

6.1   Ministry of Agriculture and Water

The function of the Ministry of Agriculture and Water is to implement Government economic plans and programs concerned with agriculture, water development, desalination, irrigation and conservation of scarce water.

The Ministry is also responsible for animal resources, fisheries, grain silos and locust control.

6.2   Ministry of Commerce

The function of the Ministry of Commerce comprises foodstuff quality control, consumer protection, the registration of companies and commercial agents, labelling regulations and standards.

The Ministry is now divided into three major sections, each headed by a Deputy Minister. These three sections are:

- Commerce
- Supplies
- Administrative and Financial Affairs

The Ministry is responsible for vetting all applications for the establishment of all types of company and for ensuring that any revisions of commercial contracts conform to current regulations. Also, in the commercial sector, the Ministry has responsibilities for both domestic and foreign trade.

The Supplies sector has the task of estimating the Kingdom's needs for basic food commodities and calculating the quantities which must be imported to ensure continuous availability. It also monitors stores of basic commodities held within the Kingdom and exercises control over prices.

Consumer protection which also falls within the Supplies sector involves the maintenance of quality control laboratories in a number of cities, the prevention and detection of commercial fraud, and the introduction of clearly marked pricing of commodities to enable consumers to make informed choices.

> The Ministry at present (1409 AH: 1989) has 18 branches in Abha, Arar, Baha, Buraida, Dammam, Ha'il, Hofuf, al-Jawf, Jeddah, Madinah (*sic*), Makkah, al-Mujamma'a, Najran, Jizan, Tabuk, Taif, Unaiza and Yanbu.
>
> The services of these branches cover limited areas of the Kingdom and none of these branches, except for Dammam and Jeddah, have permanent sites. There is an urgent need for the establishment of more branches and the construction of permanent buildings to house them.
>
> The number of quality control laboratories at present is 7. These are located in Dammam, Halatu Ammar, Haditha, Jeddah, Jizan, Jubail and

Chart VIb *Ministry of Commerce*

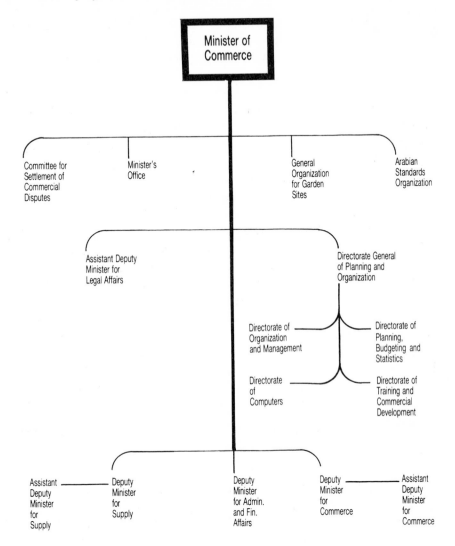

Riyadh. The number of such laboratories is expected to rise to ten by the end of 1410 AH (1990), but there is still an urgent need for the provision of laboratories at all land, sea and airports, as well as [for the upgrading of some existing facilities].

The Ministry's commercial attache's offices abroad are located in Britain (London), Kuwait, Lebanon (Beirut), Switzerland (Geneva), Turkey, Singapore and the United States of America (Washington).

Source: Ministry of Commerce – 1409 AH (1989)

6.3 Ministry of Communications

The function of this ministry is to undertake the design, building and maintenance of the Kingdom's network of roads. The Ministry is also responsible for the co-ordination of all surface transportation, including bus services and railways.

> The Ministry of Communications came into existence during the early days of the Kingdom of Saudi Arabia. The founder of the country, the late King Abdul Aziz Al Sa'ud, recognized the role that transportation and communication would play in the development and progress of the newly born Kingdom.
>
> In keeping pace with the progress achieved in other sectors in the Kingdom, the transportation and communication sector has witnessed amazing changes during the last few decades. As the material resources of the Kingdom have grown in recent years, the role of transportation and communication has continued to expand. This sector has played a key role in the overall development of the Kingdom's economy and has had a significant impact on the lives of the Kingdom's citizens.
>
> In addition to the vastness of the Kingdom, Saudi Arabia is characterized by extremes of climate and geography ranging from high, rugged mountain ranges to rocky plains and vast deserts of sand. In carrying out its vital assignment, the Ministry of Communications has had to deal with the complex problems caused by such extremes.
>
> It is our goal to link all the Kingdom's population centres with a first-class road system of about 30,000 kilometers of paved roads.
>
> Hussein Al-Mansouri, Minister of Communications

6.4 Ministry of Defense and Aviation

The Ministry of Defense and Aviation is responsible for the Kingdom's Army, Navy and Air Force. The Ministry also has responsibility for the construction of civilian airports (as well as military bases), and for meteorology.

The current Minister of Defense and Aviation is the Second Deputy Prime Minister, Prince Sultan bin Abdul Aziz. The Minister and the Vice Ministers perform similar functions and exercise similar authority, despite the fact that the Vice Ministers are second on the administrative scale of the Ministry. His Royal Highness, the Minister, delegates his authority to the Vice Ministers at all times, whether the Minister is in the country or abroad.

A similar delegation of authority applies to the General Chief of Staff and the Assistant Chief of Staff.

Saudi Arabia's armed forces, according to seniority, are composed of:

Chart VIc *Ministry of Communications*

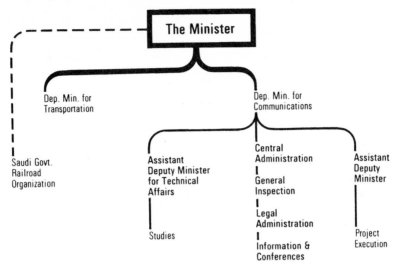

Note: The October 1975 Cabinet established a new Ministry of Post, Telecommunications and Telephones, thus curtailing the scope of this Ministry.

Source: Obtained by author from the Ministry of Communications, Riyadh. Author's translation.

1 The Army
2 The Air Force
3 The Navy

There is no compulsory draft; recruiting is conducted purely on a voluntary basis. Once a person is recruited, he joins a training center; then, as a private, he is referred to one of the army's special units according to the needs of the Army.

A candidate seeking to join one of the Saudi military academies after high school enrols for a period of three years, graduating at the end of the third year as a second lieutenant without specific specialty. He would then be sent to one of the Army's schools for specialization, after which he would become a member of one of the Army's corps. Currently, in Saudi Arabia, there are four military academies. These are:

1 King Abdul Aziz Military College (Riyadh)
   Confers a Bachelor of Military Science degree
2 King Faisal Air Force College (Riyadh)
   Offers a Bachelor's degree
3 Command and Staff College (Riyadh)
   Offers a degree which equals a Master of Science degree in Military Science

4 Internal Security College
Offers a Bachelor's degree in Internal Security Science. This college is under the supervision of the Ministry of the Interior.

This section will be restricted to the Army of Saudi Arabia. There will be no elaboration on either the Navy or the Air Force as they were not included in the interviews conducted by the author.

The Saudi Arabian Army consists of the following units:

Combat Units
1 Infantry
2 Artillery
3 Armoured
4 Air Defense

Support Units
5 Signal
6 Maintenance
7 Transportation
8 Engineering

Supply Units
9 Ordnance
10 Supply

Naturally there are various schools in the army which train men for the ten major units of the army. These schools are as follows:

1 Maintenance
2 Infantry
3 Artillery
4 Armoured
5 Air Defense
6 Engineering Corps
7 Signal Corps
8 Airborne Corps
9 Administrative Affairs

Moreover, the Saudi Arabian Army, believing strongly in good quality education at all levels and in various fields, incorporates within its structure the following institutes and schools:

1 Foreign Languages Institute

2   Technical Institute of the Air Force
3   Musical Institute of the Armed Forces

As for the general schools of the Army, they are:

1   School of Medical Services
2   School of Clerical Training
3   School of Physical Education
4   Military Police School

The period of training at these four general schools varies from two to two and a half years. They graduate Non-Commissioned Officers (NCOs).

Moreover, the Ministry of Defense carries the burden of further educating its military personnel as well as spreading and making available adult education throughout the various units of the armed forces.

It also sends men for further training in different countries – to Belgium, Britain, France, West Germany and the United States, and, in Asia, to Pakistan and Nationalist China (Taiwan). Within the countries of the Middle East, some Ministry of Defense personnel are sent to the Arab Republic of Egypt and to Jordan. By 1980, in accordance with the Second Five Year Plan, the Ministry of Defense and its armed forces had achieved a level of efficiency which has enabled the Kingdom to pursue with greater ease its perceived role in the Gulf area.

The Fifth Five Year Plan (1410–15 AH: 1990–95) sets out the following basic strategic principle for the Ministry of Defense:

> To continue the development of the Kingdom's ability to protect itself; to maintain the existence of a protective defense and security system; and to deepen the citizenry's feelings of loyalty and affiliation.

A further extract from the Fifth Five Year Plan which is worthy of note is:

> To introduce compulsory military service; and to introduce basic military courses into secondary school curricula.

All this attests to the Kingdom's commitment to maintaining and enhancing its defense capability.

6.4.1   SAUDI ARABIAN NATIONAL GUARD

In the context of defense, reference must be made to the National Guard, which is an independent force presided over by Crown Prince Abdullah bin Abdul Aziz, the Deputy Prime Minister. The Saudi National Guard's duties parallel those of the National Guard of the United States. In case of emergency, it can join with the armed forces for the defense of the Kingdom.

Chart VId *Ministry of Defense and Aviation*

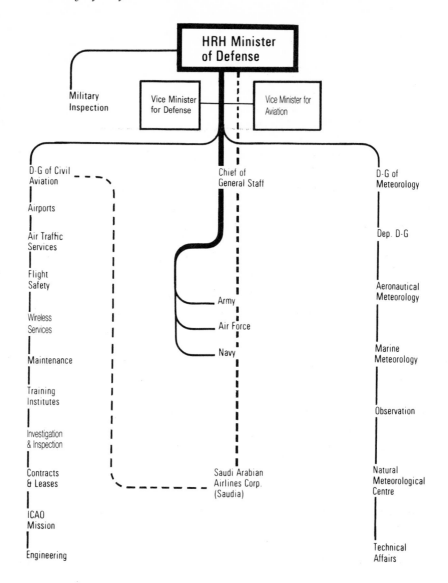

The National Guard is both an integral cultural institution and a military force. It was formed of the sons and grandsons of those Mujahideen who offered their arms, their wealth and their lives to assist the late King Abdul Aziz in unifying the Arabian peninsula.

In 1348 AH (1928), after the borders of the Kingdom had been settled and conditions in the peninsula had calmed, King Abdul Aziz ordered that an office for Jihad and Mujahideen should be established to gather and unite the Mujahideen and to assure them and their families of a good standard of living. This office was the nucleus of the National Guard.

In 1374 AH (1954), it was decreed that the National Guard should be formed in all parts of the Kingdom. An independent budget was provided and the regulations governing its work were issued.

In the early years of its existence, the Saudi National Guard, under the command of a succession of princes, passed through a formative period which lasted until 1382 AH (1962). In these years select brigades of Mujahideen, armed with guns and light weapons, were formed.

The year 1382 AH (1962) marked an important turning-point in the history of the National Guard. In that year a Royal Decree was issued, appointing HRH Prince Abdullah bin Abdul Aziz Commander of the National Guard, and the process of converting the National Guard from simple units of Mujahideen and volunteers into a major cultural and military institution began. All the military and administrative systems of the National Guard were reorganized to enable them to accommodate the ambitious development and modernization programs.

The scope of these programs was so extensive that it was decided by Royal Decree in 1387 AH (1967) that HRH Prince Badr bin Abdul Aziz should be appointed Deputy Commander of the National Guard, to provide HRH Prince Abdullah with the strong support required throughout the developmental and modernization process.

To grasp the unique role of the Saudi National Guard in the life of the Kingdom of Saudi Arabia, it is important to understand the cultural as well as the military function of the institution.

On the military front, the National Guard has become a sophisticated fighting force, benefiting from the latest military theories on organization, armaments and training.

On the cultural front, great energy and resources have been devoted to the implementation of a wide range of social programs, including programs for religious affairs and spiritual guidance, for medical services, for housing and new cities, for culture and education, for information and communications, and for sport.

The spirit of community service is strong in the National Guard and its many social programs include participation in the provision of services for the pilgrims during the annual *Hajj*.

6.5 Ministry of Education

The Ministry of Education is responsible for the provision of free general education in primary, intermediate and secondary schools, and the establishment of educational services for the handicapped. It also has a responsibility for antiquities and museums.

Chart VIe   *Ministry of Education*

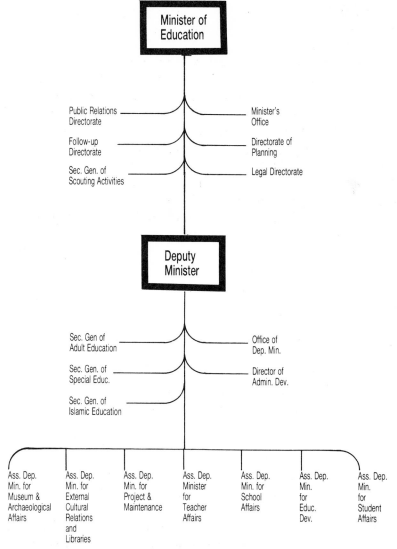

From the very formation of the Kingdom, education was seen to be of primary importance. One of the first acts of King Abdul Aziz bin Sa'ud was to convene an educational gathering in the Holy City of Makkah with a view to initiating the promotion and establishment of educational resources throughout the land. The Ministry of Education continues this tradition of emphasis on the importance of education begun by the Kingdom's founder.

The Kingdom's first Minister of Education was King Fahd. It was his far-sighted perception of the crucial importance of education in general for the development of Saudi Arabia which has led to the extensive educational system (in schools and in vocational training institutions, as well as in the Kingdom's seven universities) which Saudi Arabia enjoys today.

6.6   Ministry of Finance and National Economy

The function of the Ministry of Finance and National Economy is to manage all Government finance, including the budgeting and expenditure of all ministries and government agencies, and to control national economic growth. Its responsibilities include the administration of *Zakat*, income tax and customs duties. Both the Central Department of Statistics and the National Computer Center fall under the Ministry of Finance and National Economy.

It is of interest to note two of the Ministry's objectives under the fifth Five Year Plan (1990–95). The first is to rationalize the system of direct and indirect subsidies on the many goods and services provided by the state. The second is to adopt a fiscal policy which keeps the level of government expenditure in line with government revenues. (*Source*: Fifth Five Year Plan.)

6.7   Ministry of Foreign Affairs

The Ministry of Foreign Affairs has responsibility for the Kingdom's political, cultural and financial relations with other countries. Through the Kingdom's embassies, the Ministry monitors diplomatic relations between Saudi Arabia and the outside world.

In the context of international relations, we should mention a unique project – the Diplomatic Quarter in Riyadh. The Diplomatic Quarter is an area of Riyadh dedicated to the needs of foreign embassies and their staff. The construction of the Quarter has involved the building of not only the essential infrastructure but also full residential and recreational facilities. These include an international schools complex, sports fields and recreation centers, Arabic language schools, a diplomatic club and thirteen mosques (nine in the residential area and four in the central area). Much care has been given to the appearance of the Diplomatic Quarter. A large area around the Quarter has been landscaped.

6.8   Ministry of Health

The Ministry of Health, originally a government department but given full ministry status in 1370 AH (1950 AD), is responsible for the supervision of health care and hospitals in both the public and private sectors of the Kingdom of Saudi Arabia.

Chart VIf *Ministry of Finance and National Economy*

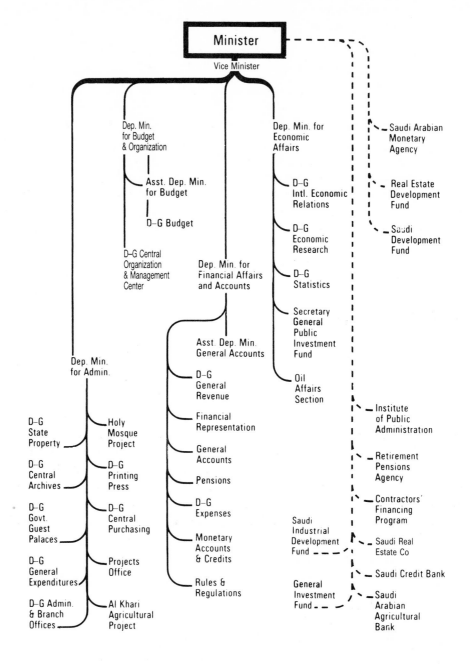

Chart VIg   *Ministry of Foreign Affairs*

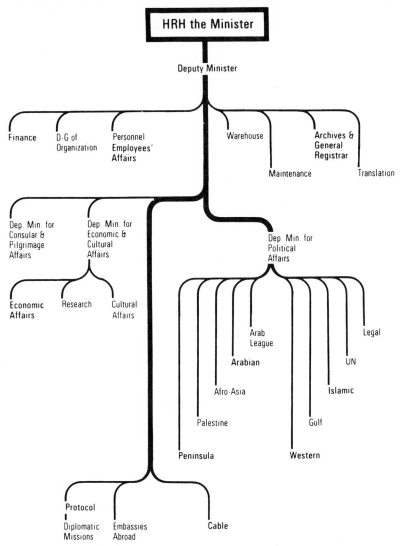

Source: Obtained by author from the Ministry of Foreign Affairs. Author's translation.

6.9   Ministry of Higher Education

The Ministry of Higher Education is responsible for all universities and institutes of higher education in the Kingdom of Saudi Arabia.

To illustrate how Islam permeates every aspect of education in the Kingdom of Saudi Arabia, it may be useful briefly to quote selected passages from the Ministry of Higher Education's report on progress in the ten year period 1395 AH–1405 AH (1975–85):

Chart VIh   *Ministry of Health*

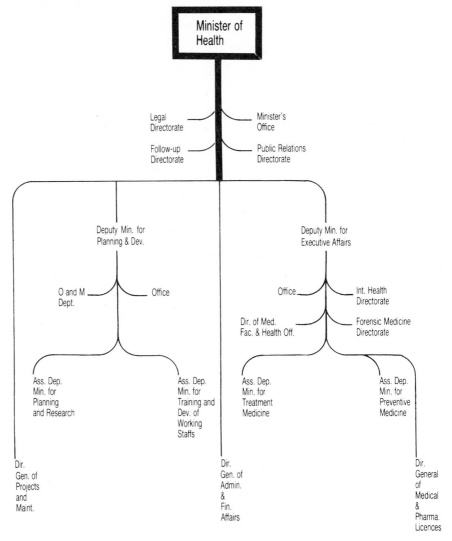

The general progress of the Kingdom's development is characterized by the originality of its philosophy, the concentration of its aims, and its close links to Islamic principles and values and to the cultural heritage of Saudi Arabia as a Muslim society.

The development plans of the Kingdom place great emphasis on the human element – by providing care, education and training for its citizens – as the main basis of successful development.

Since higher education is one of the specialized academic stages of education required for the fulfilment of the present and future needs of society, the aims of higher education emerge from the core of social and

Chart VIi   *Ministry of Higher Education*

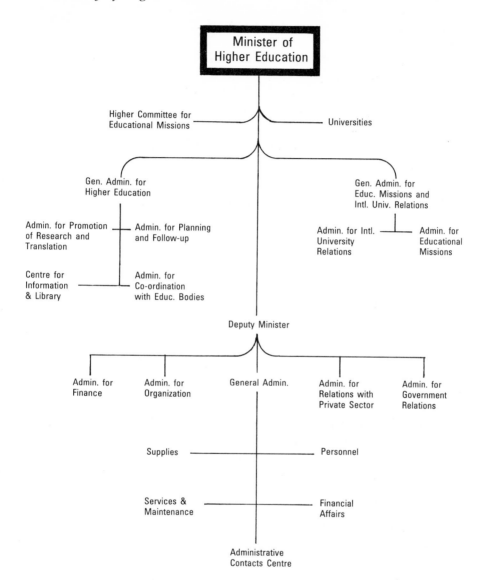

economic needs determined by the Kingdom in its ambitious quest for development.

The educational policy defines the general aims of education as follows:

The purpose of education is the sound and complete understanding of Islam, inculcating and disseminating the Islamic faith and promulgating Islamic values, instruction and ideals to students, as well as enabling them to acquire different aspects of knowledge and skills, developing constructive behavioral trends, reforming society economically, socially and culturally, and preparing individuals for a useful and constructive role in society.

Based on this policy, the aims of higher education in the Kingdom represent Islamic principles and values, while ensuring and complementing the general aims of the comprehensive development plan.

6.10   Minister of Industry and Electricity

The Ministry of Industry and Electricity is responsible for the development of the Kingdom's industrial infrastructure and for all electrical power generation projects. Industrial licensing, the protection and encouragement of national industrial activity and the collation and provision of industrial statistics, all fall within the Ministry's responsibility.

6.11   Ministry of Information

The Ministry of Information is responsible for the Kingdom's television broadcasting, radio broadcasting, the press and the publication of printed material. It is also responsible for the Kingdom's relations with the foreign press.

Within the Kingdom, the Ministry provides a focal point for all information about Saudi Arabia. Through its country-wide network of Information Centers it offers to Saudi Arabian citizens a ready source of data on the history and culture of the Kingdom.

Overseas, the Saudi Arabian Information Center in London (Cavendish House, 18 Cavendish Square, London W1), fully equipped with a library, lecture room and viewing theater, offers a similar facility to the public there. There is also a Saudi Arabian Information Center in Tunis.

The Saudi Press Agency which forms part of the Ministry of Information, has offices in Bonn, Cairo, London, Tunis and Washington DC.

Chart VIj   *Ministry of Industry and Electricity*

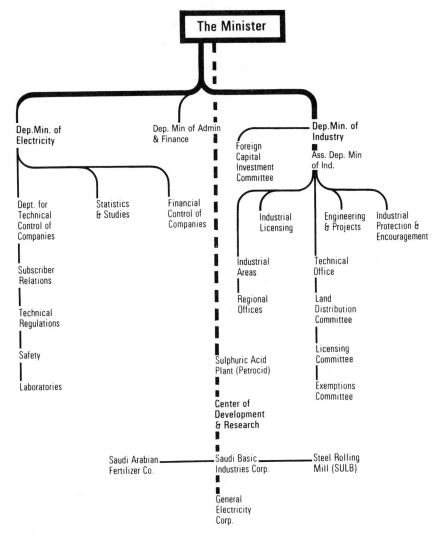

Note: The Ministry was formed out of the former Ministry of Commerce and Industry in October 1975

6.12   Ministry of the Interior

The Ministry of the Interior is responsible for all aspects of government related to security and the protection of human life and property. Within its jurisdiction fall Public Security, Civil Defense, the Fire Service, the Police and the Special Security and Investigation Forces.

Chart VIk   *Ministry of Information*

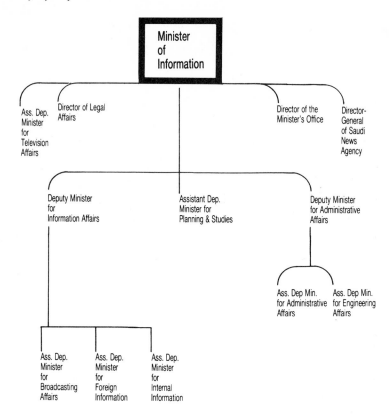

The Ministry of the Interior has as a prime responsibility the maintenance o the Kingdom's laws, based on Islam, and one of its functions is to carry ou sentences passed on offenders by the courts.

It is especially noteworthy that the Kingdom of Saudi Arabia is the first state t be governed entirely according to Islamic law.

6.13   Ministry of Justice

The Ministry of Justice is responsible for the administration of *Shari'ah* law and the provision of legal services for all Saudi citizens.

6.14   Ministry of Labor and Social Affairs

The Ministry of Labor and Social Affairs is concerned with the development and use of the Kingdom's human resources. It is responsible for manpower planning, labo

Chart VII *Ministry of the Interior*

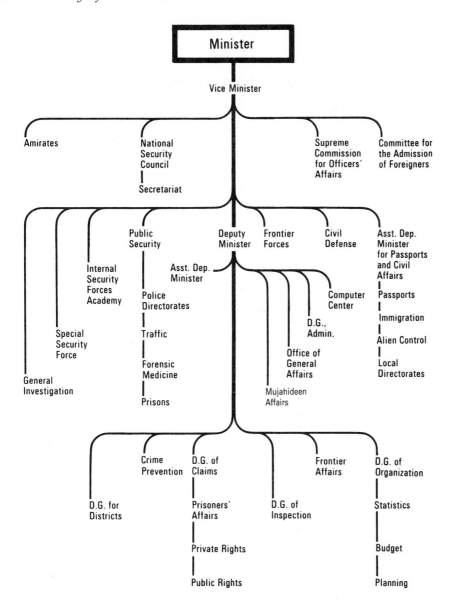

Chart VIm *Ministry of Justice*

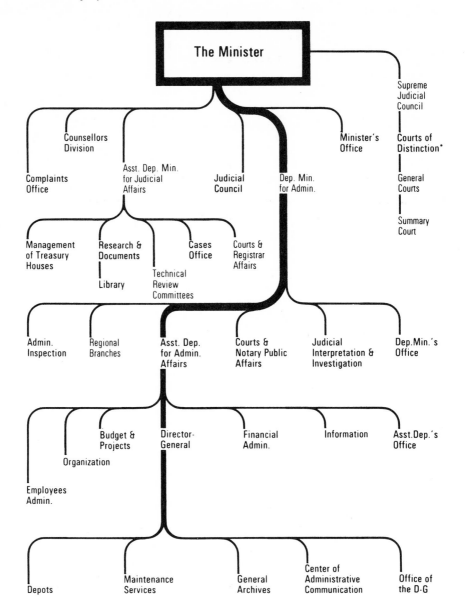

*Parallels the Supreme Appellate Courts in the United States.
Source: Obtained by the author from the Ministry of Justice, Riyadh. Author's translation.

Chart VIn   *Ministry of Labor and Social Affairs (A)*

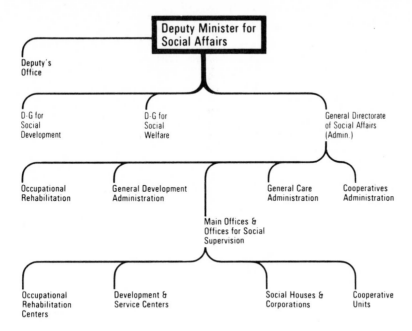

Chart VIo   *Ministry of Labor and Social Affairs (B)*

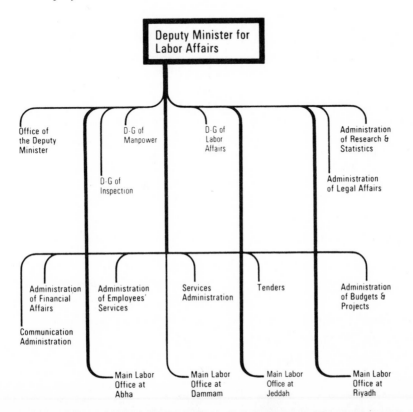

Chart VIp   *Ministry of Labor and Social Affairs (C)*

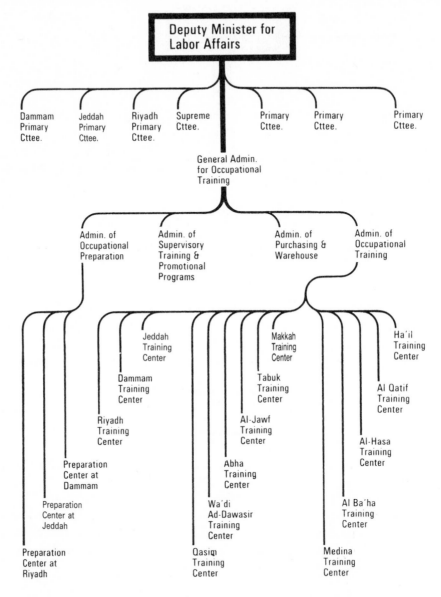

relations and the general monitoring of all matters relating to employment, as well
as for social security affairs.

In keeping with the Kingdom's Islamic foundation, the Ministry is charged
with ensuring that the less fortunate citizens of Saudi Arabia, the physically or
mentally handicapped, the aged and the destitute, are cared for within a humane
society. Throughout the Kingdom, facilities for the disabled and those needing
rehabilitation have been established.

Chart VIq   *Ministry of Labor and Social Affairs (D)*

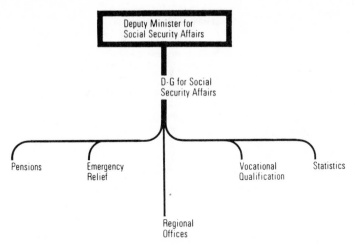

Source: Obtained by author from the Ministry of Labor and Social Affairs, Riyadh. This Ministry is now divided into three major units, the Deputy Ministry of Social Affairs, that of Labor and that of Social Security Affairs.

6.15   Ministry of Municipal and Rural Affairs

The Ministry of Municipal and Rural Affairs, which was established in 1395 AH (1975), is responsible for the administration of the municipalities throughout the Kingdom. Its primary functions include city and town planning, and the development and maintenance of the basic infrastructure, such as roads, town cleaning and hygiene.

6.16   Ministry of Petroleum and Mineral Resources

The Ministry of Petroleum and Mineral Resources is responsible for the administration, development and exploitation of the Kingdom's oil, gas and mineral resources. In discharging its wide responsibilities, the Ministry works in conjunction with Petromin, the General Petroleum and Mineral Organization.

6.17   Ministry of Pilgrimage (*Hajj*) and Endowments (*Awqaf*)

The Ministry of Pilgrimage and Endowments is responsible for the provision of facilities for the visits of pilgrims to the Holy Cities of Makkah and Medina and to other holy places within the Kingdom of Saudi Arabia. This ministry is also responsible for the building and maintenance of mosques throughout the Kingdom, as well as the administration of land held by religious trust.

Chart VIr *Ministry of Municipal and Rural Affairs*

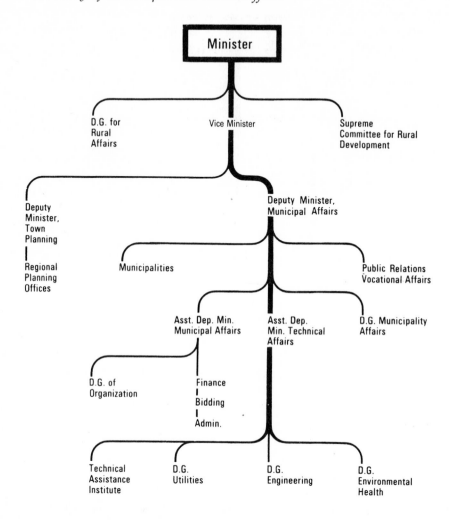

Conscious of the commitment of the Government of the Guardian of the Holy Mosques to provide every assistance and convenience for the pilgrims on *Hajj*, the Ministry of *Hajj* and *Awqaf* has spared no effort to ensure that the Kingdom is able to offer

> the best services to the guests of the All Merciful, pilgrims to God's Sanctuary, from the moment of their arrival in, until their departure from, the Holy Lands.

Source: Minister's Office, Ministry of *Hajj* and *Awqaf*, 1988

This endeavour covers a wide range of concerns. These include:

Chart VIs *Ministry of Petroleum and Mineral Resources*

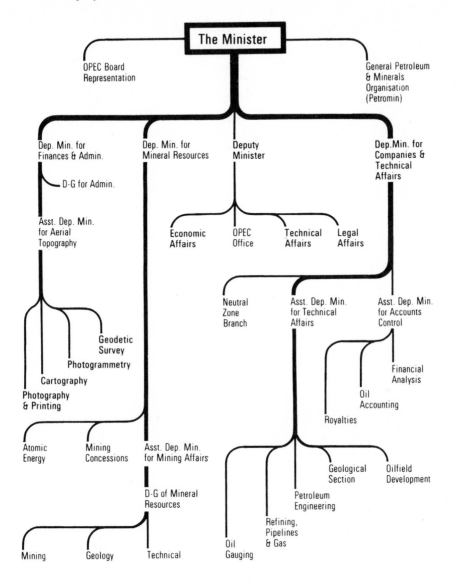

Source: Obtained by the author from the Ministry of Petroleum and Mineral Resources, Riyadh. Author's translation.

- ensuring that the service offered by all pilgrim guides is of an acceptable standard
- improving procedures for pilgrim passport control
- providing pilgrim land stations and reception centers at the Holy Places, with assistance for pilgrims who may become lost
- overseeing the improvement in pilgrim transportation services
- publishing educational materials designed to assist pilgrims in the correct performance of the rites of the *Hajj*
- erecting canopies, shelters and signposts for the convenience and guidance of pilgrims
- undertaking annual maintenance of all buildings and facilities provided for pilgrims on *Hajj*

For Muslims, the *Hajj* is the greatest of all journeys and the Kingdom of Saudi Arabia, conscious of its responsibilities, has done all in its power to permit the maximum number of pilgrims to perform *Hajj* in safety and security.

In the last decade, the Kingdom of Saudi Arabia has invested billions of Saudi riyals in the development of both the Makkah and Medina areas, as well as in the development of the sacred areas in both Mina and Arafat.

6.18   Ministry of Planning

Planning plays a key role in the development of the country.

A supreme planning board was established in 1960. This was replaced by the Central Planning Organization (CPO) in 1964 in accordance with the Council of Ministers' Resolution No 430 (dated 11–12 Ramadhan 1384 AH).

This Resolution set out the CPO's basic functions and objectives. Article 4 of the Resolution read:

4   The said Organization [CPO] shall be charged with the following functions:

a)   To prepare a periodic economic report on the Kingdom, containing an economic analysis and showing the scope of progress achieved and prospective developments.

b)   To prepare economic development plans, provided that the first plan be a five year plan and be approved by the Council of Ministers before being put into effect.

c)   To estimate the total funds required for the implementation of the development plans approved by the Council of Ministers.

d)   To conduct economic studies required for relevant projects and to submit its recommendations thereon.

e)   To assist Ministers and independent agencies in their planning

Chart VIt   *Ministry of Pilgrimage and Endowments*

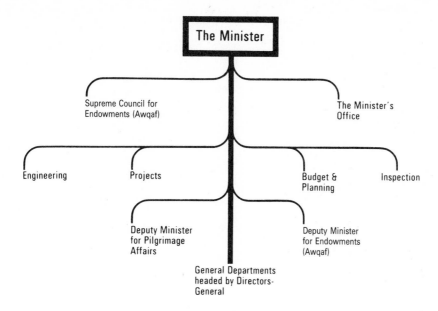

Source: Obtained by the author from the Ministry of Pilgrimage and Endowments, Riyadh. Author's translation.

affairs. To submit technical advice on matters raised by the Custodian of the Two Holy Mosques.

Members of the Organization's staff, at May 1975, numbered 194 persons. Work in the CPO was divided into two categories, administrative and technical. Out of the total number of CPO employees, 93 held administrative jobs; their educational level was beneath that of a Bachelor's degree. Another 101 occupied technical or specialized positions in the CPO. All of these were university graduates and a moderate percentage had a Master's degree in various fields (eg Engineering, Economics, Public Administration, Business Administration). The Central Planning Organization also co-operated with foreign advisory groups in the field of planning and development.

The CPO implemented the Kingdom's First Five Year Plan (1390–95 AH: 1970–75). Thereafter, responsibility for the construction and supervision of succeeding Five Year Plans has been vested in the Ministry of Planning.

We have emphasized elsewhere that the pace of development in the Kingdom in the last twenty years has been extraordinary. Such progress would not have been possible without a highly efficient central planning function.

Chart VIu *Ministry of Planning*

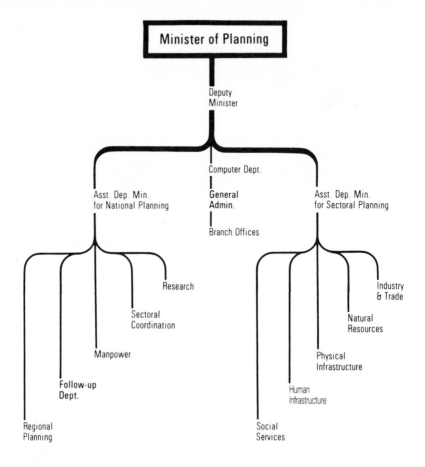

6.19 Ministry of Post, Telegraphs and Telephones (PTT)

The size of the Kingdom and the implementation of its ambitious development program necessitated the creation of a highly efficient postal and telecommunications system.

The Ministry of Post, Telegraphs and Telephones was established in 1396 AH (1976), taking over responsibility for post and telecommunication from the older Ministry of Communications. The new Ministry immediately set about creating the highly sophisticated telecommunications service which all those in the Kingdom (government, industry, commerce and the public) now enjoy.

Chart VIv   *Ministry of Post, Telegraphs and Telephones*

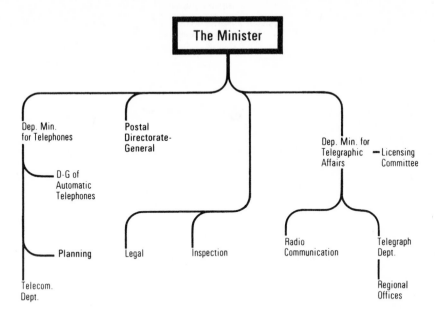

6.20   Ministry of Public Works and Housing

The Ministry of Public Works and Housing is responsible for the construction, supervision and maintenance of government building and housing projects. The Ministry is also responsible for the evaluation of tenders and the allocation of contracts for public housing projects.

6.21   General Presidency of Youth Welfare

Amongst the wide range of major development activities undertaken by the Government, the interests and well-being of the young have not been ignored. The Kingdom is well aware that the youth of today are the men and women of tomorrow and that, since any country's greatest wealth is its people, every care must be taken to provide the young with the means of self-development, physical as well as mental.

> The idea of Youth Welfare in the Kingdom of Saudi Arabia goes back to the year 1365 AH (1945 AD) when interest in football [soccer] began to spread all over the Kingdom.
>
> *Source: Riyadh, City of the Future* (King Saud University Press, Riyadh, date unknown)

Chart Viw *Ministry of Public Works and Housing*

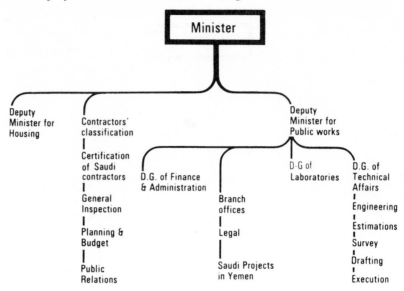

In response, it was realized that facilities and an organizational framework must be set up.

> The first Department responsible for the organization of the sport movement was established in 1952 at the Ministry of the Interior. In 1960 the Youth Welfare Department of the Ministry of Education became the authority responsible for Youth activities in both the national and scholastic sectors.
>
> In 1962, the task of national sector Youth Welfare became the responsibility of the Youth Welfare Department of the Ministry of Labor and Social Affairs.
>
> In 1394 AH (1974 AD), Resolution No 560 of the Council of Ministers decreed that Youth Welfare should become an independent Department under the name "The General Presidency for Youth Welfare", administratively responsible to the Supreme Council for Youth Welfare.

> *Source: Ibid*

With the required investment, the General Presidency of Youth Welfare has pursued its aim of providing young people in the Kingdom with a means of employing their leisure time to develop their athletic talents, to strengthen their bodies and to instil in themselves the genuine traditions of Arabian Islamic culture. There were in 1988 some 70 major sports centers widely distributed throughout the towns and districts of the Kingdom;

huge structures which enable Saudi youth to practise different sporting activities and to utilize their energy and gifts for the good and benefit of their society.

> *Source: Youth and Sport: Structures, Facts and Features* (General Presidency of Youth Welfare, 1408 AH (1988))

The implementation of these policies has been rewarded with many oustanding successes for young Saudi athletes in international competitions, most recently in the form of victory in the final of the FIFA Under-16 World Football Competition in Scotland in June 1989.

Chapter 7

Description of major Government Agencies

This chapter provides information on four major Government Agencies:

1 Audit Bureau
2 Civil Service Bureau
3 Institute of Public Administration
4 Investigation and Control Board

These four independent agencies are usually presided over by an official with the rank of Minister of State.

At the end of this chapter, similar information is provided on the:

1 Central Department of Statistics
2 Meteorological and Environmental Protection Administration (MEPA)
3 Saudi Arabian Standards Organization (SASO)
4 Saudi Ports Authority (SPA)

7.1 Bureau of General Auditing

The Bureau of General Auditing was set up in 1373 AH (1953) with the crucial task of monitoring the performance of the executive units of Government to ensure that the state's revenues were correctly and efficiently deployed in the implementation of the development programs for the general benefit of society.

The Bureau, which was formed as a subsidiary of the Council of Ministers, was made up of four departments:

1 General Secretariat
2 Monitoring of the State's Accounts
3 Technical Experts
4 Grievances

The independence of the Bureau was confirmed in the following terms by Royal Decree No M9, issued on 11/2/1391 AH;

> In order to consolidate the agency's authority and to enable it to perform its responsibilities effectively, it was decided that it would be independent of all other ministries and governmental agencies. The nature of the agency's duties necessitates its complete independence, for its task is to monitor the performance of the ministries and governmental agencies.

In its function of financial monitoring, the Bureau aims:

- to find out any deviation from the set goals in the course of implementation
- to study the cause of such deviations, correcting errors and ensuring they do not recur
- to provide the ministries and governmental agencies which it monitors with guidance on the right methods of managing their allocated budgets and assigned projects

The organizational structure of the Bureau of General Auditing is shown in Chart VIIa.

7.2   Civil Service Bureau

It is the function of the Civil Service Bureau to plan the civil manpower required in the government sector and to ensure that the competence of civil servants matches the requirements of the Kingdom as it implements its various development programs.

The Civil Service Bureau is responsible to the Civil Service Board which was established in Riyadh in 1395 AH (1975). The Board is chaired by the King and the Crown Prince is Deputy Chairman. The duties of the Board are:

- to suggest civil service laws
- to issue regulations and statutes related to the civil service and to decide on issues relating to civil servants, referred to it by ministries and government departments
- to co-operate and co-ordinate with responsible bodies in the following areas:
  - to draw up general policies for public service and to decide the relevant executive plans and programmes
  - to develop manpower in government units and to raise their efficiency and productivity by training

Chart VIIa   *Audit Bureau*

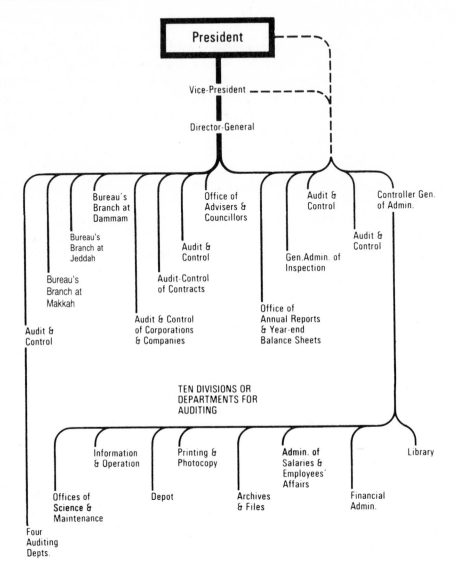

Source: Obtained by the author from the General Auditing Bureau, Riyadh. Author's translation.

- to develop the present administrative structure and systems in government and to improve work procedures
- to practise strict administrative supervision on all the activities of government units, including public corporations, to ensure they operate within the context and spirit of the rules and regulations
- job classification

Chart VIIb   *Civil Service Bureau*

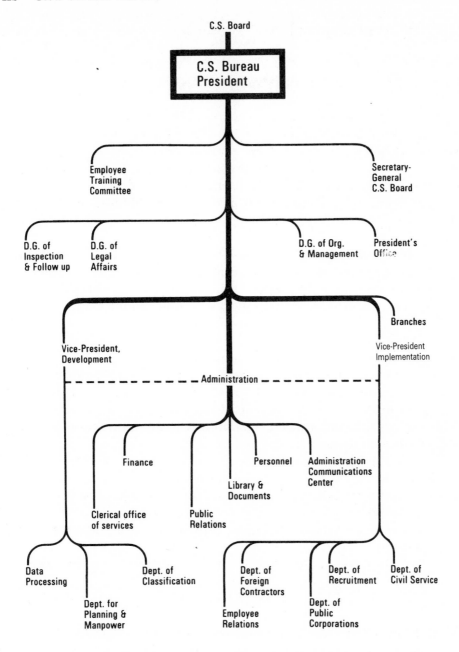

Source: Obtained by the author from the Civil Service Bureau. Author's translation.

– to study rates of salaries and wages and to suggest any alterations; also to issue regulations concerning payment and extension of allowances and remuneration to civil servants

7.3   Institute of Public Administration (IPA)

One of the essential needs of a developing nation is the capacity to deal swiftly and efficiently with its administrative problems. A prerequisite for this is the proper administrative training of the country's civil servants at all levels. This is best accomplished by the systematic administrative training of existing government employees rather than by wholesale replacement. Indeed, in the case of Saudi Arabia, replacement would have been almost impossible at the time the country started its reform programs, if the majority of government employees were not to be expatriates.

The government agency responsible for administrative reforms in the Kingdom is the Institute of Public Administration (IPA) in Riyadh, founded by Royal Decree No 93, dated 10th April 1961 (24 Shawwal 1380 AH).

The Institute of Public Administration is a government entity whose functions are as follows:

– to raise the degree of efficiency among the government's employees
– to prepare those employees in a practical and scientific manner, so that they are able to shoulder their responsibilities and exercise their authority in a fashion which will lead to higher administrative standards and the consolidation of the foundation of the country's national economy
– to organize training courses
– to participate in the administrative organization of government
– to render advice on all administrative problems submitted by various ministries
– to conduct and encourage research in the field of administrative affairs
– to strengthen cultural relations in the realm of public administration

The IPA is governed by a Board of Directors composed of the following:

1 Minister of Finance and National Economy (President)
2 Vice Minister of Finance and National Economy (Vice-President).

and the following members:

3 Deputy Minister of Education

4 Deputy Director of Riyadh University
5 Director General of the Civil Service Bureau's Administration
6 Director General of the IPA

The Board is entrusted with formulating the general policy of the Institute and supervising its execution. The Institute is autonomous and possesses the necessary authority for the achievement of its objectives. The Board may also issue whatever regulations and instructions may be necessary to guarantee the efficient execution of the Institute's work. This unusual autonomy is suggested by the composition of the Board, whose president is the Minister of Finance.

Throughout its three decades of operation, two purposes have been dominant for the IPA: (1) to train civil servants through a range of skill and experience levels and (2) to advise and consult in the resolution of administrative problems within departments and agencies of government.

The major activities of the IPA reflect its functional divisions: (1) manpower development, (2) administrative consultancy, (3) administrative research, (4) information services, (5) employment and training, and (6) projects. Activities within these divisions are summarized below.

7.3.1   MANPOWER DEVELOPMENT

Training activities fall within 'manpower development'. The following are major training activities at IPA:

- Senior Management Development: This program seeks to acquaint senior government and Gulf Co-operation Council (GCC) officials with trends and developments in their areas of responsibility.
- Pre-Service Training: Pre-service training is conducted for new civil service employees who are recent graduates (ie holders of Intermediate and Secondary Certificates, as well as university graduates).
- In-Service Training: In-service training aims at skill and capability development among government employees in common administrative specialties. Some sixteen different fields (public administration, finance, accounting, clerical work, computer usage, etc) are currently offered.
- Special-Purpose: Special-purpose programs are arranged for training needs not met by continuing programs.
- English Language: The English language program was developed to help ensure that scholarship holders going to English-speaking countries for study will possess sufficient competence in English. The program is attended by both government employees and holders of government scholarships who are scheduled for study abroad in an English-speaking country.

   – Educational Methods: Devices and methods to support instruction at the IPA are obtained or developed through the methods programme. An array of teaching aids and audio-visual devices is available.

7.3.2   ADMINISTRATIVE CONSULTANCY PROGRAM

Advisory services in administrative matters are a central feature of IPA activities and may be obtained by any government agency requesting such services. Consultancies cover such topics as communications, organization, economics, financial affairs and budgeting.

   Advisory services provided by the IPA are extended to various parts of the Arab world.

   Administrative reform is a special type of advisory service performed by the IPA and is offered through the general secretariat of the High Committee for Administrative Reform (HCAR).

7.3.3   ADMINISTRATIVE RESEARCH

The IPA carries out research on all topics related to IPA activities. In recent years, the emphasis has been on field research. During the first three years of the third Development Plan, 52 research assignments were completed and an additional 32 studies were scheduled for completion by the end of that Plan period.

7.3.4   INFORMATION SERVICES

Information services include four related activities: (1) library, (2) document center, (3) microfilm center and (4) computer services.

7.3.5   EMPLOYMENT AND TRAINING

Employment refers to IPA personnel, and training includes both local training and study abroad to increase the competence of IPA staff. The IPA has exerted unusual effort to ensure a staff of high quality.

7.3.6   PROJECTS

Projects covers construction work to house the Institute's activities.

   Table 7.1 gives a good indication of the demand for trained administrators in the Kingdom, and how the IPA has responded, between the years 1390/91 and 1406/07 AH (1970/71–86/87).

Table 7.1   *Graduates in different programs of the Institute of Public Administration*

Year		On-the-job training	Pre-job training	Special training	English language	Participants in Higher management	Total
1390/91	(1970/71)	487	—	67	115	58	727
1391/92	(1971/72)	536	—	24	127	29	716
1392/93	(1972/73)	569	184	10	166	69	998
1393/94	(1973/74)	796	132	40	151	—	1,119
1394/95	(1974/75)	899	165	214	166	94	1,538
1395/96	(1975/76)	640	104	204	147	204	1,299
1396/97	(1976/77)	808	158	182	240	184	1,572
1397/98	(1977/78)	2,497	92	137	560	93	3,379
1398/99	(1978/79)	2,574	140	216	571	239	3,740
1399/00	(1979/80)	2,306	189	295	533	286	3,608
1400/01	(1980/81)	2,913	245	306	1,376	565	5,405
1401/02	(1981/82)	3,402	356	423	1,345	497	6,023
1402/03	(1982/83)	3,959	334	301	1,584	775	6,953
1403/04	(1983/84)	3,694	499	910	1,042	855	7,000
1404/05	(1984/85)	3,932	610	679	1,941	607	7,769
1405/06	(1985/86)	3,964	751	427	1,064	503	6,709
1406/07	(1986/87)	5,478	1,226	195	965	482	8,346
Total		39,454	5,184	4,630	12,093	5,540	66,901

Source: Government Statistics

7.4   Investigation and Control Board

Chart VIId illustrates the organization of the Investigation and Control Board.

7.5   Central Department of Statistics

The Central Department of Statistics falls under the authority of the Ministry of Finance and National Economy and is the principal agency in the Kingdom for the collation, analysis and distribution of statistical information. Data processing of the information is the responsibility of the National Computer Center, which is also under the authority of the Ministry of Finance and National Economy.

The objectives of the Central Department of Statistics, as defined in the current Five Year Plan, are as follows:

 − to provide users with reliable statistical information in support of the strategic guidelines of the Development Plan
 − to improve the range, quality and timeliness of statistical information
 − to continue to provide and improve centralized automatic data

Chart VIIc *Institute of Public Administration*

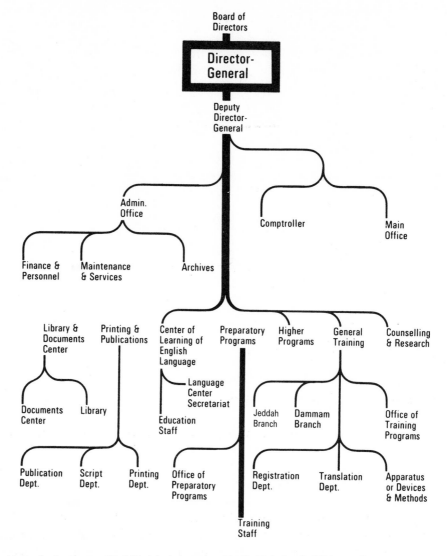

Source: Guide to the Institute of Public Administration (Da'liel Ma'had al'l'dara al'am'a) no 22, page 18. Author's translation.

processing support to the Ministry of Finance and National Economy and to other government agencies
– to improve the range and level of qualifications of Saudi statisticians and staff in allied fields at all levels

The Department has instituted demographic surveys, labor force surveys and consumer expenditure surveys and carries out quarterly the Saudi Arabian

Chart VIId   *Investigation and Control Board*

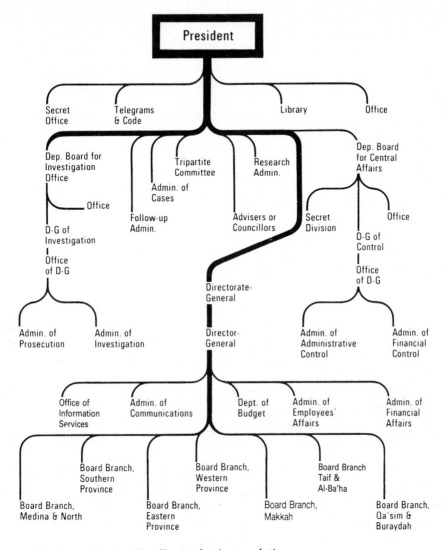

Source: Obtained by the author in Riyadh. Author's translation.

Multipurpose Household Survey, which has become a key source of statistical information.

7.6   Meteorological and Environmental Protection Administration (MEPA)

The meteorological services of MEPA provide essential information to both the defense services and to the industrial sector of the Kingdom's economy.

These services are used by commercial aviation, air traffic control stations, oil drilling platforms, ships in the Red Sea and the Arabian Gulf, and the general public. Climatological services include long-term weather information to assist all government organizations and commercial establishments.

Source: Fourth Development Plan (1405–10 AH: 1980–85)

MEPA is also responsible for protection of the environment, a crucial role, especially in a country which has undergone such a rapid development of its infrastructure and industry.

7.7   Saudi Arabian Standards Organization (SASO)

The Saudi Arabian Standards Organization, set up in 1392 AH (1972), has responsibility for determining and enforcing approved standards of services, facilities, utilities and products within the Kingdom of Saudi Arabia.

The establishment of a comprehensive national system of standards and specifications is of great importance to consumers and the producing sectors of the economy alike. With growing emphasis on economic diversification and the development of export capabilities of Saudi manufacturing, the adoption of standards acts as an important technical and quality control channel for products, in both domestic and international markets.

Source: Fourth Development Plan (1405–10 AH: 1985–90)

SASO is a member of the International Standards Organization (ISO) and is an active member of the Arab Standards and Metrology Organization (ASMO).

Of particular significance is SASO's involvement in implementing the decision of the Supreme Council of the Gulf Co-operation Council (GCC) to create a unified standards organization for the member states.

In pursuit of the Kingdom's economic development goals, SASO clearly has a crucial role to play.

The Minister of Commerce is the Chairman of the Board of SASO.

7.8   Saudi Ports Authority (SPA)

The Saudi Ports Authority is responsible for providing port and shipping facilities to meet the Kingdom's present and forecast future needs.

The building of the Kingdom's infrastructure made extraordinary demands on the Kingdom's port facilities and inevitably, for periods during the first two Development Plans, there were delays in processing some of the imports needed for the ambitious construction programs.

It must count as one of the most outstanding examples of efficient port management that the problems of congestion were entirely resolved and the general efficiency of the ports greatly improved in the course of the Third Development Plan (1400–05 AH: 1980–85).

For details of the Kingdom's port facilities, see Section 14.1.4, pp 221–23.

Chapter *8*

Saudi Arabia and Petroleum

The devotion of a whole chapter to the role of petroleum in Saudi Arabia needs no justification. Oil has been imperative to the development of the Kingdom and, despite the Kingdom's successes in expanding the industrial and agricultural sectors of the economy, oil will continue to be the Kingdom's primary source of revenue in the foreseeable future.

8.1   Oil: historical background and Aramco

Before dealing with this subject in detail, it will be of interest briefly to recount once more the fascinating story of the discovery of oil in the Kingdom and the early efforts to exploit it.

The history of oil in the Middle East and the Arab world goes back many centuries during which seepages of oil and tar were used for a multitude of purposes. A mission of German experts visited Iraq in 1871 and reported plentiful supplies of oil. In 1907, another mission said Iraq was a veritable "lake of petroleum". In Iran, oil was found in quantity in 1908. The major Iraqi field was discovered at Kirkuk in 1927 and began producing oil in commercial quantities; oil flowed abroad in 1934. In 1932, petroleum was discovered in Bahrain.

In 1923, a New Zealander, Major Frank Holmes, acting on behalf of a British syndicate, the "Eastern and General", had obtained the first Saudi Arabian oil concession from King Abdul Aziz bin Sa'ud, an exclusive concession to explore for oil and other minerals in an area of more than 30,000 square miles in the Al-Hasa region. The concession, at a bargain price of £2,000 per annum to be paid in gold, came to nothing. The Eastern and General syndicate were unable to persuade any oil company to invest sufficient funds for exploration and, after paying the £2,000 for two years, they ceased to fulfil their part of the agreement. The King waited for three years and then, in 1928, revoked the concession. From the viewpoint of Major Frank Holmes and his London-based syndicate, this episode must represent one of the world's greatest lost opportunities.

In 1930, King Abdul Aziz was faced with a substantial fall in revenues,

96

resulting from a drop in the number of pilgrims caused by the worldwide recession. The King invited a wealthy American businessman and philanthropist, Charles R Crane, to visit the Kingdom. Crane had already shown an eagerness to meet the King. In the course of Crane's visit, it was agreed that he should send a mining engineer to conduct a survey of Saudi Arabia to assess the Kingdom's water, mineral and oil resources.

In 1931, the engineer, Karl Twitchell, arrived in Jeddah. Twitchell was a civil and mining engineer, with Middle East experience, having worked for Crane in the Yemen. After an extensive survey of many months, Twitchell submitted his report to the King. A key finding was that the geological formations in Eastern Province around Dhahran strongly indicated the presence of oil.

While Twitchell's survey was proceeding, Socal, the Standard Oil Company of California, which had sent two geologists to Bahrain, was becoming increasingly interested in the oil potential of the mainland of Saudi Arabia.

In 1933, Twitchell arrived in Jeddah with a Socal representative, Lloyd Hamilton. Despite some impressive competition from the Iraq Petroleum Company, Hamilton succeeded in negotiating a concession for exclusive rights to oil in the Eastern Province. The agreement which had a 60-year life (later to be extended for a further six years), received royal assent in July 1933. Thus, the Kingdom broke what had been virtually a British monopoly of oil concessions in that part of the world.

Articles 1 and 2 of the agreement defined the nature and geographical limits of the concession. Article 2 stated:

> The area cover[s] . . . all of eastern Saudi Arabia, from its eastern boundary (including islands and territorial waters) westward to the westerly edge of Dahana and from the northern boundary to the southern boundary of Saudi Arabia, provided that from the northern end of the western edge of Dahana the western boundary of the area in question shall continue in a straight line north thirty degrees west to the northern boundary of Saudi Arabia, and from the southern end of the westerly edge of the Dahana such boundary shall continue in a straight line south thirty degrees east to the southern boundary of Saudi Arabia. For convenience this area may be referred to as "the exclusive area".
>
> *Source: Agreement between the Saudi Arab Government and the Arabian American Oil Company*, 2nd edition (Makkah: Government Press, 1383 AH (1964))

Initial exploration produced disappointing results but in 1935 a well drilled in Dhahran found oil in commercial quantities. The following year, Socal, now operating through its subsidiary the Californian Arabian Standard Oil Company (Casoc), put into effect Article 32 of the 1933 agreement and sold one-half of its concession interest to the Texas Oil Company.

Oil production began in 1938, by which time the vast extent of the oil reserves was becoming apparent.

With this confirmation of the commercial viability of the oil reserves, another supplementary agreement was signed on 31st May 1938, adding six years to the 60-year life of the original agreement. This second instrument, known as the Supplemental Agreement, enlarged Socal's concession area by almost 80,000 square miles. It also included rights in the Saudi Government's half interest in the two neutral zones shared with Iraq and Kuwait.

> It is noteworthy that in 1937, Ibn Saud had received a very advantageous offer from Japan but, believing it to be motivated by political considerations, he rejected it. Germany also had designs on Saudi oil and, in the same year, Dr Fritz Grobba, German Minister to Iraq and Saudi Arabia, who was stationed in Baghdad, visited Jidda [sic]. Nevertheless, Ibn Saud preferred to continue his association with the Americans; it had the advantage of assuring the economic development of the country without incurring political liabilities.
>
> *Source: The Middle East in World Affairs* by George Lenczowski, 3rd edition (Ithaca, NY, Cornell University Press, 1961)

In 1944, the Californian Arabian Standard Oil Company was re-named the Arabian American Oil Company – Aramco. In 1948, Aramco invoked an Article of the Supplemental Agreement of 1939 by selling a 30 per cent interest to Standard Oil of New Jersey and a ten per cent interest to Socony Vacuum. The redistributed ownership of Aramco was then: Standard Oil of California (now known as California Standard) – 30%; Texas Oil Company (now known as Texaco) – 30%; Standard Oil of New Jersey (now known as Exxon) – 30%; and Socony Vacuum (now known as Mobil Oil), the last 10%.

In 1949, the Getty Oil Company was able to acquire a 60-year exclusive oil concession in the neutral zone which the Saudi Government shared with Kuwait. This concession included exploration and production rights in territorial waters for a distance of six miles. Later, the Government of Saudi Arabia concluded an agreement by which it granted the Japan Petroleum Trading Company Ltd, a 44-year concession covering

> the government's undivided share in all that offshore area outside the territorial waters limit of the Saudi Arab–Kuwait Neutral Zone over which the government now has or may hereafter, during the period of this agreement, have right, title and interest. It is understood that such offshore area extends to the delimitation in the middle both of the mean low water coastlines of the Saudi Arab–Kuwait Neutral Zone and of Iran on the Arabian Gulf, and that such offshore area shall include shoals,

reefs, waters, wholly or partly submerged lands and submarine areas, seabed and sub-soil.

> *Source: Agreement between the Saudi Arab Government and the Japan Petroleum Trading Company, Ltd,* 2nd edition, (Makkah: Government Press, 1384 AH (1964))

Drilling started in 1959; oil was discovered in January 1960.

In January 1965, the Saudi Government concluded another concession agreement with the French-owned Société Auxiliaire de la Régie Autonome des Pétroles (abridged to Auxirap) to explore for oil in the Red Sea. It was agreed that the French company should bear all the exploration costs until oil was discovered. Then a joint operating company would be founded in which Petromin (the Saudi National Oil Company, itself founded in 1962) would acquire a 40 per cent equity, but would enjoy 50 per cent of the voting power. Furthermore

> under this agreement [with Auxirap] the government will receive a 15% royalty which will be increased to 20% if production exceeds 80,000 barrels a day. Other payments are bonuses amounting to $5.5 million, $4 million of which is payable only when production reaches the level of 70,000 barrels of crude oil a day for 90 consecutive days, and rental charges ranging from $5 per square kilometer for the first 5 years to $500 during the last 5 years of a 30-year period. In addition, the company will pay 40% income tax. (8)

> *Source: Area Handbook for Saudi Arabia,* 2nd edition (Washington, DC: US Government Printing Office, 1971)

Whilst accepting the importance of all these concessions, it is clear that the Saudi–American agreement on oil was in a class by itself in terms of its economic magnitude. It is therefore informative to trace some of the financial and economic aspects of Saudi–Aramco relations, especially because an understanding of the relationship constitutes a useful preface to the later discussion of the formation of the Organization of Petroleum Exporting Countries (OPEC).

Both the first "Saudi Arab Concession" of 1933 and the Supplemental Agreement of 1939 had separate articles dealing with the financial aspects of Saudi-Aramco relations. Article 14 of the Saudi Arab concession of 1933 stated that

> The company shall pay the government a royalty on all net crude oil produced and saved and run from field storage, after first deducting:
> 1 water and foreign substances; and
> 2 oil required for the customary operations of the company's installations within Saudi Arabia; and
> 3 the oil required for manufacturing the amounts of gasoline and

kerosene to be provided free each year to the government in accordance with Article 19 hereof. The royalty portion of such net crude oil shall be either:

a) four shillings gold; or its equivalent; or

b) at the election of the company at the time of making each royalty payment, one dollar, United States currency, plus the amount, if any, by which the average rate of exchange of four shillings gold, during the last half of the semester for which the royalty payment is due, may exceed one dollar and ten cents, United States currency. Thus, for example, if such average rate should be one dollar and fourteen cents, United States currency (that is to say, five dollars and seventy cents per gold pound), the royalty rate would be one dollar and four cents, United States currency, per ton of such net crude oil. [After the payment of the United States tax which, *a priori*, means less revenue for the Saudi government.]

> *Source: Agreement between the Saudi Arab Government and the Arabian American Oil Company*, 2nd edition (Makkah: Government Press, 1383 AH (1964))

Article 4 of the Supplemental Agreement of 1939 concerned the new financial situation that had developed due to the enlargement of the area of concession in Saudi Arabia along with the new rights in the Saudi–Iraqi–Kuwaiti Neutral Zones. Yet no conflict occurred between articles dealing with the financial arrangements in the Saudi Arab concession and the Supplemental Agreement of 1939. It was not until

December 30, 1950, [that] Aramco and Saudi Arabia [had] made a major change in the concession by concluding a fifty-fifty profit-sharing agreement. This agreement was of great importance in as much as it set a precedent for similar formulae in other oil-producing countries of the Middle East. A further [significant] step was the agreement of both parties on October 2, 1951, to apply the new formula before the payment of United States taxes rather than after, as had been done until then.

> *Source: Oil and State in the Middle East* by George Lenczowski (Ithaca, NY: Cornell University Press, 1960)

Equally relevant was the fact that it was only in November 1950 that the first income tax was issued by a Royal Decree. The imposition of taxes affected both personal income and corporate profits with minimum exemptions in both categories. Thus, by 1951, in addition to paying royalties at the rate of about 22 cents a barrel, Aramco was paying a 50 per cent income tax on its net profits. Moreover, it was agreed upon by 1952 that the Saudi government should be represented in the company's policy deliberations and that the company's headquarters should be located in Saudi Arabia . . . [consequently], Aramco's headquarters were moved to Dhahran, and in 1959 two Saudi government representatives were elected to Aramco's 15-man board of directors.

> Source: *Area Handbook for Saudi Arabia*, 2nd edition (Washington, DC: US Government Printing Office, 1971)

It is crucial to the following part of this chapter, which deals with the Organization of Petroleum Exporting Countries (OPEC), to make mention of the Saudi–Iraqi agreement of 1953, which provided for the exchange of petroleum data as well as for the holding of periodic consultations regarding petroleum policy. This agreement may very well be considered as an early catalyst towards the subsequent establishment of OPEC.

From the late 1940s through the late 1950s, relations between the Saudi government and Aramco went smoothly. It was not until the 1959–60 unilateral reductions in petroleum prices by the major petroleum companies in the area of the Gulf that relations began to change. A more complete analysis of these cuts will be made in subsequent sections of this chapter, since they became the most influential factor leading to the creation of the Organization of Petroleum Exporting Countries in 1960.

At this point in the discussion of Saudi–Aramco relations it is important to note the creation of the General Petroleum and Mineral Organization (Petromin) in 1962, the nation's first national petroleum company, which is empowered to formulate and execute projects for the development of the petroleum, petrochemical and mineral industries of the nation, and to deal

> with the progressive relinquishment of acreage by Aramco and the entry of new oil companies in the country. Petromin is acquiring growing importance. Its stature was further enhanced and its responsibilities widely extended with the implementation of the principle of participation in the equity of Aramco. (12)

> Source: OPEC, *Past and Present* by Abdul Amir Kubbah (Vienna: Petro-Economic Research Center, 1974)

It was inconceivable in the political and economic context of the second half of the twentieth century that so important a national resource as oil, representing as it did most of the country's national income, should remain under the ownership of foreign companies. In 1973, the Saudi Arabian Government took a 25 per cent stake in Aramco. In 1974, this share was increased to 60 per cent and in 1980 it was amicably agreed that Aramco should become 100 per cent Saudi-owned, with the date of ownership back-dated to 1976.

At the same time, and of equal importance, the Saudi Arabian Government implemented a consistent policy of Saudi-ization, replacing foreign expertise and labor with Saudi nationals as far as possible. In this context, it is interesting to quote a newspaper account of a major step in this process, published by the *New York Times* (6th April 1989):

> At a quiet dinner a few days ago, the last American to preside over the world's largest oil company handed over power to its first Saudi boss. The Saudi, a man who started working there more than 40 years ago as an office boy, earned engineering and management degrees as he climbed up the ladder.
>
> The transfer of the Arabian American Oil Company from the American John J. Kelberer, to the Saudi Ali Naimi, took place at Hamilton House, named after an American lawyer who negotiated the first agreement that opened this kingdom to American oil companies 56 years ago and led to the formation of Aramco, as the company is known to the world.
>
> While the formal transfer of power was low-key, in the Aramco tradition, the event was one of great moment both in Saudi and international terms.

Thus the oil of the Kingdom which had lain for so long beneath Saudi Arabia's deserts and which then, for decades, had been exploited by foreign interests became at last a national resource controlled and managed by those under whose soil it lay.

8.2   Petromin

To develop the entire natural resource sector and harness it to the service of overall development, the government established Petromin as the State Petroleum Company in 1962.

Petromin's role is to maximize the usefulness of the Kingdom's oil, gas and minerals. It is thus engaged in the production of natural resources (including, for example, the engagement of foreign partners), in the exploitation of natural resources (such as the evolution of a wide range of hydrocarbon products, like petroleum, LPG and asphalt), and in the marketing, both domestically and internationally, of these products. Its range of activity is therefore vast. Refining, pipelines, storage, power generation – all fall within Petromin's province.

For the period of 1975–80 Petromin's activities were governed by its own five year plan. This in turn was circumscribed by a number of basic governmental policies. These included that of avoiding adverse influence on local life through excessive concentrations of population; hence, decentralization has prevailed in development. At the same time, industrial development would take place with as much vertical and horizontal integration as possible. Good husbandry was stimulated by the emphasis on profitability. Long-term planning – beyond the span of any five-year period – was a further requirement. There was the caution that Petromin, with all its potential, should not encroach into fields already within the authority of other government bodies or ministries, but should integrate its planning with theirs. Lastly, Petromin would give priority to projects which might provide opportunities for private Saudi investment, and, wherever possible, look to the expansion of job opportunities for Saudis.

Under its plan, Petromin listed five principal areas of activity: the exploitation of gas; the diversification of industries within the field of fossil fuels and minerals; developing the refining of oil, including the production of benzene, toluene and xylene for the Kingdom's burgeoning petro-chemical plants; the marketing and transportation, at home and abroad, of LPG; and the speeding up of the production of mineral industries and of the prospecting for and development of precious metal resources.

Currently, a major restructuring of the Kingdom's oil industry is taking place. In 1988, Petromin formed Petrolube, a company jointly owned with Mobil. Petrolube is responsible for the production and marketing of the Kingdom's lube oil blending plants in Jeddah, Jubail and Riyadh. In the same year, the Saudi Arabian Oil Company (Saudi Aramco) was formed to manage the assets of Aramco.

Even more recently, the Kingdom has formed the Saudi Arabian Marketing and Refining Company (SAMARIC), which will be responsible for refining and domestic marketing operations. SAMARIC is to take over the three domestic refineries, at Yanbu (170,000 barrels a day), at Jeddah (90,000 barrels a day) and at Riyadh (134,000 barrels a day). The new company will hold a 50 per cent share in the two joint venture export refineries at Yanbu (with Mobil) and at Jubail (with Shell). SAMARIC will also take responsibility for the marketing of the Kingdom's oil products, both at home and abroad.

In this context, it is noteworthy that, in 1988, the Kingdom of Saudi Arabia took a major step towards its objective of moving "downstream" in the oil business by purchasing a 50 per cent stake in Texaco's petrol refining and retailing business in 23 eastern and southern states of the US.

The restructuring of the Kingdom's oil industry is not yet complete. Nevertheless, it is generally expected that Petromin will become primarily a State holding company, with shares in the newly-formed specialized oil company subsidiaries.

8.3   Oil reserves, levels of oil production, pricing and value of oil revenues

Between 1970 and the present the Kingdom's level of production and its share of

Table 8.1 *Saudi crude oil production and reserves*

		Million barrels		
Year	Reserves at the beginning of the year	Production	Gross increase in reserves	Reserves at year end	Production as percentage of world production
1970	136,700	1,387	3,387	138,700	8.3%
1971	138,260	1,741	1,301	138,260	9.9%
1972	138,260	2,202	1,012	137,070	11.8%
1973	137,070	2,773	2,533	136,830	13.7%
1974	136,830	3,095	7,305	141,040	15.2%
1975	141,040	2,583	6,123	144,580	13.3%
1976	144,580	3,139	9,969	151,410	15.0%
1977	151,410	3,358	21,428	169,480	15.4%
1978	169,480	3,030	428	167,060	13.8%
1979	167,060	3,479	4,809	168,390	15.1%
1980	168,390	3,624	2,694	167,460	16.6%
1981	167,460	3,580	940	164,820	17.5%
1982	164,820	2,366	5,867	168,321	12.2%
1983	168,321	1,668	2,367	169,020	8.7%
1984	169,020	1,516	1,496	169,000	7.6%
1985	169,000	1,182	1,365	169,183	5.7%
1986	169,183	1,718	2,182	169,584	8.1%

(Figures for 1987 and 1988 are not available)

the oil market have shown great fluctuations. This fact is most readily illustrated by Table 8.1, derived from the statistical information produced by the Ministry of Petroleum and Mineral Resources and OPEC.

The oil production figures show a remarkable increase, followed by an equally remarkable decline. From 1976 to 1981, the Kingdom's oil production exceeded 3,000 million barrels a year, but, in 1985, production had fallen to little more than 1,000 million barrels, below the figure for 1970.

The main purpose in providing Table 8.1 is to illustrate the massive fluctuation in oil production levels but, of longer-term significance, it is also noteworthy that throughout the period reserves at the end of the year have been close to or above the estimated reserves at the beginning of the year. Furthermore, in January 1989, the Saudi Arabian Oil Company (formerly Aramco) released new estimates of the Kingdom's recoverable oil reserves, raising the figure to 252,380 million barrels. Thus, while many oil fields in the United States of America and other parts of the world are close to exhaustion or at least showing a decline in reserves, the estimated oil reserves of the Kingdom are almost double what they were in 1970.

The price of oil itself has shown equally remarkable fluctuations. Table 8.2 shows both the official price and the spot market price in US$ for Light Oil (API 34) from 1970 through 1988.

Table 8.2   *Light Oil prices 1970–88 (US$)*

Year	Quarter	Official price	Spot market price
1970		1.35	1.21
1971		1.75	1.74
1972		1.90	1.87
1973	1st	2.10	2.08
	4th	13.65	4.10
1974	1st	8.65	13.00
	4th	10.40	10.30
1975	1st	10.46	10.42
	4th	10.46	10.46
1976	1st	11.51	11.51
	4th	11.51	11.90
1977	1st	12.09	12.50
	4th	12.70	12.68
1978	1st	12.70	12.66
	4th	12.70	13.50
1979	1st	13.48	18.35
	4th	22.84	38.17
1980	1st	27.17	36.58
	4th	31.22	38.63
1981	1st	32.60	37.32
	4th	34.16	33.73
1982	1st	33.80	31.00
	4th	33.23	31.75
1983	1st	30.58	29.05
	4th	28.75	28.38
1984	1st	28.62	28.06
	4th	28.75	27.81
1985	1st	28.17	27.68
	4th	28.00	27.86
1986	1st	28.00	17.96
	4th	27.83	13.55
1987	1st	17.59	17.20
	4th	17.59	17.10
1988	1st	17.06	14.99

Source: Ministry of Petroleum and Mineral Resources and OPEC

Behind the figures in Tables 8.1 and 8.2 lies a fascinating story of political and economic maneuvering.

In 1973, when the Arab–Israeli war broke out, the Kingdom of Saudi Arabia, in concert with other Arab oil-producing countries, cut off oil supplies to the United States of America and reduced supplies to some West European countries in an effort to persuade those countries to adopt a more even-handed approach to the Israeli–Palestinian conflict. There was not, however, unanimity amongst these

Arab countries on how far the "oil weapon" could safely be used. The Kingdom of Saudi Arabia, aware of the dangers of immoderate use of oil as a means of exerting political pressure, persuaded the other Arab members of OPEC to join it in resuming supplies to the United States of America and dissuaded the more radical elements within OPEC from attempting to raise the oil price still higher. (As Table 8.2 shows, the oil price had already quadrupled.)

Then, towards the end of 1978, the Iranian revolution gained impetus. With the collapse of Iranian oil production and despite Saudi Arabian efforts to hold the oil price steady by increasing production, the alarm of the West at the possibility of another disruption of supplies sent the oil price soaring. The spot market price of a barrel of Light rose from US$ 13.50 in the last quarter of 1978 to US$ 38.63 by the last quarter of 1980.

This second massive increase in the oil price sent shock waves through the Western industrialized countries. Oil exploration outside the OPEC countries was hastened, energy conservation measures were introduced, and the provision and exploitation of alternative sources of energy were given a high priority.

In the course of 1982, world demand for oil fell and, with it, by the end of that year, the price of oil. The figures show a gradual decline in the oil price from 1983 to the end of 1985 but, in reality, the price was sustained at these levels only by the willingness of the Kingdom of Saudi Arabia to act as a "swing" producer within OPEC – systematically reducing its own oil production to prevent a collapse of the oil price. By the end of 1985, the Kingdom's production of oil had fallen to less than one-third of its 1980 level.

It was in 1985 that the Kingdom decided that it could no longer sustain the role of "swing" producer. Throughout OPEC's efforts to control oil production by means of a system of agreed production quotas, the willingness of member states to adhere to quota agreements had been questionable. Indeed, Iraq, involved in the Iraq/Iran war, had openly declared that it would not be bound by any quota and, in general, it is fair to say that the quota system was "more honored in the breach than the observance". By the middle of 1985, the Kingdom of Saudi Arabia was the only OPEC member fully adhering to the "official" OPEC oil price, with the result that its sales were little more than 2 million barrels a day, less than half its official OPEC quota of 4.35 million barrels a day, and well below the 3.85 million barrels a day level of sales at the "official" OPEC price which the Kingdom required to cover the costs of its current budget.

Since adherence to the "official" OPEC price had failed to instil discipline into OPEC, the Kingdom decided to adopt an alternative approach. By the end of 1985, it had become obvious that Saudi Arabia intended to produce its full quota of oil (4.35 million barrels a day) under the OPEC quota agreement. This decision meant that the price of oil, so long sustained by the Kingdom at around the US$ 28 a barrel mark, would fall. The main objectives of this strategy were:

– to persuade other OPEC members that only by strict adherence to

production quotas could the Organization exert its influence over the
market
    – to persuade non-OPEC oil producers that they should co-operate with
    OPEC in working for a stable oil market

Within a few months the new strategy had eliminated approximately three-
quarters of a million barrels a day of global oil capacity by closing down mainly
North American facilities which could not produce oil economically at the reduced
price which, by mid-1986, had fallen to US$ 10 a barrel. Norway, a major North Sea
oil producer, had expressed some willingness to co-operate with OPEC, if OPEC
itself could devise and impose a practical system of production control on its own
members. Britain, wedded to a simplistic "free-market" economic philosophy and
strongly influenced by the United States of America which, as a net importer of oil,
favored a weak oil price and a weak OPEC, remained obdurately opposed to any
form of co-operation with OPEC, despite a substantial decline in British oil
revenues.

But the cost of what has been described as a "price war" was high and,
although it promised benefits to OPEC in the longer term (especially those whose
oil reserves would long outlast the oil reserves of the non-OPEC oil producers), the
less wealthy members of OPEC could not afford to take a long-term view.

In the last quarter of 1986, King Fahd of Saudi Arabia proposed a fixed price in
the region of US$ 18 a barrel, a proposal which was supported by all OPEC
members. In terms of its total oil production, OPEC agreed to a reduction of around
five per cent for the first half of 1987. OPEC's renewed resolve to regain some
degree of control over the oil market, combined with increased tension in the
Arabian Gulf, where a direct confrontation between the United States of America
and Iran seemed distinctly possible, had an effect. The oil price gradually firmed.
By the middle of 1987, the oil price had reached the benchmark of US$ 18.

In 1988, efforts continued within OPEC to maintain a united front but tensions
between those wishing to increase market share and those wishing to obtain the
highest price per barrel (aggravated by Iraq's refusal to be bound by any production
quota) precluded any real progress, other than a renewal of the existing
understanding on production quotas.

At the time of writing, the struggle to maintain stability in the oil price
continues. In April 1989, the price of a barrel of oil rose above US$ 20 but the view
is now widely held that, until market factors alter significantly, the price proposed
by King Fahd of around US$ 18 a barrel is sensible from both the producers' and
consumers' point of view and should remain as a benchmark.

Bringing together the figures for production and price, it is possible to compile
a table showing the oil revenues received by the Kingdom of Saudi Arabia in the
twelve years from 1976 to 1987:

Year	Oil revenues (US$ millions)
1976	33,500
1977	38,000
1978	36,700
1979	59,200
1980	104,200
1981	113,300
1982	76,000
1983	46,000
1984	43,700
1985	28,000
1986	20,000
1987	23,000

Source: Royal Dutch Shell Group, 1988

Bearing in mind the dominant role that oil revenues play in the economy of Saudi Arabia, it will be obvious that both the increase and the fall in revenues posed unique problems for the government of the Kingdom. The table shows, in effect, a trebling of the Kingdom's GNP between 1976 and 1981, followed by a fall of 80 per cent in GNP between 1981 and 1987. It is not perhaps surprising that so many analysts and commentators, unaware of the significance of the Islamic foundation of the Kingdom, predicted first that the Kingdom would be unable to absorb its increased wealth and then that it would be unable to adjust to so dramatic a decline in its revenues. The above table amply indicates the challenges the Kingdom has faced and the magnitude of the Kingdom's achievement in successfully meeting them.

8.4   OPEC (the Organization of Petroleum Exporting Countries)

Because Saudi Arabia holds some 25 per cent of the world's oil reserves, it is inevitable that the Kingdom should play a pivotal role in the affairs of the Organization of Petroleum Exporting Countries. It is also inevitable that the role which the Kingdom discharges should attract the continuing attention of foreign governments and the world's media.

In these circumstances, it is of value to study in some detail the genesis, past performance and likely future of this always controversial organization. This section on OPEC is divided into three parts:

1 Historical background

2 The establishment of OPEC
3 A discussion of its role, past, present and future

8.4.1 HISTORICAL BACKGROUND

Since its creation in 1945 in Cairo, the League of Arab States had considered establishing a petroleum organization to develop a common policy towards major petroleum companies operating within their boundaries. After some study it became evident that such an organization would have to include non-Arab exporters of petroleum, such as Iran and Venezuela. Serious diplomatic negotiations with these countries started in Washington, DC, in 1947, aimed at achieving a co-ordinated petroleum policy among large exporters. Another major step occurred in 1949 on the initiative of the Venezuelan government, which, in an effort to ally itself with the petroleum states of the Gulf, despatched a special three-man delegation to visit Iran, Iraq, Kuwait and the Kingdom of Saudi Arabia. The Venezuelan delegation exchanged views on petroleum policies and explored the possibilities of developing a permanent channel of communication between both sides. The Venezuelan government also extended an invitation to both Iranian and Saudi Arabian petroleum experts to visit Venezuela in 1951.

The fruitful result of such contacts first became evident in Iraq, Kuwait and the Kingdom of Saudi Arabia, when these countries demanded 50 per cent of the oil companies' net profits, instead of a fixed royalty on each barrel of petroleum produced.

Another step towards the establishment of an OPEC-like body was the Saudi–Iraqi Agreement of 1953. But perhaps the most important preliminary event was the convening of the first Arab Petroleum Congress in Cairo in 1959, under the auspices of the League of Arab States. Both Iran and Venezuela were invited to attend as observers. This conference is considered by many leading petroleum experts to have been the immediate predecessor of OPEC.

8.4.2 THE ESTABLISHMENT OF OPEC

During 1959, the existence of a large global petroleum surplus led to the weakening of the international market. In addition, the United States, in the same year, imposed import controls in an effort to lessen its dependency on foreign petroleum. For the major companies operating in the Gulf area, this decision meant the closure of the profitable United States market. Faced with such a situation, the petroleum companies

> had either to risk angering their host countries and at the same time increase their own profits by lowering posted prices, or to maintain good relations with the producing nations by freezing prices at their current levels, even if it meant angering the consumers and foregoing some

profits. The companies chose the first alternative. In February, 1959, they decided, without prior consultation with the governments concerned, to cut the prices of Middle Eastern oil by about 18 cents a barrel.

[Furthermore, the oil companies, ignoring the serious situation caused by the cut and the demand of the Arab states that they should be consulted before such decisions were taken], cut prices again in August, 1960, by an average of about 9 cents a barrel.]

Source: OPEC, Past and Present, Kubbah

These two cuts meant that, using 1960 as a base, Kuwait, Iran, Iraq and the Kingdom of Saudi Arabia were losing $231,241,000 annually in the value of their exports.

These two successive unilateral and arbitrary cuts in 1959 and 1960 by the petroleum companies operating in the Middle East were important determinants towards establishing OPEC. They "generated a feeling of economic insecurity in oil exporting countries and emphasized the need for a collective defense to arrest the downward drift of prices and government-per-barrel revenues".

Source: Ibid

Structural organization of OPEC

The governments of Saudi Arabia and Venezuela, in accordance with the objectives of the Arab Petroleum Congress of 1959, issued a declaration on 13 May 1960, recommending that petroleum exporting countries pursue a common policy in order to protect their rightful interests. The declaration also advanced the idea of establishing an organization to achieve this end. None the less, the countries concerned did not take immediate action. It was the sudden and arbitrary decrease in petroleum prices for the second time in 1960 that made them feel the danger which encouraged them to unite in a common front. Consequently, the major petroleum producing countries declared, after the Baghdad Conference of 10–14th August 1960 (at which the Kingdom of Saudi Arabia, Republic of Iraq, Iran, Venezuela and Kuwait were represented), their intention to establish the organization which became known as the Organization of Petroleum Exporting Countries (OPEC). One of the major decisions of that meeting declared a cardinal objective of the organization to be the standardization of petroleum prices among its members and agreement on the best methods of protecting its individual and collective interests. As a result, OPEC was founded in September 1960

as a permanent intergovernmental organization with an international status. In accordance with Article 102 of the United Nations Charter, the agreement creating OPEC was duly registered with the Secretariat of the

United Nations on November 6, 1962, under No. 6363. [Moreover, it is quite important to refer to the fact that] OPEC is not a business entity; it does not engage in any commercial transactions. [It concerns itself with the formulation of a common policy toward the industrialized countries of the world and the fixing of petroleum prices in a unified manner.] The legally authorized representative of the organization is its Secretary General. The staff of the Secretariat are international civil servants.

Source: Ibid

Member States of the Organization

State membership	Date of membership	Status
Iran	September 1960	Founder member
Iraq	September 1960	Founder member
Kuwait	September 1960	Founder member
Saudi Arabia	September 1960	Founder member
Venezuela	September 1960	Founder member
Qatar	December 1960	Full member
Libya	December 1962	Full member
Indonesia	December 1962	Full member
United Arab Emirates	November 1967	Full member
Algeria	July 1969	Full member
Nigeria	July 1971	Full member
Ecuador	November 1973	Full member
Gabon	December 1973	Associate member

Source: Author's design, drawn from *OPEC: Past and Present* by Abdul Amir Kubbah, pp 17–18

OPEC's headquarters were in Geneva, Switzerland, from 21st January 1961 through to August 1965, when they moved to Vienna. Both sites were chosen because of the host country's political neutrality.

As can be seen from the above table, only seven of OPEC's thirteen members are Arab states.

For a state to qualify, it must first possess a "substantial net export of crude petroleum". Secondly and more significantly, the state applying for membership must "[have] fundamentally similar interests to those of Member Countries".

The precise criteria governing the admission of new member states are set forth in Article 7, para C, of OPEC's statute of November 1971:

Any other country with a substantial net export of crude petroleum, which has fundamentally similar interests to those of Member Countries, may become a Full Member of the Organization, if accepted by a majority of three-fourths of Full Members, including the concurrent vote of all Founder Members.

Source: The Statute of the Organization of Petroleum Exporting Countries (Vienna, 1971)

Any member state has the right to withdraw from OPEC. According to Article 8, section A,

No member of the Organization may withdraw from membership without giving notice of its intention to do so to the conference. Such notice shall take effect at the beginning of the next calendar year after the date of its receipt by the conference, subject to the Member having at that time fulfilled all financial obligations arising from its membership.

Source: Ibid

Article 2 (sections A/B/C) of OPEC's statute, delineates the aims and objectives of the Organization:

A   The principal aim of the Organization shall be the co-ordination and unification of petroleum policies of the Member Countries and the determination of the best means for safeguarding their interests individually and collectively.

B   The Organization shall devise ways and means of ensuring the stabilization of prices in international oil markets with a view to eliminating harmful and unnecessary fluctuations.

C   Due regard shall be given at all times to the interests of the producing nations and to the necessity of securing a steady income to the producing countries; an efficient, economical and regular supply of petroleum to consuming nations; and a fair return on their capital to those investing in the petroleum industry.

Source: Ibid

The global impact of the Organization of Petroleum Exporting Countries was clearly felt during and in the aftermath of the Ramadan War of 1973, when the Arab petroleum-producing countries imposed a gradual embargo with an initial five per cent cut of their total production. This was to be followed by another five per cent cut each month, until a peaceful and just solution for the Middle East conflict was found. But President Nixon's decision to provide Israel with military aid of over $2,000 million caused the Arab petroleum-producing nations to impose a total embargo against the United States while maintaining the previous policy of successive five per cent cuts towards the rest of the Western world.

The effect of the embargo is best illustrated by the fact that the Arab petroleum-producing countries' normal production of 20 million barrels per day was cut back to between 13 and 14 million barrels per day. Of that reduction of 6.0 to 6.5 million barrels, United States cuts amounted to 2 million barrels per day. The rest was split between Europe and Japan. The total production of the members of OPEC normally runs at 30 million barrels per day, so the 6.0 to 6.5 million barrels the Arabs cut represented a twenty per cent reduction in what was available for the world market. Although the reduction was relatively small, the effect was widespread. The embargo was lifted in March 1974. Previously OPEC had existed and functioned without much attention from the rest of the world, but 1973 revealed the actual and potential influence of OPEC on the world economy.

Controversial theories emerged regarding OPEC's prospects. The first of these theories, held by the United States Secretary of the Treasury, William Simon, argued that OPEC was soon destined to decline. Simon repeatedly declared that the laws of supply and demand, along with the conditions of the international petroleum market, would bring about a lower price for petroleum. Consequently, the power of OPEC in world affairs would gradually diminish.

Three years after Secretary Simon's prediction relating to the future of OPEC none of his prophecies had been fulfilled. It is true that most of the OPEC members had been forced to reduce their petroleum production because of a relative decline in world demand. Nevertheless, such a decline provided most of the member states of OPEC with a success in reverse; that is, the reduction of their petroleum production enabled them to maintain their posted price for petroleum.

Five eminent analysts from Iran, Japan and the United States similarly speculated that

> the United States seems to expect consuming countries to shrink their consumption of oil quite naturally as they proceed further in adapting to the increase of the oil price. It is apparently expect[ed] that the producing countries will be unable to agree on shares of a shrinking market [due to a relative decrease in petroleum] consumption and will consequently begin competing among themselves at declining oil prices [and] that the "cartel" will break apart.
>
> Source: "How can the world afford OPEC oil?", Foreign Affairs, Vol 53, (1975)

An alternative theory was that OPEC would maintain a relatively strong posture for some length of time. Therefore, a common and firm policy had to be developed by the western industrialized nations in order to cope forcefully with OPEC. Such a policy, it was argued, could be developed only by the Western powers alone and without any previous consultation with the world's major petroleum producers; that is, the OPEC member states. In other words, "the United

States propose[d] to organize the developed countries first, as a prerequisite to other contacts and negotiations involving either the developing countries or the oil-producing countries" (*Ibid*). This approach was supported by United States Secretary of State, Henry Kissinger. By 1978, OPEC still wielded considerable power in the world economy and was expected to maintain such a lead for a considerable time to come. It must be admitted, at this point, that Secretary Kissinger's statement regarding the future of OPEC was not specific; it made no precise predictions like those of Secretary Simon.

A third approach was for the Western industrialized world to pursue a policy of accommodation and co-operation with the OPEC member states rather than a policy of confrontation. This approach assumed that the post-1973 events proved that confrontation with OPEC had failed. The collapse of the Energy Conference, which the United States convened in Washington, DC during the first quarter of 1975, attested to this fact. That conference included all the western European industrialized countries, Japan and the United States of America. The ulterior motive was to develop a policy of confrontation against the OPEC nations. Instead, another conference was held in Paris in April 1975 between the leading industrial nations and the OPEC representatives to establish an on-going dialogue that would serve the objectives and interests of all parties.

> The inability of [that] preparatory meeting called by President Giscard D'Estaing in April [1975] to agree a concept for future discussions between producers and consumers [should under no circumstances dissuade the parties from constructive future talks]. [This is illustrated by the] bilateral contacts to organize a new meeting [which] are already under way, and the search for that concept will go on, for there can be no equilibrium in the world economy or in the world until a more balanced relation of power between oil producers and industrial countries is reached, defined, institutionalized.
>
> *Source*: "OPEC and the Industrial Countries", by Thomas O Enders, *Foreign Affairs*, Vol 53 (1975)

8.4.3   THE ROLE OF OPEC, PAST, PRESENT AND FUTURE

The image of the Organization of Petroleum Exporting Countries, controversial from its inception, varies according to the interests of the perceiver.

The Organization itself, (*OPEC at a Glance*, 1988) describes the Organization's birth in the following terms:

> OPEC was born of protest – protest against the high-handedness of the major international oil companies, the so-called "Seven Sisters". Before the advent of OPEC, these seven multi-national oil companies – Exxon,

Texaco, Royal Dutch Shell, Mobil, Gulf, British Petroleum and Standard Oil of California – had created "States-within-States" in the oil producing countries, controlling the amount of oil extracted, how much was sold, to whom it was sold, and at what price. On these matters of vital importance to the livelihood of the oil producing countries, the host governments were never consulted. They were paid a meagre royalty, while the oil companies made vast profits and built huge financial empires for themselves at the expense of the producing countries.

In the West, it was generally agreed that the new Organization of Petroleum Exporting Countries constituted a cartel,

> a producer cartel designed to hold up prices in a falling market and to harmonize the conflicting interests of its members.
>
> *Source*: Christopher Tugendhat, *Oil, the Biggest Business* (New York: G.P. Putnam and Sons, 1968)

This view of OPEC as a cartel has persisted in the West. For example, references to OPEC as a cartel and, almost always, implicitly or explicitly as an "evil cartel", in the Western press are legion.

And yet it is arguable that the Organization of Petroleum Exporting Countries never fulfilled the requirements of a classical definition of a cartel and certainly never matched the true cartel nature of the oil companies themselves. The definition of the Organization's original objectives is illuminating:

> OPEC's principal objectives as stipulated at the founding meeting have not changed – to co-ordinate and unify the petroleum policies of Member Countries and to determine the best means of safe-guarding their individual and collective interests; to seek ways and means of ensuring the stabilization of prices in international oil markets, with a view to eliminating harmful and unnecessary fluctuations; to provide an efficient, economic and regular supply of petroleum to consuming nations and a fair return on capital to those investing in the petroleum industry.
>
> *Source: OPEC at a Glance*, 1988, published by OPEC

The fact that OPEC recognized, from the start, that it must take into account the interests of the oil companies and the consuming nations in the oil market equation, is difficult to reconcile with the description of the organization as a "cartel". But two other factors undermine such a description of it still more persuasively.

First, OPEC consisted not of a group of commercial firms (with inevitably a high degree of homogeneity in interests and outlook) but of a grouping of nations with widely varying political and economic backgrounds. The imposition of the discipline necessary to operate an effective cartel was always, in such circumstances, likely to be problematical.

Secondly, the oil companies still controlled the refining and marketing of the producers' product – and, since it was the refining, marketing and distribution of petroleum which gave access to the consumers, much economic and commercial power remained, and still remains, with the oil companies.

In recent years, following the two major price increases of the 1970s (one caused by the Arab/Israeli war, the other by the Iranian revolution and the Iraq/Iran war), there has been considerable hostility towards OPEC, both at governmental level and in the Western media. The most prolific image has been of OPEC as a kidnapper "holding the West to ransom". The popular press in Britain, for example, frequently argues that OPEC has, and would like again to have, the West "over a barrel".

Perhaps such imagery is inevitable. The West needs oil and the OPEC countries possess great reserves. To that extent, the West is dependent on OPEC (less so now than in the past, but surely more so in the future, as non-OPEC reserves of oil become exhausted). Such dependence and potential vulnerability tend to foster feelings of hostility.

And yet any serious analyst of OPEC's conduct and, in particular, of the Kingdom of Saudi Arabia's influence within OPEC, would certainly come away with a more complex interpretation of OPEC's objectives and role. OPEC has continually striven to stabilize the price of oil, acknowledging that massive increases and decreases in price, resulting from a "free market" approach, are damaging to both producing and consuming nations.

OPEC has also been aware that, in determining price levels, due account should be taken of the fact that oil is an essential and, at the same time, finite resource. Profligate use of oil, engendered in a "free market" by low prices, is scarcely in the interests of the world economy or the environment. It is indeed arguable that OPEC, in its continuing efforts to promote a coherent global oil policy, by balancing the interests of the producers and the consumers, has acted far more responsibly than consumer nations which have tended to base their response on a simple "supply/demand" formula. It seems that even the energy conservation programs and programs for the development of alternative sources of energy in the West have been motivated more by narrow political and economic considerations, rather than by a responsible overview of global energy requirements and how these can best be met in future centuries.

In the context of determining the true nature of OPEC, we should give at least a brief mention to the OPEC Fund for International Development. This Fund was set up by the Organization in 1976 to provide financial assistance to developing countries (within and outside OPEC) in their efforts to achieve social and economic improvement.

Since its inception, the Fund has implemented seven lending programmes, and is currently engaged in the eighth, which began in January, 1988. By the close of its 11th year of operation, (December, 1987), the Fund had committed $3.3 billion to 91 countries in Africa, Asia, Latin America and the Caribbean, and disbursed $2.6 billion – representing 77.2% of contributions – in 448 loans and 213 grants. In its total project lending, the Fund has covered the following sectors: energy, transportation, agriculture and agro-industry, national development banks, water supply and sewage, industry, education, health and telecommunications.

Source: OPEC at a Glance, 1988, published by OPEC

It is particularly noteworthy that the aid provided by the OPEC Fund for International Development does not involve the recipient in any obligation to purchase goods and services from the donor country (though some preference is given to sources of supply in developing countries). This degree of freedom compares very favorably with aid from the industrialized OECD countries, where a common condition of aid is the spending of much of it with the donor countries.

8.5   The Organization of Arab Petroleum Exporting Countries (OAPEC)

In the summer of 1967, the Kingdom of Saudi Arabia submitted a proposal to both Kuwait and Libya for establishing an Arab organization of petroleum exporting countries. As a result, and after further studies, the three countries met in Beirut and signed an agreement on 9th January 1968, initiating the first institutionalized Arab co-operation in the field of petroleum – the Organization of Arab Petroleum Exporting Countries (OAPEC). It was agreed that Kuwait would be the organization's headquarters.

Article 7 of OAPEC's statute sets forth the criteria for admission. The principal criterion is that petroleum must constitute the main source of the applicant state's national income. Later it was realized that such a condition was highly selective and would restrict the membership of the organization to some, rather than most, of the Arab countries. This was not in harmony with the basic objective of the organization; that is, greater co-operation between all Arab states. Consequently the Saudi government suggested an amendment to Article 7 whereby any Arab petroleum exporting country in which petroleum represents an important (rather than the main) source of income may join. Abu Dhabi, now the capital of the United Arab Emirates (UAE), Algeria, Bahrain and Qatar were admitted to the organization during an extraordinary ministerial board meeting on 24th May 1970, as a direct result of this amendment to Article 7. Another group of new member states, Egypt, Iraq and Syria, joined the organization during 1972. Both Iraq and

Syria became full members during 1972, but, because of the late deposition of Egypt's ratification documents at the Kuwaiti Foreign Ministry, Egypt did not officially become a member of OAPEC until 1973. So the members of the Organization of Arab Petroleum Exporting Countries are:

- Algeria
- Bahrain
- Egypt
- Iraq
- Kuwait
- Libya
- Qatar
- Saudi Arabia
- Syria
- United Arab Emirates

The organization's objectives are summed up in these three main aims:

A   To carry out common projects that would achieve a diversified economic investment for the members. This, in turn, would lessen their dependency on petroleum as a sole source of income. And consequently, this would slow down the consumption of their petroleum and prolong the period of its investment for future generations.

B   To consider the legitimate rights of the consumer by making sure that petroleum reaches the market under just and reasonable conditions.

C   To develop and promote the international petroleum industry by means of providing suitable circumstances for capital and experience to be invested in the member countries. The text, in this general sense, is applied to both national and foreign capital and experience as long as it is invested in the petroleum industry of member states.

> *Source: Al A'Hkam Ala'Ama*, by Algohonami (author's translation)

Since its creation, the Organization of Arab Petroleum Exporting Countries has made great efforts toward achieving its goals and serving the economies of all Arab, as well as member, countries. Acting as an effective co-ordinator, OAPEC has played an important role in reducing duplication of effort and investment and in rationalizing many aspects of oil and gas production.

Among the most important projects which OAPEC has undertaken has been the formation of the following organizations;

1 The Arab Maritime Petroleum Transport Company (AMPTC), which began its activities in 1974 with capital of US$ 500 million.
2 The Arab Shipbuilding and Repair Yard Company (ASRY), which was officially inaugurated in 1974 with capital of US$ 120 million.
3 The Arab Petroleum Investments Corporation (APICORP), which was officially inaugurated in September 1974 with capital of almost $1 billion.
4 The Arab Petroleum Services Company (APSC), which was formed in 1977.
5 The Arab Petroleum Training Institute, which was founded in 1979.
6 The Arab Engineering Company (AREC), formed in 1981.

Article 8 of the Organization's statutes sets out its organizational structure. OAPEC consists of:

- Ministerial Board [referred to as the Council]
- Executive Bureau (or office) [referred to as the Office]
- Secretary General [referred to as the Secretary]
- Judicial Organization [referred to as the Organization]

> Source: Agreement: Organization of Arab Petroleum Exporting Countries, (Kuwait: OAPEC – Author's translation)

The underlying economic strength of the member countries of OAPEC is obvious. Nevertheless, the decline in the oil price in the 1980s and the consequent drop in the revenues of the member states of OAPEC, together with political

Table 8.3 *Worldwide oil production (000 barrels per day)*

Year	North America	Latin America	Western Europe	Saudi Arabia	Middle East (other)	Africa	Asia and Australasia	CPEs*	Total
1978	11,850	4,965	1,735	8,315	13,110	6,100	2,780	14,200	63,055
1979	11,905	5,530	2,295	9,555	12,355	6,750	2,890	14,495	65,775
1980	11,895	5,895	2,475	9,990	8,765	6,180	2,745	14,810	62,755
1981	11,725	6,295	2,635	9,985	6,030	4,980	2,875	14,850	59,375
1982	11,685	6,550	3,020	6,695	6,580	4,785	2,760	14,985	57,060
1983	11,760	6,485	3,450	5,225	6,885	4,745	2,995	15,145	56,690
1984	12,150	6,680	3,765	4,760	7,095	5,200	3,215	15,235	58,100
1985	12,360	6,685	3,960	3,565	7,335	5,290	3,270	15,130	57,595
1986	12,090	6,615	4,075	5,150	7,955	5,310	3,470	15,660	60,325
1987	11,815	6,600	4,195	4,365	8,750	5,225	3,370	15,880	60,200

* CPE = Centrally Planned Economy
Source: Derived from BP Statistical Review of World Energy, 1988

Table 8.4 *Saudi Arabian, OPEC and world oil production (000 barrels per day)*

Year	Saudi Arabia	OPEC	SA as % of OPEC	World	SA as % of world
1978	8,315	30,280	27.5	63,055	13.2
1979	9,555	31,465	30.4	65,775	14.5
1980	9,990	27,445	36.4	62,755	15.9
1981	9,985	23,380	42.7	59,375	16.8
1982	6,695	19,930	33.6	57,060	11.7
1983	5.225	18,425	28.4	56,690	9.2
1984	4,760	18,470	25.8	58,100	8.2
1985	3,565	17,215	20.7	57,595	6.2
1986	5,150	19,555	26.3	60,325	8.5
1987	4,365	19,030	22.9	60,200	7.3

(Author's calculations)

factors, has not left the Organization untouched. At the end of 1986, some US$ 14 million of contributions was owed to the Organization by the member states. Furthermore the 1988 budget for the Organization (US$ 5.3 million) showed a 27% decline against the 1987 budget (US$ 7.3 million).

Despite tighter budgetary constraints, OAPEC continues to make a valued contribution to the co-ordination of diverse aspects of the Arab oil industry. In association with other Arab organizations, it organizes conferences and seminars on oil-related topics and acts as a channel of communications between oil research institutions. The current OAPEC programme (1987–91) focuses on the encouragement of trade in petroleum and petrochemicals between Arab countries.

8.6   The status of oil, present and future

Earlier sections of this chapter have centered on oil in the Kingdom of Saudi Arabia. It may be helpful to begin a review of the present and future status of oil within the Saudi Arabian economy by setting the Kingdom's oil (production and reserves) into a wider historical and geographical context.

Table 8.3 examines the Kingdom's production of oil between 1978 and 1987, set against world oil production, and Table 8.4 expresses the Kingdom's oil production as a percentage of (a) OPEC's production and (b) world oil production.

These figures show the Kingdom's share of world oil production falling from nearly 17% in 1981 to a low of just over 6% in 1985. Within OPEC, Saudi Arabia's share of total OPEC production halved in the same period, falling from 43% to 21%. Seen in the context of these figures, the Kingdom's decision in 1985 to end its role as the oil world's "swing" producer is entirely comprehensible. Had the decline in its production continued at the same pace for four more years, the country endowed with the world's largest oil reserves (reckoned in January 1989 to amount to 25 per cent of the world's total) would have ceased to produce any oil at all. With its heavy dependence on oil revenues and its commitment to the implementation of its development programs, the Kingdom of Saudi Arabia could no longer reduce its own oil production simply in order to maintain a higher price for others, within and outside OPEC.

It is fair to say that the attitude of the Kingdom of Saudi Arabia to the exploitation of its own oil reserves and to the oil market in general has, from the earliest years, shown a considerable degree of sophistication. From 1974, the Kingdom of Saudi Arabia has continuously used its influence to try to impose some degree of stability on the oil market. It has consistently shown an understanding of the economic needs of consuming nations, as well as those of its fellow producers. Indeed, by accepting the dollar as the currency for oil payments, Saudi Arabia has shared the consequences of dollar inflation and the devaluation of the money paid for oil.

It is the Kingdom's view that, in the exploitation of a finite resource as precious as oil, international and global considerations, as well as national needs, should be taken into account. It is damaging to the world economy to have major rises or falls in the price of such an essential source of energy. This fact alone suggests that rather than presenting the producer/consumer relationship as one of conflict, it would be more constructive to recognize it as one of interdependence. It must also be true that, as the world's reserves of oil diminish, and the value of that diminishing resource increases, agreement between the producers and consumers on how best to manage this economic process would seem to be highly desirable. Such an approach would surely be preferable to the vagaries of the "free market" which presumably would simply mean that the producers should extract the maximum price from their remaining oil reserves, regardless of the political or economic consequences for the consumers – much as the consuming nations have quite happily taken advantage of excess supply in the 1980s to reduce the oil price as far as possible.

In passing, it is perhaps worth adding that the "free-market" approach to oil, advocated by Britain in the 1980s, is self-evidently inappropriate in the context of a resource such as oil. The oil market cannot be free of governmental decisions which are politically motivated and have little or nothing to do with market mechanisms. For example, the level of tax imposed by governments on oil companies is no less a determining factor of the price of oil than is the decision of a producer to increase or decrease production. Both can be "external" factors which dramatically affect the "supply and demand" equation. The notion that it is possible for government policy to have no bearing on the decisions of oil companies or on the oil market is either naïve or disingenuous. The decision of a government with substantial oil export revenues not to co-operate with OPEC, apparently against its own economic self-interest, may well be politically astute, but it has little to do with *laissez faire* economics. More importantly, management of the oil market raises global considerations, stretching into the next century and beyond, which the "free-market" approach simply does not accommodate, but which governments, with a responsibility for the well-being of future generations, must assuredly address.

What will happen to the oil market in the next few years is difficult to predict. So many factors are involved. How quickly will the world's recoverable reserves of oil be depleted? How far and how quickly will alternative sources of energy be employed to replace oil in some of its applications? What impact will environmental considerations have upon national and international energy policies? What scientific advances will be made which might radically alter the total energy resources of the planet? Will nuclear fusion become a practical, as distinct from a theoretical, source of virtually limitless energy? And what of the international political environment within which the oil market game has always been played?

Because of the uncertainties, most analysts of the oil market confine their predictions to the next few weeks or, at most, months. *The Economist*, in "The World in 1989" is an exception:

> We think that the price of crude oil will remain low – perhaps very low, but don't cheer too soon because this could be deceptive. We also think margins on products from oil will rise. Behind-the-scenes manoeuvres among OPEC (the Organization of Petroleum Exporting Countries) producers are complicated even for OPEC. The new word to watch is "reintegration" which can mean either the return of Iraq to the OPEC fold or the integration of crude production with downstream operations like refining and making chemicals.

After examining the question of Iraq's relations with OPEC, the author of this article, Paul Barker, turns to the other sense of reintegration:

> Kuwait now sells the majority of its crude oil through its own network, and several other OPEC members, including Saudi Arabia and Abu Dhabi, have begun to follow suit. OPEC purchases of downstream operations in major markets is called "reintegration", because in the days before OPEC and the nationalization of oil reserves, the oil majors used to produce, refine and market their own Gulf oil. They kept the price of crude low to keep royalty payments low. Profits were made on the value-added margins of their branded oils etc.

The Economist, perhaps wisely, does not attach a time scale to any of these predictions but it seems certain that, in the next few years, the efforts of oil producers to gain some control of "downstream" (refining, distribution and marketing) operations will be a major feature of the market.

On price, this much may be said. There is, of course, nothing sacrosanct about the present benchmark price of US$ 18 a barrel but it does represent an informed estimate of the price level at which the interests of oil producers and oil consumers are currently best reconciled. The price is high enough to justify further oil exploration, but not so high as to make alternative forms of energy irresistibly attractive. The price is low enough to help the economies of the consumers in both the developed and developing worlds but not so low as to undermine the economies of the oil producers.

As the years pass and as oil reserves diminish, it seems inevitable that the oil price will rise. If this process is managed sensibly, the rise should be gradual, causing the minimum economic disruption. If it is left to the market, there are likely to be sudden and substantial rises in price which the consuming economies will no doubt find difficult to absorb – as difficult to absorb as the producing economies found the falls in price of the 1980s.

The real question is this. Will the main consumers, the industrialized nations, persist in seeing oil as simply another commodity to be obtained from the source at the lowest possible "market" price – or will they recognize that, in an increasingly inter-dependent world, the interests of producer and consumer, while not identical, must in the end be brought together in the interests of the global economy?

In terms of the economy of the Kingdom of Saudi Arabia, oil will continue to play a key role. The Kingdom's development plans have used the oil revenues to diversify the Saudi Arabian economy, expanding the non-oil industrial sector and the agricultural sector. The achievements in these areas are adequately delineated in subsequent sections of this book. It remains nevertheless true that oil will continue to represent the major sector of the economy. Latest official estimates of Saudi

Table 8.5   *Proven oil reserves 1st January 1989, million barrels*

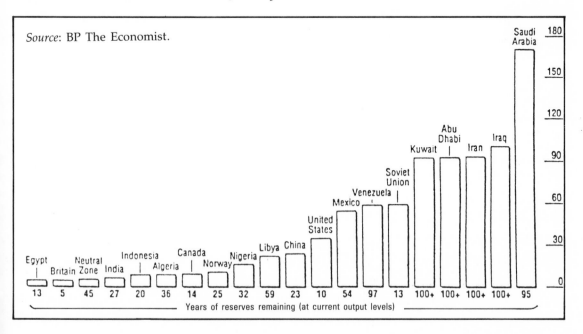

Source: BP The Economist.

Arabian oil reserves (January 1989) top 250,000 million barrels; reserves of proven gas reserves are currently estimated at 177 trillion cubic feet. Even these latest estimates are considered conservative by many who have suggested that reserves of oil could be as high as 315,000 million barrels of oil and 253 trillion cubic feet of gas. It is therefore inevitable that in the next decade and in the next century the Kingdom of Saudi Arabia will continue to derive most of its income from the black gold that lies within its territory. It is also inevitable that the Kingdom's role in the politics and economics of the Middle East, and indeed, on the wider international stage, will grow in importance, as the smaller oil reserves of other countries become more difficult and more expensive to exploit – or, finally, are exhausted.

Table 8.5 (produced by British Petroleum and published in *The Economist*, 15th–21st July 1989), shows the proven oil reserves of the main oil producing countries. The numbers at the base of each column indicate the number of years these reserves would last, assuming current levels of production and no further discoveries. The table, which shows that, on these assumptions, the Kingdom of Saudi Arabia will be able to maintain present production levels for another 95 years, does not take into account the January 1989 upgrading of Saudi Arabia's estimated reserves. Latest estimates suggest that the Kingdom now has up to 150 years of reserves at current output levels beneath its soil. The remarks in this section should be seen in this context.

Chapter **9**

The Economy

The last two decades have seen an extraordinary rise in the Kingdom's Gross Domestic Product, followed by an equally dramatic fall. It is not perhaps easy to grasp the scale of these economic phenomena or the magnitude of the Kingdom's achievement in absorbing them.

9.1   Introduction

Following the peak years of oil revenues in 1400/01–02/03 (1980/81–82/83), it became necessary to undertake a very considerable downward adjustment of the government's level of expenditure. At the same time, the economy as a whole had to come to terms with more modest circumstances. The most remarkable feature of this process is the relative ease with which both the government and the private sector have come to terms with the new circumstances. This is not to say that the process has not been difficult, demanding, even painful. But it is true that a decline in revenues which could have destabilized or even destroyed other economies has been taken as an opportunity to consolidate past achievements and to engender a more commercially realistic and efficient approach to all types of venture.

To a very large extent, Saudi Arabia's success in adjusting to reduced revenues is attributable to the Kingdom's national planning process. The planning function which permeates all areas of government activity ensures that the country enjoys the benefits of a long-term economic strategy. Just as the earlier Development Plans ensured that the Kingdom's revenues were applied to the essential task of developing Saudi Arabia's infrastructure, its industry and agriculture, so the Fourth Development Plan, taking into account the prevailing economic climate, was able to focus resources more on consolidation.

In many ways, a period of retrenchment may be seen as a blessing in disguise. The years of the boom were years of great achievement but they brought with them economic and social strains. The need to develop the Kingdom economically as quickly as possible meant that speed sometimes took precedence over cost effectiveness. The need to import very large numbers of foreign workers (skilled and unskilled) from many different countries and cultural backgrounds to implement the ambitious development program posed a considerable social challenge. It is therefore the view of many Saudi Arabian citizens that a period of consolidation will prove in the long run both economically and socially beneficial.

In this context, it is useful to quote from the Basic Strategic Principles of the Fifth Five Year Plan (which is to run from 1410 to 1415; 1990–95):

> Emphasis should be laid on improving the economic productive standards of services, utilities and products provided by the Government for the citizens, both directly (such as education and security services) and indirectly (such as electricity, transport and basic commodities).

> Economic performance may be improved by means of:
> 1 Reducing production costs of public services and utilities.
> 2 Ensuring that services are appropriate and not excessive; eg by limiting specifications for construction or operation of projects to what is actually required.
> 3 Utilizing technology in all public service sectors, through mechanization and the use of advanced methods.
> 4 Concentrating on those technologies that are available for the needs of the national economy, such as automation, the use of saline-water agriculture and other methods.
> 5 Judging the economic feasibility of projects of all types by including operational and maintenance costs, including management costs, not only the capital costs.
> 6 Encouraging the citizens to invest in feasible, worthwhile industries, dependent on local raw materials which will use production methods requiring minimum labor and minimum quantities of critical resources, such as water.
> 7 Emphasis should be given to diversifying the agricultural productive base, through encouraging investment and the establishment of joint stock companies on a large scale; and by feasible agricultural projects employing modern equipment and machinery in irrigation, and continuing to encourage individual investment therein.
> 8 Supporting the trend towards investment in projects applying new technologies, where the Kingdom has economic advantages or which are urgently needed (eg solar energy projects, modern irrigation methods and the use of greenhouses).
> 9 Supporting the centers and programs for applied research.
> 10 Making full provision in the planning of any projects for all foreseeable future maintenance and operational requirements. In projects, design consideration should be given to reducing maintenance requirements as far as possible.

Table 9.1 *Saudi Arabian GDP*

| Year | Millions of Saudi Riyals (SR) | | |
	GDP in producers' values	Import duties	GDP in purchasers' values
1389/90 1969/70	17,153	246	17,399
1390/91 1971/71	22,581	340	22,921
1391/92 1971/72	27,857	400	28,257
1392/93 1972/73	40,087	464	40,551
1393/94 1973/74	98,840	475	99,315
1394/95 1974/75	139,224	376	139,600*
1395/96 1975/76	163,893	633	164,526
1396/97 1976/77	203,942	1,114	205,056
1397/98 1977/78	223,818	1,583	225,401
1398/99 1978/79	247,624	1,917	249,541
1399/00 1979/80	383,589	2,217	385,806
1400/01 1980/81	517,996	2,595	520,591
1401/02 1981/82	522,177	2,542	524,719
1402/03 1982/83	411,801	3,433	415,234
1403/04 1983/84	368,399	3,624	372,023
1404/05 1984/85	322,919	3,916	326,835
1405/06 1985/86	274,719	3,943	278,662
1406/07** 1986/87	264,074	3,571	267,645

*   the figures from 1394/95 on are not strictly comparable with those of the earlier years
** a ten-month fiscal year, figures annualized
Source: Central Department of Statistics, Kingdom of Saudi Arabia

11 Including safety protection programs in project maintenance schedules based on the life of the unit or rate of operation.

12 Standardizing the technical specifications of projects to facilitate and reduce the cost of maintenance.

13 Developing training programs for machine operation, thereby reducing operational errors.

14 Employing general principles of maintenance and safety as part of the educational curricula for the post-elementary educational stage to enable individuals to carry out simple maintenance tasks.

15 Encouraging the private sector to invest in maintenance projects.

16 Laying emphasis on the employment of Saudi manpower in important and permanently productive sectors.

17 Developing appropriate administrative and financial organization to serve the new needs of the community.

Already, efforts to increase economic efficiency have paid dividends. Waste has been reduced and costs have fallen in both the public and private sectors of the economy.

9.2   Basic statistics on the Saudi Arabian economy

9.2.1   GROSS DOMESTIC PRODUCT

Table 9.1 sets out the Kingdom's Gross Domestic Product, at Producers' and Purchasers' Values, from 1389/90 AH (1969/70) to 1406/07 AH (1986/87). These figures show the extraordinary growth in the Kingdom's economy, fuelled by oil, in the early years, followed by a very steep decline in recent years.

The first major oil price increase shows up in the figures for 1393/94 AH (1973/74), with GDP more than doubling in one year. The second major oil price increase shows through in the figures for 1399/1400 AH (1979/80), with a greater than 50 per cent increase in GDP in that year. By 1400/01 AH (1980/81), the GDP was double the figure for 1398/99 AH (1978/79) and that level of GDP was maintained in the following year, 1401/02 AH (1981/82). The figures thereafter show a steep decline until, by 1406/07 AH (1986/87), the GDP was at its pre-1398/99 AH (1978/79) level.

9.2.2   GROSS DOMESTIC PRODUCT IN PRODUCERS' VALUES, BROKEN DOWN BY OIL AND NON-OIL SECTORS

Table 9.2 clearly shows the key role that oil plays in the Kingdom's economy, but, on closer inspection, it also reveals the Kingdom's determination to develop the non-oil sector, thereby reducing the Kingdom's dependence on oil and creating a

Table 9.2   *GDP by oil and non-oil sectors*

Year	Oil sector			Non-oil sector			Total
	SR (millions)	% Share	% Growth	SR (millions	% Share	% Growth	
1389/90 1969/70	9,566	55.8	—	7,587	44.4	—	17,153
1390/91 1970/71	14,328	63.5	+ 50	8,253	36.5	+ 9	22,581
1391/92 1091/72	18,674	67.0	+ 30	9,183	33.0	+ 11	27,857
1392/93 1973/74	28,684	71.6	+ 54	11,403	28.4	+ 24	40,087
1393/94 1973/74	83,410	84.4	+191	15,430	15.6	+ 35	98,840
1394/95 1974/75	111,101	79.8	+ 33	28,123	20.2	+ 82	139,224*
1395/96 1975/76	116,570	71.1	+ 5	47,323	28.9	+ 68	163,893
1396/97 1976/77	136,249	66.8	+ 17	67,693	33.2	+ 43	203,942
1397/98 1977/78	133,935	59.8	− 2	89,883	40.2	+ 38	223,818
1398/99 1978/79	140,384	56.7	+ 5	107,240	43.3	+ 19	247,624
1399/00 1979/80	252,705	65.9	+ 80	130,884	34.1	+ 22	383,589
1400/01 1980/81	360,741	69.6	+ 43	157,255	30.4	+ 20	517,996
1401/02 1981/82	337,884	64.7	− 6	184,293	35.3	+ 17	522,177
1402/03 1982/83	206,360	50.1	− 39	205,441	49.9	+ 11	411,801
1403/04 1983/84	157,989	42.9	− 23	210,410	57.1	+ 2	368,399
1404/05 1984/85	121,467	37.6	− 23	201,452	62.4	− 4	322,919
1405/06 1985/86	90,004	32.8	− 26	184,715	67.2	− 8	274,719
1406/07** 1986/87	85,513	32.4	− 5	178,561	67.6	− 3	264,074

*   the figures from 1394/95 on are not strictly comparable with those of the earlier years
**   a ten-month fiscal year, figures annualized
Source: Saudi Riyal figures – Central Department of Statistics, Kingdom of Saudi Arabia (percentages calculated by author)

more broadly-based economy. Of course, the non-oil sector has shared in the general economic recession but the figures indicate the Kingdom's success in pursuing its policy of economic diversification.

9.2.3 ANNUAL RATE OF GROWTH OF GROSS DOMESTIC PRODUCT BY OIL AND NON-OIL SECTORS, IN PRODUCERS' VALUES, AT CONSTANT PRICES

To provide an index of economic performance, Table 9.3 sets out the growth in the Kingdom's Gross Domestic Product (producers' values), based on constant prices.

9.2.4 GOVERNMENT REVENUES AND EXPENDITURE

There can be no clearer illustration of the magnitude of the economic challenges and problems faced by the Government of the Kingdom of Saudi Arabia than the figures for government revenues and expenditure (1389/90 AH–1406/07 AH: 1969/70–86/87). These figures follow the same pattern as those for GDP but with steeper rises and steeper falls. Figures for government expenditure are also given, clearly showing the scale of the adjustment required by both the rise and fall in revenues and the difficulties the government has faced in reconciling falling revenues with its commitments (Table 9.4).

9.2.5 SOURCE OF GOVERNMENT REVENUES (OIL AND OTHER SOURCES) IN PERCENTAGE TERMS

In terms of understanding the Kingdom's overall economic development strategy, these figures are of particular interest (Table 9.5). Clearly the declining share of government revenues provided by oil in recent years is primarily the consequence of falling oil revenues. But, also within these statistics is a further indication of the Kingdom's determination to diversify the Saudi Arabian economy, making it less dependent on oil.

9.2.6 IMPORTS, EXPORTS AND THE BALANCE OF TRADE

Figures for the total value of imports and exports, and their value by region, are presented in Table 9.6 and Table 9.7.

9.3   Oil revenues

Over the twelve-year period from 1976 to 1987, the Kingdom's oil revenues (in millions of US dollars), including revenues from natural gas, refined products and revenues from the Neutral Zone (shared with Kuwait), have been:

Year	Millions US$
1976	33,500
1977	38,000
1978	36,700
1979	59,200
1980	104,200
1981	113,300
1982	76,000
1983	46,000
1984	43,700
1985	28,000
1986	20,000
1987	23,000

Source: Royal Dutch Shell Group, 1988

It should be noted that these figures are expressed in US dollars. In considering the implications of these figures for the Saudi Arabian economy, the fall in the value of the US currency against other hard currencies since 1985 should be taken into account.

9.4   Banking and finance

In the last twenty years, there has been a very considerable development of the banking system in the Kingdom of Saudi Arabia.

It should perhaps first be pointed out that, in a Muslim society, Islam sets the guiding principles for banking as for all else. In the *Quran*, usury is expressly forbidden. Because of this prohibition, the introduction of Western banking systems and procedures into the Kingdom has not always been possible and, indeed, in many cases, the Western and the Saudi Arabian attitudes to banking have not been compatible.

The challenges posed to the Islamic world by the interest-based financial institutions of the West have encouraged the development of the Islamic banking movement, under which Islamic banks perform all the functions of their Western counterparts without recourse to usury. Prince Muhammad ibn Faisal of Saudi Arabia has played a leading role in the development of the Islamic banking movement.

For the Kingdom, which, from a financial viewpoint, operates internationally as well within its own borders, the problems of reconciling the Muslim and the Western attitudes to banking remain.

Table 9.3 *GDP growth (percentages based on constant prices 1399/1400)*

Year	Oil sector % Growth	Non-oil sector % Growth	Total % Growth
1390/91 1970/71	21.2	5.2	16.6
1391/92 1971/72	22.6	7.3	18.7
1392/93 1973/74	24.4	13.1	21.6
1393/94 1973/74	15.7	16.7	15.9
1394/95 1974/75	−5.2	17.4	−0.3
1395/96 1975/76	1.1	22.0	6.4
1396/97 1976/77	13.2	16.9	14.3
1397/98 1977/78	−0.7	12.4	3.2
1398/99 1978/79	2.3	8.7	4.4
1399/00 1979/80	8.1	9.4	8.5
1400/01 1980/81	3.5	11.9	6.4
1401/02 1981/81	−9.5	10.7	−2.2
1402/03 1982/83	−37.6	4.3	−20.6
1403/04 1983/84	−10.3	0.7	−4.4
1404/05 1984/85	−14.5	−5.0	−9.1
1405/06 1985/86	−5.5	−8.6	−7.3
1406/07* 1986/87	28.2	−4.3	9.3

* a ten-month fiscal year, figures annualized
Source: Central Department of Statistics, Kingdom of Saudi Arabia

Table 9.4   *Government revenues and expenditure*

	Millions of Saudi Riyals		
Year	Revenues	Expenditure	Balance
1389/90 1969/70	5,741	6,028	(287)
1390/91 1970/71	7,954	6,293	1,661
1391/92 1971/72	11,116	8,130	2,986
1392/93 1972/73	15,326	10,158	5,168
1393/94 1973/74	40,597	18,595	22,002
1394/95 1974/75	100,103	35,039	65,064
1395/96 1975/76	103,384	81,784	21,600
1396/97 1976/77	135,957	106,737	29,220
1397/98 1977/78	132,241	137,110	(4,869)
1398/99 1978/79	131,505	146,306	(14,801)
1399/00 1979/80	211,196	185,724	25,472
1400/01 1980/81	348,119	230,416	117,703
1401/02 1981/82	368,006	283,258	84,748
1402/03 1982/83	246,182	244,912	1,270
1403/04 1983/84	206,419	230,186	(23,767)
1404/05 1984/85	171,509	216,363	(44,854)
1405/06 1985/86	131,736	181,500	(49,764)
1406/07* 1986/87	76,498	137,422	(60,924)

* a ten-month fiscal year, figures annualized
Source: Ministry of Finance and National Economy, Kingdom of Saudia Arabia

Table 9.5 *Source of government revenues*

Year	Oil %	Others %
1389/90 1969/70	89.2	10.8
1390/91 1970/71	89.5	10.5
1391/92 1971/72	87.1	12.9
1392/93 1972/73	88.0	12.0
1393/94 1973/74	97.3	2.7
1394/95 1974/75	94.1	5.9
1395/96 1975/76	90.4	9.6
1396/97 1976/77	89.1	10.9
1397/98 1977/78	86.2	13.8
1398/99 1978/79	87.5	12.5
1399/00 1979/80	89.6	10.4
1400/01 1980/81	91.7	8.3
1401/02 1981/82	89.3	10.7
1402/03 1982/83	75.6	24.4
1403/04 1983/84	70.3	29.7
1404/05 1984/85	70.8	29.2
1405/06 1985/86	67.1	32.9
1406/07* 1986/87	55.5	44.5

* a ten-month fiscal year, figures annualized
Source: Ministry of Finance and National Economy, Kingdom of Saudi Arabia

9.4.1   THE SAUDI ARABIAN MONETARY AGENCY – SAMA

The Saudi Arabian Monetary Agency – SAMA – which was founded in 1372 AH (1952), is the Kingdom's central bank. The Agency's charter requires it to act as the central government bank, to issue currency (paper and coin), to support the value of the Riyal at home and abroad, and to supervise and encourage the development of the Kingdom's banking system in both the public and the commercial sectors.

SAMA is also the Kingdom's investment authority. In this role, it is responsible for managing the country's foreign assets, most of which are held in Europe and the United States of America. At the end of 1407 AH (1987), the Kingdom's international reserves stood at US$ 22,912 million (International Financial Statistics published by the International Monetary Fund).

9.4.2   COMMERCIAL BANKS

There are eleven commercial banks in the Kingdom:

1   The National Commercial Bank (Head Office: Jeddah), founded in 1938 as a financial trading house and acquiring its present name in 1954, is the Kingdom's largest wholly-owned Saudi bank. In 1987, the NCB had 27 branches in Riyadh, 28 in Jeddah, ten in the Holy City of Makkah, thirteen branches in Dammam, Al-Khobar and Dhahran in the Eastern Province, and others spread throughout the Kingdom, making a total of 183 branches.
2   The Riyadh Bank (Head Office: Jeddah) was established in 1957 and is also wholly Saudi owned. In 1987, it had seventeen branches in Jeddah, fourteen in Riyadh, four in each of the Holy Cities of Makkah and Medina, eleven in Dammam, Al-Khobar and Dhahran and a network of other branches throughout the Kingdom, making a total of 144 branches.
3   The Arab National Bank (Head Office: Riyadh) had 93 branches in the Kingdom in 1987.
4   Al-Bank Al-Saudi Al-Fransi (Head Office: Jeddah) had 55 branches in the Kingdom in 1987.
5   The Saudi Cairo Bank (Head Office: Jeddah) had 45 branches in the Kingdom in 1987.
6   The Saudi American Bank (Head Office: Jeddah) had 31 branches in the Kingdom in 1987.
7   The Saudi-British Bank (Head Office: Riyadh) had 30 branches in the Kingdom in 1987.
8   Al-Bank Al-Saudi Al-Hollandi (Head Office: Jeddah) had 27 branches in the Kingdom in 1987.
9   The Al-Jazirah Bank (Head Office: Jeddah) had 26 branches in the Kingdom in 1987.

10   The United Saudi Commercial Bank (Head Office: Jeddah) had thirteen branches in the Kingdom in 1987. The United Saudi Commercial Bank is wholly Saudi owned.

11   In 1988, the Kingdom's leading money-changing company, Al-Rajhi, formed in 1978 when the four Al-Rajhi brothers merged their operations, was accorded commercial bank status under the name the Al-Rajhi Banking and Investment Company. The Al-Rajhi Banking and Investment Company is reckoned to be the third largest commercial financial institution in the Kingdom, after the National Commercial Bank and the Riyadh Bank.

9.4.3   INVESTMENT INSTITUTIONS

In addition to the commercial banks, there are a number of financial institutions specializing in investment:

1   Arabian Industrial Investment Company (Head Office: Riyadh)
2   Arab Investment Company (Head Office: Riyadh)
3   Arab Investment Company SAA (Head Office: Riyadh)
4   Saudi Arabian Investment Company Limited (Head Office: Jeddah)
5   Saudi Investment Bank (Head Office: Riyadh)
6   Saudi Investment Group (Head Office: Jeddah)
7   Saudi Investment Group Limited (Head Office: Riyadh)

9.4.4   SPECIALIZED CREDIT INSTITUTIONS

To assist in the Kingdom's development, the Government established several specialized credit institutions:

1   The Saudi Agricultural Bank was established in 1382 AH (1962) to provide government finance for farmers to enable them to contribute to the Kingdom's agricultural development.

2   The Public Investment Fund was established in 1391 AH (1971) to provide finance for medium and long-term industrial development projects.

3   The Real Estate Development Fund was established in 1394 AH (1974) to provide home loans to individuals and to provide companies with finance for private and commercial real estate projects.

4   The Saudi Credit Bank was established in 1394 AH (1974).

5   The Saudi Industrial Development Fund was established in 1394 AH (1974) to provide support for industrial (primarily electricity) companies, lending up to 50 per cent finance for ventures which are at least 25 per cent Saudi owned.

Table 9.6 *Total value of imports, exports and the balance of trade, 1394–1406 AH (1974–86)*

| Year | Saudi Riyals (millions) | | Balance of trade |
	Imports	Exports	
1974	10,149	126,223	+116,074
1975	14,823	104,412	+ 89,589
1976	30,691	135,154	+104,463
1977	51,662	153,209	+101,547
1978	69,180	138,242	+ 69,062
1979	82,223	213,183	+130,960
1980	100,350	362,886	+262,536
1981	119,298	405,481	+286,183
1982	139,335	271,090	+131,755
1983	135,417	158,444	+ 23,027
1984	118,737	132,299	+ 13,563
1985	85,564	99,536	+ 13,972
1986	70,781	74,378	+ 3,597

Source: Central Department of Statistics, Kingdom of Saudi Arabia

Table 9.7 *Value of imports and exports by region expressed in millions of Saudi Riyals and as percentages of the total for 1406 AH (1986)*

Region	Imports (SR mill)	%	Exports (SR mill)	%
Europe	30,509	43.1	24,986	33.6
Asia and Far East	21,522	30.4	24,935	33.5
North America	12,785	18.1	12,658	17.0
Gulf Co-operation Council	1,441	2.0	4,851	6.5
Other Arab League countries	1,489	2.1	2,480	3.3
Australia and Oceania	1,341	1.9	758	1.0
Latin America	1,083	1.5	3,012	4.0
Africa	272	0.4	465	0.6
Other, not defined	338	0.5	231	0.3
Total	70,780	100.0	74,377	100.0

Source: Statistics published by the Saudi Arabian Embassy, Washington DC, USA

9.4.5 BANKING AND FINANCE: THE FUTURE

In the Fourth Development Plan (1405–10 AH: 1985–90), it was recognized that a major turning point in the development of the financial and banking sector of the economy had been reached:

> The changing economic and business environment will place new demands on the financial sector: falling oil revenues have identified more clearly the need to harness the private sector capital in the development process. With increased demands being placed on private enterprise to help maintain the pace of economic development, new needs will arise for greater involvement of the financial sector in private project financing. This will require significant changes in the sector; new services and specialist capabilities and skills will be required; and new financial intermediaries will need to be established for the effective channelling of surplus capital to development projects. Changes are also called for in the public sector; new attitudes to finance will be required by the Government funding agencies in order to increase the private sector participation in long-term financing, and thereby develop its investment activities.

Source: Fourth Development Plan

In 1989, the Ministry of Commerce made the following comments on the status of fixed bank investments in the Kingdom and on the increasing participation of the private sector in the country's economic life:

> Fixed investments for the year 1406–07 AH (1986–87) have shown a decrease compared with the previous year; this is mainly due to the completion of the infrastructure projects in the Kingdom, and the drop in the nominal value of oil exports which led to lower Governmental revenues and in turn to lower Governmental spending (a 31.8% fall compared with the previous year).
> The share of the public sector has dropped from 48.8% in 1404–05 AH (1984–85) to 40.5% in 1406–07 AH (1986–87); while the private sector share, other than oil, rose from 41.1% in 1405–06 AH (1985–86) to 46.% in 1406–07 AH (1986–87). This clearly indicates that the private sector has expressed increasing confidence and interest in investment.
> It has been noted that there is growing interest in investment in shares. The shares of national joint stock companies have won the investors' confidence. This development has necessitated the regulation of share transactions and the establishment of management to encourage share transactions and to discourage harmful speculation. The expansion

in the formation of joint stock companies and the achievement of economic harmony and integration with the Gulf Co-operation Council states necessitate the establishment of a joint stock exchange for share dealings.

9.5   Commercial services

Although the commercial services (trade, finance, real estate and personal services) have traditionally been important activities, it was not until the mid-1390s [mid-1970s], in response to the surge in demand for imports, that their growth really began to take off. Many new companies were established, most of which were connected to construction activities. Several of these companies have grown into diversified multi-national corporations – some with turnovers estimated to exceed SR three billion.

The new Saudi companies are typified by their corporate structure – few having limited liability and almost none being public companies. Control usually remains with a family or is shared with a foreign joint-venture partner.

Complementing the multinationals are numerous commercial companies, ranging in size from very small traders to substantial retail and industrial companies. While smaller than the giants, these companies can be quite substantial – a great many achieving turnovers in excess of SR 250 million. A large proportion still have ties to the construction sector.

Source: Fourth Development Plan (1405–10 AH: 1985–90)

In the years since this was written, the Kingdom's economy has experienced a further fall in oil revenues and a number of companies, both large and small, have faced financial difficulties in trying to adjust to less expansive market conditions.

As a broad indication of the growth and then the slow-down in the commercial services sector, it is useful to consider the number of commercial registrations in the Kingdom between 1401 AH (1981) and 1407 AH (1987) (Table 9.8).

These figures should be taken only as a general indication, since they take no account of the number of employees in each company. Inevitably, in a period of economic consolidation, there is a tendency for the more dynamic companies to continue their expansion, while others, faced by a more competitive market-place, will fail.

Table 9.8 *Commercial company registrations 1401–08 AH (1981–88)*

Year	Number of registrations	Percentage comparison
1401 AH (1981)	139,221	
1402 AH (1982)	169,596	+22%
1403 AH (1983)	219,349	+29%
1404 AH (1984)	243,542	+11%
1405 AH (1985)	267,192	+10%
1406 AH (1986)	281,726	+ 5%
1407 AH (1987)	297,316	+ 6%
1408 AH (1988)	303,657	+2%

Source: Ministry of Commerce

9.5.1 DISTRIBUTIVE TRADES

Traditionally, and still today, the distributive trades (wholesale and retail) are dominated by a very large number of relatively small establishments. In line with other sectors of commercial services, there has been a tendency for some companies in this sector to grow in size, and the number of very small organizations (employing less than five people), although still large, has dropped considerably as a percentage of the total.

Early in 1989, the Ministry of Commerce made the following comment on the distribution and retail operations:

> The sector of wholesale and retail trade still suffers from low productivity despite the large size of the labor force. Foreign labor represents more than 90% of the total numbers employed. The traditional selling methods are still preferred by a large number of traders. Services offered to consumers are still limited and, with few exceptions, establishments have no retail sales outlets of their own. The general characteristic of the distribution [wholesale and retail] sector is a lack of specialization which leads to the division of managerial efforts amongst different products. [This division] works against the acquisition of in-depth product knowledge and makes efficient supervision and stock control difficult.

Table 9.9   *Number of hotels and number of rooms 1400–07 AH (1980–87)*

Year	Number of hotels	Number of rooms	Percentage change in number of rooms
1400 1980	231	17,526	—
1401 1981	232	19,992	+14
1402 1982	240	21,263	+ 6
1403 1983	233	20,568	− 3
1404 1984	239	21,196	+ 3
1405 1985	245	21,510	+ 1
1406 1986	245	22,129	+ 3
1407 1987	246	22,298	+ 1

Source: Ministry of Commerce

This has resulted in a surplus of some goods and products which are difficult to market locally. There is still an urgent need for more efforts to support and subsidize exports and traders' capacity to re-export.

9.5.2   HOTELS

During the period of the building of the Kingdom's infrastructure, there was a heavy demand for hotel rooms to accommodate the many visiting businessmen and expatriate workers. Consequently, hotel capacity expanded at a very fast rate, with the result that by the end of the Third Development Plan (1405 AH: 1985), by which time most of the major infrastructural projects had been completed, there was substantial over-capacity. This led to low average occupancy, the cutting of room-rates and the closure of some hotels (see Table 9.9).

9.5.3   EXHIBITIONS

In its efforts to promote knowledge of locally-produced goods amongst consumers and to encourage the Kingdom's export trade, the Ministry of Commerce has, in the period of the Fourth Development Plan (1405–10 AH: 1985–90) issued a number of licences for temporary national and foreign trade exhibitions in Saudi Arabia and has encouraged participation by Saudi companies in exhibitions abroad. Nevertheless, the Kingdom's cities still lack the presence of permanent centers for national exhibitions. . . . And there is still a tangible need for travelling exhibitions inside the Kingdom and abroad.

Source: Ministry of Commerce (1409 AH: 1989)

9.5.4   CHAMBERS OF COMMERCE AND INDUSTRY

With the expansion of the Kingdom's economy and the need to consolidate the commercial base, the network of Chambers of Commerce has played an increasingly active role in the development of the Kingdom's commercial activity.

The Council of Saudi Arabian Chambers of Commerce is based in a new building in Riyadh. There are eighteen local Chambers in Abha, Arar, Al-Hassa, Al-Majma, Baha, Dammam (for the Eastern Province), Ha'il, Jeddah, Jizan, Jouf, the Holy City of Makkah, the Holy City of Medina, Najran, Qassim, Riyadh, Tabuk, Taif and Yanbu.

A number of specialized departments have been established within the chambers of commerce with the purpose of improving the services offered. In addition, a number of meetings and conferences of interest to businessmen and commercial/industrial groups have been organized in conjunction with the Ministry of Commerce.

Source: Ministry of Commerce (1409 AH: 1989)

The Union of Chambers of Commerce and Industry in the Gulf is located in Dammam, and the Union of Arabian Chambers of Commerce and Industry has its office in Riyadh.

9.6   The economy: discussion

Since 1403/04 AH (1983/84), despite substantial economy measures, the Kingdom of Saudi Arabia has been running a budget deficit and, although the strategic principles of the Fourth Development Plan have been adhered to, the pace of implementation has inevitably been slowed.

But the results have been far from uniformly negative. One beneficial effect of the decline in oil revenues has been a fall in the cost of living. During the years of very fast development and expansion the cost of living soared. Between 1394 AH and 1403 AH (1974 and 1983), the cost of living index more than doubled. If we take the index for 1403 AH (1983) as 100, the cost of living index, since then, has progressively declined:

Year	Cost of living index
1403 1983	100.0
1404 1984	98.8
1405 1985	95.6
1406 1986	92.7
1407 1987	91.9

Source: Central Department of Statistics (1987)

The largest fall has been recorded in housing, where the index of 100 in 1403 AH (1983) has fallen to 71.8 in 1407 AH (1987).

There have been equally important social effects. The program of Saudi-ization (replacement of foreign labor by Saudi nationals) has accelerated. To some extent, the surge in revenues engendered by the oil price increase of 1399/1400 AH (1979/80) tended to foster false expectations amongst the population. The realization that the "boom" period could not continue indefinitely has encouraged the Saudi workforce to adopt a more realistic and, in the longer run, much healthier attitude to the role they can and must play within the Saudi Arabian economy, both in the public and private sectors.

It is perhaps worth pointing out that this change of attitude would have occurred in due course even if the oil price had not fallen. By the end of the Third Development Plan (which ran from 1400–05 AH: 1980–85), most of the Kingdom's infrastructure was in place. Industrial sectors such as construction were inevitably facing a very considerable contraction. It is also true that the rationale behind all the Kingdom's development plans has been to create a diversified economy, with thriving agricultural and industrial sectors, manned and managed by Saudi citizens. It is therefore fair to say that diminished revenues have simply hastened a process which was an essential element in the government's long-term plans.

The contraction that followed the completion of the main infrastuctural program also meant the departure from the Kingdom of large numbers of expatriate workers. The influx of foreigners, so necessary for the building of the Kingdom's infrastructure and the development of its industrial and agricultural base, brought with it social strains. The Kingdom of Saudi Arabia is a strictly Muslim country, with a society based on the Islamic puritanism promulgated by Imam Muhammad bin Abdul Wahhab more than 200 years ago. The millions of expatriate workers arriving in Saudi Arabia came from many different countries with diverse cultural backgrounds. The expatriates faced the problems of adjusting to Saudi society and there were those in the Kingdom who feared that Saudi society itself could be damaged by the influence of alien cultures. These fears have proved groundless.

In terms of the immediate future, budgetary constraints have necessitated a clear formulation of strategic priorities. For the government, the highest priorities are likely to be defense, education and health. At the same time, the government will look to the private sector to play a much greater role in the industrial and agricultural development of the Kingdom. The infrastructure is in place and the groundwork has been completed for the development and the expansion of Saudi Arabia's economy. There will be an increasing reliance on private sector investment to achieve further advances.

In the longer term, much will depend on oil. As we have seen, there has already been a remarkable diversification in the country's economy, but it must be true that the Kingdom's oil and gas reserves remain its greatest natural asset and its largest single source of revenue.

The Kingdom of Saudi Arabia possesses a quarter of the world's known recoverable oil reserves. Other exploitable oil fields in other parts of the world will, no doubt, be found and existing or even new alternative forms of energy will be developed, but it seems certain that, in the course of the first decades of the next century, the oil reserves of many countries, currently net exporters, will be exhausted. It is to be hoped that, as this happens, the decreasing number of producing nations and the increasing number of oil importing nations will develop a sane, global economic policy which will be fair to both sides and will make the best use of a dwindling energy resource.

Whatever the case, the Kingdom's revenue from oil is likely to rise again. Precisely how that increased revenue will be deployed cannot be determined now, but we can be certain that the same principles which have governed the Kingdom's Development Plans will be brought to bear in formulating new plans for the maintenance of Islam, for the enhancement of the quality of life of Saudi Arabian citizens, and for the continued development of the Kingdom's economy.

Chapter 10

Planning

Throughout this book, the reader will find frequent mentions of the various Development Plans which the Kingdom has produced. To date, there have been four such plans:

> First Development Plan: 1390–95 AH (1970–75)
> Second Development Plan: 1395–1400 AH (1975–80)
> Third Development Plan: 1400–05 AH (1980–85)
> Fourth Development Plan: 1405–10 AH (1985–90)

The Fifth Development Plan, which will run from 1410 to 1415 AH (1990–95), is almost completed and will shortly be published. (The author has been given early access to the draft of the Fifth Development Plan and has made use of it where appropriate.)

It is the purpose of this chapter to explain how the planning process operates within the Kingdom and to summarize the objectives and achievements of the four Development Plans which have been implemented. The final section of this chapter looks ahead to the objectives of the Fifth Development Plan.

10.1   The planning process

In order to understand how the Kingdom of Saudi Arabia has achieved in two decades what many thought would take far longer, it is necessary to appreciate the contribution that long-term strategic planning has made to the developmental process.

The Development Plans have considered every aspect of the Kingdom's economy, identifying its infrastructural, agricultural, industrial and commercial needs and formulating strategies, all compatible with each other, to achieve defined national goals. Oil revenues have made the government the driving force behind the economy and, out of those oil revenues, the government has provided the essential infrastructure without which the economy could not mature. At the same time, it should be understood that Saudi Arabia operates a market economy in which free enterprise can flourish. Indeed, as the country's agricultural and industrial base expands, the part played by the private sector in the economy will grow in importance, reducing the role played by government.

This chapter looks in some detail at the four Development Plans which have governed the Kingdom's development over the last twenty years and will consider the content and implications of the Fifth Development Plan. Such a survey of the Plans provides a valuable insight into the guiding principles which have governed what is probably the greatest national development program that any country has ever seen. But, before we embark on this survey, it may be helpful to provide a little more information on how the planning process itself functions.

Planning is the primary instrument of development in the Kingdom. As conceptual frameworks the Five Year Development Plans represent structural designs for society's development; as organizational frameworks they provide guidelines for implementation. While all government agencies are involved in the planning process, the key role is assigned to the Ministry of Planning, which is responsible for the preparation and co-ordination of all sectoral plans at the national level.

Although Saudi planning experience includes the setting of long-term objectives, the actual planning system is based on these comprehensive five-year plans. The Five Year Plan is prepared according to the guidelines of the national development strategy, as approved by the Council of Ministers. Specifically, it includes both the Plan Document, which outlines the medium term economic policies and development strategy, and the detailed Operation Plans for each Ministry and public agency, which set all government expenditure and development programs. Hence, the Plans (both national Plan Document and the agency Operation Plans) integrate the main elements of development: the structural priorities and directions of the economy, and the development and expenditure programs of government. The latter become the guidelines for the annual budgets, which, as the first stage of Plan implementation, function as the main annual instruments of economic policy.

For the various government agencies this combined system of Five Year Plan and annual budget determines the level and pattern of expenditure, with all the associated implications for the progress and direction of sectoral development.

For the private sector, the system defines the regulatory and economic framework in which to operate. In a broader sense, the Five Year Plans provide orientation for the private sector on the likely course of the economy, on related government policies, and on potential business opportunities.

Source: Fourth Development Plan

It would be wrong to conclude from the above description of the Saudi approach to planning that the process is in any way rigid. It is recognized that in the course of implementation many factors, internal to a government agency or external to it, may affect progress, the priority, and/or the cost of individual projects. Increasingly, the Kingdom's planners have emphasized a program-based approach which, by taking a broad view of each agency's defined objectives and role, allows the agency itself a degree of flexibility in its selection and management of individual projects. The government agency must, of course, implement all "priority" projects but it is allowed some degree of discretion in its selection of other "acceptable" projects, as defined and approved by the overall program structure.

The Fourth Development Plan has been implemented in a period of great uncertainty. Oil revenues, which remain the major source of finance for all government activity, have been unpredictable and the reduction in this source of funding has had an inevitable effect on the implementation of the Plan. It is nevertheless true that, within the constraints imposed by this factor, the principles and objectives of the Plan have been adhered to throughout the five-year period.

10.2 The four Five Year Plans, 1970 to 1990 (1390–1410 AH)

The five-year planning phenomenon started in Saudi Arabia in 1970 (1390 AH) with the country's First Five Year Plan, which ran to the end of the fiscal year of 1975 (1395 AH). The beginning of the new fiscal year of 1975–76 (1395–96 AH) marked the official inauguration of the country's Second Five Year Plan which covered the period through to 1980 (1400 AH). The Third Five Year Plan ran from 1980 to 1985 (1400–05 AH). The Fourth Five Year Plan covered the period 1985 to 1990 (1405–10 AH).

The purpose of this section is to summarize and discuss the achievements of the First, Second, Third, and Fourth Five Year Plans. Only the most important aspects of these Plans will be analyzed, but it is hoped that even this brief statement of objectives and results will be sufficient to indicate the nature and scope of the Kingdom's planning process.

10.2.1   THE FIRST FIVE YEAR PLAN 1970–75 (1390–95 AH)

The Central Planning Organization (CPO), elevated to the Ministry of Planning in 1975, prepared a report, which was submitted to the King, on the findings and achievements reached during the Kingdom's First Five Year Plan. This report outlined the basic goals of the Plan:

> The general objectives of economic and social development policy of Saudi Arabia were to maintain its religious and moral values, and to raise the living standard and welfare of its people, while providing for material security and maintaining economic and social stability. These objectives were to be achieved by:
>
> 1 Increasing the rate of growth of gross domestic product (GDP)
> 2 Developing human resources so that the several elements of society will be able to contribute more effectively to production and participate fully in the process of development, and,
> 3 Diversifying sources of national income and reducing dependence on oil through increasing the share of other productive sectors in the gross domestic product.
>
> Furthermore the purpose of the plan is to provide a rational and orderly approach to achieving the nation's development objectives. The plan was not intended to be a rigid, restrictive set of rules and regulations but a means of bringing increased rationality into public sector programs by establishing priorities and integrating activities to avoid bottlenecks and ensure co-ordination.
>
> *Source*: *Report of the Central Planning Organization*, prepared by the CPO, 1394 AH (1974) (Jeddah, Banawi Printers, 1974)

In its examination of recorded progress during the opening years of the First Five Year Plan, the CPO reported the establishment by Royal Decree of a new classification system and salary scale for both civil servants and non-cadre employees in 1971, in accordance with the Plan's aim for more institutional and administrative reforms. Furthermore, a public investment fund was established during the fiscal year of 1971–72 (1391–92 AH) with an initial budget of SR 350 million, with further additions of SR 250 million in 1972–73 (1392–93 AH) and SR 600 million in 1973–74 (1393–94 AH). The final target of the fund was to reach SR 2,000 million. The basic objective of this public investment fund was to finance investments in production projects of a commercial nature. The fund's affairs were entrusted to a board of directors consisting of the President of the Central Planning Organization, the Minister of Finance, the Governor of the Saudi Arabian Monetary Agency (SAMA) and two members chosen from the Council of Ministers. The immediate intention behind the establishment of this fund was to use the financial backing of the government to encourage and promote commercial projects needed in the country's development plan.

Vocational training, student enrolment and school construction expanded considerably in accordance with the Plan's gradual acceleration of these fields. In a developing nation, it is believed, development and progress are not overnight creations; rather they are the result of sound, long-range planning and the rigorous efforts of personnel in charge of planning affairs. The concentration on education, both vocational and academic, should undoubtedly fill the urgent needs for technically educated manpower who are expected to shoulder properly the responsibilities of continued progress.

Another improvement, in the Kingdom's telecommunication network, was made with the establishment of new television stations, the study for the eventual introduction of color television and the expansion made in the automatic telephone program from 134,700 lines to 172,000. Postal service improvement began in the fiscal year 1972–73 (1392–93 AH), aiming at the construction of new and well-equipped complexes in the major cities (a very impressive complex was completed in 1975 at the Holy City of Makkah). Also, improvements in training and operations, urgently needed to meet the ever-increasing task confronting the postal services, were made with the ultimate goal of the total mechanization of postal operations.

Further progress was made in the realm of social services, which included institutional care, social security, community development and service centers. The concern of the social welfare program is reflected in providing care for orphans, the aged, handicapped persons and delinquents. Through 1971–72 (1391–92 AH) the government was operating ten social centers, seven for boys and three for girls. These centers provided care – food, clothing, lodging, education and training – for 682 boys and 177 girls between the ages of six and eighteen.

In 1972 (1392 AH) the Council of Ministers approved the establishment of an orphanage at the Holy City of Makkah to provide care for foreign children. Four resident homes for the aged and handicapped throughout the Kingdom caring for 92 persons as of 1972 (1392 AH) were founded, and preparations were on the way to establish a fifth in the Asir area by 1973 (1393 AH).

A social security program was initiated in the fiscal year 1962–63 (1382–83AH) to include financial disbursements for almost 77,412 persons with an allocation of SR 16.6 million. By the 1970–71 (1390–91 AH) fiscal year, social security payments reached SR 47.6 million, covering 225,642 beneficiaries. Pension disbursements increased from 1970 through 1974 by 51 per cent while the number of persons covered increased by 53.7 per cent.

Impressive progress was made in health services. Total budget appropriations for the overall improvement of health services increased from SR 259.8 million in the fiscal year 1969–70 (1389–90 AH) to SR 659.0 million in 1972–73 (1392–93 AH) and to SR 1,085.9 million for 1973–74 (1393–94 AH). In terms of manpower operating in the medical sphere, there were, in 1971, 1,138 physicians and 5,078 paramedical personnel providing public and private medical services within the Kingdom. New allocations for 450 more physicians and an additional 1500 para-medical personnel were approved for the 1972–73 (1392–93 AH) fiscal year.

Another crucial advance was being made in the development of the country's water resources. Desalination facilities at Jeddah were reported complete, while two more desalination plants at Khobar and Khafji were finished by 1973–74 (1392–94 AH). Construction of two smaller desalination plants was to begin at Um-Laj and Jubail during the same year. Development of 24 water supply systems throughout the Kingdom was already in progress and construction of seventeen more was commissioned to start by 1972–73 (1392–93 AH). Needless to say, the development and preservation of water resources in Saudi Arabia is of vital importance to the country's developmental planning and the well-being of its citizens. A great effort has been made to meet the ever-increasing demands on the water supply on which depends much of the country's development.

Exhaustive efforts were being made in town planning to further the surveys and studies already commissioned which would eventually lead to detailed and sound planning for cities and adjacent areas. The final goal was gradual integration of such plans into the Second Five Year Plan.

In the area of transportation and communications, the Plan's target was met on time, and in many instances, in advance of schedule. Over 500 kilometers of the 1,000 kilometer target for main and secondary roads were completed in 1970–71 (1390–91 AH), and a total of twenty new projects, representing over 900 kilometers of new roads, had been authorized in the 1972–73 (1392–93 AH) budget. Construction of the Jeddah port was completed in 1972 (1392 AH), and the expansion of Dammam's port facilities, which began in the first year of the Plan, was in progress and would meet with scheduled plans. Moreover, the national airports development plan proceeded well as new airports were completed at Medina, Taif, Tabuk and Khamis Mushayt. The Medina Air Terminal was completed by 1974 (1394 AH), while work on the Khamis Mushayt Air Terminal was begun in 1973 (1392–93 AH). Saudia, the Kingdom's national airline, was making progress and by 1972 (1392 AH) it was operating a fleet of nine jet and eleven piston engine aircraft. The latter were eventually to be phased out upon the completion of the country's airports program. In 1975 (1395 AH) Saudia concluded a contract with McDonnell-Douglas Corporation for the purchase of five to seven Tri-Star commercial jets. Delivery started in July 1975 (1395 AH).

Finally, the Plan's

> policy of intensifying production on developed land was being pursued through the programs of the Agricultural Extension Services, the Agricultural Research Centers, and the Agricultural Credit Bank . . . The policy of expanding arable land is being accomplished through the large irrigation projects at Al-Hasa and Wadi Jizan, the settlement project at Haradh, and the Fallow Land Distribution Program.
>
> *Source: Report of the Central Planning Organization,* prepared by the CPO, 1394 AH (1974) (Jeddah, Banawi Printers, 1974)

The achievement of the Kingdom's First Five Year Plan

> is modestly described as "mixed", in the sense that not every program was fully implemented. Nevertheless, [the] achievement was great. Water supply projects were carried out for six major cities. Five desalination plants were built on the Red Sea and two on the Arabian Gulf Coast. . . . Principal towns and cities were linked by a network of 6,800 miles of paved roads. Twenty domestic airports were served by Saudia Airline . . . [Moreover] during the Fist Plan the construction industry doubled its activity . . . education system [in addition] was established on a strong base . . . health and social security services expanded steadily. On the other hand, housing did not keep pace with urban growth, and development of a national telecommunications system did not meet demand.

> Source: Wall Street Journal, 6th October 1975

The *Wall Street Journal* went on to suggest that perhaps the most significant outcome of the First Five Year Plan was the planning experience gained by the Central Planning Organization. Undoubtedly, "the Saudi planners are no beginners at the game. They are now [with the beginning of the Kingdom's second Five Year Plan] ready to tackle a job nine times bigger than that of the first Plan."

Table 10.1 *Financial appropriations of the Second Five Year Plan (1975–80/ 1395–1400 AH)*

Appropriations	Saudi Riyals (millions)	US Dollars (millions)
Economic Resource Development	92,135	26,063.00
Human Resource Development	80,124	22,665.91
Social Development	33,213	9,395.47
Physical and Infrastructure Development	112,945	31,995.75
Administration	38,179	10,800.28
Defence	78,196	22,120.50
External Assistance, Emergency Funds, Food Subsidies, Transfers to General Reserve	63,478	17,957.00
Total	498,270	140,997.91

NB: At constant 1974–75 prices
Source: The *Wall Street Journal*, October 6 1975

10.2.2   THE SECOND FIVE YEAR PLAN 1975–80 (1395–1400 AH)

The following pages will examine the major objectives and policies of the Kingdom's Second Five Year Plan, effective for the period 1975–80 (1395–1400 AH), with an overall allocation of $140,997 million. Table 10.1 provides a breakdown of the financial appropriations of the plan in both Saudi and United States currency.

Two fundamental guidelines were carefully delineated in the country's Second Five Year Plan. The first was the construction of large factories, eg petrochemical, petroleum refinery, steel and iron, glass, aluminum complexes. The recommendation was to build these factories on the western and eastern coasts of the Kingdom, specifically in the towns of Jubail and Yanbu. These towns have now become the country's major industrial areas, exporting petroleum and petrochemical products throughout the world. Secondly, there was great emphasis on the maximum utilization of the Kingdom's mineral resources. Feasibility explorations proved the existence of large deposits of these resources which are internationally marketable and were considered to be a major source for certain mineral industries. The government granted certain concessions to international specialized companies for the exploration of mineral resources in various parts of the country.

The Second Five Year Plan put much emphasis on educational and training programs in the Kingdom. Free universal education was expected to "inculcate the spirit of honest work". Thomas Jefferson's early and righteous assertion and belief in the effectiveness and importance of education for the development of nations is clearly manifested through the advanced and sophisticated technical status the United States has attained. (Chapter 16 summarizes the Kingdom's vigorous and ambitious efforts in the educational field.)

From a survey of data about the Second Saudi Five Year Plan in 1978, three goals could be identified. The Kingdom was striving for the diversification of its economic base by establishing new industries which would enable it in the distant future to lessen its reliance on petroleum as the major source of the country's revenues. Secondly, the plan focused on improving and enlarging its manpower base to carry out more effectively the nation's development. There was heavy emphasis on vocational and technical training; it provided for the establishment of new vocational schools from which would graduate, through the five years of the plan, 2,800 students. The plan asserted that:

> the enormous education program intended by the Government is one (essential) way of increasing the efficiency of the work force at all levels. At the same time, it is planned to increase reliance on non-Saudi labor. The Saudi work force will increase from 1,236,000 to 1,518,000, while non-Saudis will more than double from 314,000 to 812,000 by the end of the present plan.

Source: The *Wall Street Journal*, 6th October 1975

The third major objective of the plan was to develop non-petroleum industries throughout the country. For that purpose and to achieve overall industrial integration in the Kingdom, the plan provided for the establishment of various industries such as canning, minerals, water supply, cement, glass, lumber, fisheries, marble, cotton weaving, leather and synthetics.

The Kingdom's oil reserves were considered ample to sustain any foreseeable level of production required, either for revenues to finance the Plan, or to meet the needs of the extensive hydrocarbon-based industrial complexes which were being planned for the next decade. Nevertheless, economic planning for the optimum utilization of these depletable resources was essential to ensure that the long-run objective of economic diversification and reduced dependence on oil could be achieved.

Petromin, the Saudi National Oil Company (a government corporation) had allocations for projects which were the largest in the Second Five Year Plan, ie ten per cent of the total financial allocation of the Plan. This is attributed to the fact that Petromin was considered:

> the corner-stone of the Kingdom's strategic industries and within the next few years will place the country among the leading industrial nations. The total sum allocated for Petromin projects during the plan is SR 50,000 million . . . Among its projects are two pipelines for gas and petroleum extending from the Eastern Province to the Western Province, with a natural gas collecting plant in the former province, an aluminum smelter, two oil refineries, three petro-chemical complexes and an ammonia fertilizer plant which will make the city of Jubail the most important industrial town in the Middle East and perhaps in Asia.

Source: Al-Riyadh, 23rd May 1975 (author's translation)

Agricultural projects were also given heavy emphasis in the Plan. During the First Five Year Plan, a sharp disparity between domestic food production and consumption was noted. Stress was therefore placed on increased productivity in agriculture; the target at the end of the second Plan was to produce 50 per cent of the total domestic wheat consumation. The annual wheat production of approximately 4,200 tons was to be increased to 250,000 tons annually by the end of the second Plan.

Desalination projects were given great attention. The target of the Second Plan was to increase the capacity of existing desalination plants, due to the expectedly high demand for water both for industrial and household use. It was expected that Riyadh would need up to three times as much water. In 1975, Riyadh consumed 58 million gallons daily and total daily consumption was expected to reach 130 million gallons during the plan period. Jeddah's consumption (57 million gallons daily) was expected to reach 142 million gallons during the Second Five Year Plan. New desalination plants were to be established in Hakl, Umm Lij, Rabigh, Al Lith, Al Qunfudhah and Jubail and they, besides producing water, would aid in increasing electricity output for certain parts of the Kingdom, as well as helping to provide electricity to neighboring factories.

In the field of education, the greatest emphasis was manifested in the concern of the Saudi planners to expand and increase the quality of education at all levels. At the elementary level, the goal was universal education through the year 1980 for boys and girls. Enrolment of boys would increase to 677,500 a year through the Plan's period, from a 1975 figure of 401,300; enrolment of girls, to 353,400 from 214,600 annually. At the secondary level, the target was to increase boys' enrolment from 99,300 to 179,200; and girls', from 46,200 to 100,700. The tremendous increase in enrolment at these two levels of education would require the further construction of approximately 2,000 new schools and enlargement of the present schools during the Second Five Year Plan, 1975–80 (1395–1400 AH).

At the university level, the objective was to increase the current enrolment figure of 14,500 to 49,000 by the end of the Plan period.* This would be accomplished through the then six universities in Saudi Arabia which, along with the new Umm al-Qura University, are described in Chapter 16.

Goals of public and personal health in Saudi Arabia were uncommonly ambitious; health services for both the Saudis and non-Saudis resident in Saudi Arabia would be increased by increasing the number of out-patient treatment clinics from 215 to 452. The number of hospital beds was to increase from 4,000 to 11,400. The number of physicians per patient would increase to six for each ten thousand persons.

Information projects have also been the focus of the Saudi planners. To suit and cope with the present information needs of the country, the Plan's objective was to increase television broadcasting to cover 90 per cent of the total area of the Kingdom as well as the western parts of neighboring countries of the Arabian Gulf area, United Arab Emirates, Qatar, and Bahrain. Daily television broadcasting would be doubled from five hours to ten. The establishment of new rediffusion stations was planned for Do'ba, Al-Gurayat, Jeddah and Jizan, and twenty medium wave broadcasting stations would be constructed throughout the Kingdom. All existing and new information projects must be guided by the Kingdom's overall commitment to enhance and develop a better understanding of Islam and to apply the principles of Islam in all domestic and international activities.

In communications, the construction of 13,000 kilometers of main roads as well as the construction of 10,000 kilometers of rural roads was planned for the Plan period. This would double road mileage in the country, making Saudi Arabia among the leading nations of the Middle East in respect of quality and mileage of roads.

Twenty new piers would be constructed at Jeddah port, sixteen new piers at Dammam, three at Yanbu, and two at Jizan. In addition, a new seaport was to be established near the Port of Yanbu to export petroleum and gas products across the Red Sea.

Telephone services would be expanded from 93,400 to 666,535 lines, and telex lines from 450 to 1,500. The establishment of two permanent ground Telstar stations at Riyadh and Jeddah was included in the second Plan, along with the transfer of the two temporary stations from Riyadh and Jeddah to Tabuk and Abha. This would eventually mean twenty telephone sets for every hundred citizens in major cities and five telephone sets for every hundred citizens in smaller cities, with the ultimate goal of further expansion to reach the level found in the United States.

An analysis of Saudi Arabia's first two Five Year Plans seems appropriate at this stage. First, a comparison of the first two Five Year Plans reveals the tremendous increase in budget allocation in the Second Five Year Plan, compared with the First. The total financial allocation for the first Five Year Plan amounted to SR 41,300 million. The financial allocation for the Second Five Year Plan was SR 498,300 million. In other words, the allocation of the Second Five Year Plan represented a twelve-fold increase over the allocation for the First Five Year Plan.

Secondly, examination of categories of the two plans indicates that major categories of the country's First Five Year Plan were in the fields of administration, defense, education, vocational training and cultural affairs, health and social affairs, public utilities and urban development, transport and communications, industry, agriculture, and, finally, trade and services. But the Second Five Year Plan's main emphases were: economic resource development, human resource development, social development, physical infrastructure development, administration, defense, external assistance, emergency funds, and, finally, food subsidies.

The explanation for this shift in emphasis is clear. The objectives and nature of the country's First Five Year Plan were general in scope, and experimental in nature. The Kingdom's developmental needs in its different areas were almost even in terms of their priorities. The stress was on improving existing conditions in the various development fields, eg agriculture, communication, education, vocational training. By contrast, the Second Five Year Plan resembled a rocket launched from an existing launching pad, namely the First Five Year Plan.

The emphasis of the country's Second Five Year Plan was focused on the vital objective of diversifying the Saudi economic base by developing the agricultural and industrial sectors. A comparison of the financial appropriations of the two Plans devoted to the objective of diversifying the Kingdom's economic and agricultural structure reveals the predicament of the Saudi planners *vis-à-vis* their Second Five Year Plan. While financial allocations of the First Five Year Plan for industry, agriculture, education, vocational training and cultural affairs reached the US$ 2,780 million mark, financial allocations in the Second Five Year Plan devoted to these same purposes were $31,400 million, an eleven-fold increase.

Finally, being aware of its international responsibility:

> the Saudi Arabian government takes very seriously the responsibility of wealth, not only in seeking to use it creatively at home . . ., but also assisting less fortunate [LDCs] of the "Third World". [As new allocations in the Second Five Year Plan were appropriated for international aid] . . .

it seems fair to assume that the "assistance" element in the [appropria-
tions item of the Second Plan] must be over SR 20 billions. This can be
deduced from the budget for the current fiscal year, which is the first
year of the Plan. Funds are provided for SR 4.25 billions to be disbursed
directly as loans or grants . . . to developing countries.

Source: The *Wall Street Journal*, 6th October 1975

This foreign aid appropriation by Saudi Arabia amounts to $1.300 million annually,
that is, 5.75 per cent of its $22,600 million total revenues in 1974.

Table 10.2 shows the total appropriation for development projects in major
cities in the country which were executed during the second Five Year Plan.

Table 10.2   *Total allocation of the planned projects for Saudi Arabia during the Second Five
Year Plan*

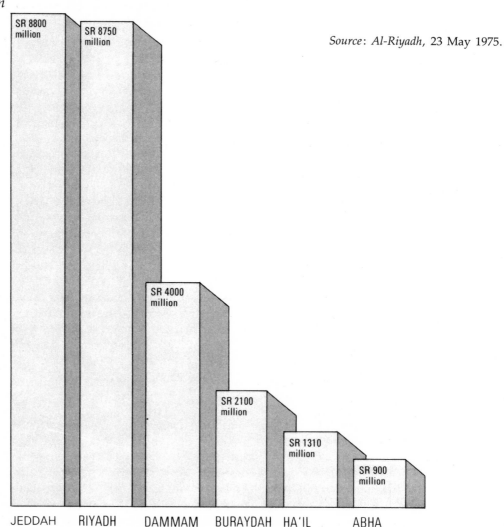

Source: *Al-Riyadh*, 23 May 1975.

SR 8800 million — JEDDAH
SR 8750 million — RIYADH
SR 4000 million — DAMMAM
SR 2100 million — BURAYDAH
SR 1310 million — HA'IL
SR 900 million — ABHA

10.2.3   THE THIRD FIVE YEAR PLAN 1980–85 (1400–05 AH)

Examination of the First Five Year Plan (1970–75) reveals that the scope of that Plan was comprehensive in nature, ie it was an exploration – theoretical and empirical – of the planning process in Saudi Arabia and of all the various aspects of its development. It must be admitted that the Plan was not implemented *in toto*. Yet the biggest achievement of that Plan was the experience gained by Saudis in the field of developmental planning.

The Second Five Year Plan (1975–80), compared with its predecessor, was a phenomenal achievement both in volume and value. As indicated by the preceding section, the thrust of the Second Plan was towards the establishment of the infrastructure and the industrial sources of the Saudi national economy.

The Third Five Year Plan (1980–85) was distinguished by its determination to consolidate past achievements and to continue progress in a planned and controlled fashion. Diversification of the economy into productive sectors (agriculture, industry and mining) was considered essential for future economic prosperity. At the same time, human resources were firmly identified as the Kingdom's most valuable asset. The desire to ensure stability by broadening the economic base, by developing Saudi manpower and thus, in both economic and social terms, increasing the Kingdom's independence and self-sufficiency permeated the thinking behind the Plan. The Third Five Year Plan emerged as a rational development of the previous Plan and the government's experience of implementing it. There were no abrupt changes of policy, rather an increasing sharpness in the definition of the basic objectives of the Second Five Year Plan.

It is not possible here to give more than the briefest of summaries of the Third Five Year Plan, and such a summary cannot, in any way, do justice to the comprehensive scope of the plan or the integration of the economic and social philosophy which underlined it. It is nevertheless useful in giving a broad indication of how the government of Saudi Arabia responded to the challenges of a society which was developing at an unprecedented rate.

The Third Five Year Plan (1980–85) set three fundamental objectives.

1.   Structural changes in the economy
　　　　　– to conserve the natural resources of oil and gas in order to increase the long-term potential for value-added development; to fix levels of crude oil production to generate sufficient revenue, together with revenue from monetary reserves, to cover the financial requirements for the development plan
　　　　　– to diversify the economy, in particular into the sectors of agriculture, industry and mining, concentrating investment in these productive activities
　　　　　– to continue development of the physical infrastructure of the Kingdom but at a reduced rate in relation to other sectors of the economy to

permit maximum investment in agriculture, industry and mining

2. Increased participation and social welfare in development
    – encouragement of all Saudi citizens to make a contribution to the development of the nation; to give all regions of the country the opportunity to develop their full potential; to assist Saudi society with the problems associated with rapid economic growth; to control inflation and reduce subsidies while, at the same time, protecting lower income groups; to expand and improve the social services

3. Increased economic and administrative efficiency
    – to increase the present and long-term efficiency of the economy itself, the management of the economy and government administration
    – *Objectives for Administrative Development* to introduce, where necessary, basic changes in government administration; to attain optimum utilization and performance of manpower; to ensure that all managerial and senior administrative positions are held by Saudi citizens.
    – *Objectives for Manpower Development* to increase the total numbers of available manpower; to increase the productivity of manpower in all sectors; to deploy manpower in those sectors with the greatest potential for growth; to reduce dependence on foreign manpower.
    – *Objectives for the Preservation of National Fixed Capital* to preserve national fixed capital and to ensure that sufficient manpower and financial resources are available to operate the infrastructure to full capacity.
    – *Objectives for Fiscal Management* to achieve the planned growth rate for the various sectors and to prevent the rate of inflation from exceeding tolerable levels.

One or two of the objectives of the Third Five Year Plan are particularly worthy of comment. It was (and still is) government policy that diversification of the economy (which was a primary objective of the Plan) should be undertaken largely by the private sector. The government's role is to set priorities for investment; to provide information and research on which the private sector can sensibly base investment decisions; and to supply the necessary infrastructural support for the development by the private sector of productive enterprises. Clearly, it was and remains the government's wish that an increasing number of Saudi citizens should become directly involved in and committed to this phase of the Kingdom's development, thus reducing the importance of the role of the agent (the Saudi citizen who represents foreign companies) and increasing the importance of Saudi companies in the implementation of local industrial and agricultural projects.

Under the Third Plan, manpower development was given the highest national priority. Education at the primary, intermediate, secondary and university levels was geared to the needs of the society. Above intermediate level, there was to be streaming of the students to ensure that sufficient students remained in formal

Table 10.3 *Total government expenditure on development,* 1400–05 AH (1980–85)*

Function of expenditure	SR million current prices
Economic Resource Development	261,800
Human Resource Development	129,600
Social Development	61,200
Physical Infrastructure	249,100
Subtotal: Development	701,700
Administration	31,400
Emergency Reserves, Subsidies	49,600
Total Civilian Expenditure	782,700

* Total excludes transfer payments; non-civilian sectors; foreign aid
Source: The Third Development Plan

education and that the Kingdom's requirements for skilled technicians were taken into account. The private sector was encouraged to expand training programs and government loans were to be made dependent upon the provision of a full training scheme for Saudi citizens in the project. At the same time, Saudi citizens were encouraged, through incentives, to enrol in training courses for technical and skilled jobs. Surplus manpower, currently employed in areas with limited economic potential, was encouraged to move to work in high growth sectors of the economy. A special effort was made, through government sponsored research, to devise plans for the most effective use of manpower in general.

Both the policy of requiring the Saudi private sector to play a crucial role in diversifying the Saudi economy and the emphasis on the training and use of Saudi manpower indicated the government's awareness of the need to involve Saudi citizens as much as possible in the future development of their own society.

10.2.4   THE FOURTH FIVE YEAR PLAN 1985–90 (1405–10 AH)

On 20th March 1985 (29 Jamad Al-Thani 1405 AH), the Ministry of Planning published the following document which gave a brief summation of the objectives of the Fourth Development Plan.

1. *Fourth Plan Themes*
Although the objectives of the Fourth Plan are mostly continuations of the principles and policies of the Third Plan there are four broad themes

which characterize it and differentiate it from its predecessors. These are:

1) a greater concern with the efficiency of operations and usage of the Kingdom's resources and facilities and with the discovery and development of renewable alternatives

2) a strong focus of the diversification strategy on development of the producing activities, particularly manufacturing, agriculture and finance

3) a commitment to reduce the number of unskilled and manual foreign workers in the Kingdom by more than half a million

4) a clear and definite emphasis on promoting the private sector's involvement in economic development

2. *Elements of the Fourth Development Plan*

2.1 Objectives

In its resolution No.36 dated 24.2.1404 AH, the Council of Ministers specified eleven objectives for the Fourth Plan as follows:

1) To safeguard Islamic values, duly observing, disseminating and confirming Allah's Shari'ah

2) To defend the faith and the nation; and to uphold the security and social stability of the Realm

3) To form productive citizen-workers by providing them with the tributaries conducive thereunto – ensuring their livelihood and rewarding them on the basis of their work

4) To develop human resources thus ensuring a constant supply of manpower and upgrading and improving its efficiency to serve all sectors

5) To raise cultural standards to keep pace with the Kingdom's development

6) To reduce dependence on the production and export of crude oil as the main source of national income

7) To continue with the real structural changes in the Kingdom's economy through continuous transformation to produce a diversified economic base, with due emphasis on industry and agriculture

8) To develop mineral resources and to encourage discovery and utilization thereof

9) To concentrate on qualitative development through improving and further developing the performance of the utilities and facilities already established during the three development plan periods

10) To complete the infrastructural projects necessary to achieve overall development

11) To achieve economic and social integration between Arab Gulf Co-operation Council countries

2.2 **Basic Strategic Principles**

In the same resolution, the Council of Ministers specified eight basic strategic principles to achieve the objectives mentioned in the resolution. They were as follows:

1) Emphasis should be laid on improving the economic productive standards of the services, utilities and products which the Government provides for citizens – both directly (such as education and security services); and indirectly (such as electricity, transport and basic commodities)

2) Adopt a policy giving the private sector the opportunity to undertake many of the economic tasks of the Government, while the Government would not engage in any economic activity undertaken by the private sector

3) Rationalize the system of direct and indirect subsidies on many goods and services provided by the state

4) Consideration of the economical use of resources should predominate in many government investment and expenditure decisions

5) Continue the development of Saudi manpower, through the evaluation of education and training programs and curricula as well as by the further development or modification of these in conformity with the Islamic Shari'ah, the changing needs of society, and the requirements of the developing process

6) Attention should be given to the development of Saudi society; to the provision of social welfare and health care for all; and to the support given to society's participation in the implementation of the programs of the plan as well as reaping the benefits of development

7) In order to carry out the second objective the defense and security authorities shall plan their strategy in order to ensure the defense of the nation, and shall submit that strategy to the National Security Council preparatory to presenting it for consideration to the Council of Ministers

8) Adopt a fiscal policy which keeps the level of expenditure in line with the Government's revenues through the Fourth Plan period

These basic strategic principles included a total of 61 detailed policies which as a whole formed a comprehensive policy framework to provide a base for government expenditure and development operations. Most of the policies had a close relationship with each sector, and have been summarized in the following sections. Some of these policies were more applicable to the government agencies and some to the private sector:

– Reducing production costs of public services and utilities.
– Ensuring that services are appropriate and not excessive, e.g. by

limiting specifications for construction or operation of projects to what is actually required.

– Utilizing technology in all public service sectors through mechanization and the use of advanced technology.

– Judging the economic feasibility of projects (of all types) by including operational and maintenance costs (including management costs) and not only capital costs.

– Developing appropriate administrative organizations to serve the new needs of the community.

– Giving the private sector the opportunity to operate, manage, maintain and renovate many of the utilities currently operated by Government provided that this results in lower costs, better performance, and employment opportunities for Saudi citizens.

– Re-considering some of the prevailing methods, policies and regulations so as to allow private sector to operate more freely and more flexibly and to assist it in becoming more creative and developed.

– Reducing subsidy rates in ways that will rationalize consumption without significantly affecting low income consumers.

– All government departments which administer public services should make economic efficiency a fundamental objective by adopting two basic principles. First, the cost of producing such services to the Saudi community should be reduced, and second, the price of such services should not be less than production costs, except in rare areas and with the proviso that the prices should be periodically reviewed.

3. *The Economic Context of the Fourth Plan*

The Fourth Plan was prepared at a time of new economic conditions which have been gradually developing since the end of the Second Plan. These were:

1) Completion of the greater part of the basic infrastructure.
2) Considerable progress made in the diversification of the economy
3) Increased capabilities and efficiency of Saudi manpower.
4) More efficient government administration.
5) Greater maturity and business skills of the private sector.
6) Lower levels of oil revenues.
7) Increased oil production by non-OPEC countries.
8) The world economy had begun its recovery from the longest economic recession period in its recent history.

4. *Planning Approach to the Fourth Development Plan*

The Fourth Development Plan introduced a new planning methodology – the program approach. It derived directly from the 8th basic strategic principle. As well as stipulating fiscal balance, this principle included a policy directing that all authorized projects must comply with development objectives and principles as summarized above.

The "Program Approach" has introduced certain new emphases in planning government expenditure: on whole programs rather than on individual projects, on structure of expenditure rather than the component items; on responsibility for priorities and proportions rather than detailed commitments.

The program-based method also introduced other major changes in the planning process and in the allocation of government expenditure for the Plan. It has provided increased flexibility for the government agencies to select projects within the specific allocations for the program, taking into consideration the objective of co-ordinating regional development.

5. *Role of the Private Sector during the Fourth Development Plan*

The Fourth Development Plan introduced a major change in the respective roles of the government and the private sector. Many of the key goals and objectives of the Plan were to be achieved through the private sector. In particular great reliance was placed on the private sector to continue the strategy of economic diversification through the development of agriculture, industry and mining, and to improve the efficiency and productivity of existing economic units.

To facilitate this, financial provision was made within the total Fourth Development Plan expenditure to support and encourage the private sector to increase its contribution to development.

6. *Civilian Expenditure during the Fourth Development Plan*

In the light of the Kingdom's recent experience, the importance of Saudi Arabia's strategy of diversification away from oil has been underlined. Government expenditure in the Fourth Development Plan reinforced this strategy.

The total government expenditure in the Fourth Development Plan was set at SR 1,000 billion (in current prices). Of this SR 500 billion was to be devoted to development expenditure. The largest share of development expenditure, 27.1% (SR 135.3 bn), was allocated to human resources development; economic resources received 26.1% (SR 130.7 bn), health and social services 17.9% (SR 89.7 bn), transport and telecommunications 15.4% (SR 76.9 bn) and municipalities and housing 13.5$ (SR 67.4 bn).

The amount allocated for the economic and human resources and health and social services was more than the actual spending on these sectors during the Third Development Plan. The percentage increase ranged between 28.9% for health and social services and 8.6% for economic resources. However, the basic infrastructure allocation was lower. The reasons for this are first, conformity with the strategic principle that emphasizes development of the producing sectors; second, most of the infrastructure projects had already been completed; and third, it was expected that project costs would be reduced through the implementation of programs concerned with the modification of construction specifications, reducing the scope of projects and through higher competition in the market.

The number of projects to be completed over the plan period totalled 3226 of which 1444 were new, and 1782 under construction and scheduled to be completed during the Fourth Development Plan period.

The budgetary sums envisaged for government expenditure in the Fourth Development Plan were not realized. In the year 1985 (1405 AH), oil production amounted to an average of only 3.565 million barrels of oil a day, compared with almost 10 million barrels a day in both 1980 (1400 AH) and 1981 (1401 AH). Revenues from oil had fallen from SR 361,000 million in the year 1980/81 (1400/01 AH) to SR 90,000 million in the year 1985/86 (1405/06 AH).

Inevitably, many government projects, especially in the area of public utilities, have had to be postponed. The reduction in government spending has had serious consequences for the private sector. The reduction of economic activity, partly the result of falling oil revenues and partly engendered by the completion of most of the major infrastructural projects, has had the most obvious impact on the construction industry. It is estimated that up to a million foreign workers in the construction and related service industries had returned home by 1987. This significant fall in the population has had an inevitable effect on other sectors of the economy, especially on retailers who had become accustomed to the level of turnover generated by catering for the larger workforce.

Despite budgetary restrictions, the Fourth Development Plan has provided firm guidelines for the implementation of government policy in all areas of the Saudi Arabian economy.

10.3   Objectives of the Fifth Five Year Plan 1990–95 (1410–15 AH)

This section sets out the objectives of the Fifth Development Plan (1410–15 AH: 1990–95). The completion of the infrastructure and many industrial/agricultural development projects, together with the down-turn in oil revenues, have reinforced the shift in strategy first clearly discernible in the Fourth Development Plan. Apart from the preservation of Islam, defense of the realm and education of the citizenry, the emphasis now is firmly on encouraging the private sector to build upon the economic foundations laid by government.

I   *The objectives of the Fifth Development Plan for the Kingdom of Saudi Arabia (1410–15 AH) are defined as follows:*

  1   To preserve Islamic values, duly observing, promulgating and confirming Allah's *Shari'ah* (God's Divine Law).

  2   To defend the faith, and nation, and uphold the security and social stability of the Realm.

  3   To form productive citizen workers by providing them with the tributaries conducive thereunto, ensuring their livelihood and rewarding them on the basis of their work.

  4   To develop human resources thus ensuring a constant supply of manpower, and upgrading and improving its efficiency to carry out the requirements of national economy.

  5   To raise cultural and informational standards to keep pace with the Kingdom's development.

  6   To reduce dependence on the production and export of crude oil as the main source of national income.

  7   To continue with real structural changes in the Kingdom's economy through continuous transformation to produce a diversified economic base with due emphasis on industry and agriculture.

  8   To develop mineral resources and to encourage the discovery and utilization thereof.

  9   To concentrate on qualitative development through improving and further developing the performance of the utilities and facilities.

 10   To complete the infrastructural projects necessary to achieve overall development.

 11   To continue with encouraging the private sector's participation in social and economic development.

 12   To achieve balanced development between the different regions of the Kingdom.

 13   To achieve economic and social integration between the Arab Gulf Co-operation Council countries.

II *The strategic bases upon which the aforementioned objectives may be achieved are as follows:*

The First Basic Strategic Principle:
Continue the development of the Kingdom's self-protection abilities, and support the existence of a protective defense and security system, and deepen the citizens' feelings of loyalty and affiliation.

    The defense and security authorities shall plan their strategy in order to ensure the defense of the nation, and shall submit that strategy to the National Security Council preparatory to presenting it for consideration by the Council of Ministers.

The Second Basic Strategic Principle:
Emphasis should be laid on improving the economic productive standards of services, utilities and products which the Government provides for the citizens, both directly, such as education and security services, and indirectly, such as electricity, transport and basic commodities.

[For a detailed account of how the economic performance of government services, utilities and products is to be improved, see the quotation from the Fifth Development Plan in Section 9.1 above.]

The Third Basic Strategic Principle:
Adopt a policy giving the private sector the opportunity to operate many of the economic tasks of government, while the government would not engage in any economic activity undertaken by private sector.

This policy may be implemented through:

1   Giving the private sector the opportunity to operate, manage, maintain and renovate many of the utilities currently operated by government, provided that this results in lower costs, better performance and the employment of citizens.

2   Creating suitable means and methods to encourage the private sector to provide employment opportunities for Saudi citizens.

3   Offering for public subscription the shares of SABIC and Petromin Companies, thus giving the private sector the opportunity to share in the ownership and management of basic industries set up by the government.

4   Reconsidering some of the prevailing methods, policies and regulations so as to allow the private sector to operate more freely and more flexibly and to assist it in becoming more creative and developed. This includes

   a) the equitable adjustment of price control on private hospitals and clinics, thus ensuring fairness to citizens and investors alike

   b) the development of the procedures for commercial courts and notary public officers etc

5   Encouraging co-operatives, as well as private benevolent and commercial societies and institutions to undertake social and economic projects, eg the management of private sanitaria, hospitals and clinics, tourist areas and recreation centers.

6   Urging commercial banks to extend their credit facilities to

production projects, instead of concentrating on the import trade.

7   Encouraging the incorporation of more joint stock companies to undertake large projects with economies of scale so that the greatest number of citizens may benefit from investment transactions.

8   Creating an organized financial market under government supervision for the exchange of companies' shares, with the objectives of encouraging investment and avoiding the pitfalls of financial speculation.

9   Participation of the private sector in formulating and implementing training programs.

10   Making information available to citizens by increasing the quality and frequency of special programs for identifying investment opportunities in the productive sectors.

11   Carrying out more studies of investment and marketing opportunities and the feasibility of projects in the productive sectors.

12   Acquainting investors with the results of the accurate quarterly studies relating to mining; encouraging investors to start utilization and development of available minerals; allowing companies to invest in discovered minerals; and encouraging investment by various means, such as the provision of basic infrastructures.

13   Continuing the policy of giving preference to Saudi contractors – qualified and classified – in implementing various projects. When a foreign company is awarded a contract, it should subcontract a portion of the work to a Saudi contractor.

14   Confirming the division of projects, whenever possible technically or economically, into multiple contracts or sub-projects to enable the participation of Saudi companies in their execution.

15   Encouraging the national financial institutions to invest funds within the Kingdom.

16   Facilitating the private sector's participation in providing opportunities for scientists and researchers to conduct scientific and technical research projects, and to co-operate with King Abdul Aziz City for Science and Technology in research fields, with the emphasis on applied research.

The Fourth Basic Strategic Principle:
To rationalize the system of direct and indirect subsidies on many goods and services provided by the State.
    This may be implemented through:

1 Reducing subsidy rates in ways that will rationalize consumption without significantly affecting low income consumers.
2 All government departments which administer public services should make economic efficiency fundamental to the function of these services by adopting two basic principles:
    First, the cost of providing such services for the Saudi community should be reduced.
    Second, the prices of such services should not be less than production costs except in rare cases.

The Fifth Basic Strategic Principle:
The consideration of ensuring the economical use of resources should predominate in the government's investment and expenditure policies. This may be implemented through:
1 Considering water as a basic factor and an important determinant of efficiency in government projects, as is the case with expatriate labor or inflation.
2 Developing economically promising natural resources – eg the exploration of mineral and sea resources; the mapping of their location; their further development and utilization; and the processing of available gas to maximum extent possible.
3 Horizontal and vertical expansions in the petrochemical industries as well as in the production of gas and petroleum derivatives, through the private sector or mixed companies, whenever economic feasibility is proven.
4 Increasing the capacity for manufacturing refined petroleum products to the maximum potential within the bounds of economic feasibility.

The Sixth Basic Strategic Principle:
To continue the development of Saudi manpower through the evaluation of the educational and training programs and curricula, as well as by the further development or modification of these in conforming with the Islamic *Shari'ah*, the changing needs of society and the requirements of the development process.
1 Primary education for all boys and girls shall be mandatory.
2 To identify, at each educational stage beyond the intermediate level, the proportion of students qualified to receive higher education so that the remainder can be guided towards specialized technical institutes.
3 To direct the university admissions policy in accordance with the requirements of development for the long range, and developing appropriate educational programs and curricula.

4 To confirm the integration and flexibility of channels and tributaries of education.
5 To increase Saudi women's participation in manpower in accordance with the Islamic *Shari'ah*.
6 To limit university barriers to proficient students and to the fields of specialization, including technical education and vocational training.
7 Attention should be given to the quality of training by concentrating on the use of modern technology at the intermediate and advanced levels.
8 Training programs should qualitatively reflect actual needs of the economy, and be set at the level of efficiency required.
9 There should be a greater concentration on training, with the aim of encouraging on-the-job training.
10 Attention should be given to industrial safety and vocational health, in both the public and private sectors.
11 To give considerable importance to libraries in order to encourage students to make use of and to familiarize themselves with library facilities.

The Seventh Basic Strategic Principle:
Attention should be given to the development of Saudi society; to the provision of social welfare and health care for all; and to the encouragement of society's participation in the implementation of the development programs from which the social benefits ensue.
   Therefore it is necessary:
1 To create in Saudi citizens an awareness of the objectives and requirements of development, and all the tasks involved. This calls for:
   – Information through the public media giving religious and social values to work as an important and respectable activity in order to change attitudes towards certain occupations which at present are not acceptable to some people.
   – The dissemination of culture by encouraging literary authorship and the spread of public libraries, as well as by establishing museums and the preservation of archaeological and historical sites.
   – The establishment of a national library with a collection of books which would include every Saudi author.
2 Attention should be given to children in all fields and at all levels.
   This may be implemented through:
   – Giving attention to mothers through increasing their aware-

ness and eliminating illiteracy.
- Reserving sections for children in public libraries.
- Defining the diseases which attack children during the first stages of their life.
3 Increasing the attention given to the handicapped, and introducing national programs for their rehabilitation and welfare.
4 Introducing compulsory military service.
5 Introducing some basic military subjects into the secondary schools' curricula.
6 Expanding anti-illiteracy and adult educational programs.
7 Giving more attention to local community programs based upon the effective participation of citizens in the planning and implementation of local projects.
8 Giving attention to preventive medicine and health guidance, increasing the effectiveness of the preventive and curative institutions in safeguarding the health of citizens.
9 Improving the capabilities of individuals to increase their income.
10 Paying more attention to social welfare programs in all fields, and extending private sector participation by encouraging the establishment of yet more private benevolent societies.
11 Continuing the development of environmental programs.
12 Safeguarding and developing natural life.
13 Paying more attention to the beautification and improvement of the Kingdom's cities, the establishment of promenades, and encouraging citizens' participation in these projects.
14 Paying more attention to youth welfare programs, to develop the capabilities of young people, and to enable them to gain mental and physical skills in the fields of culture, science and sports.

The Eighth Basic Strategic Principle:
Realizes a balanced development between the different regions of the Kingdom through:
- Considering the development centers as a basis for regional development according to chosen standards.
- the complete utilization of services and utilities available in the different regions of the Kingdom.

The Ninth Basic Strategic Principle:
Adopting a fiscal policy which keeps the level of expenditure in line with the government revenues throughout the Fifth Development Plan.
1 Studying means and methods which aim at increasing the State's revenues.

2 Ensuring that authorized projects comply with the development objectives and the above-mentioned strategic principles.

3 Ensuring that authorized projects are undertaken on the combined basis of their operational and maintenance costs, including management and replacement costs, over the life of the project.

Source: "Objects of the Fifth Five Year Plan" published by the Ministry of Planning.

Chapter **11**

Industrial development

A key element in the Saudi Arabian government's economic strategy is industrial diversification, a process which has as its primary objective the reduction of the Kingdom's dependence on oil revenues. This chapter looks at various aspects of this strategy and provides statistics which give some measure of the achievements to date. Such a subject merits a book of its own but it is hoped that this brief survey of the main areas of industrial activity will at least indicate the the scale and the scope of the industrialization process.

11.1   Growth of manufacturing outlets in the Kingdom

To reduce dependence on the production of crude oil as a primary source of national income and to reduce the Kingdom's need for imported goods, the government has encouraged the development of a wide range of manufacturing industries.

Table 11.1 (taken from the Statistical Year Book, 1407 AH (1987), published by the Central Department of Statistics) on the number of local factories licensed and the number of workers employed in each industrial activity between 1401 AH (1981) and 1407 AH (1987) gives a good indication of the progress made in diversifying the industrial base of the economy.

The government has provided a range of incentives to encourage the private sector to participate in the Kingdom's industrial effort. Eight industrial estates provide private Saudi manufacturing companies with the necessary infrastructure and services at a very low cost. Credit facilities on generous terms are readily available for such enterprises.

11.2   The Saudi Industrial Development Fund (SIDF)

A good indication of the government's determination to expand the industrial base of the economy and a measure of the government's success are the loans disbursed

Table 11.1   *Licensed factories and total workers employed by industry sector*

	No of factories	No of workers
1 Foodstuffs, drinks		
1401 AH (1981)	260	15,170
1402 AH (1982)	277	15,702
1403 AH (1983)	287	15,954
1404 AH (1984)	302	16,248
1405 AH (1985)	310	13,506
1406 AH (1986)	321	17,388
1407 AH (1987)	329	18,461
2 Ready-made clothes and textiles		
1401 AH (1981)	28	2,776
1404 AH (1982)	29	2,881
1403 AH (1983)	32	2,911
1404 AH (1984)	38	2,934
1405 AH (1985)	39	2,308
1406 AH (1986)	39	3,534
1407 AH (1987)	42	3,740
3 Manufacture of leather goods		
1401 AH (1981)	7	519
1402 AH (1982)	7	519
1403 AH (1983)	8	577
1404 AH (1984)	10	723
1405 AH (1984)	10	723
1406 AH (1985)	10	535
1407 AH (1986)	10	535
4 Manufacture of wood products		
1401 AH (1981)	53	3,479
1402 AH (1982)	60	3,672
1403 AH (1983)	62	3,696
1404 AH (1984)	62	3,696
1405 AH (1985)	63	2,735
1406 AH (1986)	65	4,183
1407 AH (1987)	67	4,470
5 Manufacture of paper and paper products, printing and publishing		
1401 AH (1981)	99	4,857
1402 AH (1982)	110	5,150

Table 11.1–cont.

	No of factories	No of workers
1403 AH (1983)	112	5,150
1404 AH (1984)	116	5,227
1405 AH (1985)	121	4,182
1406 AH (1986)	122	6,188
1407 AH (1987)	125	6,588
6 Chemical industries, including petrochemicals rubber and plastics		
1401 AH (1981)	231	17,202
1402 AH (1982)	251	18,318
1403 AH (1983)	273	18,318
1404 AH (1984)	286	18,681
1405 AH (1985)	294	10,554
1406 AH (1986)	295	21,888
1407 AH (1987)	302	23,649
7 Manufacture of china, earthenware, pottery, porcelain and glass		
1401 AH (1981)	6	1,416
1402 AH (1982)	6	1.416
1403 AH (1983)	6	1,416
1404 AH (1984)	6	1,416
1405 AH (1985)	6	1,327
1406 AH (1986)	6	1,505
1407 AH (1987)	6	1,505
8 Manufacture of building materials		
1401 AH (1981)	438	29,898
1402 AH (1982)	464	31,003
1403 AH (1983)	486	32,253
1404 AH (1984)	501	34,857
1405 AH (1985)	517	31,292
1406 AH (1986)	525	40,080
1407 AH (1987)	532	40,929
9 Metal industries		
1401 AH (1981)	463	29,339
1402 AH (1982)	490	30,444

Table 11.1–cont.

	No of factories	No of workers
1403 AH (1983)	527	31,617
1404 AH (1984)	551	32,136
1405 AH (1985)	562	21,062
1406 AH (1986)	570	33,277
1407 AH (1987)	581	38,494
10 Manufacture of other products		
1401 AH (1981)	16	630
1402 AH (1982)	19	698
1403 AH (1983)	24	774
1404 AH (1984)	29	774
1405 AH (1985)	33	613
1406 AH (1986)	36	1,064
1407 AH (1987)	39	2,249
11 Storage		
1401 AH (1981)	28	668
1402 AH (1982)	28	668
1403 AH (1983)	28	668
1404 AH (1984)	28	668
1405 AH (1985)	28	642
1406 AH (1986)	28	852
1407 AH (1987)	28	—
Summary of totals		
1401 AH (1981)	1,629	105,951
1402 AH (1982)	1,741	109,919
1403 AH (1983)	1,845	113,334
1404 AH (1984)	1,929	117,360
1405 AH (1985)	1,983	88,943
1406 AH (1986)	2,017	130,494
1407 AH (1987)	2,061	140,620

by the Saudi Industrial Development Fund. The Saudi Industrial Development Fund (SIDF), which was set up in 1394 AH (1974), is a government agency charged with the responsibility of providing a source of funds to private sector industries and public utility companies.

Table 11.2 shows the scale of the SIDF's involvement in Saudi Arabia's rapid industrial expansion over the seven years 1977/78 to 1983/84.

Table 11.2   *Loans disbursed by the SIDF (SR millions)*

Fiscal year	Industry	Electricity gas and water	Total
1977/78	1,268	3,883	5,151
1978/79	1,117	5,729	6,846
1979/80	1,307	5,184	6,491
1980/81	1,172	5,489	6,661
1981/82	797	4,551	5,348
1982/83	878	4,238	5,116
1983/84	1,056	4,169	5,225

Source: SIDF

In the first ten years of its existence (1974–84), the SIDF approved 906 loan applications to finance 788 projects with cumulative loan commitments of SR 11,200 million (about 77 per cent of total loan commitment).

The SIDF's loans cover a wide range of industrial sectors, including construction materials; industrial products and equipment; transportation and automotive products; and consumer products.

In the electricity sector, the SIDF has played an even more crucial role. In the years 1974 to 1984, the SIDF disbursed loans of SR 36,300 million to this sector, facilitating the expansion of power generation facilities throughout the Kingdom. The capacity of the electric companies rose from 1,080 megawatts in 1975 to 9,000 megawatts in 1982 and, by 1987, generating capacity exceeded 14,000 megawatts.

Behind these figures lies the sustained strategy of reducing Saudi Arabia's dependence on oil. It is a daunting task. Saudi Arabia possesses 25 per cent of the world's oil reserves and, therefore, the economy must remain oil-based in the foreseeable future. Nevertheless, by judicious use of the oil revenues, the government of Saudi Arabia is expanding the industrial base and other economic sectors, and reducing the degree of dependence.

The expansion of non-oil activities brings with it the acute need to make best use of manpower at all levels. Saudi Arabia has a small population relative to the size of its economy. Much of the economic expansion during the construction of the Kingdom's infrastructure necessitated the use of expatriate labor. The sections of this book which deal with education and training are a clear indication that, just as the government is reducing dependence on oil, so it is determined to reduce dependence on foreign labor, especially in the areas of science and technology.

The SIDF has played a key role in creating local Saudi industrial enterprises and the employment opportunities which they present. The wide range of locally manufactured goods now available in the Kingdom attests to the success of the SIDF's contribution.

11.3   The Saudi Arabian Basic Industries Corporation

The Saudi Arabian Basic Industries Corporation (SABIC) is an example, *par excellence*, of the practical results of the Kingdom's blend of long-range planning, long-term major investment and the judicious use of public and private sources of finance.

SABIC was established by Royal Decree in 1976 – its task to set up and operate hydrocarbon and mineral-based industries in the Kingdom of Saudi Arabia. The Public Investment Fund provides long-term loans to SABIC on highly concessional terms. The balance of SABIC's capital requirements comes from SABIC's joint venture partners. In addition, SABIC can make use of normal commercial loans. With these sources of finance, SABIC is able to undertake industrial projects considerably in excess of its own authorized capital of SR 10,000 million.

The main features of the first phase of the industrial program launched by SABIC were:

- ethylene-based petrochemical complexes with a total annual capacity of 1.6 million tons of ethylene
- chemical-grade methanol plants with a total annual capacity of 1.25 million tons
- urea plant with an annual capacity of 500,000 tons
- iron and steel plant at Jubail with an annual capacity of 800,000 tons
- expansion of the Jeddah Steel Rolling Mill to produce 140,000 tons per annum

Project implementation began in 1979. In that year, SABIC concluded four joint venture agreements with foreign companies. In the following year, the joint venture Saudi Yanbu Petrochemical Company was set up with the objective of producing 450,000 tons of ethylene per annum. At the same time another joint venture, the Jubail Petrochemical Company, was established to produce 260,000 tons of low density polyethylene. Later in 1980, the Saudi Petrochemical Company was set up with the objective of producing 656,000 tons of ethylene in Jubail and new joint venture operations followed in 1981.

In 1981 the Jeddah Steel Rolling Mill began production, to be followed by the Jubail Iron and Steel Plant in 1982.

SABIC's major role in the development of petrochemical and mineral-based industries in Saudi Arabia is clear. Less obvious but perhaps more important is the function SABIC fulfils in providing a mechanism for the acquisition by Saudi citizens of the managerial, professional and technological skills required to control and expand a modern industrialized economy.

The challenges which SABIC faces (not all of them technical) are far from over.

By 1985, the year in which exports of Saudi Arabian petrochemicals to Europe were scheduled to begin, the governments of Europe, persuaded by the lobbying of the European petrochemical companies, set extremely small duty-free quotas for Saudi Arabian petrochemical imports. The effect was that any substantial quantities of Saudi Arabian petrochemicals exported to Europe were handicapped by duties of up to 20 per cent.

For Saudi Arabia, this act of protectionism has been doubly disappointing. First, the development of a petrochemical industry is of central importance to the Kingdom's plans to reduce economic dependence on the export of crude oil. The setting up of what are, in effect, tariffs against Saudi petrochemicals in the large European market is unhelpful. Secondly, Saudi Arabia believes in a free market and free trade. It has shown this belief in allowing almost all imports into the Kingdom duty-free. It is surely unfair that those who have enjoyed the benefits of free trade in Saudi Arabia for so long should adopt a protectionist stance as soon as they are faced by competition from the products of Saudi industry, which represent a mere 4–5 per cent of petrochemical production worldwide.

There must also be disappointment that Europe was not prepared to take a longer-term view in this matter. In an issue of *The Economist* in January 1985, an article on this subject included the following comment:

> European protectionism has so far left Saudi faith in the free market undented. Nearly all imports enter Saudi Arabia duty-free – despite the temptation to use tariffs to protect fledgeling local industries. If the Europeans succeed in blocking Saudi petrochemicals from their markets, the Saudis have high hopes of selling the stuff to others.

It should have been clear that, in the long run, such a stance would not help European economies to compete in world markets if they relied for their petrochemicals on the product of an expensive, tariff-protected petrochemical industry.

Despite the unhelpful attitude of Europe, SABIC has been a success. *The Financial Times* (13th April 1988) gave this assessment:

> The company [SABIC] now has 14 operating plants, producing products including steel, plastic, fertilizer and petrochemicals. Output in 1987 reached 9.7m tonnes.
>
> The surprise is that the petrochemical and plastics market have accepted the Saudi output with so little disruption. SABIC output is higher than planned, because bottlenecks in its plants have been released. On average, production now is nearly 18% higher than the designed capacity.

The article goes on to explain how market factors have helped SABIC to succeed:

> The reason SABIC products were not disruptive was two-fold. First, the

Japanese, American and European petrochemical industries underwent restructuring and plants closed. Second, world demand for petro-chemical products rose faster than anticipated. This produced a market-place that was actually eager for Saudi petro-chemicals.

Certainly market factors have helped but this should not in any way detract from the remarkable achievements of an organization that holds a central position in the Kingdom's program of industrial diversification.

11.3.1 SABIC'S INDUSTRIAL POLICY

The following notes on SABIC's industrial policy were supplied by the management of SABIC.

> SABIC's policy and strategies are directly derived from its planned objectives. Having been established as one of the principal vehicles for diversifying the Saudi economy, SABIC's strategies were drawn along three basic lines of action.
>
> The first is to make use of the comparative advantages of local industrial production by utilizing and adding value to available natural resources . . . Hence, the setting up of basic industries that are based upon hydrocarbon and mineral resources.
>
> The second is to construct related downstream and supporting industries, thus contributing to the expansion of the Kingdom's industrial base, and at the same time providing investment opportunities for private capital either directly in SABIC's industries or in related industries and services.
>
> The third line of action is to participate in training and building Saudi technical and managerial capabilities in industrial planning, implementation, operation, maintenance and development.
>
> Now, with SABIC's projects moving from the construction and implementation phase to that of actual production, there have emerged the elements of efficient, safe and profitable operation of industries – together with the most important requirement for the continued development of SABIC as a successful commercial enterprise, and as a corporate vehicle for marketing its products.
>
> In this direction, SABIC is careful to enter the petrochemical markets as a world wide producer worthy of its name:
>
> Seeking the best and most appropriate qualities in its products;
> Pursuing serious, fair and honest competitions in its business dealings; and
> Endeavouring in a gentlemanly way, and within its direct interests, to work for the benefit of both the consumer and world industry as a whole.

As a measure of the scale of SABIC's operations and the extent of its success, it is noteworthy that SABIC's profits in the first eight months of 1988 amounted to more than SR 2,500 million, with its exports reaching 65 countries. It has undoubtedly become a major force in the world market for high-quality petrochemicals.

Table 11.3, listing SABIC projects and products (taken from *A Guide to Doing Business in the Kingdom of Saudi Arabia*, published by the Royal Embassy of Saudi Arabia in Washington, DC), gives a further indication of the scope and scale of SABIC's operations.

11.4   Jubail and Yanbu: the industrial cities

In its efforts to broaden the industrial base of the Saudi Arabian economy, it was obvious that the Kingdom should take advantage of its copious hydrocarbon energy resources.

The industrial cities at Jubail and Yanbu have played a key part in the Kingdom's determination to develop hydrocarbon-based and energy-intensive industries. The Royal Commission for Jubail and Yanbu (PO Box 5964, Riyadh 11432), established in 1395 AH (1975), has created the basic infrastructure for these two cities, often described as the jewels in the Kingdom's industrial crown.

By the end of the Third Development Plan (1405 AH: 1985), fifteen primary industrial projects (ten at Jubail and five at Yanbu) were operational.

The provision of training facilities has formed an important part of the development program at Jubail and Yanbu. Both cities have training centers for basic and advanced vocational skills.

As in other aspects of the economy, the government is eager to encourage private sector involvement in the future development of Jubail and Yanbu. As the Fourth Development Plan (1405–10 AH: 1985–90) stated:

> Where appropriate, the public sector will delegate responsibilities to the private sector and will make particular efforts to assist in the establishment of privately-owned secondary industries. The support to be given to the private sector will include ownership and management opportunities in secondary industries, incentives to Saudi businessmen, attractive lease contracts, and the establishment of a strong retail and commercial base in the industrial cities.

11.5   Other aspects of industrial diversification

Inevitably, any consideration of the Kingdom's industrial diversification program centers on the establishment and development of large-scale state-owned industrial

Table 11.3   *SABIC's projects and products*

Project name	Partner	Partnership formed	Feedstocks	Products	Capacity MTPA–000	On stream	Location
Saudi Petro chemical Co. (SADAF) (SABIC's largest ethylene complex; one of world's largest petro-chemical projects)	Pecten Arabia Ltd., subsidiary of Shell Oil Co., U.S.A. 50%	9/28/80	Ethane	Ethylene	760	First Unit: Ethylene On-stream Oct. 1984	Al-Jubail
			Salt	Ethylene Dichloride	560	Last Unit: Styrene in late 1985	
			Benzene	Styrene Monomer	360		
				Crude Indus-trial Ethanol	300		
Caustic		450					
				Soda			
Saudi Yanbu Petrochemical Co. (YANPET)	Mobil Oil Corp., U.S.A. 50%	4/19/80	Ethane (from East-West pipeline)	Ethylene	560	Ethylene on-stream Dec. 1984	Yanbu
				Linear Low Density Polyethylene	332		
				High Density Polyethylene	98		
				Ethylene Glycol	250		
Al-Jubail Petrochemical Co. (KEMYA)	Exxon Chemical Co., subsidiary of Exxon . Corp. 50%	4/26/80	Ethylene (from SADAF plant)	Linear Low Density Polyethylene	332	On-stream Nov. 1984	Al-Jubail
Saudi Methanol Co. (AR RAZI)	Japanese Consortium headed by Mitsubishi Gas Chemical Co., Japan 50%	11/24/79	Methane	Chemcial Grade Methanol	610	On-stream since mid-1983	Al-Jubail
National Methanol Co. (IBN-SINA) (One of world's largest methanol producing complexes	Celanese, (25%) Texas Eastern, (25%) U.S.A.	2/3/81	Methane	Chemical Grade Methanol	770	On-stream since 7/84	Al-Jubail
Arabian Petrochemical Co. (PETROKEMYA)	100% SABIC-owned	5/20/81	Ethane	Ethylene Burlene-I Polystyrene	650 50 100	Mid-1985 mid-1988 mid-1988	Al-Jubail

Table 11.3–cont.

Project name	Partner	Partnership formed	Feedstocks	Products	Capacity MTPA–000	On stream	Location
Eastern Petrochemical Co. (SHARQ)	Japanese consortium headed by Mitsubishi, Japan 50%	5/23/81	Ethylene (from PETROKEMYA plant)	Linear Low Density Polyethlene Ethylene Glycol	140 330	On-stream mid-1985	Al-Jubail
National Industrial Gas Co. (GAS)	Saudi private sector	2/14,83	Air	Oxygen Nitrogen	438 400	On-stream since 1984	Al-Jubail
Saudi Iron and Steel Co. (HADEED)	Deutsche Ent- wickbung Gesell schaft of W. German government 4.5%	3/20/79	Iron Ores Limestone Natural Gas Scrap Iron	Rein- forcing Rods and Bars	800	On-stream since mid- 1983	Al-Jubail
Jeddah Steel Rolling Mill (SULB)	100% HADEED-owned (SABIC & D.F.G. of W. Germany	5/29/79	Steel Billets from HADEED)	Rein- forcing Bars	140	On-stream since 1981	Jeddah
Al-Jubail Fertilizer Co. (SAMAD)	Taiwan Fertilizer Co., Taiwan	12/4/79	Methane	Urea	600	On-stream since mid- 1983	Al-Jubail
Saudi Arabian Fertilizer Co. (SAFCO)	SABIC 41% Saudi share- holders 49% SAFCO employ- ees 10%	1965	Methane	Urea Sulfuric Acid Melamine	330 100 20	On-stream since 1970 since 1985	Dammam
National Plastic Co. (IBN HAYYAN)	Lucky Group, S. Korea 15%	12/18/83	Ethylene (from PETROKEMYA Ethylene Dichloride (from SADAF)	Vinyl Chloride Monomer Polyvinyl Chloride	300 200	On-stream early 1986	Al-Jubail
Gulf Petroleum- ical Industries Co. (GPIC)	Petrochemical Industries Co. of Kuwait 33.3% Government of the State of Bahrain 33.3%	12/5/79	Methane	Ammonia Methanol	330 330	On-stream early 1986	Bahrain
Aluminum Bahrain (ALBA)	Government of the State of Bahrain 57.9% Kaiser Aluminum 17% Breton Invest- ments 5.1%	1/23/69	Aluminum	Ingots, "Rolling" Slabs "Pellets"? Bullets, Liquid Metal	170	On-stream mid-1971	Bahrain

Table 11.3–cont.

Project name	Partner	formed	Feedstocks	Products	Capacity MTPA–000	On stream	Location
	Saudi Public Investment Fund 20%						
GARMCO Aluminum Rolling Mill	20% Saudi Arabia 20% Bahrain 20% Kuwait 20% Iraq 10% Qatar 10% Oman	10/2/81	Aluminum	Sheets, Circles, Corrugated Sheets, Can Stocks	40	On-stream mid-1985	Bahrain
Saudi European Petrochemical Company (IBN-ZAHR)	APICORP Neste Oy (Finland) ENI Corp.	12/16/84	Butane Chemical Grade Methanol	MTBE	500,000	On-stream 1988	Al-Jubail

companies engaged in oil refining and petro-chemical production.

But there is another sector, smaller but in terms of employment and in terms of the future, of considerable significance. There are today some 2,000 general manufacturing companies licensed by the Ministry of Industry and Electricity, and some 20,000 light industrial workshops licensed by the municipalities.

Another feature of the Kingdom's strategy in seeking industrial diversification is the type of industrial projects which are appropriate to Saudi Arabia's geography and demography. Although Saudi Arabia is vast in size, the population of the Kingdom is small, and, despite the reduction in numbers of immigrant workers in recent years, it remains true that the economy still requires a large foreign work-force to complement the indigenous population. It is not therefore appropriate for the Kingdom to encourage the development of labor-intensive industries. Rather, it favours the introduction and expansion of high-technology industrial ventures with a high productivity/worker ratio, which will provide suitably trained Saudi citizens with well-paid and challenging occupations.

Because of government policy and support, the non-oil industrial sector has increased in both size and efficiency of operation and can now claim to have achieved output-per-worker figures which are amongst the highest in the Arab world.

Table 11.1 gave statistics on the number of factories in the Kingdom (1401 AH–07 AH: 1981–87). Table 11.4 gives statistical information on the number of offices of self-employed professionals in the Kingdom in 1407 AH (1987), which, as a service sector, indicates the employment opportunities for skilled personnel, opportunities which have inevitably accompanied the Kingdom's industrial diversification policies.

Table 11.4   *Offices of self-employed professionals 1407 AH (1987)*

Type of office	Saudi	Non-Saudi	Mixed	Total
Engineering consultancy	241	7	13	261
Chartered accountancy	153	51	5	209
Civil engineering	167	30	5	202
Legal consultancy	163	20	2	185
Translation	124	3	1	128
Architecture	61	33	5	99
Temporary permit eng. co.	80	0	0	80
Admin. and organisation	54	1	0	55
Agricult. and hydro consult.	28	0	1	29
Survey services	28	0	1	29
Economic consultancy	23	1	1	25
Partnership companies	16	1	8	25
Electrical engineering	16	3	0	19
Financial consultancy	11	0	0	11
Geological and hydro cons.	10	0	0	10
Chemical engineering	7	0	0	7
Mechanical engineering	6	1	0	7
Soil examination	5	0	1	6
Computer consultancy	4	0	0	4
Industrial engineering	4	0	0	4
Organisation and stats.	2	0	0	2
Petroleum engineering	1	1	0	2
Safety consultancy	2	0	0	2
Education consultancy	1	0	0	1
Electronics engineering	1	0	0	1
Health consultancy	1	0	0	1
Security consultancy	1	0	0	1
Total	1,210	152	43	1,405

Source: Central Department of Statistics, 1987

11.6   Industrial development, the present and the future

The Fourth Development Plan (1405–10 AH: 1985–90) gave a clear and succinct description of the industrial sector of the Saudi economy.

> Industrial development of the Kingdom is of comparatively recent origin and essentially comprises three components:
> First, are the SABIC (Saudi Arabian Basic Industries Corporation) enterprises, which comprise mainly the downstream hydrocarbon industries and, to a lesser degree, the heavy metals industry. These industries are capital and energy-intensive, utilizing raw material

feedstock from the oil and gas industries, and their petrochemicals output is primarily for export. The production plants are technologically very advanced, and the controlling companies are usually joint ventures with foreign partners who have varying degrees of control, but never above 50 per cent. These industries are normally referred to as the "basic" industry sector.

Second, is the large group of factories licensed by the Ministry of Industry and Electricity (MIE) and best described as the "formal" manufacturing sector. Most of these enterprises are privately sponsored and eligible for Saudi Industrial Development Fund (SIDF) loans. Their output is geared primarily to the domestic market, which is very open and competitive. A range of investment incentives is available to companies, following a screening procedure; for example, sites with subsidized energy and utility services, industrial estates, SIDF loans, preferential purchases by state organizations, training grants and, in some cases, tariff protection.

The third group can be referred to as the "informal" manufacturing sector, and is composed largely of labor-intensive small workshops in repair and small-scale production activities. These workshops require neither an MIE license nor its screening procedure, but do require a license from the municipalities and registration as companies with the Ministry of Commerce. Furthermore, the Ministry of Industry is not responsible for monitoring their activities. The financing needs of this sector relate mainly to working capital requirements such as raw material, rather than premises and equipment. Finance comes mainly from the owners of the workshops, and this can be supplemented by grants from the Saudi Credit Bank, if the owner has completed GOTEVT vocational training.

Key Issues

Despite the advances made towards a more diversified economic base, industrial development during the Third Plan was not without problems. The fundamental changes occurring in the industrial sector have raised a number of issues that need to be addressed to a greater or lesser extent by the government, Saudi industrialists and the trading partners. It is anticipated that these problems and issues, outlined below, will have an important influence on the future development of the industrial sector, particularly over the Fourth Plan period.

Capital-Intensive Development

One of the Third Plan's major objectives was to minimize the need for foreign manpower. However, the large number of foreign laborers recruited by domestic factories has been an obstacle to the achievement of this objective. This objective will be realized gradually during the Fourth Development Plan and beyond, through manpower training, and establishing capital-intensive factories using modern technology that requires less manpower.

Project Planning

A substantial part of industrial investment by the private sector has been based on short-term market indicators. This kind of investment planning has resulted in excess capacity, thus lowering productivity in many industrial activities, and particularly those which are construction-related. The programs of the Fourth Development Plan will provide support to industrialists to undertake feasibility studies for their new projects, based both on short-term and long-term expectations, thus enabling them to make more successful investment decisions.

Market Protection

In an increasingly competitive trading environment, measures may be sought both to protect domestic manufacturers from foreign competition and to assist them in gaining footholds in markets abroad. The government, however, is committed to free trade, recognizing that increased protection is likely to induce inefficiency in domestic industry, and could result in higher prices for imported raw material and other manufacturing inputs, to the detriment of the population as a whole.

Structure of Incentives

A major objective for the Fourth Plan is not only to maintain the growth rate in the formation of new factories, but also, more pressingly, to improve the performance of existing industrial establishments. The present excess capacity in the industrial sector, in terms of both capital equipment and manpower, has resulted in low productivity. Significant productivity gains could be realized if output from these establishments were to expand.

The present system of government support – loans, incentives and serviced sites – is geared primarily to new operations and is not related to output performance. The government recognizes that, if the objective is to increase output from existing establishment and to encourage those sections of industry that are now well established, then emphasis should shift towards operational assistance: export promotion, organizational and management support, re-equipment incentives, and training pro-grams. This type of support measure will enable Saudi manufacturing to sustain output at higher levels of efficiency and asset utilization, consequently enhancing its ability to expand and compete in foreign markets.

Regional Dispersion of Industry

The Fourth Plan strategy gives priority to the growth and productivity of the manufacturing sector across the Kingdom, including areas outside the main urban centres. At the same time, because of the social aspects involved, the need is recognized to accommodate production projects in areas of appropriate development potential. These areas will serve as development centres attracting people from places which lack the necessary potential. In this way industrial development and the growth of linkages will utilize environmental advantages to the best effect and contribute to the reduction of costs and rise of productivity.

Export Markets

It is not easy for a newly industrializing country to export its products to compete in international markets. However, by exporting SABIC products to international markets the Kingdom has realized an objective that assured the importance of expanding the implementation of industrial development programs and projects, thus increasing the contribution of exports to GDP.

In the field of manufacturing industry operated by the private sector, the Fourth Development Plan has included programs for encouraging and supporting industrial products to reach foreign markets, since these products have proved to be competitive in the domestic market.

Saudi-ization

The fourth objective of the Fourth Development Plan has identified the importance of manpower development, thus ensuring a constant supply of manpower and upgrading and improving its efficiency to serve all sectors. Industrial development will provide opportunities for the upgrading and employment of Saudi manpower through training programs in all producing and industrial sectors. It is fully recognized that the transfer of modern technology to young Saudis is no less important than realizing profits in industrial projects. For that reason the Fourth Plan has concentrated on creating training programs for SABIC industries and the private sector to promote Saudi manpower skills.

It is a prime objective that SABIC should increase substantially the proportion of Saudi nationals in all strata of its activities, but particularly in its technical and managerial functions. In doing so SABIC needs also to consider the requirements of other sectors of the economy, and give attention to developing its own supply of qualified nationals through more extensive training programs, rather than relying principally on the open market.

The government's scope for resolving many of these issues in the context of the Fourth Plan is limited. Some issues will require longer-term solutions than are possible within a five-year planning period; others have wide implications and cannot be addressed from the viewpoint of industrial development alone. Furthermore, some issues can only be resolved by the private sector itself. Nevertheless, a series of public sector programs in the Fourth Plan has been designed to overcome many of the short-to-medium-term constraints, while setting in motion initiatives for longer-term solutions.

The Fifth Development Plan (1410–15 AH: 1990–95) indicates the government's future intentions for the continuing development of the country's economy:

> Consideration of the economical use of resources should predominate in government investment and expenditure decisions and this may be implemented through:
> 1 Considering water as basic factor and an important determinant of efficiency in Government's projects as is the case with expatriate labor or inflation.
> 2 The development of economically promising natural resources – e.g. the exploration of mineral and sea resources; the mapping of their location; their further development and utilization; and processing of available gas to the maximum extent possible.
> 3 Horizontal and vertical expansions in the petrochemical industries as well as in the production of gas and petroleum derivatives, through the private sector or mixed companies, whenever economic feasibility is proven.
> 4 Increasing the capacity for manufacturing refined petroleum products to the maximum potential within the bounds of economic feasibility.

(See Section 10.3 for full details on the objectives of the Fifth Development Plan.)

11.7 The private sector

It will be clear from previous sections of this chapter that, although the state must continue to play a key role in the Kingdom's economy, the government is eager to see the private sector assume increasing responsibility for the country's economic development.

The Kingdom of Saudi Arabia follows a free trade policy, believing that such a policy and the competition it engenders is the most effective way of utilizing resources efficiently, of employing those resources to meet the changing needs of society, and of providing consumers with the greatest degree of choice.

This policy leads the government to encourage the private sector of the economy to become as efficient and competitive as possible. Fledgeling Saudi industries need help (in the form of grants, soft loans, or, in some instances, even protective tariffs), but the longer-term aim is to generate a private industrial sector capable of facing local and fair foreign competition, of meeting the Kingdom's own industrial needs as far as practical and, indeed, of exporting Saudi goods to other Arab states and beyond.

As part of this economic strategy, the government is progressively privatizing public organizations, encouraging both domestic and foreign investment in the Kingdom's industrial sector. (The fourth conference of the Council of Saudi Chambers of Commerce and Industry, which was held in Riyadh in May 1989, had this topic on its agenda for discussion.)

The clearest indication of the Kingdom's future policies for the private sector is provided by the Fifth Development Plan (1410–15 AH: 1990–95). See the Third Basic Strategic Principle in Section 10.3 above.

11.8   Mineral resources and mining

Geological surveys and mineral exploration have revealed that, in addition to the vast oil reserves, the Kingdom of Saudi Arabia possesses large deposits of various minerals, including bauxite, copper, gold, iron, lead, silver, tin and a number of non-metallic minerals.

Responsibility for geological surveying of the Kingdom rests with the Deputy Ministry of Mineral Resources, which is also the agency responsible for mineral exploration. The task of exploiting the mineral wealth of the Kingdom is primarily allocated to the private sector, operating in joint ventures either with foreign companies (whose expertise in this highly technical field is often needed) or Petromin.

In line with government policy in other sectors of the economy, the government is most eager to train Saudi nationals so that they play the fullest possible part in the exploitation of the Kingdom's mineral wealth. The Fourth Development Plan set as a specific objective the training of Saudi nationals in the practical application of the geo-sciences and mining engineering.

Chapter 12

Agricultural development

In view of the geography and climate of the Kingdóm, the reader might expect a chapter on Saudi Arabian agriculture to contain little of note. A country consisting largely of desert terrain, with modest natural ground water resources and subject to extremes of temperature, is scarcely ideal for agricultural development. The extent to which Saudi Arabia has managed to develop the agricultural sector of the economy over the last two decades is, therefore, one of the Kingdom's most spectacular achievements.

12.1   Agricultural achievements

The Fourth Development Plan (1405–10 AH: 1980–85) explains why agriculture has been given such a high priority, pointing out the importance of social and ecological, as well as economic, considerations in the government's thinking:

> The development of agriculture was given a high priority by Government during previous development plans, and will continue to play a leading role in the national strategy to diversify the economic base during the Fourth Plan. It has long been recognized that the importance of agriculture to the Kingdom extends beyond that of its contribution to national output alone. At the end of the Third Plan period almost half of the Kingdom's population was living in rural areas and a significant proportion of total Saudi employment was in agriculture. Apart from the strategic significance of increasing domestic food production for a growing population, the planned development of agriculture fulfils other important roles. It generates employment both within the sector and in closely related agro-industries. It contributes to the diversification of the economic base and to import substitution, while raising income levels and improving rural living standards for both settled and nomadic communities alike. This has a positive influence on the population balance and helps to prevent population drift to urban centres. A further

important aspect of agricultural development in the Kingdom is its role in maintaining the ecological balance through combating desertification.

Progress in agricultural development has been achieved largely through a policy of governmental incentives for private sector participation:

> The encouragement of large-scale mechanized agriculture was identified in the Third Plan as a priority for investment in the Kingdom's efforts to induce structural change in the economy. The positive investment response from the private sector to a high level of Government support exceeded even the high expectations of the Plan. Substantial private sector funds were channelled into agriculture, attracted by profit opportunities which, particularly in wheat production, were almost guaranteed. Many large-scale farms, utilizing the latest technology, machinery and equipment, were established. The output effect of this level of private investment and Government support has been one of the Kingdom's major successes during the Third Plan period.

The Ministry of Agriculture and Water is responsible for the implementation of the Kingdom's agricultural policy. The Ministry takes direct responsibility for irrigation and drainage projects if they are beyond the means of local farming communities, and, through the Arable Land Distribution Scheme, identifies land suitable for reclamation and allocation to Saudi citizens for agricultural applications. The Ministry of Agriculture and Water describes the progress of agricultural development as follows:

A brief Introduction to Agriculture Development in the Kingdom of Saudi Arabia

Introduction
During the past eight years, agriculture in the Kingdom of Saudi Arabia has developed so rapidly that the agricultural sector has become one of the most productive and fast-expanding economic sectors in the Kingdom.

Extensively subsidized by the State, the agricultural sector has achieved a complete revolution based on the most up-to-date scientific technology which has been applied to farming methods, irrigation, and animal and fishing resources.

This unique revolution stemmed from a clear philosophy concentrating on agricultural self-development. The State has been responsible for drawing up policies and setting aims, supporting and guiding the private sector, and following up private sector activities; while the private sector itself has implemented all stages of productive operation without State interference, or unhealthy competition among individual or corporate members of the private sector.

Arising from this philosophy, and as a result of subsidies and incentives, the great transformation from a traditional to a modern agricultural system has been accomplished, both on the level of experienced and able individual farmers and on the level of large agricultural companies, either limited or corporate; in addition, the Kingdom has seen the development and modernization of research and training centres and agricultural education, running in parallel with the rapid development and expansion of agricultural productivity.

With the care, supervision and support of the Custodian of the Two Holy Mosques, King Fahd bin Abdul Aziz, and his Highness, his Heir Apparent, Prince Abdullah bin Abdul Aziz, the Kingdom of Saudi Arabia has been able, under King Fahd's reign, to attain self-sufficiency in one of the world's major strategic crops: wheat. In 1985, the Kingdom's wheat produce amounted to about 1.7 million tons. Eight years earlier it was no more than three thousand tons.

While the Kingdom has concentrated on self-sufficiency, it has not neglected its obligations to humanity. It has supported the World Food Program in its fight against global food inequalities. Its efforts and contribution in this field are widely recognized, be they through local or regional or international funds or through bilateral aid.

Expansion of Cultivated Land
In 1975, cultivated land in the Kingdom of Saudi Arabia did not exceed 150,000 acres: at the beginning of 1985 it had reached 2,300,000 acres.

Wheat Production
The total wheat produce of the Kingdom of Saudi Arabia in 1975 did not exceed three thousand tons; in 1985, the Kingdom's production reached 1,700,000 tons, representing an astronomical rise in wheat production in the Kingdom in eight years, surpassing all expectations in a desert country like the Kingdom. Thus, by 1985, Saudi Arabia exceeded its own requirements for this major globally-strategic crop.

Dates
Dates are one of the richest and oldest alimentary products in the Kingdom. Date production has risen in eight years from 200,000 tons to approximately 500,000 tons, an increase which has enabled the Kingdom to export to neighboring countries – in addition to the large quantities it offers as aid to the World Food Program which in turn distributes it to countries in need of this major source of nutrition.

Meat

There has been an increase in projects involving the raising and fattening of sheep and cattle, which have had important implications in terms of the need for the cultivation of fodder, subsidized by the Government. These developments have contributed to the fulfilment of the country's requirements for good quality meat.

Vegetables

The Kingdom of Saudi Arabia produces a variety of essential vegetables, including potatoes, both for local consumption and for export to neighboring States. Vegetable cultivation is carried out on modern agricultural principles of controlled environment; and the operations of preparation and packing of produce employ the most modern techniques, as required for modern markets.

Milk and Dairy Products

In 1975, there was no significant milk or dairy production in the Kingdom of Saudi Arabia. Total production supplied 5% of the local demand; in 1985 the Kingdom was not only meeting the self-sufficiency limit of milk and dairy products and their derivatives but was also exporting part of its production to its neighboring sister States.

Poultry

In 1975, the poultry industry in the Kingdom of Saudi Arabia did not cover 10% of local demand; by 1985 the Kingdom had achieved self-sufficiency in egg production and surpassed it, exporting to its neighboring sister States. As for the production of slaughter chickens, it now covers 60% of local demand.

Piscatorial Resources

The Government has given special attention to this sector along all its coasts of the Arabian Gulf and the Red Sea. It has carried out concentrated studies and provided various means of support and incentives to small fishermen, facilitating the purchase of boats equipped with modern fishing gear and offering effective marketing facilities.

Aware of the importance of piscatorial resources, the State has encouraged, and five years ago contributed to, the formation of a company with a capital of 100 million Riyals: the Saudi Fishing Company, in which, in addition to the State; some 16,000 citizens hold shares. This company has successfully built its private fleet and provided a large variety of fish and prawn for local and export markets.

State Aid to Farmers

Since the agricultural sector makes a major contribution to the diversification of income resources, and in view of the importance of encouraging farmers to continue working the land, agricultural development projects have been given top priority. The Government of the Kingdom of Saudi Arabia has adopted an intensive program of farming subsidies including interest-free loan offers and generous aid to agricultural investment and production projects. The Government offers aid to the value of 50% of the cost of agricultural machinery and equipment imports, as well as for seeds, fertilizers and fodder. It also contributes to the cost of insecticides and air transport of milking cows from abroad. Moreover, the Saudi Agricultural Bank and other governmental trust funds offer interest-free loans in order to finance investments and operations in various agricultural projects. The Government also offers free arable land to farmers and agricultural companies; it has drawn up a policy for the subsidy of wheat and date prices; and has imposed a customs tax to protect the production of eggs for consumption.

Agricultural Companies

The pinnacle of the efforts of the Kingdom of Saudi Arabia in achieving agricultural development has been its encouragement of the private sector to build up and establish agricultural companies, be they public corporations or large private limited companies.

In the last few years, large public corporations have been established for various agricultural purposes, with capital varying between three hundred and five hundred million Saudi Riyals each. These companies are active in Harad and Ha'il, Wadi'l-Dawasir, al-Qasim, Tabuk, the Eastern Province and other regions. The success of these companies in fulfilling their objectives is evident from the increase in the local agricultural productivity of wheat, fodder and milk, as well as in the processing and packaging of dates, and cattle breeding and fattening. Further evidence of these companies' dynamism is seen in their future plans for diversification of agricultural production, the development of food industries and the adoption of modern marketing systems. Moreover, a Saudi company for fish industries has been established and has achieved tangible success in efficiently providing the local market with clean fish and exporting a variety of its produce.

Agricultural Research Stations and Centers

As a result of its awareness of the importance of research and its responsibility for achieving the best results, the Ministry of Agriculture and Water has established a number of centers and stations, which through experimentation, and economic and analytical studies, aim to employ the most modern means for the development of agricultural and animal resources. Moreover, Saudi cadres are being trained in these centers and stations in order to raise their efficiency and level of qualifications. The results of all such research is being published and distributed among farmers and other relevant institutions in order to share the ensuing benefits.

Training

In view of the importance of training human resources for the preparation of technical cadres highly efficient in different agricultural fields, the Ministry of Agriculture and Water has established several training centres in numerous agricultural regions, like Riyadh, al-Qasim, al-Hofuf and Jizan, to train officials from the Ministry and farmers and their children. Also, ministry officials and some farmers are being sent for training in international centers and universities which are advanced in specialized fields, so that, on their return, they can apply their knowledge in the Kingdom, after adapting it to the agricultural needs and conditions of Saudi Arabia.

Forests and Grazing Land

Forests spread south-west of the Kingdom in an area of about 18 million Donum. The State has undertaken many procedures for their protection and conservation, in addition to the building of twenty nurseries in different areas to produce the necessary seedlings for the development and expansion of forests. It has planted tree barriers in the form of defensive lines to stop creeping sands, and has used trees for similar purposes alongside the main roads outside the cities in the Eastern Province.

Natural grazing land accounts for approximately 75% of the land in the Kingdom of Saudi Arabia. This has led the Ministry of Agriculture and Water to establish a centre specialising in the study of the development and protection of pastures, as a basis for increasing animal resources.

Supplies of Potable and Irrigation Water

1   Desalination

The Kingdom of Saudi Arabia occupies the highest rank among all the States of the world in the production of potable water from the sea.

The General Organization of Sea Water Desalination was formed to supervise all desalination projects in the Kingdom. The volume of production capacity of the desalination stations in 1985 had reached

500,000,000 gallons per day, which enabled the Kingdom, after covering the needs of the cities and villages on its eastern and western coasts with potable water, to introduce desalinated sea water into the heart of the Arabian Peninsula for the first time in its history. It now feeds Riyadh, the capital, with potable water from the Gulf, 500 kilometers away, and feeds the Holy City of Madinah with potable water from the Red Sea 200 km away. At present, work is being undertaken to transport desalinated water to the Holy city of Makkah, the summer resort of Ta'if, and the region of Asir in the south of the Kingdom, which has meant that subterranean water can be allocated to agricultural purposes.

2   Subterranean Water Projects

The Ministry of Agriculture and Water has established several large and self-contained projects to extract subterranean water in order to provide the population of the Kingdom in different areas with good quality water. The largest are the water project in the city of Riyadh, and the Jeddah water project feeding the city of Jeddah. If the other self-contained water projects covering different towns and villages and bedouin centres are included, the Kingdom can now boast that pure water is available to every home in all corners of Saudi Arabia.

3 Dams and Reservoirs Projects

In order to exploit rain and flood waters as efficiently as possible, the Ministry has concentrated on building several dams in different areas. Before 1975, there were 16 dams; the number had increased to 180 by 1984. These dams contribute to the increase of subterranean water reserves and the provision of potable water, as well as helping to protect plantations and some villages against the flooding which previously threatened them as a result of sudden torrential rises in the level of water.

Among the major dams in the Kingdom is the dam of Wadi Najran with a storage capacity of 85 million cubic metres, the dam of Wadi Jizan with a storage capacity of 75 million cubic metres, and the dam of Wadi Fatima on the outskirts of the Holy City of Makkah with a storage capacity of 20 million cubic meters.

4   Recycling of Purified Sewage Projects

These projects aim at recycling purified sewage water for agricultural and industrial use. The first project was established in the city of Riyadh and saves about 200,000 cubic meters of purified water per day, water which is transported through pipes to plantations in the regions of al-Dara'is and Dairab. Similar projects are planned for the cities of al-Qasim and al-Dammam.

National Parks

The Kingdom of Saudi Arabia, through its vastness, enjoys a diversity of good natural scenery ranging from mountains covered by a variety of natural vegetation and trees, and wide plateaux with attractive plants in spring, to beautiful green oases in the middle of the desert, distinguished by their wild fauna, and the rich coastal regions in the Red Sea and the Arabian Gulf.

The government of the Kingdom of Saudi Arabia has realized the importance of the protection of these natural resources which are for the enjoyment of present and future generations. It has thus been concerned with the establishment of parks, like the National Park of Asir on the large mountainous and hilly landscape of Asir around the city of Abha. There are also studies and designs in preparation for the establishment of modern parks in Riyadh, al-Hassa, al-Baha and in other places.

12.2   Agricultural statistics

The development of the Kingdom's agriculture is, in some ways, the most exciting of all the developmental programs. At a time when desertification is a major issue amongst environmentalists and one which, with global warming, is becoming an issue of primary international concern, the Kingdom is channelling resources into turning the desert into agriculturally productive land. The scale of the task is

Table 12.1   *Agricultural development and production 1983/84–1985/86*

	1983/84 1403/04 AH	1984/85 1404/05 AH	1985/86 1405/06 AH
Total crop area in Donums	7,826,947	9,463,587	10,821,742
Wheat production in tons	1,401,644	2,134,930	6,303389
Tomato production in tons	149,060	167,490	174,982
Cucumber production in tons	7,085	13,825	17,933
Date production in tons	454,420	455,730	459,829
Number of broiler chickens produced by specialized projects (millions)	138	177	186
Number of eggs produced by specialized hatcheries (millions)	1,852	2,394	2,497
Number of sheep in specialized projects	1,116,803	1,170,939	1,234,150
Milk production in liters (millions)	97	125	166

Source: Central Department of Statistics, 1987

enormous, but anyone who has seen the great circles of wheat growing in the desert between Riyadh and Jeddah will realize that the Kingdom's commitment is equal to the challenge.

The Kingdom of Saudi Arabia is now self-sufficient in many types of agricultural produce and is, in many cases, able to export. Table 12.1 presents a selection of key statistics on the estimated level of agricultural development and production in the years 1983/84 (1403/04 AH) to 1985/86 (1405/06 AH).

These are truly remarkable figures when set against the background of traditional agricultural production in Saudi Arabia before the Kingdom's development plans were initiated.

13

Population and manpower resources of the Kingdom

The population of the Kingdom of Saudi Arabia is homogeneous. All citizens share the same cultural heritage, the same religion and the same language. Because this is so, the problems sometimes associated with multi-cultural societies (polycommunality) do not arise. In many developing countries, any study of the ethnic composition would immediately involve the concept of polycommunality. By this we mean that in countries like India, the Lebanon, Nigeria and Pakistan, where problems of cultural and religious heritage, language and ethnic origin exist, the concept of polycommunality

> allows for the varying mixtures and interlacings of ethnic, caste, tribal, religious, and different systems. It . . . has the qualities of range and precision. The prefix "poly-" directs attention to the inter- rather than the intra- group nature of the problem.
>
> *Source: External Inducement of Political/Administrative Development: An Institutional Strategy*, by Ralph Braibanti (Durham, NC: Duke University Press, 1969)

But the Kingdom of Saudi Arabia is among the

> few polities [of the world] whose political culture . . . approximates homogeneity [a condition which can be largely attributed to the cohesiveness of Islam]
>
> *Source: The Politics of the Developing Areas*, eds Gabriel Almond and James Coleman (Princeton, NJ: Princeton University Press, 1960)

It is, of course, true that expatriate workers have come to the Kingdom from all over the world, many with cultural backgrounds very different from the indigenous population but, because of the Kingdom's unique position as the Custodian and

Guardian of the Holy Places of Islam, a responsibility vested in the King, the homogeneity of Saudi Arabian culture and society has been entirely unaffected.

13.1   Population characteristics

The population of Saudi Arabia falls conveniently into three categories. The first and second are indigenous; the third is composed of aliens.

The first category contains the major tribes of the country. The second contains the bulk of the population: the native residents of cities, towns and villages. The final category includes all the foreigners living and working in the country.

In this section, we consider the tribes of Saudi Arabia, and here we rely heavily on the authoritative work dealing with Arabian tribes, entitled *Qalb Al-Jazira Al Arabia* ("The Heart of the Arab Peninsula"). The author of this work, Fouad Hamza, was for some time a Deputy Minister of Foreign Affairs in the reign of King Abdul Aziz Al Sa'ud. All his work on the tribes of Saudi Arabia had received the approbation of the late Prince Abdullah bin Abdul Rahman, the late King Khalid's uncle, who was himself considered to be a leading authority on tribal affairs. As Hamza rightly said,

> it is very difficult for a researcher to comprehend and account for the origin of all the Arabian tribes that exist at the present time, due to the loss of a rather large section of the genealogical records which their predecessors wrote, and [to] the loss of several links in the lineage chain during the Middle Ages, a period of decline for Arabian states [as well as of] disagreement among its princes and tribes.

For obvious reasons, no effort was made to trace the branches of these various tribes back to their ancient roots.

Tribes, according to Fouad Hamza, consist of a five-tier hierarchical structure:

1 Tribe = (*Kabila*)
2 Group = (*Batin*)
3 Division = (*Fakhed*)
4 Clan = (*Fasila*)
5 Family = (*Raht*)

As an example, the family (*Raht*) of Sahlan belongs to the Al Mir'ad clan (*Fasila*), of the group (*Batin*) of Al Rola, of the division (*Fakhed*) of Dani Muslim of the tribe (*Kabila*) Anza.

Tables 13.1 and 13.2 present the tribes of the entire country arranged alphabetically according to the Arabic alphabet, disregarding the alternative categories of pride, wealth, ability and lineage. The two tables designate the major tribes of the Arabian Peninsula and the main tribes of Saudi Arabia, respectively.

King Abdul Aziz Al Saud, the founder of the Kingdom of Saudi Arabia

King Fahd Bin Abdul Aziz, Custodian of the two Holy Mosques

H.R.H. Crown Prince Abdullah Bin Abdul Aziz, Deputy Prime Minister and Head of the National Guard

H.R.H. Crown Prince Sultan Bin Abdul Aziz, Second Deputy Prime Minister, Minister of Defence and Aviation, and the Inspector General

View of Jeddah today

The Holy Mosque in Makkah

(*top*) King Khalid International Airport in Riyadh (internal view)

(*bottom*) Traditional architecture in Riyadh city

King Fahd Bin Abdul Aziz, laying the foundation stone for one of the major developmental projects in the Kingdom: to the right of the King stands H.R.H. Prince Abdullah Bin Abdul Aziz, and to the left H.R.H. Prince Sultan Bin Abdul Aziz.

Table 13.1   *Names of major Arab tribes in the Arabian Peninsula (arranged in alphabetical order)*

Ahmar	Rabiy'ah al Tihham	Awof
Asmar	Rabiy'ah Warfidah	Awazim
	Rabiy'ah at Yaman	Ayr
Barik	Rashaydah	
Bahr bin Sukayna	al Rayesh	Gamed
Baqum	Rigal al Ma'a	
Bili		Fodole
	Zubeid	Fahme
Tamin	Zahran	
	Zeid	Qahtan
Thaqif		Karne or Garne
Thamalah	Subel'a	Quraysh[1]
Thawab	Sa'd	
	Sufyan	Malek
Gahadlah	Su'kaynah	Malek Asir
Ga'afrah	Sahl	Muhammad
Go'dah		Marwan
Gohaynah	Shoubail	Masarehah
	Shararat	Motair
Harith	Shareef	Ma'a
Ho'rath	Shou'abah	Me'gyed
Harb	Shamran	Manaseer
Hasan	Shammar	Mongehah
Hala	Shehre	Mahdy
Howaytat	Shahran	Mosa
	Shalawah	Morrah
Khaled		
Kath'am	Salboh	Hager
Kotha'ah		Hotaym
Kidayr	Zufayer	Hothayl
Kamiseen		Helal
	Abse	
Doriab	Utaybah	Nogo'a
Da'Kaiyah	Ogman	Nashar
Dawasir	Aryan	Nomoor
	Asir	Nagran
Zabyan or Thabyan	Atayah	
	al Kam al Howl	Ya'la
Rabiy'ah	Amre	Yam
Rabiy'al Mokatirah	Anzah	

[1] Descendants of the Prophet Muhammad
Source: Hamza, *Qalb, Al-Jazira Al-Arabia*, pp 136–137 Author's transliteration

Table 13.2   *Names of major tribes in Saudi Arabia*

Belahmer	Kath'am	Kabilat al Ogman
Belasmer	Kotha'ah	Kabilat Harb
Ahle Bareg[q]	Kamiseen	Kabilat al Howaytat
Bahr bin Sukayna	Bano Kidayr	Ahle Hala
Baqum	Al-Aldorayeb	Thoo Hasan
Bili	D'akyah	Khaled
Bano Tamim	Dawasir	Shamran
Bano Thawa'h	Rabiy'ah	Bano Shehre
Thamalah	Rigal al Ma'a	Shahran
Thaqif	Al Rashaydah	Al Sha'lawah
Al Gahadlah	Al Raysh	Shammar
Al Ga'afrah	Zubeid	Al Selbeh
Go'dah	Zahran	Kabilat Twowayreg[q]
Gohaynah	Bano Zeid	Al Zufayer
Belhareth	Saby'a	Kabilat Anzah
Kabilat al Howaytat	Bano Sa'ad	Kabilat Utaybah
Asir	Sufyan	Kabilat Bani Atayah
Al Kam al Howle	Al Sahol	Al Awazim
Al Ashraf	Al Shararat	Bano Abse
Quraysh	Kabilat Fahme	Bano Shobayl
Bano Malek	Belgarn	Qahtan
Al Masarehah	Bano Malek Asir	Al Mahdy
Kabilat al Morrah	Bano Muhammad	Bano Marwan
Al Mongehah	Me'gyed	Kabilat Motayer
Al Nogo'a	Al Mosa	Al Manasir
Amre	Bano Nashar	Nagran
Kabilat Bani Hager	Bal'eyre	Al Nomoor
Hothayl	Kabilat Bani Hager	Gamid
	Helal	Hotaym
	Bano Ya'ly	Yam

Source: Hamza, *Qalb Al-Jazira Al-Arabia*, pp. 138–212 Author's transliteration

All Saudi Arabian citizens are Muslims and the vast majority of these are Sunni, subscribing to Wahhabite Unitarianism. As a distinct minority, there are the Shi'ites, who live mainly in the Eastern Province (especially at the Qatif-Sayhat-Safwu oasis and in Al-Hasa). Shi'ites represent about five per cent of the Saudi Arabian population. In recent years, the Kingdom has devoted very substantial resources to improving the lot of the Shi'ite minority.

13.2   Urbanization and nomadism

The development of the Kingdom's infrastructure and, in particular, its industrialization program, has had a predictable effect on old patterns of life.

In general,

> there has been a steady trend toward settlement on the part of nomads, who pass through semi-nomadic stages. There may be no more than 200,000 to 300,000 wholly nomadic bedouin in the Kingdom of Saudi Arabia out of a total population of six to seven million. . .
>
> *Source: Area Handbook for Saudi Arabia* (Washington DC: US Government Printing Office, 1971)

Perhaps five per cent of the Saudi population are wholly nomadic today.

As to native residents of cities, towns and villages, little can be said, except that the population of Saudi Arabia is ethnically homogeneous. The most conspicuous difference is that of dialect, by which one can distinguish whether a person is from the Western Province (the Holy Cities of Makkah and Medina, or Jeddah) or from the Central or Eastern Provinces (Riyadh, Dammam, or Al-Hasa).

In recent times the trend has been towards further urbanization and away from nomadism, a trend encouraged by the government.

13.3   Age distribution of the Kingdom's population

It is estimated that more than half of the population of the Kingdom of Saudi Arabia are under twenty years of age. Although no official population growth rates are available, it is believed that in 1978 the rate was around two per cent.

13.4   Geographical distribution of population

Population is concentrated not only in the major cities of the Kingdom but in approximately parallel north-south bands down the middle of the Peninsula. The map on page 204 indicates this distribution. The first band includes the cities of Hijaz and the settled agricultural areas of Asir and Hijaz oases. The second comprises the belt of oases in the Tuwaiq escarpment area. The third includes the Al-Hasa (Hofuf and environs) oases, which had a total population in the late 1970s of about 160,000, and the oases and towns in the Arabian Gulf coastal plain, of which the agricultural center of Qatif, the administrative capital of Dammam, and the Aramco headquarters of Dhahran are the most important.

13.5   Foreign manpower

The third stratum of population raises an issue of considerable significance to the future of the country: foreign manpower, the minority ethnic groups. These groups

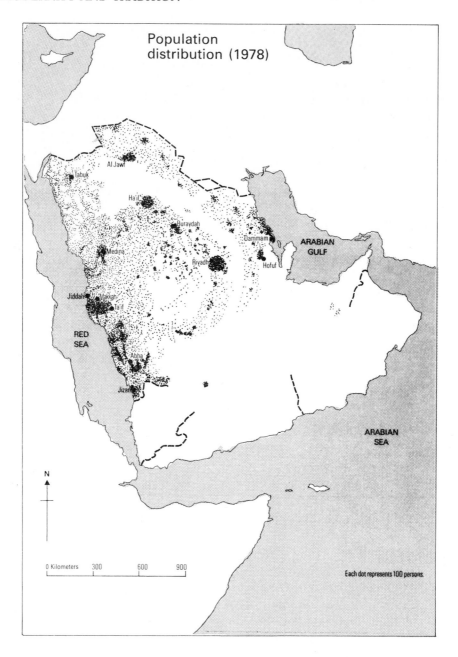

Population distribution (1978)

Source: Saudi Arabia – A Case Study in Development, Kegan Paul International, 1986

can be divided into Arabic and non-Arabic speaking people. Any review of the numbers of these expatriates during the past two decades reveals a significant increase, followed by a substantial decline. In 1962–63 the Saudi Ministry of Finance and National Economy sponsored a census, limited to the five largest cities of the country, which revealed that the foreign population of those cities comprised from fifteen to 35 per cent of the total number of residents and about 30 per cent of the owners and employers of businesses and service establishments. The tremendous wealth of the nation at the beginning of the 1970s, along with the critical and crucial need for foreign manpower, contributed to a significant increase in the number of aliens working in Saudi Arabia. The Second Five Year Plan (1975–80) projected a further increase in imported foreign manpower.

The implementation of this Plan was basically contingent upon the increase of both Saudi and non-Saudi manpower through the following five years. The Plan's goal was to increase "the Saudi work force from 1,236,000 to 1,518,000, while the non-Saudi work force would more than double – from 314,000 to 812,000". The increase of Saudi manpower would require more time for reaching its optimum capacity. Training and educating Saudis in the various fields of industrial technology according to the plan would need about ten years. The focus was therefore on foreign manpower to satisfy the immediate and foreseeable industrial needs of the Kingdom.

Besides importing this urgently needed foreign manpower from the Arab and Muslim world, Saudi Arabia sought a labor force from the Western countries as well as from Asia and, in later years, from North Africa. The manpower of the countries of North Africa was doubly useful. These were Western-trained workers who speak Arabic, so there was no communication barrier at the lower level of the industrial base. *Al-Hawadith* of Beirut, Lebanon, stated that "the Kingdom of Saudi Arabia has declared its need of a quarter of a million workers in addition to various kinds of experts". The British *Daily Telegraph* indicated that the shortage of manpower in the Arabian states forced those who were in charge of planning in Saudi Arabia to turn towards North African workers, among whom unemployment was increasing.

The then Saudi Central Planning Organization (which sought the aid of the International Bank to help it in studying its labor force needs) estimated that between 180,000 and 250,000 skilled and semi-skilled workers were needed for the Second Five Year Plan. Dr Fayz Badr, the then Vice President of the CPO, hoped that Saudi Arabia might acquire those "guest workers" from Morocco and Algeria, where a large number of expert laborers with experience of European industry existed. And a plan was made to draw up contracts with those workers through an international advisory consultative company specializing in labor affairs.

Table 13.3 indicates the volume of foreign manpower in Saudi Arabia in 1973/74 as well as the nationality of the groups constituting this foreign labor force. Table 13.4 shows the number of dependents of foreign manpower in Saudi Arabia during the same period.

Examination of Table 13.3 reveals that foreign manpower in Saudi Arabia in

Table 13.3 *Foreign manpower in Saudi Arabia, 1973–74*

(Workers only; not dependants)

Country of nationality	1973AD 1393AH	1974 1394	Increase/ decrease 74/73	1978 1398	Increase/ decrease 78/74
Afghanistan	88	51	−37	1,037	+986
Algeria	62	140	+78	297	+157
Argentina	0	1	+1	86	+63
Austria	0	0	0	225	+225
Australia	0	0	0	236	+236
Bahrain	1	1	0	0	−1
Bangladesh	0	0	0	2,319	+2,319
Belgium	37	57	+20	733	+676
Barbados	0	0	0	2	+2
Bolivia	0	0	0	1	+1
Burundi	2	3	+1	0	−3
Brazil	6	4	−2	166	+162
Britain	4,493	5,002	+509	12,139	+7,137
Burma	12	151	+139	6	−145
Cambodia	1	1	0	0	−1
Cameroon	13	7	−6	11	+4
Canada	163	179	+16	1,451	+1,272
Ceylon	24	21	−3	2,777	+2,756
Chad	19	77	+58	219	+142
Chile	1	10	+9	5	−5
China (Taiwan)	73	193	+122	4,629	+4,436
Columbia	0	0	0	24	+24
Costa Rica	0	0	0	4	+4
Cyprus	46	72	+26	1,062	+990
Dahomey	10	4	−6		−4
Denmark	27	44	+17	359	+315
Dominican R.	0			2	+2
Ecuador	0	1	+1	6	+5
El Salvador	0	0	0	136	+136
Egypt	17,491	23,086	+5,595	92,956	+69,870
Eritrea	3		−3	3,753	+3,753
Ethiopia	619	1,318	+699	1,295	−23
Fiji	1	0	−1	0	0
Finland	17	8	−9	330	+322
France	454	532	+78	2,980	2,448
Gambia	4	1	−3	0	−1
Germany (F.R.)	558	723	+165	4,333	+3,610
Ghana	16	10	−6	38	+28
Greece	240	359	+119	3,228	+2,869
Guinea	2	2	0	15	+13
Guyana	3	4	+1	0	−4
Holland	271	183	−88	1,959	+1,776
Hong Kong		2	+2	10	+8
Hungary	7		−7	0	0
India	1,130	1,912	+782	32,842	+30,930

Table 13.3–cont.

Country of nationality	1973AD 1393AH	1974 1394	Increase/ decrease 74/73	1978 1398	Increase/ decrease 78/74
Indonesia	251	383	+132	3,326	+2,943
Iran	110	120	+10	414	+294
Iraq	782	919	+137	898	−21
Ireland	60	76	+16	204	+128
Italy	531	733	+202	7,206	+6,473
Ivory Coast	0	0	0	4	+4
Jamaica	0	1	+1	3	+2
Japan	612	405	−207	1,833	+1,428
Jordan	12,199	15,211	+3,012	14,036	−1,175
Kenya	16	35	+19	263	+228
Lebanon	2,784	3,683	+899	18,396	+14,713
Liberia	0	2	+2	1	−1
Libya	0	2	+2	4	+2
Malagasy R.	1	0	−1	1	+1
Mali	37	78	+41	43	−35
Maldive Islands	2	4	+2	0	−4
Malta	7	20	+13	57	+37
Malaysia	0	0	0	622	+622
Mauritania	50	42	−8	64	+22
Mauritius	0	3	+3	1	0
Mexico	0	1	+1	3	+2
Morocco	62	48	−14	1,188	+1,140
Nepal	0	1	+1	0	−1
New Zealand	23	22	−1	62	+40
Niger	12	19	+7	289	+270
Nigeria	40	47	+7	341	+294
N. Korea	0	29	+29	0	−29
Norway	0	0	0	104	+104
Oman	32	39	+7	5	−34
Pakistan	5,401	8,884	+3,483	59,400	+50,516
Palestine	5,723	8,541	+2,818	3,570	−4,971
Panama	0	0	0	1	+1
Peru	1	1	0	1	0
Philippines	363	206	−157	16,672	+16,466
Poland	0	1	+1	3	+2
Portugal	5	1	−4	1,965	+1,964
Qatar	1	2	+1	0	−2
Rwanda	1	3	+2	0	−3
Senegal	15	13	−2	84	+71
Sierra Leone	5	4	−1	38	+34
Singapore	3	6	+3	497	+491
Somalia	228	743	+515	2,542	+1,799
S. Africa	30	22	−8	53	+31
S.W. Africa	0	0	0	10	+10
S. Korea	8	277	+269	41,035	+40,758
Spain	25	15	−10	327	+312
Sudan	n/a	n/a	n/a	12,933	
Sweden	54	145	+91	641	+496
Syria	3,991	5,599	+1,608	20,878	+15,279

Table 13.3–cont.

Country of nationality	1973AD 1393AH	1974 1394	Increase/ decrease 74/73	1978 1398	Increase/ decrease 78/74
Switzerland	n/a	n/a	n/a	1,098	
Tanzania	12	11	−1	35	+24
Thailand	59	52	−7	13,159	+13,107
Togoland	3	4	+1	0	+4
Trinidad	1	1	0	7	+6
Tunisia	85	170	+85	354	+184
Turkey	231	235	+4	7,404	+7,169
Uganda	7	14	+7	10	−4
U.A.E.	5		−5	1	+1
Upper Volta	16	11	−5	7	−4
Uruguay	0	0	0	38	+38
U.S.A.	2,552	4,319	+1,767	14,701	+10,382
Vietnam	53	2	−51	0	−2
Venezuela	0	0	0	3	+3
W. Somalia	0	0	0	95	+95
N. Yemen	62,091	90,006	+27,915	66,988	−23,008
S. Yemen	6,573	7,077	+504	3,092	−3,985
Yugoslavia	0	0	0	7	+7
Zaire	0	0	0	9	+9
Unknown or Non-Nationality	3	20	+17		
Totals	131,050	182,449	+51,339	488,685	+306,236

Source: Figures for 1978 derived from completed data sheets supplied to the author through the courtesy of the Deputy Minister of Interior (Passport and Immigration Affairs) Government of Saudi Arabia, June 1979

1973/74 increased significantly. Of 100 different foreign and ethnic minorities, only 36 showed a decrease; most of the other 64 showed significant increases.

> Among most developing countries data on the labor force are limited and of poor quality . . . Furthermore, it would be inappropriate to criticize strongly the data base for the region [of the Gulf area] because, for any country, developing a reliable systematic data collection system is expensive and requires years of effort. Moreover [it is quite true to assert that] the rationale for such a system has until recent times been lacking.
>
> *Source: Demographic Changes in Iran, Pakistan and the Gulf Area with Particular Emphasis on the Developing Labor Force Need,* by Lee L Bean, (Unpublished paper submitted to the International Conference on Islam, Pakistan and Iran and the Gulf States, Bellagio, 1986)

Since there were no official figures available from the Ministry of Labor and Social Affairs, it seemed that the best way of calculating the foreign labor force was

Table 13.4   *Dependants of foreign manpower in Saudi Arabia, 1973–74*

	1973	1974	Increase or decrease 1974 over 1973
Workers	131,148	182,505	+51,357
Dependants	66,124	97,872	+31,748
Total	197,272	280,377	+83,105

Source: Figures for 1973 and 1974 derived from handwritten data supplied to the author through the courtesy of the Deputy Minister of Interior (passport and immigration affairs) Government of Saudi Arabia, in an interview in Riyadh, June 1975 (SF translations)

to obtain the figures for aliens residing in Saudi Arabia during 1973 and 1974. The figures in these tables were for aliens granted annually renewable residence permits. Arab Muslims and non-Arab Muslims, along with Christian Arab workers, were those most needed to carry out the Kingdom's development needs. Manpower from the Western world was needed for its technical know-how and efficiency. The figures in both categories show an increase in 1974 over 1973. The inflow of Western manpower increased steadily over the years immediately following the country's Second Five Year Plan.

The categories of professional foreign manpower also showed an increase in the Arab Muslim and non-Arab Muslim labor force. The increase in Egyptian manpower in 1974 was almost 40 per cent over that of 1973. This reflected an impressive undertaking in the educational system of the Kingdom, since most of these Egyptians worked as teachers at all levels of the system.

The high increase in Lebanese, Syrian and Palestinian manpower indicated the growth in trade and business. The third, and most important, element was the increase in the inflow of American, British, French, Italian, Swedish and Nationalist Chinese manpower in 1974 over that of 1973. These groups, to which have to be added a very substantial Korean element, represented a potential factor in the development of Saudi Arabia at the highest industrial, technical and commercial level. Indeed, the increase or decrease of this foreign labor force was seen as a good index of the economic development of the Kingdom.

In spite of the critical need for more foreign manpower in order to achieve the objectives and projects of the Second Five Year Plan, the ratio of foreign manpower to the total population of the country had to be kept at a certain level which, for all practical purposes, required that it should not exceed one-fifth of the total population of the nation – that is, 1.25 million workers. While it is true that Saudi Arabia was not confronted with the problem the United Arab Emirates was experiencing, of its citizens possibly becoming a minority within their own country, a carefully thought-out manpower policy was certainly required.

The most crucial problem arising from this massive need for foreign manpower was the social impact which such an alien labor force might have on the country.

Too many foreigners with their own alien customs and way of life could have disturbed the existing unique Islamic social pattern of the Kingdom. Despite the fact that most foreign workers were and are drawn from the Islamic countries, there was no precedent in history for the idea that a commonly shared creed – Islam – would suffice to prevent or delay rapid social change. Ralph Braibanti's assertion that "[occasionally] advisers and other agents of change from similar cultures are less respectful of the indigenous context in which they work than are foreigners from a totally different society" underlined the need for concern.

The problem of the effect of alien customs and habits on the country's social mores posed a critical challenge for the future. Over the previous two decades there had always been a foreign labor force residing in Saudi Arabia, but the issue was never raised. The situation in the mid-1970s did not involve a small foreign community, as it had done in the past; it arose from the need for a huge foreign labor force over the next decade. At the most conservative estimate, the figure would reach a million; but if dependents were included, it would be much higher. Saudi Arabia was indeed confronted with a critical dilemma: whether to strive for this crucially needed foreign manpower in order to carry out developmental projects essential to future prosperity, or to curtail the inflow of foreign laborers in order to safeguard a social system based on "orthodox" Islam.

Undoubtedly, this was the most grave choice which the country had to face. Concern over the adverse social impact which the massive foreign labor force could have on Saudi Islamic society might justify a recommendation to slow down the country's urgently needed developmental projects. On the other hand, future prosperity was largely dependent upon rapid implementation of the Second Five Year Plan. The enormous wealth of Saudi Arabia derived totally from a depletable natural resource – petroleum. All the existing signs, such as the trend towards conserving energy, and the industrialized world's vigorous efforts to develop other sources of petroleum or alternative sources of energy, suggested that Saudi Arabia had only until the turn of the century to develop a new industrial and economic base, not entirely dependent upon petroleum. It was an awesome task, to be completed within a relatively short period of time.

The second alternative therefore seemed preferable; namely, the rapid and sound industrialization of the country, even if an excessive influx of foreign manpower was required.

This decision should, by no means, be construed as acceptance of the unwanted, anticipated social change which might have occurred as a result. On the contrary, the problem was treated with great urgency by the Saudi planners.

It was not possible to prescribe an exact formula for solving this critical problem. But an important factor which helped to minimize the impact of alien social customs and norms was that once the purpose of each individual or group had been accomplished their services would be terminated. In other words, there would be a pre-designed policy for their dispersal rather than allowing them to settle permanently in the country.

Another recommendation was the maintenance of a fixed and balanced ratio between the inflow of foreign manpower and the total population. This would serve to control leverage against the spread of alien social norms, and thus help the Kingdom to preserve its existing way of life.

Perhaps the final answer lay in the resilience and strength of the Saudi ethos. Saudis were able to accept, absorb and perceive the necessary measures for the development of their country without losing their enormous pride in a truly distinctive Islamic social order.

With the completion of the Third Development Plan, the awesome task of building the Kingdom's infrastructure was more or less completed and the requirement for foreign manpower began to diminish. The period covered by the Fourth Development Plan has seen a further reduction in the need for foreign manpower, while development of the indigenous workforce has been sustained, thus greatly diminishing the problems posed by the importation of a massive foreign labor force.

The following figures give an indication of the reduction in the Kingdom's reliance on foreign workers in more recent years. They show the number of residence permits issued to foreigners in the years 1403 to 1407 AH (1983 to 1987).

Year AH	Number of residence permits issued to foreigners
1403	819,613
1404	950,726
1405	802,859
1406	563,747
1407	591,261

It is an extraordinary tribute to the self-confidence and resilience of Saudi society that it has been able to face the challenges posed by such a large, albeit temporary, immigration – without any weakening of its religious, moral and social convictions.

14

Infrastructure

Throughout preceding chapters of this book there has been frequent mention of the building of the Kingdom's infrastructure. Indeed, it is certainly true that the first three Development Plans concentrated most of the government's energy and most of the Kingdom's resources on the infrastructure program.

This chapter therefore sets out to describe the main areas of infrastructure development, giving key facts and statistics as an indicator of the magnitude of the task the Saudi Arabian government undertook and as a measure of its achievement.

Sections of this chapter will look at the Kingdom's infrastructure under three broad headings:

- transportation
- post and telecommunications
- electricity

14.1 Transportation

In this section, we look at all the features of transportation of people and goods in the Kingdom – roads, railways, air and sea. We include a brief section on overall transportation strategy.

The statistics on each aspect of transportation give further evidence of the speed with which the infrastructure of the Kingdom has been built to meet the demands of the Kingdom's development plans in the industrial and agricultural sectors of the economy.

14.1.1 ROADS

The Ministry of Communications, which is responsible for the Kingdom's road network, has played a crucial role in the successful implementation of the Kingdom's economic development.

THE HIGHWAY NETWORK OF SAUDI ARABIA, 1980

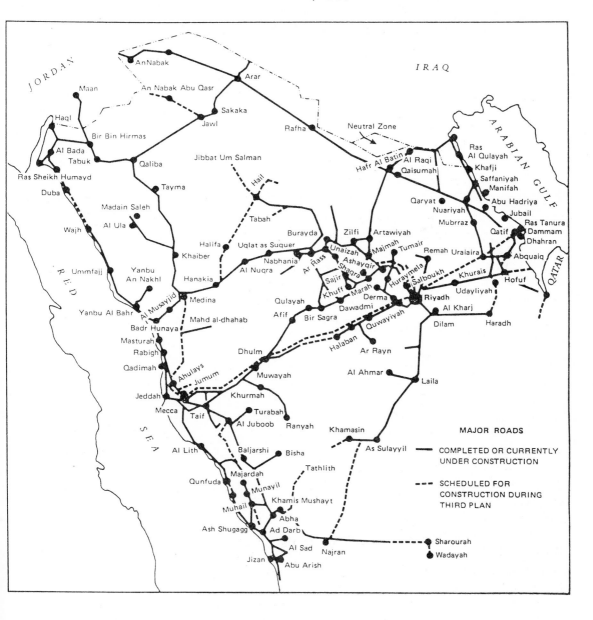

Source: Summary of Saudi Arabian Five Year Development Plan 1980–1985

During the first [development] plan 1390–1395 AH (1970–1975), most of the districts and main cities were linked by a network of paved roads. By the end of this plan 1,219 km of asphalt roads and 8,510 km of agricultural roads had been built.

With the second development plan 1395–1400 AH (1975–1980), the major projects were completed. The total length of paved roads had grown to 21,583 km and agricultural roads had increased to 24,186 km. Most of the Kingdom's districts were now connected by a modern road network.

By the end of the third development plan in 1405 AH (1985), the Kingdom had 29,655 km of paved highways. Agricultural roads had been increased to 50,655 km.

The fourth development plan has a target of increasing the road network in the Kingdom to 116,000 km which will include 35,000 km of paved highways (primary, secondary and feeder roads) and 81,000 of agricultural roads.

Source: Transport and Communications in the Kingdom of Saudi Arabia, published by the Ministry of Communications, 1986

With the massive increase in traffic that has ensued from the Kingdom's industrial and agricultural development, it has been necessary to upgrade many of the inter-city roads to expressways, with anything up to eight lanes for traffic. The cities too have become congested by the growth in traffic and a number of cities now enjoy the benefits of modern ring-roads which serve to speed vehicles on their way and reduce congestion and pollution in city centers.

A further development is the construction of networks of over- and under-passes within the cities which again serve to facilitate driving in city centers.

While a major effort has been devoted to inter-city and in-city road-building, agricultural communities have not been neglected. Even isolated villages are now connected by road to the main road network, so that the Kingdom can now boast a fully integrated, modern, nationwide network of roads.

The climate and the terrain of the Kingdom is inimical to road-building. Burning hot deserts and high mountain ranges each pose different but equally challenging problems for contractors. Nowhere were these problems more intimidating than in the south-west of the Kingdom, where mountain ranges soar to 3,000 meters. A series of projects, involving the construction of magnificent viaducts, has been undertaken so that even the more inaccessible parts of the Kingdom in this region may now be reached by road.

Probably the most spectacular road construction project of all has been the building of the Bahrain Causeway, connecting the Saudi Arabian mainland with the island of Bahrain. Building works, financed entirely by the Kingdom of Saudi Arabia, were completed in 1986 and the Causeway was opened to traffic at the end of that year.

SAPTCO inter-city bus services

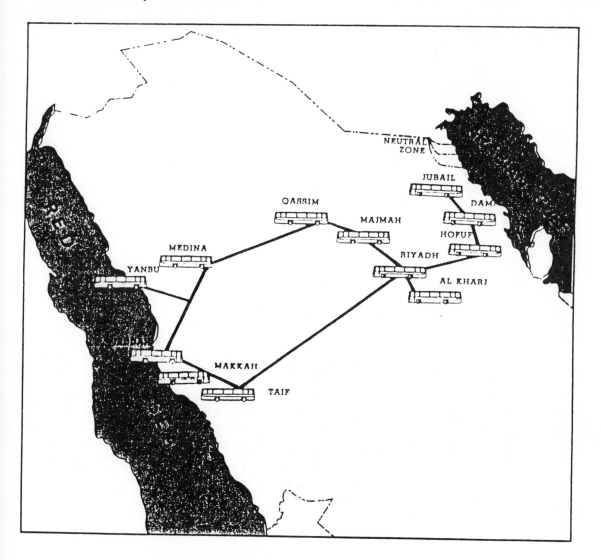

Source: Fourth Development Plan (1985–1990)

Table 14.1 *Progress of road construction 1397/98 AH to 1406/07 AH (1977/78–1986/87)*

Year	Main roads			Agricultural roads		
	Completed in the year	Total	Index 1977/78 = 100	Completed in the year	Total	Index 1977/78 = 100
	(kilometers)			(kilometers)		
1977/78	2,162	17,200	100.0	3,641	16,948	100.0
1978/79	1,700	18,900	109.9	3,171	20,119	118.7
1979/80	1,338	20,238	117.7	4,076	24,186	142.7
1980/81	916	21,154	123.0	4,401	28,587	168.7
1981/82	990	21,926	127.5	4,332	33,310	196.5
1982/83	1,827	23,753	138.1	5,334	38,644	228.0
1983/84	1,717	25,470	148.1	8,192	46,836	276.4
1984/85	1,667	27,137	157.8	5,390	52,226	308.2
1985/86	968	28,105	163.4	5,276	57,502	339.3
1986/87	778	28,883	167.9	4,006	61,508	362.9

Source: Central Department of Statistics, 1987

With the building of the road network, it became possible to expand the public transport services. In 1399 AH (1979), the Saudi Public Transport Company (SAPTCO) was established. From small beginnings, SAPTCO has grown into a national bus service, providing cheap public transport within and between major population centers. SAPTCO's services continue to expand as it increases the size of its fleet and upgrades the quality of its vehicles. Each year, SAPTCO faces and meets a particular challenge when pilgrims arrive from all over the Kingdom and from all over the world to perform the annual pilgrimage to the Holy Cities of Makkah and Medina.

14.1.2 RAILWAYS

Railways remain the least developed means of transportation in the Kingdom. With such vast distances to cover, in often adverse environmental conditions, it is inevitable that airline services seem to be a more practical mode of transportation to a country undertaking a major development program in the second half of the twentieth century.

The Kingdom's railways currently consist primarily of a single track, standard-gauge line, running for 570 km from Riyadh to Dammam in the Eastern Province. This line, which was opened in 1951, passes through Dhahran, Abqaiq, Hofuf, Harad and al-Kharj and has benefited from substantial renovation in recent years. An additional line joining Hofuf with Riyadh was opened in 1985.

Chart XIVa   *Development of the road network in Saudi Arabia: 1951–85*

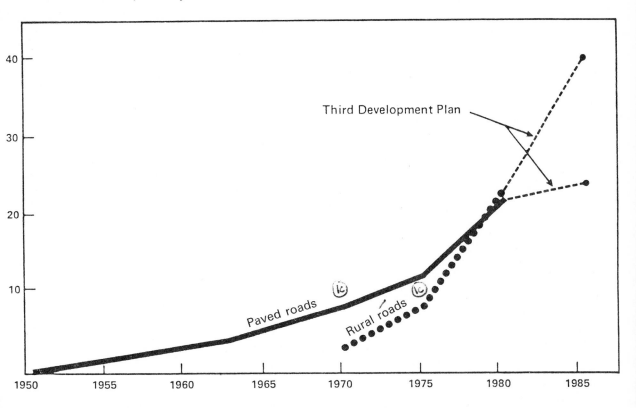

The Kingdom's railways are managed by the Saudi Arabian Railway Corporation (now the Saudi Government Railroad Organization), established in 1396 AH (1966 AD), as an independent public utility, governed by a board of directors.

Of particular interest is a project currently under consideration. According to the Fifth Development Plan (1990–95):

> The Ministry of Communications is studying the feasibility of reviving the Hijaz Railway which at one time linked the Kingdom with Syria and Jordan. One major benefit of the line would be its service to pilgrims wishing to visit the Holy Places. However, it is hoped that international connections to Iraq, the Lebanon and Europe will be arranged to make the line economically viable.

The original Hijaz railway was built between 1900 and 1908 and was primarily intended by its sponsors, the Turks, as a means of transporting their troops and supplies to Medina. The railway, always bedevilled by maintenance problems and attacks by Bedouin who saw it as a threat to their trade of supplying camels to

Table 14.2   *Railway passenger traffic 1398–1407 AH (1978–87)*

Year AH	Ton/Kilometer		Passengers/Kilometer	
	Million	*Index* 1398 = 100	*Million*	*Index* 1398 = 100
1398 (1978)	148.7	100.0	63.4	100.0
1399 (1979)	210.0	141.2	74.2	117.0
1400 (1980)	261.0	175.5	82.0	129.3
1404 (1981)	272.1	183.0	95.8	151.1
1402 (1982)	393.8	264.2	104.6	165.0
1403 (1983)	194.3	130.7	86.8	137.0
1404 (1984)	525.0	353.1	78.5	123.8
1405 (1985)	415.2	279.2	71.6	112.9
1406 (1986)	321.1	215.9	70.7	111.5
1407 (1987)	491.2	330.3	81.4	128.4

Source: Saudi Government Railroad Organization, 1987

pilgrims, was finally closed by the determined attacks of T E Lawrence and his men in 1917.

Chart XIVb   *Saudi Government Railroad Organization passenger traffic 1400–10 AH (1980–90)*

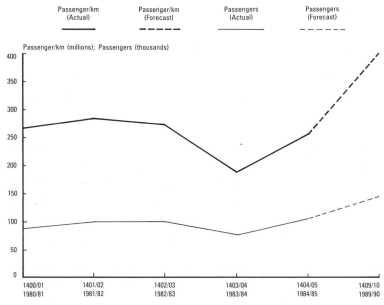

Source: Fourth Development Plan

Chart XIVc *Saudi Government Railroad Organization freight transport 1400–10 AH (1980–90)*

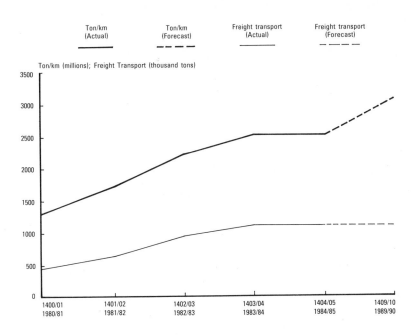

Source: Fourth Development Plan

14.1.3   AIR TRANSPORT

Civil aviation occupies a special place in any account of the Kingdom's transportation systems.

In 1364 AH (1945), Franklin D Roosevelt, President of the United States of America, presented a DC-3 Dakota to the late King Abdul Aziz. Quick to realize the contribution that air travel could make to the development of the Kingdom, the King promptly ordered two more planes.

These three planes formed the embryo of what has grown into Saudia, the Kingdom's flag carrier, and now one of the world's leading airlines – an airline which has in its fleet today more than 100 aircraft (including a number of Boeing 747s, Tristars and Airbuses), which carried 10.5 million passengers and 187,000 tons of cargo in 1986, and which continues to expand to meet increasing demand.

The Kingdom has three international airports. In 1981, the late King Khaled opened the King Abdul Aziz International Airport in Jeddah. This airport, which has special facilities for handling the annual influx of pilgrims performing *Hajj*, has a land area of 105 square kilometers.

The King Khaled International Airport was opened in 1983. Located 35 kilometers north of Riyadh, with a land area of 225 square kilometers, the King Khaled International Airport is a masterpiece of modern architecture, blending traditional Arab design with the requirements of efficiency, and incorporating into the whole the essential Islamic character of the Kingdom. It has four terminals and, from its inauguration, had the capacity to handle 7.5 million passengers a year. By the year 2000, its capacity will have been doubled.

The third international airport, the King Fahd International Airport, is at Dhahran and is currently under construction. This airport, scheduled to begin operations in 1990, will replace the existing international airport in the Eastern Province.

In addition to the construction of these three international airports, domestic airports are being systematically expanded.

Civil aviation has grown in parallel with the Kingdom's ambitious development plans. Its advantage over road and rail, in terms of speed for users, has made it the transportation mode of choice and its contribution to the Kingdom's successful progress cannot be over-estimated.

Of its history, Saudia makes the following proud claims:

> The airline has played a vital role in the development of the country. Well before the Kingdom's road network was built, Saudia made possible access to the most remote areas of the country, providing a network of transport and communication that was essential for the development of commerce and industry, education, health care and other urban amenities.
>
> Internationally, Saudia has also played an important role in the Kingdom's development. Within two years of its founding, Saudia began operations outside the Kingdom. Within the space of a little more than a decade, it became the region's largest airline. Today, with over 10 million passengers carried each year and an international network linking 50 cities on four continents, Saudia is one of the world's major airlines and ranks 15th among the 165 member airlines of the International Air Transport Association (IATA)

And Saudia is determined to maintain and enhance its position in terms of advanced technology and the highest standards of service.

> In the field of technical services, Saudia's capabilities meet the highest international standards. It has implemented several programmes to enhance fleet reliability, to improve the quality of services, to generate

Table 14.3   *Passengers and cargo traffic on all Saudi airlines 1986*

Items	Outgoing	Incoming
Foreign airports		
Passengers	1,732,488	1,737,729
Cargo (kg)	91,421,291	29,984,960
Domestic airports		
Passengers	8,618,571	8,613,105
Cargo (kg)	76,324,903	137,774,177
Total		
Passengers	10,351,059	10,350,834
Cargo (kg)	167,746,194	167,759,137

Source: Saudi Airlines

more revenues from the technical support services offered to other international carriers, and to develop the technical skills of its staff.

Saudia's Communications Division is constantly developing its systems, equipment and quality of services, and has invested heavily to improve all areas of its communications network, now one of the most advanced telecommunications systems in the world. Aircraft flying in Saudia's network around the globe can keep in touch with the communication base in Jeddah, and communicate with any telephone subscriber anywhere in the world.

It is surely true that Saudia has played a key role in facilitating the Kingdom's rapid development.

14.1.4   SHIPPING AND PORTS

The Kingdom has five major commercial ports and two major industrial ports. The commercial ports are at Jeddah, Dammam, Jizan, Jubail and Yanbu. The industrial ports are the King Fahd Industrial Port at Jubail and the King Fahd Industrial Port at Yanbu. There is also the oil port of Ras Tanura, as well as a number of minor ports.

To indicate the total growth pattern in terms of number of berths, handling capacity and volume of import cargo unloaded at all these ports, we provide the following table, derived from data supplied by the Central Department of Statistics and the Saudi Ports Authority:

Year	Number of berths	Handling capacity (000 tons)	Volume of import cargo unloaded (000 tons)
1975	27	6,102	6,084
1976	39	10,629	10,570
1977	53	17,850	16,415
1978	75	21,530	19,879
1979	95	31,100	25,477
1980	101	37,800	28,564
1981	113	41,300	33,351
1982	137	46,700	41,427
1983	159	48,800	49,398
1984	159	48,800	57,227
1985	168	52,000	52,055
1986	168	52,000	59,631
1987	174	52,000	69,617

The Jeddah Islamic Port is the busiest of all the Kingdom's ports. It is the principal commercial port and the main port of entry for pilgrims on their way to the Holy Cities of Makkah and Medina. In 1975, Jeddah imported 2,811,000 tons which represented almost half of all imports to the Kingdom in that year. In 1984, the volume of imports reached a peak of 20,762,000 tons. In 1987, Jeddah was visited by a total of 5,341 ships and imported 14,935,000 tons. This represented 21% of all imports by weight to the Kingdom in that year.

The King Abdul Aziz Port at Dammam ranks second to Jeddah as a commercial port. Like Jeddah it boasts a fully-equipped repair yard. In 1975, Dammam imported 2,486,000 tons (approximately 40% of the total entering the Kingdom that year). Imports through Dammam reached a peak of 14,515,000 tons in 1982. In 1987, Dammam was visited by a total of 3,288 ships and imported 7,322,000 tons (10.5% of total imports in that year).

The commercial port at Jizan, which is the main port in the south of the country, imported 100,000 tons in 1975. The import figure reached a peak in 1983 (1,724,000 tons), reducing to 722,000 tons in 1987. In 1987, Jizan port was visited by 122 ships.

The Jubail commercial port imported 849,000 tons in 1978, reaching a peak of 2,199,000 tons in 1985. In 1987, the commercial port at Jubail imported 1,612,000 tons.

The commercial port at Yanbu imported 687,000 tons in 1975. Imports peaked at 2,874,000 tons in 1984. Then, after a sharp fall in 1985, imports began to rise again in 1986. The import figure for 1987 was 2,505,000 tons.

These figures indicate the Kingdom's enormous appetite for imports during its major developmental phase, with peaks being reached in the period 1982 through 1984/5.

The industrial cities of Jubail and Yanbu are still undergoing development and the import figures for the industrial ports (as distinct from the commercial ports located in those cities) testify to the continuing requirement there for large volumes of imports. In 1987, King Fahd Industrial Port at Jubail imported 19,294,000 tons: and King Fahd Industrial Port at Yanbu imported 23,227,000 tons.

Before leaving the subject of shipping, we should note the very substantial increase in tonnage of Saudi Arabia's national commercial fleet. In 1379 AH (1979), the fleet carried 530,000 tons in 70 ships. This had increased to 3,250,000 tons carried in 166 ships by 1402 AH (1981). By 1404 AH (1984), the total tonnage carried was 5,597,000, accommodated within a fleet of 372 ships.

14.1.5 TRANSPORTATION STRATEGY

The process of national planning gives the Kingdom a mechanism through which an integrated transportation strategy can be developed. The Fourth Development Plan (1405–10 AH: 1985–90) set out a series of programs for all aspects of transportation. It identified as a key issue "the need for greater co-ordination of investment in roads, railroads and domestic air transport in order to avoid over investment".

For the roads, following completion of the main road network, it defined a road construction program, concentrating mainly on secondary roads. It provided for the intimidating task of maintaining and improving the established road network. And it specified a program of transportation research which included a study of ways in which road safety could be improved.

For the railways, the plan envisaged the upgrading of existing facilities, including rolling stock, together with training programmes for staff and the commissioning of studies to improve efficiency.

For air transport, it defined "financial self-sufficiency" as a key issue and placed emphasis on "cost control and operational changes in response to changes in demand", in order to achieve further improvements in financial performance.

For the sea ports, the plan recognized that lower volumes of imports were to be expected and focused on the rationalization of cargo handling. Other features of the plan concerned training of port personnel and safety improvement programs.

14.2 Post and telecommunications

Of all the indicators of social and economic progress in a modern society, probably the most obvious is the development of postal and telecommunication services. Certainly, efficient communications are a prerequisite of success. This section looks at the Saudi Arabian telephone service, the postal service and the telex service, together with other telecommunications media.

Table 14.4 *Transport sector program expenditure under the Fourth Development Plan 1405–10 AH (1985–90)*

	Total expenditure (SR million)
Presidency of Civil Aviation	
Operation and Maintenance Improvement	8,759.2
Air Traffic Safety	3,323.9
Airport Development	2,608.3
Administrative Efficiency Improvement	1,566.6
Training	859.6
New Airports	4,547.5
Sub-total	**21,665.1**
(Expected Revenues)	(2,768.0)
Saudia	
Operating Revenue	43,058.0
Operating Expenditure	42,922.0
Operating Profit	136.0
Depreciation	3,802.0
Total Financing Resources	3,938.0
less loan repayment	(5,224.0)
Surplus (deficit)	(1,286.0)
Government Subsidy required	1,291.0
Ministry of Communications (Roads)	
Main Road Development	8,386.3
Secondary and Feeder Road Development	2,013.0
Rural Road Development	2,397.4
Settlement of Completed Projects	1,917.0
Operation and Maintenance	2,849.8
Administrative Efficiency	1,659.1
Technical and Economic Studies	61.5
Sub-total	**19,284.1**
(Expected Revenues)	(131.0)
Deputy Ministry for Transport Affairs	
SAPTCO Development	1,496.0
Land Transport Development and Performance Monitoring	12.0
Saudi Maritime Development	9.0
Transport Research, Development, Training	7.0
Transport Safety Improvement	5.0
Hajj Transport Improvement	5.0
Sub-total	**1,534.0**

Table 14.4–cont.

	Total expenditure (SR million)
Saudi Ports Authority	
Major Port Development	2,152.3
Marine Transport Safety Improvement	137.1
Minor Port Development	186.0
Training	75.3
Management, Operation and Maintenance*	6,413.8
Sub-total	**8,964.5**
(Expected Revenues)	(6,653)
Saudi Government Railroad Organization	
Management, Operation and Matinenance**	1,126.8
Track	643.7
Rolling Stock and Equipment	168.9
Maintenance Improvement	77.0
Riyadh Dry Port Development	57.0
Manpower Training	21.0
Studies	18.0
Sub-total	**2,112.4**
(Expected Revenues)	(551.5)

* Funded from revenues
** Partly funded from revenues
Source: Fourth Development Plan (1985–90)

14.2.1 TELEPHONE SERVICE

King Abdul Aziz was well aware that an efficient telecommunications system was essential to his plans for consolidating and developing the Kingdom and it was during his reign (in 1930) that the first telephone exchange was installed in Al-Dira.

In 1953 the Ministry of Communications was formed, and amongst its responsibilities were post and telecommunications. Within a year, the Saudi Arabian Radio Telecommunication Scheme RT-1 was installed, providing a multi-channel telephone and telegraph network, linking Riyadh, Dammam, Jeddah, the Holy Cities of Makkah and Medina, and Taif.

In 1977, the Ministry of Post, Telegraphs and Telephones (which had taken over PTT responsibilities from the Ministry of Communications) embarked upon an ambitious plan to establish a modern telecommunications network, comprising telephone, telegraph and telex services for the entire Kingdom. The Ministry's achievements have been remarkable by any yardstick. To give some perspective to the magnitude of this achievement, we set out below a table showing the telephone exchange capacity and the number of telephones operating between 1393 and 1407 AH (1973 and 1987):

Year AH		Exchange line capacity (000s)	No of telephones operating (000s)
1393	(1973)	76.6	62.6
1394	(1974)	99.6	75.1
1395	(1975)	131.6	90.1
1396	(1976)	134.6	108.1
1397	(1977)	177.0	126.0
1398	(1978)	216.0	156.8
1399	(1979)	397.2	227.3
1400	(1980)	587.3	319.6
1401	(1981)	841.9	512.2
1402	(1982)	1,060.5	664.6
1403	(1983)	1,150.4	793.7
1404	(1984)	1,182.7	857.2
1405	(1985)	1,272.6	913.4
1406	(1986)	1,297.0	950.8
1407	(1987)	1,367.1	1,014.0

By 1989, the number of installed exchange lines had risen to 1,413,372, serving a total of 349 towns and villages throughout the Kingdom.

14.2.2   POSTAL SERVICES

The development of the Kingdom's economy has generated a massive increase in the volume of mail which the postal services have had to handle. In a continuing process of expansion, the fourth Development Plan provided for five new central post offices (in the Holy City of Medina, Abha, Burayda, Jizan and Sakaka) to complement the three main postal complexes in Riyadh, Jeddah and Dammam. Indeed, an efficient postal network now covers all the cities and villages of the Kingdom.

14.2.3   TELEX

The development of telex services in the Kingdom has kept pace with every innovation in telex technology. From the early days of electro-mechanical devices, through the installation of electronic machines in 1978, to the introduction in the 1980s of the most sophisticated equipment, capable of handling Arabic and Latin

Table 14.5   *Number of approved and operating telephones by province 1407 AH (1987)*

Province	No. of operating telephones	No. of approved telephones
Riyadh	220,998	284,072
Jeddah	172,666	231,072
Makkah	80,715	111,976
Medina	59,782	68,320
Taif	54,637	66,784
Eastern	120,475	156,552
Qaseem	46,934	57,552
Al-Ahsa	35,241	53,648
Ha'il	13,240	17,152
Al-Jouf	17,711	26,856
Al-Baha	9,262	13,312
Arar	10,985	12,288
Southern	30,647	42,448
Tabouk	29,279	36,560
Yanbu	14,541	35,832
Jubail	21,976	59,196
Najran	7,201	13,288
Jizan	9,390	17,152
Total	955,680	1,304,060

Source: Ministry of PTT

text simultaneously, the Ministry of Post, Telegraphs and Telephones has ensured that the Kingdom's ever-growing need for efficient telex communication services has been handsomely met.

Telecommunications experts agree that the Kingdom of Saudi Arabia possesses one of the most advanced telex networks in the world. It is also beyond question that this network is actively able to support the business community and with it progress and prosperity in the Kingdom.

Source: World of Communication in the Kingdom of Saudi Arabia, Ministry of Post, Telegraphs and Telephones, 1987

Having equipped the Kingdom with one of the most modern telex networks in the world, the Ministry of PTT has been able to proceed with the introduction of a high-

Table 14.6 *International calls issued from the Kingdom to world countries by continents 1407 AH (1987)*

Continents	Calls effected		Minutes	
	(000)	*Percentage distribution*	*(000)*	*Percentage distribution*
Asia	30,559	55.6	125,253	48.1
Africa	12,271	22.4	63,911	24.5
Europe	8,785	16.2	47,433	18.2
N. America	3,168	5.8	22,962	8.8
C. America	15	0.0	94	0.0
S. America	43	0.0	302	0.2
Australia & other countries	75	0.0	500	0.2
Total	54,916	100	260,455	100

Source: Ministry of PTT

Table 14.7 *Number of post offices in the Kingdom 1398–1407 AH (1978–87)*

Year AH	Number of post offices	Index 1398 = 100
1398 (1978)	371	100.0
1399 (1979)	384	103.5
1400 (1980)	396	106.7
1401 (1981)	437	117.8
1402 (1982)	437	117.8
1403 (1983)	443	119.4
1404 (1984)	441	118.8
1405 (1985)	443	119.4
1406 (1986)	443	119.4
1407 (1987)	447	120.5

Source: Post Statistical Section: G. Dept. of Post

Table 14.8   *Number of post offices in the Kingdom by regions 1407 AH (1987)*

Post regions	No. of post offices	Percentage distribution
Jeddah	25	5.6
Makkah	26	5.8
Central	82	18.3
Eastern	46	10.3
Medina	44	9.9
Qassem	34	7.6
Ha'il	9	2.0
Northern	39	8.7
Southern	91	20.4
Jizan	30	6.7
Baha	21	4.7
Total	447	100.0

Source: Post Statistical Section: G. Dept. of Post

Table 14.9   *International telex communications from the Kingdom to Arab countries 1407 AH (1987)*

Arab Countries	Communications (000)	Percentage distribution	Minutes (000)	Percentage distribution
Kuwait	99	9.2	232	1.9
Qatar	23	2.1	60	2.0
Ammam	17	1.6	45	1.5
Bahrain	252	23.5	895	30.0
UAE	171	15.9	431	14.6
Iraq	23	2.1	78	2.6
Syria	19	1.8	52	1.7
Jordan	76	7.1	183	6.0
Lebanon	128	11.9	319	10.8
North Yemen	41	3.8	114	3.8
Egypt	97	9.0	240	8.0
Morocco	21	2.0	54	1.8
Other Arab countries	107	10.0	274	9.3
Total	1074	100	2932	100

Source: Ministry of PTT

speed data transmission service (Teletex), to which existing telex subscribers will have easy access.

14.2.4 SATELLITE COMMUNICATIONS

In 1985, with the launch of two communications satellites, Arabsat (the Arab Satellite Communications Organization – formed by the Arab League in 1976) became operational. The Arabsat satellites are positioned in geo-stationary orbit above the equator.

Communications satellites facilitate the almost instantaneous transmission of many forms of data, including alphanumeric text, voice, still pictures and moving pictures. Their uses, in news dissemination, in business, in entertainment and in education are limited only by the imagination and resources of the user.

The Kingdom is playing an active role in the development and exploitation of this exciting medium of communication.

Table 14.10 *Production and supply of electricity 1390–1407 AH (1970–87)*

| Year AH | Installed capacity (MW) | Usable capacity (MW) | Peak load (MW) | Power generated (million Kwh)[1] | Power sold (million Kwh) | | Total | Number of subscribers (000) | Apparent consumption per subscriber (Kwh/year)[2] |
					Industrial purposes	Residential, commercial and other purposes			
1390	418	344	300	1,825	1,128	562	1,690	216	2,602
1391	505	418	345	2,055	1,263	639	1,902	233	2,742
1392	615	512	438	2,390	1,404	798	2,202	248	3,218
1393	800	657	577	2,908	1,722	956	2,678	265	3,608
1394	1,152	938	722	3,672	2,191	1,209	3,400	304	3,977
1395	1,349	1,173	848	4,270	2,173	1,587	3,760	352	4,509
1396	2,083	1,780	1,140	6,389	3,023	2,300	5,323	403	5,707
1397	2,829	2,367	1,633	7,263	3,142	3,223	6,365	466	6,916
1398	4,071	3,210	2,161	9,713	4,064	4,402	8,466	582	7,564
1399	5,506	4,124	2,955	15,470	6,613	6,836	13,449	727	9,403
1400	7,033	5,904	3,986	18,909	6,841	10,596	17,437	872	12,151
1401	8,566	7,359	5,227	25,061	7,626	14,018	21,644	1,042	13,453
1402	11,579	9,001	6,309	31,014	10,042	16,589	26,631	1,212	13,687
1403	11,318	10,704	7,708	35,307	8,731	22,446	31,177	1,391	16,137
1404	14,578	11,853	8,503	39,884	9,296	27,690	36,986	1,584	17,487
1405	16,744	13,923	9,424	44,502	11,656	30,248	41,904	1,758	17,206
1406	17,773	14,762	10,252	49,481	12,029	33,837	45,868	1,896	17,847
1407	18,215	14,909	10,889	54,178	12,444	36,462	48,906	2,043	17,847

[1] From 1403 onwards includes power generated by SWCC
[2] Excluding sales for industrial purposes
Source: Ministry of Planning and Ministry of Industry and Electricity

14.3 Electricity

To meet the Kingdom's growing demand for electrical power in the industrial and agricultural sectors of the economy, the government has replaced the old fragmented system of electrical power generation (provided by numerous small companies) with SCECOs – Saudi Consolidated Electric Companies – each providing electricity for a whole region of the Kingdom.

The first SCECO (SCECO-East) was created in 1977. This was followed in 1979 by SCECO-South. Electricity for the south-west of the Kingdom is provided by another consolidated company, and the central region is served by SCECO-Central.

The General Electricity Corporation (GEC) has overall responsibility for the Kingdom's electricity system and has a direct responsibility for the provision of electrical supplies to rural areas not at present covered by the consolidated companies. The GEC represents the government equity holdings in all the independent electricity generating companies and is a source of finance for those companies' capital requirements.

The Fourth Development Plan foresaw a need almost to double the Kingdom's electrical generating capacity. The key statistics, taken from that Plan, are as follows:

	Actual 1404 AH (1984)	Forecast 1410 AH (1990)
Number of customers (000)	1,527	2,354
Population served (000)	9,030	13,600
Peak load (MW)	8,336	15,691
Installed capacity (MW)	12,011*	20,050*
Steam electric (MW)	2,600*	6,140
GT and diesel (MW)	9,441	13,910

* Figures exclude electricity generated by the Saline Water Conversion Corporation (SWCC).

Table 14.10 (compiled from statistics provided by the Ministry of Planning and the Ministry of Industry and Electricity) gives a useful overview of the growth of the Kingdom's electricity generation from 1390 AH (1970) to 1407 AH (1987).

Chapter **15**

Social development

One of the underlying purposes of the building of the Kingdom's infrastructure, and the expansion of the industrial and agricultural base has been to encourage social development in its widest sense.

In this chapter, we look at a number of aspects of social development: the arts, radio, television, the press, sport, and the role of women in Saudi Arabian society. Our purpose in providing a simple overview of these aspects of social activity is to demonstrate that, amidst all the major projects undertaken as part of the developmental process, social development has not been neglected.

It is appropriate to begin this chapter with an account of the part played by the United Nations Development Program (UNDP) for the UNDP has made a substantial contribution to the research and training programs which have been a prerequisite of progress in a number of areas of social development.

15.1   United Nations Development Program (UNDP)

The United Nations Development Program started its activities and operations in 1957 under the name of the Technical Assistance Board (TAB), in accordance with an agreement between the government of Saudi Arabia and the United Nations. In 1960–61 another agreement was concluded between the government and the United Nations, still under the aegis of the Technical Assistance Board. In 1970, the name of the Technical Assistance Board was changed to the United Nations Development Program and its representation in Saudi Arabia became known as the United Nations Development Program Office at Riyadh.

In the Arabian Peninsula at that time, there were many programs and projects which were supervised by the New York Office of the UNDP, along with other of the United Nations executive and specialized agencies. The various and affiliated bodies of the United Nations which were operating in projects under the auspices of the United Nations Development Program Office Riyadh in 1978 are shown in Table 15.1.

All the agencies of the United Nations listed in Table 15.1 operated in Saudi

Table 15.1   *United Nations agencies operating in Saudi Arabia in 1978*

Name of agency of the United Nations	Regional Office (if any)	Head Office
Food and Agricultural Organization (FAO)	Cairo	Rome
Office of Technical Co-operation (UNOTC)		New York
World Health Organization (WHO)	Alexandria	Geneva
United Nations Industrial Development Organization (UNIDO)		Vienna
International Labor Organization (ILO)		Geneva
International Telecommunication Union (ITU)		Geneva
International Atomic Energy Organization (IAEO)		Vienna
United Nations International Children's Fund (UNICEF)	Beirut	New York
Economic Commission for Western Asia (ECWA)		Beirut
United Nations Educational, Scientific, and Cultural Organization (UNESCO)		Paris
International Bank for Reconstruction and Development (IBRD)		Washington
International Monetary Fund (IMF)		Washington
International Maritime Consultative Organization (IMCO)		London
Universal Postal Union (UPO)		Berne
United Nations Conference on Trade and Development (UNCTAD)		Geneva
International Civil Aviation Organization (ICAO)		Montreal
World Meteorology Organization (WMO)		Geneva

Source: Obtained by the author through an interview with Mr Mostafa Badawi, Programs Assistant in the United Nations Development Program Office at Riyadh, Saudi Arabia, in May 1975 (Designed by FF)

Arabia and the Arabian Gulf area under the auspices of the UNDP at Riyadh.

Generally speaking, projects which have been supervised by the United Nations agencies have been initiated by mutual consultation between the Government of Saudi Arabia and the United Nations, both guided by the priorities of the Kingdom's relevant Five Year Plan. Much of the UNDP effort has been devoted to the technical training of Saudi personnel.

These projects are classified into the following categories:

1 Large Scale Projects
2 Small Scale Projects (involving one foreign adviser)
   In both categories, large and small, there have been projects which

have been subsidized by the United Nations as well as by the Saudi government, while other projects, called FIT projects (Fund-in-Trust), have been individually financed by the government of Saudi Arabia. The financing of the latter has been done by the deposit of an agreed sum of money by the Saudi government at the disposal of the United Nations in order that the latter may arrange for such specific projects, sending advisory personnel and conducting studies.

3 Regular Programs: usually short-range programs with low financing
4 Country's Participating Program – UNESCO
5 Fund-in-Trust for both large and small scale projects
6 Regional and international–regional projects
   Such projects are usually financed by the United Nations along with fellowships, seminars, training courses and symposia. These activities may come under the large scale category and are sometimes directly implemented by the United Nations by sending individuals to conduct surveys, make comprehensive studies, draft plans, or carry out studies in certain fields. Such personnel dispatched by the United Nations are called visitors and consultants. Often their missions are of short duration – seven days to a month.

The United Nations Development Program has offered fellowships at two levels. In connection with the large-scale projects, these fellowships, called counterpart fellowships, have been given to Saudi Arabian nationals for the duration of the project conducted in the Kingdom. In other words, while the project is being executed in Saudi Arabia for two or three years under foreign advice, Saudis have been sent abroad (usually to Western Europe, Canada, or the United States of America) for the duration of the project, to be trained in the same field. When the project's time has expired and the foreign advisers have left for their homes, they are replaced by Saudi nationals, thus providing continuity for the projects as well as increasing the staff of the Saudi technical advisory group. Counterpart fellowships for small scale projects have been financed differently. If a Saudi national has been sent abroad under the Indicative Planning Figure (Country Program) the United Nations has financed his fellowship. But if he has been sent under the Fund-in-Trust (FIT) program, the Saudi Government has sponsored his fellowship directly.

Tables 15.2 and 15.3 show large and small scale projects planned or being implemented in Saudi Arabia in 1978.

Among successfully completed early projects implemented under the supervision and co-operation of the United Nations Development Program at Riyadh were:

1 the Faculty of Engineering, currently one of the faculties of the University of Riyadh

Table 15.2   *United Nations large scale projects in Saudi Arabia in 1978*

Large Scale Projects	Locations of Projects in Saudi Arabia	Name of UN agency* in charge
Center for Training and Applied Research in Community Development	Ad-Dir'iyah Riyadh	UNOTC
Regional and Natural Physical Planning (Town Planning)	Riyadh	UNOTC
Industrial Studies and Development Center	Riyadh	UNIDO
Irrigation Development Wadi Jizan	Jizan	FAO-completed projects, supplemental project
Farm Engineering Center	Riyadh	FAO-completed projects, supplemental project
Telecommunications and Broadcasting Training Center	Riyadh Jeddah	ITU
Center for Applied Geology	Jeddah	UNESCO
Educational Research Center (completed project)	Riyadh (faculty of education)	
Training in Civil Aviation (including fund-in-Trust)	Jiddah & Dhahran	ICAO
National Transport Survey (completed project)	Riyadh	IBRD
Road and Ports Fund-in-Trust	Riyadh	UNOTC
Agriculture and Waters Development	Riyadh	FIT-FAO

* Key
FAO: Food and Agricultural Organization
FIT: Fund-in-Trust
IBRD: International Bank for Reconstruction and Development
ICAO: International Civil Aviation Organization
ITU: Internaional Telecommunications Union
UNESCO: United Nations Educational, Scientific, and Cultural Organization
UNIDO: United Nations Industrial Development Organization
UNOTC: United Nations Office of Technical Co-operation

Source: Information obtained by the author in an interview with Mr Mostafa Badawi, Programs Assistant in the UNDP, Riyadh, Saudi Arabia in May 1975. (Designed by FF)

Table 15.3   *United Nations small scale projects[1] in Saudi Arabia in 1978*

Small Scale Projects	Locations of Projects in Saudi Arabia	Name of UN agency in charge
Agricultural Training Adviser	Riyadh	FAO
Irrigation Adviser – Senior Irrigation Adviser	Riyadh	FAO
Vocational Preparation	Riyadh	UNICEF
Telecommunication Planning and Programming Adviser	Riyadh	ITU
Education Research	Riyadh	UNESCO
National Accounts and Economic Statistics Adviser	Riyadh	UNOTC
Standardization Quality	Riyadh	OTC
Meteorology Communication Adviser	Jeddah	WMO
Sanitary Engineering and Municipal Programming Adviser – FIT[2]	Riyadh	WHO
Telephone System (automatic and manual telephone system) – FIT	Riyadh	ITU
Industrial Standardization and Quality Control – FIT	Riyadh	UNICO-SIS[3]

[1] When the project has only one foreign adviser it is termed "small scale"
[2] Fund-in-Trust
[3] Special Industrial Service

Source: Information obtained in an interview with Mr Mostafa Badawi, Programs Assistant in the UNDP, Riyadh, Saudi Arabia in May 1975. (Designed by FF)

2 the Faculty of Education, also currently a faculty of the University of Riyadh
3 a Farm Engineering Center in Riyadh
4 the Wadi Jizam Irrigation Project
5 The Qatif Experimental Farm

15.1.1   THE CENTER FOR TRAINING AND APPLIED RESEARCH IN COMMUNITY DEVELOPMENT AT AD-DIR'IYAH

The Center for Training and Applied Research in Community Development, set up with the co-operation of the United Nations Development Program, will serve as a useful model of a large scale project. This section focuses on the project's objectives, organization and achievements.

The Center was inaugurated on 16th June 1970, under an agreement between the Saudi government, represented by the Minister of Labor and Social Affairs, and the

United Nations Development Program and Technical Co-operation Office (UNDP-TC), represented by the United Nations Resident Representative in Riyadh. The project was launched on 1st July 1970. The major objectives and aims of the Center are:

To train senior level personnel, field work staff, specialists and technicians as well as local leaders in the different fields of community development.

To advise and assist the Ministry of Labor and Social Affairs and other related ministries in the implementation of procedures conducive to efficient administration, supervision and evaluation of rural development programs.

To strengthen the existing community development centers and assist in the establishment of new ones.

To assist the government in carrying out rural, social and economic development activities in selected areas; these activities will form an integral part of the training and research elements' activities.

To conduct action-oriented research whose results will be utilized in training and community development activities. To offer specialized seminars and courses in agriculture, health, education, literacy and adult education, co-operatives, and social welfare, etc.

Source: Ministry of Labor and Social Affairs and UNDP (Riyadh, 1975)

The Center's Central Committee, established by the Saudi Council of Ministers, governs its affairs. The Central Committee consists of the following personnel:

Minister of Labor and Social Affairs	Chairman
Deputy Minister for Social Affairs	Vice-Chairman and Member
Director, Community Development Administration	Member
Director General of the Center	Member and Rapporteur
Director General, Technical Co-operation Administration	Member
Representative of Ministry of Agriculture	Member
Representative of Ministry of Education	Member
Representative of Ministry of Health	Member
Representative of Central Planning Organization	Member

The Central Committee is charged with the following functions: (1) the planning and implementing of community development policy and projects throughout the country; (2) follow-up and appraisal of community development projects; (3) study of problems confronting community development programs, and the submission of recommendations for their solution; (4) acting as co-ordinator and liaison officer between the ministries concerned and agencies active in community development work; (5) submission of the budget necessary for development programs, specifying the required allocations from every contributing organization prior to each new financial year; (6) supervision of training staff as well as of research in community development; and, finally, (7) preparing periodic reports on the progress of the community development programs.

Training is the first of the Center's tasks, this being one of the most essential requirements for social and economic development. The availability of sufficient highly trained manpower in specialist fields must greatly enhance a country's development. Being aware of this fact, the Center for Training and Applied Research has adopted a tri-partite formula for the training of Saudi manpower:

1   preparation of the necessary number of specialists in fields relevant to social development
2   focus on local environmental conditions and utilization of available human and national resources in various processes
3   training local leaders and making full use of their status in community development

The Center for Training and Applied Research in Community Development plans its programs and functions within the framework of these objectives. Training activities are designed for top personnel engaged in various social and economic schemes in different regions of the Kingdom. Personnel engaged in local community development in the fields of health, education, social affairs and agriculture constitute the main groups who participate in the long and short scale courses planned by the Center.

The method and techniques of training utilized by the Center are as follows:

1   an integrated approach to socio-economic development in the community
2   linkage with development objectives, targets, needs, plans and problems of local communities in the various regions
3   co-operation and co-ordination with various local institutions within the framework of national development plans
4   scientific methods in the investigation of the environment and in the identification of needs and problems
5   application of modern techniques and even utilization of mass media and audio-visual aids tailored to activities contributing to change of

attitudes, technology and new practice

6   field work to implement the theoretical framework in both rural and urban communities

7   exchange of experiences, ideas and knowledge among trainees, supervisors, officials and experts

8   follow-up and evolution of training needs among graduates of the Center. (These approaches or techniques lead to the enrichment of the basic skills and experience of those engaged in community development schemes)

The Center's second objective is the development of social research, as well as social studies, as a basic dimension in the community development process. The Center believes that analysis of existing circumstances and further evolution of the human and material elements at hand, along with the declared need for development, are essential for planning in developing nations. The planning of social programs, aimed at the elimination of existing hindrances to the welfare and progress of society, necessitates the identification of elements influencing communities as well as of social problems that have resulted from change. Social research is described by the Center as "the scientific method for collecting, analyzing, and interpreting facts and data needed for community development".

The Center's training programs began on 19th December 1971. The community development program in Saudi Arabia is a multi-purpose and co-ordinated activity with the ultimate intention of meeting major community needs. Its final goal is to develop human resources by providing opportunities for decision making and self-reliance, for exercising responsibility and acquiring positive social attitudes. The Saudi government regards this program as an essential factor in its national development plan – the Five Year Plans – for social and economic progress. The community development program is also considered an integral part of the overall national development program of the Kingdom. According to the First Five Year Plan, started in 1970 (1390 AH), "the community development program seeks to co-ordinate government services with community efforts to maximize the use of the local, economic, and social resources for the improvement of the welfare of the country".

An interview with the Chief Adviser and Supervisor of the Training Center community development program, Dr Ali Mahjoub, revealed that the community development program was established under the auspices of the ministries of Education, Health, Agriculture, Labor and Social Affairs. The first community development pilot project in Saudi Arabia was launched in the town of Ad-Dir'iyah in October 1960 with the technical co-operation of the United Nations and its international specialized agencies. One year prior to the establishment of the present center, the Ministry of Labor and Social Affairs was established and the administration of the community development program was transferred to this ministry. A division for the community development program was subsequently established with the collaboration of the Ministries of Education, Health and Agriculture. The Ministry of Labor and Social Affairs has shouldered the responsibility of promoting and supervising the community development project at Ad-Dir'iyah, assisted by the international agencies of the United Nations. By the year 1964, there were seventeen community development centers operating in Saudi Arabia – eleven in rural areas and six in cities. Seventeen additional centers were established during the Second Five Year Plan (1975–80).

The Ad-Dir'iyah Center trained only Saudi nationals with specialties in various aspects of community development. Training courses conducted outside the Ad-Dir'iyah Center included both Saudis and non-Saudis. Moreover, they included both males and females working as specialists in various community development centers. A survey of participants in various community development centers in the Medina, Al-Hasa and Qasim areas showed that of 54 who had taken part in various training programs twenty had been female.

In the Center's second field of activity (ie applied research), it concluded several descriptive and evaluative studies of training programs and trainees. The

Chart XVa   *Center for Training and Applied Research in Community Development*

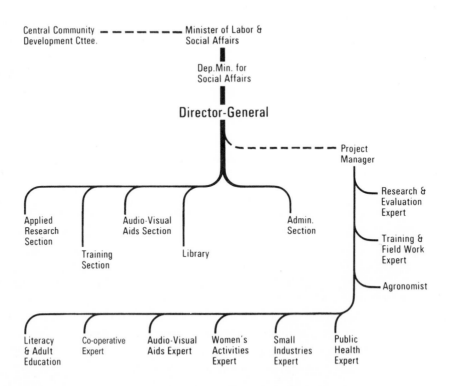

Source: Kingdom of Saudi Arabia, Ministry of Labor and Social Affairs. 'Center for Training and Applied Research in Community Development', page 16. Author's translation.

purpose of such evaluations was to obtain the reactions of the trainees to the courses of study, the material used, the duration of the courses and the means and methods employed in conducting these courses. The trainees' suggestions were welcomed and thoroughly studied.

The organization of the Center is shown in Chart XVa.

15.2 The arts

It would be understandable if the reader imagined that, amidst all the infrastructural, industrial and agricultural developments in the Kingdom, the arts had been somewhat neglected. This is not the case.

The General Presidency of Youth Welfare is responsible for the formative arts movement in the Kingdom of Saudi Arabia. It prepares both an annual and a five-year plan for the encouragement and development of the arts.

Within the Kingdom it organizes regular competitions and exhibitions. Abroad, it arranges exhibitions of Saudi Arabian art, to provide Saudi artists with an international forum and to strengthen cultural ties with the host countries. The Presidency has organized exhibitions of Saudi Arabian art in the following Arab countries: Algeria, Bahrain, Jordan, Kuwait, Morocco, Oman, Qatar, Tunisia and the United Arab Emirates; and outside the Arab world in India, Italy, Mexico, Sweden, Turkey, West Germany and the United States of America (Source: General Presidency of Youth Welfare, 1988).

The Presidency is also an active participant in the Arab Youth Festivals and Exhibitions, the Kuwait Exhibition for Formative Artists and other periodic exhibitions in Europe, Asia and India, and takes part in the Biannual Arab Exhibition which is supervised by the Arab Formative Artists Union.

In 1392 AH (1972), a Royal Decree was issued to form the Saudi Arabian Arts Society. In 1398 AH (1978), the name of the Society was changed to the Saudi Arabian Society for Culture and Arts. This society is responsible for protecting and nurturing the culture of the Kingdom. Its duties are defined as follows:

1   to develop progressively the level of culture and arts in the Kingdom
2   to look after the welfare of Saudi artists and work towards raising their cultural, artistic and social standard
3   to sponsor talented young people and provide an opportunity for them to develop and display their talents
4   to represent the Kingdom in all matters relating to the development of culture and arts at both Arab and international levels

The work of the Society is managed by four committees:

1   The Cultural Committee
    This committee is responsible for encouraging Saudi men of letters

and for raising public literary and cultural taste.

2   The Plastic Arts Committee
This committee assists in the development of the plastic arts. It encourages Saudi artists and promotes their work by arranging exhibitions both within and outside the Kingdom.

3   The Music and Vocal Arts Committee
This committee encourages music and singing, with special attention to the rich folk art of poetry and song found in the various regions of the Kingdom.

4   The Information and Publications Committee
This committee is not only responsible for the dissemination of all culturally related information to the Society's branch offices and to local newspapers but also maintains an archive of artistic productions and events in the Kingdom.

The Society also maintains a Cultural Video Film and Recording Library and is responsible for the Kingdom's first Cultural Center in Riyadh, set up to revive and popularize the Kingdom's cultural heritage.

Currently under construction in the capital is the King Fahd Cultural Center, a building which in the grace and beauty of its design suitably reflects the riches of the Kingdom's artistic productions, both past and present, which are to be displayed there. The building occupies an area of 10,000 square meters and within it are housed a theater with a seating capacity of 3,000; a library; a training theater; a restaurant; and a cafeteria, as well as the necessary administrative offices.

15.3   Radio

In 1932, King Abdul Aziz set up his own private radio network in the Kingdom, primarily to enable him and his officials to keep themselves informed of events.

In the full sense of public broadcasting, transmissions began in the Kingdom of Saudi Arabia in 1368 AH (1948) from a small station in Jeddah. This was followed three years later by a station in the Holy City of Makkah. These two stations, which were on the air for no more than fourteen hours a week, broadcast recitations from the Holy *Quran*, the sayings of the Prophet, news and cultural programs and some music (military marches).

From these relatively modest beginnings the Saudi Radio Broadcasting Service emerged. In 1384 AH (1964), the Riyadh broadcasting station and the Call of Islam station (based in the Holy City of Makkah) began transmissions.

In the discharge of its duty as the guardian of the Holy Places and its role as the center of the Islamic world, the Kingdom has employed radio to strengthen Islam within and outside Saudi Arabia. In 1393 AH (1973), the Kingdom began short-wave and high-frequency broadcasting in Bembari, Bengali, English, French,

Indonesian, Pharsi, Somali, Swahili, Turkestan, Turkish and Urdu.

In 1399 AH (1979), radio broadcasts from the various stations were unified into the General Service. The programming policy governing the General Service is based on the following principles:

- the essential emphasis must be on religious, social and cultural programs
- particular attention should be given to news and political programs
- outstanding thinkers should be encouraged to give talks on important topics
- provision should be made for educational programs for the enlightenment of the listeners
- there should be special programs catering for the family, for childcare and for health education
- eminent men of letters should be encouraged to write religious, cultural and social dramas for broadcast as serials.

In addition to the General Service, there are now a number of other radio channels:

- the Second Program Service, which broadcasts folklore, dramatic, recreational, literary and scientific programs
- Foreign Language Broadcasting (Directed Programs), which place the emphasis on Islamic solidarity and which also have a proselytizing function
- the Call of Islam Broadcasting Station, which promulgates the message of Islam and defends the Islamic faith against the assaults of hostile ideologies
- the Holy *Quran* Broadcasting Service
- the European Languages Station, which broadcasts religious and informational programs in English and French

The Fourth Development Plan, 1405–10 AH (1985–90), made provision for a number of new radio facilities, including two radio stations, to be built in Dariyah and Jizan, and a further 25 radio stations to be built around the country.

15.4 Television

In 1384 AH (1964), the late King Faisal commissioned the American National Broadcasting Company (NBC) to construct a national television network. The first test television transmissions in the Kingdom took place in 1385 AH (1965) from stations in Riyadh and Jeddah.

Throughout the development of the Kingdom's television services, the Ministry of Information has ensured that only the most advanced technology has been utilized. The result is certainly the best-equipped and most sophisticated television facilities in the region.

The television complex in Riyadh stands as a fine example of this commitment to technical excellence. This complex includes the most advanced production and transmission studios, a complete film production facility, a theater (with seating capacity for 800) and, rising majestically above it all, the transmission tower, a 170-meter high edifice, topped by a glass, jewel-shaped structure from which all of Riyadh is visible.

When color television was introduced, obviously a major event in the development of television services in the Kingdom, the Ministry of Information, in conjunction with the Ministry of Post, Telegraphs and Telephones, selected the French SECAM-3B system, since it was considered to be the most advanced color television system in the world.

There are currently two television channels: one in Arabic; the other in English. Programming is a balanced blend of religious and cultural programs, entertainment and music, Arabic drama programs, non-Arabic films and serials, children's programs, and news and current affairs programs. Special programming is produced for all the major events in the Islamic calendar, especially for Ramadan and for the period of the *Hajj*, the annual pilgrimage to the Holy Places.

The Fourth Development Plan 1405–10 AH (1985–90) provided for the introduction of a satellite television service and for the construction of a new television station in Jeddah.

15.5   Publications

Prompted by the Kingdom's general development and, in particular by the Kingdom's extensive and intensive educational program, a thriving publications industry has grown up. Daily newspapers, weekly publications, other periodicals and a wide selection of books now compete for the reader's interest.

The main daily publications are:

- *Arab News*, an English language daily newspaper with local and foreign news coverage
- *Ashaq al-Awsat*, an Arabic language daily newspaper published simultaneously in Jeddah and London
- *Al-Bilad*
- *Al-Jazirah*
- *Al-Medina al-Munawara*
- *Al-Nadwah*
- *Okaz*

- *Al-Riyadh*
- *Saudi Gazette*, an English language daily newspaper with local and foreign news coverage
- *Saudi Review*
- *Al-Yaum*

Many foreign news publications are available in the Kingdom, including the following British publications:

- Dailies: *The Daily Telegraph, The Financial Times, The Guardian, The Daily Mail, The Times*
- Weeklies: *The Economist*

Also available are *Newsweek* and *Time*.

The growth in the number of newspapers and periodicals has engendered an active advertizing business in the Kingdom of Saudi Arabia.

15.6   Sport

The General Presidency of Youth Welfare has been responsible for the rapid development of sport within the Kingdom.

As part of its program to provide the young people of the Kingdom with facilities for all sporting activities, the Presidency has built twelve integrated sports "cities" in different districts of the Kingdom. Three further "cities" are under construction.

North-east of Riyadh is the King Fahd International Stadium, one of the largest, and widely regarded as one of the most beautiful, sports stadia in the world. The stadium occupies an area of 500,000 square meters. The seating has been cleverly designed to provide all spectators with an unimpeded view.

The Kingdom is an active member of the Olympic movement. The Saudi Arabian Olympic Committee, established in 1964, included the fourteen federations for the sports then practised in the Kingdom. In 1404 AH (1984), Saudi Arabia competed in the Olympic Games for the first time, in football and rifle-shooting.

The efforts of the Saudi athletes culminated in the success of the Saudi national football team in 1404 AH (1984), when the team won the Asian Football Cup.

The Kingdom currently caters for more than twenty different sporting activities. Table 15.4 lists these sports and gives key statistics for the year 1407 AH (1987) on the numbers of players, matches, trainers and referees.

Table 15.4 *Numbers of players, trainers, matches and referees involved in sport, 1407 AH (1987)*

Type of sport	No of players	No of trainers	No of matches	Referees
Football	9,032	150	640	499
Basketball	5,800	50	245	118
Volleyball	8,973	120	363	245
Handball	5,537	100	305	184
Table tennis	2,870	60	320	112
Cycling	2,476	38	95	139
Swimming	520	6	30	72
Athletics and Marathon	4,640	90	260	205
Gymnastics	1,724	35	53	44
Karate	298	20	30	27
Boxing	180	9	30	27
Weightlifting	120	9	20	41
Bodybuilding	220	9	20	20
Wrestling	220	12	30	19
Taekwondo	250	20	25	15
Judo	409	20	25	11
Lawn tennis	240	30	150	72
Diving	205	2	20	16
Fencing	460	20	23	16
Waterpolo	190	8	70	16
Sighting	400	6	16	14

Source: General Presidency for Youth Welfare

15.7   The role of women in Saudi Arabian society

The position of women in Islamic society in general and in Saudi Arabian society in particular is a complex and frequently misunderstood issue. It is certainly true that Muslim and Western views of the role of women show sharp cultural differences, but the stereotype of Muslim women as uneducated, down-trodden creatures with no rights and no opportunities is a caricature born of ignorance or malevolence.

The Holy *Quran* gave women economic and social rights long before such rights were attained by Western women. From the beginning of Islam, women have been legally entitled to inherit and bequeath property, holding their wealth in their own names even after marriage, without obligation to contribute that wealth to their husband or their family. The important role played by the wives of the Prophet Muhammad (peace be upon him) in the course of his ministry sorts ill with the view that Islam in any way undervalues the female half of humanity.

It is nevertheless true that, under Islam, a woman is enjoined to behave modestly in public and that, as in the West until recently, is generally expected to give a full commitment to making a family home – a home within which, incidentally, she enjoys a pre-eminent role. Such expectations are rather different from those now widely required of women in the West, just as the stability of family life and the security of women in Islamic society differs markedly from the conditions which women now face in Western society.

This said, it would be a mistake to think that the role of women in Saudi Arabian society is confined to home-making. The development of the Kingdom of Saudi Arabia has brought with it increasing opportunities for women in both education and employment. In 1960, the Government of the Kingdom of Saudi Arabia undertook the introduction of a national education program for girls. By the mid-1970s, about half of Saudi Arabian girls were attending school. Five years later, education was available to all Saudi girls. By 1980 (1400 AH), there were six universities for women. (For further details on the educational opportunities for women in the Kingdom today, see Chapter 16.)

In terms of employment, women now play an active role in teaching, medicine, social work and broadcasting.

15.8   Youth hostels

The first youth hostels were established by the General Presidency for Youth Welfare in 1969. In this undertaking the Presidency had two objectives:

- to develop and support the youth hostel movement in the Kingdom
- to increase young people's knowledge of all the Kingdom's regions by encouraging them to travel within the Kingdom and to broaden their knowledge of other countries by utilizing youth hostel facilities abroad

The Kingdom's youth hostels boast modern swimming pools, theaters and areas for hobbies and games, as well as sleeping accommodation. Currently, there are twenty such hostels in the Kingdom.

15.9   Social services

The social services provisions of the Kingdom of Saudi Arabia are extensive by any standards. The Fourth Five Year Development Plan (1405–10 AH; 1985–90) set out clearly the philosophy behind the Kingdom's extensive social services program:

The social services are designed to redress existing imbalances, to improve living standards and the quality of life of the population, to stimulate citizen participation in community development activities, and to provide remedial care and assistance for the disabled and the deprived.

There are a number of social service agencies whose task it is to remedy social problems, many of which are created by the process of social development itself. The Government takes the view that

> poverty and deprivation are not necessarily due to the failure of individuals to meet their own needs. Most of these problems are a result of broader external conditions in society as a whole, and will not solve themselves. Public and private interventions are necessary to improve the conditions of the individual and the community. The Social Services agencies will continue to pay attention to the development of Saudi society, to assist in improving the standard of living, and to take steps to redress some of the social imbalances which have become salient during this period of rapid economic change.

Source: Fourth Development Plan (1405–10 AH; 1985–90)

Amongst the social services provided by the state are wide-ranging programs designed to improve living conditions for the population and to smooth the processes related to the rapid transformation of the socio-economic system. There are a number of social rehabilitation, care and remedial services, designed to assist the physically or mentally disadvantaged, to protect vulnerable members of society, and to deal with such problems as juvenile delinquency. Special attention is given to raising the living standards of the poorest sections of the community, particularly in the villages and the less developed districts of the towns and cities.

In addition to these social services, there is a compulsory occupational insurance scheme, covering provisions for sickness and retirement, for employees in both the public and private sectors.

In all the social services programs, there is an emphasis on helping people to help themselves, wherever possible. The objectives set for the Fourth Development Plan were defined as follows:

- to extend the scope of integrated social development activities with other service providers and citizen groups in order to meet the basic needs of disadvantaged groups and individuals
- to emphasize the social responsibility of the population for improving the standards of local communities and poor districts within cities through private sector activities
- to assist the population in improving their real standard of living by their own efforts and without reducing incentives to work

Table 15.5 *Social security provisions 1389–1407 AH (1969–87)*

Year AH	Regular assistance			Relief assistance			All assistance			
	Number of families or cases (Thousand)	Number of beneficiaries (Thousand)	Amount received (SR million)	Number of families or cases (Thousand)	Number of beneficiaries (Thousand)	Amount received (SR million)	Number of families or cases (Thousand)	Number of beneficiaries (Thousand)	Amount received (SR million)	Amount received per family or case (Riyals)
1389/90	62	187	39.4	2	11	2.3	64	198	41.7	652
1390/91	73	226	47.6	2	10	2.3	75	236	49.9	665
1391/92	89	275	58.4	3	12	2.3	92	287	60.7	669
1392/93	104	322	68.4	4	20	3.8	108	342	72.2	1,301
1393/94	108	327	143.1	6	26	5.2	114	353	148.3	2,554
1394/95	137	427	349.0	3	16	8.5	140	443	357.5	2,638
1395/96	174	531	442.1	14	64	53.9	188	595	496.0	3,153
1396/97	199	613	625.1	19	69	62.2	218	682	667.3	3,993
1397/98	215	658	855.0	18	77	75.4	233	735	930.4	3,861
1398/99	239	723	924.3	33	103	125.9	272	826	1,050.2	3,860
1399/00	247	753	931.1	26	99	122.7	273	852	1,053.8	3,829
1400/01	256	757	969.6	21	87	91.0	277	844	1,060.6	5,128
1401/02	273	798	1,375.0	24	111	148.0	297	909	1,523.0	4,984
1402/03	284	810	1,402.0	25	114	138.0	309	924	1,540.0	5,033
1403/04	286	810	1,406.5	20	93	133.5	306	903	1,540.0	4,834
1404/05	289	806	1,394.3	25	118	123.7	314	926	1,518.0	4,826
1405/06	295	792	1,389.1	18	84	121.5	313	876	1,510.6	4,856
1406/07*	287	752	1,384.5	12	55	67.4	299	807	1,451.9	

* Ten-month fiscal year
Source: Central Department of Statistics and Ministry of Labor and Social Affairs

- to extend social service programmes to all parts of the Kingdom and to all eligible persons
- to encourage family solidarity and support the desired socialization of children
- to provide care for those requiring institutionalization if it is impossible to deliver sufficient care in the family setting

15.10   Future social policy

The clearest way of outlining the Kingdom's future social policy and, at the same time, demonstrating the continuity in Saudi Arabia's commitment to the principles of social justice entailed by Islam is to refer once more to an extract from the Fifth Development Plan (1410–15 AH; 1990–95).

> Attention should be given to the development of Saudi society, to the provision of social welfare and health care for all, and to the support given to society's participation in the implementation of the development plans, as well as in reaping the benefits of the related programs.

The government can create the conditions for social development, just as it has created the conditions for economic diversification, but, for the fulfilment of the Kingdom's aspirations, it is essential that Saudi citizens understand the objectives of the development programs and become, through their personal involvement, committed to the Kingdom's goals.

Such commitment in the social area may take many forms. It may appear as active participation in the Kingdom's cultural life (through, for example, authorship), or as an enhanced appreciation of the Kingdom's cultural traditions (by, for example, greater use of the Kingdom's libraries and museums), or in a changed perception of the value of types of work which may previously have been accorded low social status.

In short, the Fifth Development Plan places a heavy emphasis on the full participation of the citizenry in the Kingdom's future progress, at both local and national level. At the same time, the Plan foresees the need for the government to continue its investment in many areas of social development, particularly in order to ensure that children and young people in the Kingdom are given the fullest opportunity to develop their potential and to become responsible and productive citizens.

For a more detailed account of the social objectives expressed in the Fifth Development Plan, see the Seventh Basic Strategic Principle, Section 10.3.

16

Education

The true wealth of any nation is its people, for it is their ability to manage the country's existing resources and to identify and develop new ones which determines the prosperity of the economy and the health of society for present and future generations.

Mindful of the need to ensure that the Kingdom's population should be equal to the challenges of the developmental process, the government has devoted vast resources to a program covering primary, secondary and higher levels of education. This chapter gives an indication of the government's commitment to this aspect of social progress.

16.1 Background to the development of education

Surveying the total educational system of Saudi Arabia, it must be remembered that it had its real start only in 1949–50 with the personal support of the then Prince Faisal and the encouragement of Prince Fahd bin Abdul Aziz, who later became Minister of Education and President of the Saudi Higher Council of Education, the highest educational authority in the Kingdom, and is now the King.

The statement of C Arnold Anderson is applicable to the educational policies initiated and adopted in Saudi Arabia:

> In formulating educational policy, every society must compromise among three goals: (1) efficiency in allocating training to individuals most likely to profit from it; (2) equity in opening opportunities for education impartially to various groups; and (3) free choice of educational careers to maximize motivation and flexibility.
>
> *Source:* "Economic Development and Post-Primary Education", published in *Post Primary Education and Political and Economic Development* (Durham, NC: Duke University Press, 1964)

"Compromise" suggests that efficiency, equity and freedom of choice are, in that sequence, the three important elements necessary for a sound educational system. If these three elements cannot be attained in equal proportions, priority must be given to the criterion of efficiency. In most developing nations, the financial realities and sometimes poor judgement, make it impossible for their educational systems to balance these three elements effectively. For example, the Egyptian educational system, in implementing equity and freedom of choice for students, sacrificed efficiency. This result was of course not intentional on the part of the Egyptian policy makers, but was unavoidable. Inadequate financial resources and the crippling factor of over-population compounded the disparity between intention and achievement.

Some other countries, which neither lack the financial resources nor are over-populated, deprive their students of an important element of the Anderson formula, ie the freedom of choice. Indeed, the freedom of choice of an educational career is vital and essential since it "maximises motivation and flexibility". Libya is one of the developing nations which has adopted such a policy, with the rationale of producing specialists in the various fields of education. Such a result can be automatically achieved when the demand for well-trained manpower in almost all the fields of education in a developing nation like Libya absorbs all the available output of educated manpower.

Although Saudi Arabia's educational policy makers may not have been aware of the Anderson formula of efficiency, equity and freedom of choice, they were built into the Saudi educational system at all levels. Saudi Arabia's abundant financial resources have enabled the country to pursue such a policy with ease and effect. For example, the efficiency element sometimes necessitates the hiring of educational personnel from distant countries, eg the United States of America, and, despite the heavy financial requirements involved in such a case, the Saudi policy makers have encouraged it, as it is to the country's ultimate benefit, contributing to the fulfilment of the Kingdom's educational goals. The equity element is also achieved by having a free educational system open to all citizens at all levels. Yet at certain levels, such as universities, in order to maintain a high standard, a student must possess specified academic qualifications for admission. This policy is sound, for it ensures the university remains a serious institution of higher learning, rather than allowing it to be used as a boarding house for uninterested students. In Egypt during the 1960s, when universities began to admit students according to an equity criterion based on political motivations (the ideology of socialism), an enormous surplus in university graduates resulted. University graduates often waited two years after graduation only to be appointed to government positions which rarely did justice to their educational qualifications. This situation has not changed much despite the introduction of rigid entrance requirements to Egyptian universities. Surpluses of unwanted and unemployed university graduates still represent a major problem facing Egypt today. This result undermines the efforts of Egyptian educational policy makers who find it extremely difficult, even dangerous, to alter the status quo.

Table 16.1 Total educational budget by authority, 1405–1408 AH (1985–88)

Authority	1405/1406 AH (1985/1986)					1406/1407 AH (1986/1987)					1407/1408 AH (1987/1988)				
	Salaries and wages	General expenditure	Other expenditure	Projects	Total & % to total education allocations	Salaries and wages	General expenditure	Other expenditure	Projects	Total & % to total education allocations	Salaries and wages	General expenditure	Other expenditure	Projects	Total & % to total education allocations
Ministry of Education	7,569	1,147	72	1,672	10,460 / 44.4%	7,573	1,149	72	1,672	10,466 / 44.0%	7,845	908	46	1,115	9,914 / 42.8%
Presidency of Girls' Education	4,343	521	60	539	5,463 / 23.3%	4,539	658	63	655	5,915 / 24.9%	5,894	498	41	249	6,682 / 28.8%
Higher Education and Universities	2,468	2,186	237	1,801	6,692 / 28.4%	2,468	2,186	237	1,801	6,692 / 28.1%	2,497	1,768	177	1,392	5,834 / 25.2%
General Organization for Technical Education and Vocational Training	377	189	114	245	925 / 3.9%	378	189	114	45	726 / 3.0%	347	185	98	121	751 / 3.2%
Total	14,757	4,043	483	4,257	23,540	14,958	4,182	486	4,137	23,799	16,583	3,359	362	2,877	23,181

Saudi educational policy makers, viewing the Saudi educational system from another perspective, were able to cope with an important problem prevailing in other countries, namely the cultural gap resulting from the great emphasis on secular education on the one hand and the neglect of religious education on the other. The strong Islamic culture of the country enabled the Saudi Arabian educational system to avoid the persistent problem of the modernization of the educational system at the expense of religion. Secularized schools in Saudi Arabia have not created a religious and cultural gap. In Egypt, for example, religious courses at the high school and university levels are weak and inadequate. In the high school senior year, religion is taught with the understanding that the student will not have to take a final examination. As a result, religious courses are severely undermined and neglected by students. At the university level, no religious courses are offered except to students of Al-Azhar University.

In Saudi Arabia, by contrast, religious courses are taught at the high school level with full seriousness and are accorded high status. At the university level, reasonable religious courses are taught along with other secular courses in all years, and are required of all students. Islam, being a way of life, is accessible to educated and uneducated people alike. The assumption is that religion finds its way to their souls and, once this is achieved, psychological stability is attained. Consequently, the pursuit of all activities is rendered much easier and can be approached with full concentration. Even after reaching the highest levels of education in various fields, a true Muslim invariably remains faithful to his religion.

It should be noted that most, if not all, of the educational systems of the Middle Eastern countries were copied from previous colonial experiences, and that this hindered these countries' educational policies, since adjustment compatible with their indigenous needs required lengthy and tortuous attitudinal and institutional change. The situation in Saudi Arabia was different; the Saudi educational system had an initial advantage and its *de novo* start gave the Saudi policy makers, with the benefit of advice from the most advanced educational systems of the world, an excellent opportunity to gear the system's needs to the country's requirements.

16.2 Primary and secondary school education

In the Kingdom, there are four levels of education below higher education. First, there is the pre-school level, which is a small sector of educational activity, currently confined mainly to cities and towns. Secondly, there is the elementary level, which caters for the educational needs of children from the age of six to twelve. Thirdly, there is the intermediate level, which caters for children from twelve to fifteen. And fourthly, there is the secondary level, which caters for children from fifteen to eighteen and prepares those who are to take their education further for higher education.

There can be no clearer indication of the Kingdom's commitment to the

Table 16.2   *Number of pupils in primary and secondary education*

Year	Pre-school (000) Boys	Girls	Total	Elementary (000) Boys	Girls	Total	Intermediate (000) Boys	Girls	Total	Secondary (000) Boys	Girls	Total
1389/90 (1969/70)	3	1	4	277	120	397	56	5	61	14	2	16
1390/91 (1970/71)	4	2	6	296	132	428	61	9	70	18	2	20
1391/92 (1971/72)	4	3	7	321	154	475	71	13	84	20	3	23
1392/93 (1972/73)	5	3	8	347	174	521	79	21	100	23	4	27
1393/94 (1973/74)	6	4	10	380	198	578	86	30	116	27	6	33
1394/95 (1974/75)	8	6	14	411	223	634	99	38	137	32	10	42
1395/96 (1975/76)	9	7	16	439	247	686	107	48	155	35	14	49
1396/97 (1976/77)	9	7	16	460	266	726	122	56	178	42	18	60
1397/98 (1977/78)	10	8	18	475	278	753	133	64	197	50	20	70
1398/99 (1978/79)	13	10	23	504	299	803	149	71	220	59	25	84
1399/00 (1979/80)	14	10	24	537	325	862	165	80	245	64	29	93
1400/01 (1980/81)	16	12	28	570	360	930	169	88	257	66	34	100
1401/02 (1981/82)	19	16	35	601	397	998	177	97	274	74	42	116
1402/03 (1982/83)	23	18	41	637	437	1074	193	108	301	81	49	130
1403/04 (1983/84)	26	21	47	676	491	1167	212	123	335	88	59	147
1404/05 (1984/85)	30	25	55	720	522	1242	232	141	373	93	65	158
1405/06 (1985/86)	41	27	68	762	555	1317	240	148	388	100	72	172
1406/07 (1986/87)	33	27	60	811	649	1460	267	165	432	114	85	199

education of all its people than the massive investment in all four levels of education over the last two decades. Table 16.2 provides a collation of relevant statistics (1389/90–1406/07 AH: 1970–87), taken from data supplied by the Ministry of Education and the Directorate General for Girls' Education.

Primary and secondary education are largely the responsibility of the Ministry of Education, which caters for male pupils, and the General Presidency for Girls' Education. (Although there is a private educational sector, the vast majority of children are educated through the State system.) The statistics provided in Table 16.2 attest to the efforts and the success of the Ministry in working towards the Kingdom's goal of providing a high standard of primary and secondary education for all. At every level of education, the number of pupils has increased year by year. It is also worth emphasizing the number of girls who are now given the benefits of education at both primary and secondary level, an essential component of the Kingdom's policy of ensuring that the entire population is literate and numerate.

16.3   Higher education

Of all the challenges facing the Kingdom in its social and economic development, there can be no doubt that the need to create a pool of highly educated Saudi Arabian citizens, capable of managing a complex modern economy, has been paramount.

Table 16.3   *General and technical education, 1405–07 AH (1985–87)*

Level and type of Education	Sex	1405/06 AH (1985/86)				1406/07 AH (1986/87)			
		Schools	Students	Teaching staff	Adminis-trators	Schools	Students	Teaching staff	Adminis-trators
Kindergartens	Co-ed	176	11,124	831	82	194	12,603	1,141	120
Elementary ed.	M.	4,433	737,127	46,640	649	4,560	785,489	47,644	623
	F.	3,197	567,526	37,999	1,767	3,226	627,565	39,475	1,967
Intermediate ed.	M.	1,449	242,925	17,288	2,340	1,491	257,506	17,565	1,484
	F.	850	147,421	12,007	1,837	871	161,826	12,409	2,016
Secondary ed.	M.	550	101,631	5,981	824	580	109,304	6,179	575
	F.	320	72,867	5,745	944	348	82,759	6,191	1,006
Teacher ed.:	M.	63	5,585	554	80	65	5,538	477	38
(Secondary)	F.	88	4,848	467	9	95	6,111	530	6
(Junior college level)	M.	16	4,964	719	189	19	6,293	755	219
	F.	14	3,943	415	75	14	4,410	441	74
Technical ed.:									
(Secondary)	M.	34	11,023	1,440	421	34	12,782	1,448	335
(Junior college level)	M.	5	576	111	51	6	793	116	47
Other types	M.	114	26,010	2,731	741	121	18,871	2,622	741
	F.	36	2,621	459	146	36	2,666	443	156
Special ed.	M.	17	1,840	549	156	19	2,078	586	169
	F.	10	980	277	116	11	1,130	279	116
Total	M.	6,681	131,681	76,013	5,451	6,895	1,198,654	77,393	4,195
	F.	4,691	811,330	58,200	4,976	4,795	899,070	60,909	5,461
Adult ed.	M.	1,415	78,548	—	—	1,383	76,842	—	—
	F.	1,554	62,475	—	—	1,442	73,359	—	—

It is in this context that the Kingdom's massive expenditure on education at all levels, but particularly at the higher level, must be seen. Clearly, the implementation of the development plans necessitated the assistance of tens of thousands of expatriate managers, scientists, engineers and teachers. But, while the development program was pursued with their help, the Kingdom allocated resources to ensure that, as soon as reasonably possible, its own citizens should be able to assume full responsibility for their own future.

The Kingdom now has seven major universities:

– King Saud University in Riyadh, founded in 1957 as Riyadh University, renamed King Saud University in 1982

- Islamic University in the Holy City of Medina, founded in 1961
- King Abdul Aziz University in Jeddah, founded in 1967
- Imam Muhammad ibn Saud Islamic University in Riyadh, founded in 1953 and given university status in 1974
- King Faisal University in Dammam and Hofuf, founded in 1975
- King Fahd University of Petroleum and Minerals in Dhahran, founded in 1963 and given university status in 1975
- Umm Al-Qura University in the Holy City of Makkah, founded in 1979

All but two of these universities (the King Fahd University of Petroleum and Minerals and the Islamic University) admit women as well as men, and all universities admit foreign as well as Saudi Arabian students.

Later in this chapter, we will look in more detail at each of these major academic institutions.

In order to illustrate the growth and development of higher education in the Kingdom, Table 16.4 provides some key statistics on both graduates from the Kingdom's own universities and Saudi citizens obtaining degrees from universities abroad during the period 1389/90 AH to 1405/06 AH (1969/70 to 1985/86).

Table 16.4   *Saudi graduates from universities in the Kingdom and abroad*

Year	Saudi students graduating from local universities*			Saudi students graduating from universities abroad*			Grand total
	Male	Female	Total	Male	Female	Total	
1389/90 (1969/70)	795	13	808	0	0	0	808
1390/91 (1970/71)	806	27	833	310	0	310	1,143
1391/92 (1971/72)	1,106	39	1,145	306	0	306	1,451
1392/93 (1972/73)	1,184	79	1,263	134	0	134	1,397
1393/94 (1973/74)	1,839	157	1,996	404	0	404	2,400
1394/95 (1974/75)	1,699	210	1,909	192	10	202	2,111
1395/96 (1975/76)	2,044	179	2,223	156	15	171	·2,394
1396/97 (1976/77)	2,644	566	3,210	166	20	186	3,396
1397/98 (1977/78)	3,071	804	3,875	232	17	249	4,124
1398/99 (1978/79)	3,112	911	4,023	305	30	335	4,358
1399/00 (1979/80)	3,447	1,174	4,621	474	29	503	5,124
1400/01 (1980/81)	4,446	1,505	5,951	607	32	639	6,590
1401/02 (1981/82)	4,820	1,635	6,455	1,983	137	2,120	8,575
1402/03 (1982/83)	5,295	2,416	7,711	2,218	116	2,334	10,045
1403/04 (1983/84)	6,307	3,328	9,635	2,368	277	2,645	12,280
1404/05 (1984/85)	7,220	3,925	11,145	2,500	300	2,800	13,945
1405/06 (1985/86)	8,020	4,481	12,501	2,500	300	2,800	15,301

* Graduates = graduates at all levels

The subjects studied by university students in the Kingdom of Saudi Arabia may be categorized as agriculture, medicine and medical sciences, engineering, natural sciences, education, economics and administration, social sciences, humanities, and islamic studies. To give a broad indication of the spread of students amongst these faculties we show below the percentage of total students in each faculty for the year 1985/86

Faculty category	*Percentage*
Agriculture	2.4
Medicine and medical sciences	5.8
Engineering	6.9
Natural sciences	10.2
Education	19.0
Economics and administration	10.2
Social sciences	4.0
Humanities	25.8
Islamic studies	15.7
Total	100.0

16.3.1   KING SAUD UNIVERSITY

The King Saud University (PO Box 2454, Riyadh 11451), founded in 1957 as the Riyadh University and renamed in 1982, has 2,000 teachers, more than 30,000 undergraduate students and more than 600 postgraduate students (almost 40 per cent of whom are female). As one of the first institutions of higher education in Saudi Arabia, it has on its register more than a quarter of all the Kingdom's university level students (male and female) and more than one-third of all the Kingdom's university and administrative staff.

There are colleges of administrative sciences, agriculture, agriculture and vetinary sciences (in Al-Qasim), arts, computer sciences, dentistry, economics and administration (in Al-Qasim), education (also in Abha), engineering, medicine (also in Abha and Al-Qasim), allied medical sciences, pharmacy and science.

There is also a college for Graduate Studies, a Center for Women's University Studies and an Arabic Language Institute.

The faculties authorized to confer higher degrees are as follows:

1   The Faculty of Arts has conferred Masters of Arts degrees in Geography and History since 1973–74 (1393–94 AH) and in Arabic Language since 1975–76 (1395–96 AH). Since 1975, the Faculty of Arts has also offered a one-year program leading to a Diploma in

Table 16.5 *Students in higher education by level of certificate and field of study, 1985/86*

Field of study	Below Bachelor		Bachelor		Higher Diploma		Master		Doctorate	
	M & F	F	M & F	F	M & F	F	M & F	F	M & F	F
Total	1,511	68	96,422	39,422	260	34	3,251	819	698	164
Islamic studies	—	—	14,655	3,023	1	—	1,017	73	454	35
Humanities	1,338	68	24,817	14,630	—	—	355	154	73	29
Social sciences	—	—	3,943	1,597	88	—	71	18	34	2
Economics and administration	—	—	10,243	2,615	—	—	232	1	—	—
Education	73	—	18,355	10,413	171	34	799	458	88	88
Natural sciences	100	—	10,075	3,981	—	—	285	94	5	2
Engineering	—	—	5,589	144	—	—	399	—	23	—
Medicine	—	—	5,857	2,467	—	—	42	15	21*	8*
Agriculture	—	—	2,408	552	—	—	51	6	—	—
Not specified	—	—	1,047	—	—	—	—	—	—	—

* Fellowship in medicine
Source: Ministry of Higher Education

Information and now confers a Bachelor of Arts degree in that subject.

2   The Faculty of Education offers: (a) a one-year diploma program in Educational Administration, usually offered to the Directors (Principals) of the general high schools; (b) a diploma in Education. There are several other higher education programs offered by this faculty.

The King Saud University admits women. As early as 1961–62 (1381–82 AH) women were allowed to enrol as external students in the Colleges of Arts and Administrative Sciences. In 1975–76 (1395–96 AH), they were accepted as full-time students. The Center for Women's University Studies was established a year later, to provide a center for the development and supervision of all aspects of women's higher education. Women students now pursue their studies in a wide range of subjects including Arabic language, English language, geography, history, sociology and social work.

16.3.2   ISLAMIC UNIVERSITY

The Islamic University (PO Box 170, Medina), founded in 1961, has 250 teachers, more than 2,000 students at undergraduate level and almost 250 at Higher Studies level. The University has faculties of Islamic Law (*Shari'ah*), the Holy *Quran* and Islamic Studies, *Da'wa* and *Usul Al-Din*, Islamic Traditions (*Hadith*) and Arabic Language.

The Islamic University in Medina is analogous to the Al-Azhar University of Cairo. It is essentially a school of Islamic theology. While, in recent years, the Al-Azhar of Cairo has expanded its field to secular programs of study such as medicine and engineering, the Islamic University in Medina continues to focus all its resources on religious affairs.

Saudi students constitute almost 80 per cent of the total enrolment. Foreign students have come to the Islamic University from more than 70 countries.

16.3.3   KING ABDUL AZIZ UNIVERSITY

The King Abdul Aziz University (PO Box 1540, Jeddah 21441), founded in 1967, has 2,071 teachers and more than 28,000 students (registered for the academic year 1989–90).

Established initially as a private university, King Abdul Aziz University was converted to a state university in 1971. It has the following faculties: arts and humanities, earth sciences, economics and administration, education (in Medina), engineering, marine sciences, medicine and allied sciences, meteorology and science.

The University awards Masters degrees in earth sciences, economics and administration, education, humanities, marine sciences, meteorology and the environment, and sciences. It awards Doctorates in earth sciences and education.

The Research and Development Center (which forms part of the Faculty of Economics and Administration), the International Center for Research in Islamic Economics and the King Fahd Medical Research Center, (all in Jeddah), are attached to the King Abdul Aziz University.

In 1988, 2,816 students graduated from the King Abdul Aziz University – 60 students from the higher studies section and 2,756 students (either regular or affiliated) from the Bachelor degree section. In the same year, the University hosted a number of important conferences and seminars, including the 10th Computer Conference and Exhibition and the Second Seminar for Academic Guidance. The annual Books Exhibition attracted some 47 publishing houses and more than 15,000 books.

16.3.4   IMAM MUHAMMAD IBN SAUD ISLAMIC UNIVERSITY

The Imam Muhammad ibn Saud Islamic University (PO Box 5701, Riyadh), founded in 1953 and accorded university status in 1974, has more than 1,000 teachers and more than 12,000 students (including almost 900 registered for graduate studies). The total number of female students registered in 1986 (1406 AH) was 1,546.

The Imam Muhammad ibn Saud University is an international educational and cultural institution. It was formally inaugurated by Royal Decree in 1974. Currently the University is composed of several faculties. The High Judiciary Institute was originally established in 1965 (1385 AH) for the purpose of graduating qualified

Shari'ah judges. The Faculty of *Shari'ah* (Theology) was established in 1953 (1373 AH) for the purpose of meeting the demand for qualified *Ulama* and preachers throughout the country. The Faculty of Arabic Language and Social Science was originally established as the Faculty of Social Science in 1970 (1390 AH) and was expanded in 1974 (1394 AH) by adding the Arabic Language major and a program in library science.

The University currently comprises two institutes and ten faculties. These are:

> Institutes
> – Higher Institute of Islamic *Da'wa*
> – Higher Judiciary Institute
> Faculties
> – Arabic
> – Arabic and Social Sciences (in Al-Qassim and also in the south)
> – *Da'wa* and Mass Communication
> – Fundamentals of Religion
> – *Shari'ah*
> – *Shari'ah* and the Fundamentals of Religion (in Al-Qassim and also in the south)
> – *Shari'ah* and Islamic Studies (in Al-Hasa)
> – Social Sciences

16.3.5 KING FAISAL UNIVERSITY

The King Faisal University in Dammam and Hofuf (PO Box 1982, Dammam), founded in 1975, has some 500 teachers. The total student enrolment in 1988 (1408 AH) was 4,026, of which 1,880 were female.

The idea of establishing a university in the Eastern Province was originated by the late King Faisal in 1974 (1394 AH). The then Crown Prince Fahd's efforts brought into existence the King Faisal University, which was inaugurated during the academic year 1975–76 (1395–96 AH) with two campuses. The first campus is in Hofuf in Al-Hasa and it comprises the Faculties of Agriculture, and Veterinary Medicine and Animal Resources. The second campus is located in Dammam and consists of the Faculties of Medicine and Medical Sciences (established with the educational co-operation of Harvard University), and of Engineering. The campus at Al-Hasa now also caters for female students of home economics, medicine and dentistry.

One of the main objectives of the University is to modernize teaching methods. It is also committed to the development of study plans to serve the requirements of the local environment. In this context, the University offers consultancy, guidance and training programs for several bodies in the field of community service. The Community Service Center in the University encourages teaching staff to develop technical skills (in agriculture, commerce, education and engineering) to meet requirements at local community level.

16.3.6   KING FAHD UNIVERSITY OF PETROLEUM AND MINERALS

The King Fahd University of Petroleum and Minerals (PO Box 144, Dhahran 31261) was founded in 1963 with less than 100 students under the name of the College of Petroleum and Minerals. In 1964, the University decided to admit other Arab and Muslim students along with Saudi students. The College was officially inaugurated in 1965 by the late King Faisal who, on that occasion, declared that "it is a great pleasure for us to take part in inaugurating this great institution, of which the least that can be said is that it represents one of the pillars of our scientific, economic and industrial development". By 1974, student enrolment had increased to 1,500 and it was accorded university status in 1975. In December 1986 (1407 AH), the University became the King Fahd University of Petroleum and Minerals. The University has some 800 teachers and, in 1988 (1408 AH), there were 4,599 students at undergraduate level and 371 at postgraduate level.

The University is a semi-autonomous institution operating under an independent University Board, headed by the Minister of Higher Education. It has six teaching colleges:

- Applied Engineering
- Computer Science and Engineering
- Engineering Science
- Environmental Design
- Industrial Management
- Sciences

It also has a College of Educational Services, a Graduate School, a Center of Applied Geology and a Data Processing Center.

> Studies in the University concentrate on the areas of petroleum and minerals and much encouragement is given to related scientific research. The University endeavours to promote awareness and understanding of petroleum and mineral issues in the Kingdom. Most important is that the University trains skilled manpower needed for the petroleum and mineral industries in the Kingdom. The University keeps abreast of the latest technological and scientific developments in the field. The University awards the Bachelors degree in certain fields of engineering and science. There are also Masters and Doctoral programmes in some fields of science, engineering sciences and industrial management. The University also has a well-equipped research institute (the UPM Research Institute).

Source: Ministry of Education

The research institute has six divisions:

- Economic and Industrial Research
- Energy Resources
- Geology and Minerals
- Meteorology Standards and Materials
- Petroleum and Gas Technology
- Water and the Environment

The King Fahd University of Petroleum and Minerals can now claim to be a University with internationally acknowledged and respected standards of academic and technical excellence in the fields of petroleum and mineral technology.

Because of the importance of oil to the Kingdom's economy and the key role that the King Fahd University of Petroleum and Minerals plays in it, it is appropriate to give further details of the University's development since its foundation.

When the University (then a college) first started in 1963, student enrolment was 67 and there was a faculty strength of fourteen. In 1978, student enrolment was 2,350, of whom eight per cent were non-Saudi students from 25 Arabian Islamic countries. The faculty strength had reached 388 from 25 different countries, including 37 Saudi professors with PhD degrees. Over 100 Saudi "faculty" members were in training in the United States, working for their PhDs. By 1983, 3,814 students had enrolled.

Saudi students enrolled at the University received generous financial aid from the government (free tuition, monthly allowance, subsidized meals at the University's cafeteria, essential medical care, furnished and air-conditioned accommodation, free textbooks and round-trip air transportation to the student's place of residence once each academic year). The University offered similar scholarships to non-Saudi students from the Arab and Islamic world. It had students from Bahrain, Egypt, Ethiopia, Indonesia, Iraq, Jordan, Lebanon, Morocco, Pakistan, Qatar, Sudan, Syria, Tunisia and Yemen.

The University was governed by a Board consisting of prominent Saudi and non-Saudi scholars and government officials. The Saudi Minister of Petroleum and Mineral Resources was its chairman until 1976, when the Minister of Higher Education became Chairman of the Board.

The University of Petroleum and Minerals' academic program to train the manpower for the petroleum and related industries was complemented by the decision to set up a major Applied Research Institute to help solve technical problems in this field. The Institute's program included six areas of focus – petroleum and gas; alternative sources of energy (such as solar power); minerals; water and the environment; standards metrology; and economic and industrial research.

A SR 900 million ($260 million) expansion of campus facilities began in 1977,

Table 16.6 Number of students studying abroad by country and main fields of study, 1405/1406 AH (1985/86). (Table cont. on p. 265)

Country	Humanities		Education		Fine arts		Law		Sociological sciences		Physics		Engineering		Medicine		Agriculture		Others		Total		
	M.	F.	M.	F.	M.	F.	M.	F.	M.	F.	M.	F.	M.	F.	M.	F.	M.	F.	M.	F.	M.	F.	T.
1 Arab countries																							
Egypt	10	4	2	2	1	1	4	—	17	25	3	1	3	—	39	10	—	—	76	72	155	115	270
Morocco	—	—	—	—	—	—	2	—	—	3	—	—	—	—	1	—	—	—	—	12	3	15	18
Iraq	—	2	—	—	—	—	1	—	1	2	1	—	2	—	2	—	—	—	—	—	6	4	10
Jordan	4	4	2	8	—	1	—	—	8	13	1	2	2	1	1	2	—	2	—	—	18	33	51
Kuwait	3	10	1	5	1	—	3	1	15	21	4	7	—	—	2	—	—	—	19	6	48	50	98
Syria	—	4	—	3	—	1	1	1	—	1	—	1	7	—	14	9	—	—	—	—	22	20	42
Bahrain	—	—	—	—	—	—	—	—	—	—	—	—	—	—	8	4	—	—	—	37	8	41	49
Tunisia	1	7	—	—	—	—	—	—	—	—	—	—	—	—	—	1	—	—	—	—	1	8	9
Algeria	2	3	—	—	—	—	—	—	—	—	—	—	—	—	—	—	—	—	—	—	1	3	4
UAE	5	1	—	—	—	—	—	—	—	2	—	—	4	—	—	—	—	—	180	379	189	382	571
Qatar	—	1	—	15	—	—	—	—	—	—	—	—	—	—	—	—	—	—	—	—	9	16	25
Oman	—	—	—	140	—	—	—	—	—	—	—	—	—	—	—	—	—	—	—	—	—	140	140
Sudan	—	—	1	—	—	—	—	—	—	—	—	—	—	—	—	—	—	—	—	22	1	22	23
Total	25	36	6	173	2	3	11	2	40	67	8	11	18	1	67	26	—	2	275	528	461	849	1310
2 Islamic non-Arab countries																							
Pakistan	—	—	—	—	—	—	—	—	—	—	1	—	1	—	64	10	—	—	—	—	66	10	76
Turkey	—	—	—	—	—	—	—	—	—	—	—	—	—	—	2	—	—	—	1	—	3	—	3
Total	—	—	—	—	—	—	—	—	—	—	1	—	1	—	66	10	—	—	1	—	69	10	79
3 Europe																							
France	9	34	—	1	—	1	11	—	4	1	3	1	1	1	4	2	—	—	2	—	34	39	73
U.K.	33	1	7	1	—	9	4	1	96	11	194	2	54	—	120	15	26	—	521	29	1055	62	1117
W. Germany	4	—	3	37	—	—	—	2	1	—	—	—	116	—	85	3	—	—	—	—	209	51	260
Swiss	6	24	—	—	—	1	—	—	5	5	—	—	1	—	3	—	—	—	—	—	15	31	46
Italy	—	—	—	—	7	—	—	1	—	3	—	2	—	—	1	—	—	—	10	14	18	17	35
Austria	—	3	—	—	—	—	—	—	1	4	—	—	1	—	71	3	—	—	—	28	73	40	113
Total	52	62	10	39	7	11	15	4	107	24	197	5	173	1	284	23	26	—	533	71	1404	240	1644

Table 16.1 – cont.

4 United States	227	159	260	50	13	15	15	—	986	66	431	47	778	67	90	10	53	2	584	1223	3437	1639	5076
5 Other countries																							
Canada	1	—	1	86	1	—	1	—	3	—	1	—	10	—	120	12	—	—	—	—	138	98	236
China	1	1	—	—	—	—	1	—	1	1	—	1	1	—	3	—	—	—	—	7	7	10	17
Brazil	—	—	—	—	—	—	—	—	—	—	—	—	—	—	—	—	—	—	—	—	—	—	—
Total	2	1	1	86	1	—	2	—	4	1	1	1	11	—	123	12	—	—	—	7	145	108	253
Grand total	306	258	277	348	23	29	43	6	1146	158	638	64	981	69	630	81	79	4	1393	1829	5516	2846	8362

Source: Ministry of Higher Education

including a 24,000-square-meter building for the Research Institute; a building for the Graduate School, College of Industrial Management and the Data Processing Center; a conference center within the Department of Architecture; a 10,000-seat stadium; and a doubling of family and student housing.

By 1978, UPM had graduated 1,000 engineers and industrial managers. By 1988, the University, now the King Fahd University of Petroleum and Minerals, had awarded more than 4,940 degrees, including 520 Masters and 4 PhD degrees.

16.3.7   UMM AL-QURA UNIVERSITY

The Umm Al-Qura University (PO Box 407/715, Makkah), founded in 1979 and accorded university status in 1981–82 (1401–02 AH), had on its register almost 14,000 undergraduate students in the year 1986–87 (1406–07 AH), of whom more than 6,000 were female, and more than 400 postgraduate students.

Originally, this institution included colleges of *Shari'ah* and education and an institute to teach Arabic language to non-Arabs, all of which functioned as branches of the King Abdul Aziz University. Later colleges of agricultural sciences, Arabic language, applied sciences and engineering, *Da'wa* and *Usul El-Din*, education (in Taif), and social sciences were opened.

A number of scientific centers are affiliated to the colleges of this University (for example, the Educational and Psychological Research Center, the *Hajj* Research Center, the International Center for Islamic Education, the Scientific and Engineering Research Center, and the Scientific Research and Islamic Heritage Rejuvenation Center). In addition, the Umm Al-Qura University co-operates with a number of foreign universities and other academic institutions through scientific exchange and scholarships.

16.4   Saudi Arabian National Center for Science and Technology

The Saudi Arabian National Center for Science and Technology (SANCST), an independent scientific institution, is the Kingdom's principal agency for promoting scientific and technological research and development.

SANCST was established by Royal Decree in 1977 (1397 AH) with the following objectives:

1   to conduct applied research programs which will serve the development needs of the Kingdom
2   to establish an information system center on national manpower engaged in the field of science and technology
3   to establish applied research laboratories
4   to assist the national public and the national private sector in developing research on industrial and agricultural products in order to increase national productivity

5   to support joint research programs with international scientific institutions to keep abreast of scientific development

6   to establish an information centre on local and foreign scientific institutions

7   to propose the national scientific policy which will help the State to achieve scientific development

8   to award scholarships to develop the necessary skills in scientific research

9   to award research grants to individuals and institutions to carry on applied scientific research

10   to co-ordinate the activities of government units, scientific institutions and research centers in the Kingdom to avoid duplication of effort

The central purpose of SANCST is to harness science and technology to the developmental needs of the Kingdom. The Fifth Development Plan (1410–15 AH: 1990–95) requires the Kingdom's industry in both the public and private sectors, to concentrate on improving efficiency and competitiveness (see Section 10.3 above). In achieving these goals, the application of the latest scientific developments and the most advanced technology will clearly have a major role.

16.5   Education: the future

As the economy of the Kingdom increases in complexity and as the government pursues a policy of replacing foreign labor at all levels by Saudi nationals, the provision of an efficient educational system capable of producing citizens with the skills required to manage their own and the country's affairs becomes ever more important.

With this in mind, the commitment to expanding and improving the educational system permeates all levels of society. The Fifth Development Plan (1410–15 AH: 1990–95) sets out the following strategic principles for the continued development of the educational system in the Kingdom of Saudi Arabia.

> To continue the development of Saudi manpower through the evaluation of the educational and training programs. Further development or modification should be applied conforming with the Islamic *Shari'ah*, the changing needs of society, and the requirements of the development process.

The Plan goes on to set objectives for every level and every aspect of education in the Kingdom, from primary and secondary schooling through technical training to university education. The main emphasis is placed on ensuring that the educational system is geared to producing well-educated and fully trained citizens capable of discharging the responsibilities and fulfilling the tasks which the economic and social development of Saudi Arabia demands.

For a more detailed account of the educational objectives expressed in the Fifth Development Plan, see the Sixth Basic Strategic Principle, Section 10.3.

Chapter 17

Health

The Kingdom's policy on health is simply expressed – the provision of free health services for the benefit of all the citizens of Saudi Arabia. This chapter examines this policy in more detail and gives a brief account of the Kingdom's achievements to date.

Health care is the responsibility of the Ministry of Health, which provides both general and specialized hospital services. Amongst the Kingdom's specialized hospitals are the King Faisal Specialist Hospital, the Military Hospitals and some Ministry of Health hospitals which offer, amongst other advanced medical techniques, open-heart surgery, kidney transplantation and cancer therapy.

The general health service is complemented by other agencies which provide health services for their staff (for example, the Military Agencies) or segments of the general population (for example, the Royal Commission for Jubail and Yanbu). There is an active Red Crescent Society in the Kingdom which provides medical emergency services and plays a key role in providing medical assistance during the period of the annual pilgrimage, the *Hajj*. The Kingdom's universities are also involved in health care, not only by providing primary and specialized health care for their own staff and students, but through research, training and the implementation of health education programs.

In essence, the provision of health care services depends on the skills and dedication of the medical staff at all levels – human factors which sets of statistics cannot convey. Nevertheless, Table 17.1, which shows the budget appropriations for the Ministry of Health and the Red Crescent from 1402/03 to 1406/07 AH (1982/83–1986/87), gives an indication of the Kingdom's commitment to fulfilling its policy of providing free medical services of the highest quality to all.

17.1 The development of health care

The Ministry of Health policy reflects the government's national development strategy, which is committed to improving the quality of life of the Saudi people, and helping them to participate fully in the development plan and benefiting from it.

Table 17.1   *Budget appropriations for the Ministry of Health and Red Crescent Society by main sectors 1402/03–1406/07 AH (1982/83–1986/87)*

Sector	1402/03	1403/04	1404/05	1405/06	1406/07*
			(000 Saudi Riyals)		
Ministry of Health:					
1) Salaries	3,432,000	3,225,000	3,631,000	3,760,000	3,373,750
2) Recurrent expenditures	1,700,000	1,800,000	1,808,900	1,735,000	956,377
3) Op. & maint. programs	—	730,800	1,120,000	1,109,750	1,284,056
4) Development projects	3,671,700	2,645,000	4,183,000	2,209,790	1,458,750
Total	**8,803,700**	**8,400,800**	**10,742,900**	**8,814,540**	**7,072,933**
Red Crescent Society:					
1) Salaries	101,000	95,000	147,400	103,000	94,036
2) Recurrent expenditures	32,000	29,000	27,700	18,000	8,652
3) Op. & maint. programs	1,000	3,000	3,000	11,200	9,584
4) Development projects	13,437	14,400	35,670	10,260	8,721
Total	**147,437**	**141,400**	**213,770**	**142,460**	**120,993**
Grand total	**8,951,137**	**8,542,200**	**10,956,670**	**8,957,000**	**7,193,926**

Source: Ministry of Finance and National Economy

To carry out this policy, the Ministry of Health provides a whole range of health services (preventive, curative, promotive and rehabilitative) to all the population. This is achieved through a network of hospitals and primary health care centers which are distributed throughout the country.

The health system used by the Ministry of Health stresses the importance of preventive health care as the basis for providing comprehensive health services to citizens and residents, and uses a referral system for patients who need specialized diagnosis or hospital care. At the same time, the Ministry of Health gives much attention to upgrading and improving the quality of manpower in the medical field through expanding in-service training, particularly amongst Saudi personnel, as well as improving administrative effectiveness and health research.

Health care in the Kingdom has witnessed impressive improvements and progress as shown by several and varied health indicators. By 1987, 93 per cent of the population were covered by health services. Wholesome drinking water and sanitary services were available to 93 per cent and 86 per cent of the population respectively in 1983. Immunization of infants and children against infectious diseases attained a high coverage by 1987 – 89 per cent, 89 per cent, 77 per cent and 93 per cent received DPT, Polio, Measles and BCG vaccines respectively. There has been an overall decrease in the incidence of communicable diseases. There is a reduction in infant mortality and an increase in life expectancy at birth due to high socio-economic development and better health care.

The principal health policy of the Kingdom is to provide comprehensive health

Table 17.2   *The development of the Ministry of Health budget 1970–89*

Year	Budget (million Saudi Riyals)	Percentage increase	Proportion of MOH budget to national budget
1970–71	177.1	—	2.8
1974–75	1,163	557	2.5
1979–80	4,177	2259	2.3
1985–86	8,815	4878	4.4
1988–89	7,735	4268	5.5

Source: Ministry of Health

Table 17.3   *The development of health care in Saudi Arabia 1971–88*

Ministry of Health	Year 1971	1988	Percentage increase
Hospitals	49	162	230
Hospital beds	7,942	26,315	231
Health centers	521	1,477	183
Health institutes	6	32	433
Physicians	817	11,940	1361
Nurses	2,268	27,169	1098
Technicians	1,542	14,013	809
Saudi manpower:			
Physicians	103	1,081	949
Nurses	596	2,474	315
Technicians	933	4,554	388
Total Saudis	1,632	8,109	397

All health sectors	Year 1971	1988	Percentage increase
Hospitals	75	247	229
Hospital beds	9,837	38,848	295
Health centers, dispensaries, health units, clinics	599	2,766	362
Physicians	1,316	21,144	1506
Nurses	3,355	43,963	1210
Technicians	1,982	23,030	1062
Hospital beds/1000 population	1.3	3.3	
Physicians/population	1/5,900	1/548	
Nurses/population	1/2,750	1/264	

care to all citizens and residents throughout the country. To meet the increased demand for health care, the Ministry of Health budget has increased steadily – from 177 million Saudi Riyals in the fiscal year 1970/71, representing 2.8 per cent of the national budget to SR 7,735 million in 1988/89, representing 5.5 per cent of the national budget (see Table 17.2).

The expansion of health facilities has been reflected in the increased number of health centers, dispensaries, health units and clinics from 599 in 1971 to 2,766 in 1988. Hospitals and hospital beds also increased from 75 hospitals with a total of 9,837 beds to 247 hospitals with 38,848 beds in 1988 (see Table 17.3).

At the beginning of the First Five Year Plan in 1971, there were only 75 hospitals in the Kingdom, with Riyadh Central Hospital as the only referral hospital. During the Second Plan (1975–80) five large referral hospitals were constructed and opened in various parts of the country. The five hospitals had 2,275 beds and cost a total of 3,500 million Saudi Riyals. During the Third Five Year Plan (1980–85), 32 hospitals with 7,632 beds were built, costing approximately 9,100 million Saudi Riyals. By mid-1984, King Khalid Specialist Eye Hospital was opened in Riyadh with a capacity of 220 beds and intended to offer high quality ophthalmic care. In 1985, 24 new hospitals with 5,306 beds and costing about 5,700 million Saudi Riyals were in operation. By the end of the current Fourth Development Plan (1985–90), most of the eighteen hospitals currently under construction (with 4,165 beds) at a cost of 5,100 million will be in operation. Among these hospitals are King Fahd Medical City in Riyadh (1,400 beds) and Al-Khaleeg Hospital in Dammam, in the Eastern Region (640 beds).

The great expansion in health care all over the Kingdom requires a large number of health personnel and the health manpower in the Ministry has therefore increased considerably. In 1971 the total health manpower numbered 6,653 employees; this number had risen to 84,570 in 1988. The number of physicians had increased from 1,316 to 21,144, nursing staff from 3,355 to 43,963, and allied health personnel from 1,982 to 23,030 in the same period (see Table 17.3).

To meet the increased demand for health manpower, the Ministry of Health planned and opened health institutes for males and females all over the country. The number of health institutes increased from seven in 1975 to 32 in 1988, of which sixteen are for men and sixteen for women. The number of students has risen from 154 to 4,536 and the number of graduates from 281 to 1,895 in the same period.

The Ministry plans to open intermediate health colleges in various parts of the country to improve the standard of the nursing staff and allied health personnel.

Although the responsibility for providing health care to the population of Saudi Arabia rests with the Ministry of Health, there are several government agencies which also provide health services. Some of these agencies are providing health services for their employees only, such as the Ministry of Defense, the National Guard and the Ministry of Interior.

In addition to hospitals operated by the Ministry of Health, there are the university hospitals, military hospitals, King Faisal Specialist Hospital and King

Khalid Eye Specialist Hospital; most of these hospitals have highly advanced technology and operate as referral hospitals.

17.2   The Red Crescent

The Red Crescent of Saudi Arabia (the Muslim equivalent of the Red Cross) was founded in 1383 AH (1963). It provides emergency medical services in five administrative regions of the Kingdom of Saudi Arabia. By 1987, the society had 139 first aid centers.

The Red Crescent has a particular role to play during *Hajj* (the annual pilgrimage to the Holy City of Makkah), providing on-the-spot first aid and using its fleet of vehicles (780 in 1987) to take emergency cases to the nearest medical facility.

17.3   Future plans

This chapter has given a good indication of the success already achieved in meeting the Kingdom's objectives for health care. But, as every country knows, the provision of a perfect health service is an ideal to be striven for, rather than an attainable goal.

The Fifth Development Plan (1410–15H: 1990–95) gives a high priority to the protection of children against disease in the first stages of life; to improving the services and facilities for the handicapped; and to increasing the effectiveness of programs for preventive medicine.

18

Foreign relations

This chapter examines the Kingdom of Saudi Arabia's relations with the Arab world, Western Europe, the United States of America and the Communist Bloc.

Within the Arab world, the Kingdom, working tirelessly to create and enhance Arab solidarity, has persistently pursued a policy designed to resolve disputes by diplomatic means.

In its relations with the major industrialized powers (the United States of America, Western Europe and Japan), the Kingdom of Saudi Arabia has always recognized the economic inter-dependence which must exist between those who need oil and the country which holds 25 per cent of the world's oil reserves, and has endeavored to stabilize the oil price at a level which takes account of the needs of both net producers and net consumers.

At the same time, the Kingdom of Saudi Arabia is part of the Arab world and, above all, has been entrusted with the guardianship of the Holy Places of Islam. Both its Arab and its Muslim heritage mean that its basic political tenets and its foreign policy objectives are sometimes not co-incident with those of the power blocs of the East or the West. In this context, the section on Saudi Arabian relations with the United States of America will be of special interest.

18.1 Saudi–Arab relations

It is entirely appropriate that any consideration of Saudi Arabian relations with the Arab world should begin with a brief account of the establishment of the Gulf Co-operation Council (GCC) for, in many ways, the GCC demonstrates, albeit in a small regional area, what can be achieved with good will and good sense in terms of increasing Arab solidarity.

18.1.1 THE GULF CO-OPERATION COUNCIL (GCC)

The Co-operation Council for the Arab States of the Gulf, more commonly known as the Gulf Co-operation Council (GCC), was founded on 22 Rajab 1401 AH (25th

May 1981), when the heads of state of Bahrain, Kuwait, Qatar, the Kingdom of Saudi Arabia, the Sultanate of Oman and the United Arab Emirates signed the new organization's constitution.

The constitution of the GCC requires the organization to provide "the means for realizing co-ordination, integration and co-operation" in economic, social and cultural affairs. Specifically, the GCC aims:

- to achieve co-ordination, integration and close ties leading to unity between the member states
- to deepen the ties, relations and all aspects of co-operation between the peoples of the region
- to adopt similar systems and laws in: economics and financial affairs; commercial, customs and transportation affairs; education and cultural affairs; social and health affairs; communication, informational, political, legislative and administrative affairs
- to encourage progress in the sciences and technologies involved in industry, mining, agriculture, water and animal resources, and to establish scientific research centers and to undertake joint projects

The structure of the organization consists of the Supreme Council, the Ministerial Council and the Secretariat General:

- The Supreme Council (the highest authority of the GCC) comprises the heads of state of the six member countries. The Supreme Council meets once a year in ordinary session. Emergency sessions can be convened at any time by the heads of any two member states. The chairmanship of the Council is held by each member state in turn. Resolutions are carried by majority vote. The Supreme Council is responsible for determining the overall policy of the GCC and for ratifying recommendations presented to it by the Ministerial Council or the Secretariat General.
- The Ministerial Council comprises the Foreign Ministers of the six member countries. The Ministerial Council meets once every three months in ordinary session. Emergency sessions can be convened at any time by the Foreign Ministers of any two member states. The Ministerial Council draws up policies and makes recommendations on means of developing co-operation and co-ordination amongst member states in the economic, social and cultural spheres.
- The Secretariat General prepares reports, studies, accounts and budgets for the GCC. It drafts rules and regulations and is charged with the responsibility of assisting member states in the implementation of decisions taken by the Supreme and Ministerial Councils. The Secretary General is appointed for a three-year period (renewable) by

the Supreme Council on the recommendation of the Ministerial Council.

The Secretariat is based in the city of Riyadh (PO Box 7153, Riyadh, 11462). It has recently moved to new headquarters in the Diplomatic Quarter, where a substantial complex, financed by a gift from King Fahd, has been built to meet the Secretariat's present and future needs.

The GCC represents a bold move towards regional integration. The speed of its progress has been remarkable, aided by the homogeneity of religious commitment and common economic, social and cultural interests. In the past, there have been a number of grandiose schemes to unite parts of the Arab world, all of which have foundered. The GCC, more modest in ambition, has shown how, with the commitment of heads of state, a well-planned and rational program of integration is possible, given time to resolve the inevitable problems.

The Gulf Investment Corporation

In 1983, the six member states of the GCC founded the Gulf Investment Corporation. The Corporation, which is based in Kuwait (PO Box 3402, Safat, 13035), is involved in investing in a wide range of industrial and agricultural projects in the GCC countries.

Trade exchange between the Kingdom of Saudi Arabia and the other GCC countries

Table 18.1 shows the trade exchange between the Kingdom of Saudi Arabia and the other GCC countries from 1974 to 1986. Trade peaked in 1981 and has fallen since then, reflecting the diminution in trade caused by the collapse of the oil price.

18.1.2   SAUDI ARABIA'S WIDER RELATIONS WITH OTHER ARAB COUNTRIES

In its relations with the wider Arab world, the Kingdom's policy is to assist in the economic and social development of less wealthy Arab countries and to use its substantial diplomatic influence to resolve inter-Arab disputes wherever possible.

Economic and social activities

In terms of Saudi Arabia's involvement in the economic and social development of the Arab world, it may be useful to list some of the international organizations of which the Kingdom is a member:

- AAAID – Arab Authority for Agricultural Investment and Development, (PO Box 2102, Khartoum, Sudan), founded in 1976, with the primary objective of assisting in the agricultural development of the Arab world.
- AGFUND – Arab Gulf Program for the United Nations Development

Table 18.1   *Trade exchange between the Kingdom and Gulf Co-operation Council countries 1974–86*

Year	Exports		Imports	
	Value (000 SR)	Index 1974 = 100	Value (000 SR)	Index 1974 = 100
1974	2,888,414	100.0	762,335	100.0
1975	2,374,367	82.2	1,024,441	134.4
1976	2,652,760	91.8	3,693,075	484.4
1977	3,489,897	120.8	3,484,573	457.1
1978	3,418,966	118.4	671,936	88.1
1979	4,857,796	168.2	1,112,795	146.0
1980	7,553,565	261.5	1,107293	145.3
1981	10,212,378	353.6	1,624,878	213.1
1982	8,096,122	280.3	1,905,706	250.0
1983	5,386,382	186.5	1,753,438	230.0
1984	5,615,681	194.4	1,538,851	201.9
1985	5,191,265	179.7	1,808,169	237.2
1986	4,850,921	167.9	1,441,141	189.0

Source: Central Department of Statistics (Foreign Trade Statistics)

Organization (PO Box 18371, Riyadh 11415), founded in 1981, to help finance projects undertaken by the United Nations' organizations and to co-ordinate the aid efforts of the GCC countries.
- Arab Bureau of Education for the Gulf States (PO Box 3908, Riyadh 11481), which aims at the co-ordination and, wherever possible, the integration of the educational and scientific efforts of the GCC member states.
- Arab Towns Organization (PO Box 4954, Safat 13050, Kuwait), founded in 1967, with the primary objective of assisting Arab towns in resolving environmental problems.
- AFESD – Arab Fund for Economic and Social Development (PO Box 21923, Safat, Kuwait), founded in 1968, to help finance economic and social development projects in the Arab states.
- Arab Sports Federation (PO Box 6040, Riyadh), founded in 1976, to encourage the development of and regional co-operation in sport.
- Center for Research in Islamic Economics (PO Box 16711, King Abdul Aziz University, Jeddah 21474), founded in 1977, to co-ordinate and support research into Islamic economics.
- ESCWA – Economic and Social Commission for Western Asia (Amiriyah, PO Box 27, Baghdad, Iraq), founded in 1974, to expand the facilities for researching and co-ordinating developmental activities,

previously offered by the United Nations Economic and Social Office in Beirut.
- GOIC – Gulf Organization for Industrial Consulting (PO Box 5114, Doha, Qatar), with the objective of co-ordinating industrial development and mounting joint venture projects in the region.
- Islamic Institute of Defense Technology (16 Grosvenor Crescent, London SW1, England), founded in 1978.
- International Association of Islamic Banks (PO Box 4992, Jeddah), founded in 1977.
- Muslim World League (PO Box 537, Makkah), founded in 1962, to promote Islamic unity.

Through these and many other organizations, the Kingdom of Saudi Arabia deploys its energies and resources for the advancement of Islamic and Arab unity, and to assist in the economic and social development of the Arab world. (For details of the aid provided by the Kingdom of Saudi Arabia to the developing world, see Chapter 19.)

Political activities
On the political front, the Kingdom of Saudi Arabia is tireless in its efforts to resolve disputes between or involving Arab nations.

The long-running Iraq/Iran war saw the Kingdom using every diplomatic means at its disposal to bring about a cessation of hostilities. In the dispute between the Moroccan government and the Polisario, Saudi Arabia has taken an active role in trying to bring the two sides together. Closer to home, in border disputes between member states of the GCC, the Kingdom has used its good offices to bring about a peaceful solution. In Lebanon, as a member of the Arab League, the Kingdom has consistently endeavored to ameliorate a virtually anarchic situation which involves Lebanese Muslims, Lebanese Christians and Israel in a seemingly endless cycle of violence. And in the most intractable problem of all, the Palestinian/Israeli problem, Saudi Arabia has taken a number of diplomatic initiatives in an effort to secure for the Palestinians at least basic human rights.

In common with all countries, the Kingdom is mindful of the need to be able to defend itself. Yet it is fair to say that the main distinguishing feature of the Kingdom's foreign policy within the Arab world (and, for that matter, outside it) is not to make wild, provocative pronouncements or to resort to threats or military action, but to work quietly and yet energetically at the diplomatic level to promote the cause of peace with justice. In a region noted for its instability and beset by regional conflict, the value of the Kingdom's role at the political and diplomatic level should not be underestimated.

Table 18.2 *Trade exchange between the Kingdom and other Arab League countries (excluding Gulf Co-operation Council) 1974–86*

Year	Exports		Imports	
	Value (000 SR)	Index 1974 = 100	Value (000 SR)	Index 1974 = 100
1974	2,133,629	100.0	2,223,555	100.0
1975	1,275,865	59.8	2,662,049	119.7
1976	1,790,358	83.9	3,793,585	170.6
1977	2,457,294	115.2	3,927,211	176.6
1978	1,855,752	87.0	2,409,254	108.4
1979	3,839,280	179.9	2,762,067	124.2
1980	6,710,856	314.5	3,231,442	145.3
1981	10,318,938	483.6	3,748,347	168.6
1982	7,668,743	359.4	3,317,747	149.2
1983	6,356,925	297.9	2,844,225	127.9
1984	5,126,501	240.3	2,151,905	96.8
1985	4,897,050	229.5	1,737,893	78.7
1986	2,479,778	116.2	1,489,405	66.9

Source: Central Department of Statistics (Foreign Trade Statistics)

Trade exchanges between the Kingdom of Saudi Arabia and other Arab countries, excluding the GCC

Table 18.2 shows the trade exchange between the Kingdom of Saudi Arabia and other Arab countries (excluding the GCC states) from 1974 to 1986.

18.1.3 THE ARAB LEAGUE

The Arab League (officially, the League of Arab States) was formed in 1945. The founder members were the Kingdom of Saudi Arabia, Egypt, Jordan (then Transjordan), Lebanon, Iraq, Syria and Yemen (now the Yemen Arab Republic). The purpose of the League was to foster Arab co-operation and unity.

Since its formation, another fourteen Arab states have joined the League. The Palestinian Liberation Organization, representing Palestine, is also a full member of the League.

Egypt was expelled from the League in 1979, following its bi-lateral peace agreement with Israel (the Camp David Accords). After ten years of isolation, Egypt was re-admitted to the League in 1989. The present membership of the League is as follows:

– Algeria
– Bahrain

- Djibouti
- Egypt
- Iraq
- Jordan
- Kuwait
- Lebanon
- Libya
- Mauritania
- Morocco
- Oman
- Palestine
- Qatar
- Saudi Arabia
- Somalia
- Sudan
- Syria
- Tunisia
- United Arab Emirates
- Yemen Arab Republic
- Yemen People's Democratic Republic

The headquarters of the Arab League is in Tunisia (37 Avenue Khereddine Pacha, Tunis). The League's organization consists of a Council and a General Secretariat.

The Council, which is the Arab League's supreme authority, includes all the member states, each state having one vote. (The League is a voluntary association of sovereign Arab states and decisions are binding only on those states which have voted in support of a resolution.)

Attached to the League are a number of committees dealing with key aspects of policy. These are:

- The Permanent Committee for Administrative and Financial Affairs
- The Committee of Arab Experts on Co-operation
- Arab Oil Experts Committee
- Arab Women's Committee
- Communications Committee
- Cultural Committee
- Economic Committee
- Health Committee
- Human Rights Committee
- Information Committee
- Legal Committee
- The Permanent Committee for Meteorology

  – Political Committee
  – Social Committee

In addition, there is an Organization of Youth Welfare.

The General Secretariat of the Arab League is charged with the responsibility of implementing the decisions of the Council and provides a wide range of financial, research and administrative services.

18.2 Saudi Arabian relations with Western Europe

8.2.1 SAUDI-BRITISH RELATIONS

Saudi Arabia's first major contact with a major Western power occurred in 1915.

> On December 26, 1915, Britain and Ibn Saud [the late King Abdul Aziz Al Sa'ud was and still is widely known in the West as Ibn Saud] signed a treaty that secured the latter's benevolent neutrality
>
> > *Source: The Middle East in World Affairs* by George Lenczowski (Ithaca, NY: Cornell University Press, 1956)

In return, Britain recognized Ibn Saud's undisputed sovereignty over Najd and Al-Hasa. From 1915 through 1949,

> Saudi Arabian–British relations [were] determined by the encircling presence of more than a dozen political entities, vestiges of former empires still under the suzerainty of Great Britain, which dot the rim of the Arabian Peninsula.
>
> > *Source: Area Handbook for Saudi Arabia*, Washington, DC (US Government Printing Office, 1971)

Consequently, as events developed in the decade following 1915, King Abdul Aziz had become by 1926 the sole ruler of most of the Arabian Peninsula. In 1927, Saudi Arabia and Britain entered into full diplomatic relations at the ambassadorial level, when Britain recognized the sovereignty of Ibn Saud as the King of Hijaz and Sultan of Najd and its Dependencies. As a quid pro quo, Saudi Arabia acknowledged Britain's rights in Bahrain and other political entities in the area. Relations with Britain remained traditionally good up to the late 1940s, during which period Britain gained no new political or military privileges in Saudi Arabia, although British trade and business in Jeddah prospered. By 1949, relations had begun to deteriorate over the Buraimi Oasis issue, which was followed by unsuccessful boundary negotiations between the two countries. When the conflict was submitted to arbitration in Geneva in 1954–55, the British representative withdrew from the tribunal panel, thus creating a deadlock in the talks. The Saudi government, in November 1956, severed its diplomatic relations with Britain because of the latter's invasion of Egypt. It was not until January 1963 that diplomatic relations were restored.

In short, Saudi-British relations from 1925 to 1950 were mainly concerned with the fulfilment of boundary agreements concluded between the two nations.

In recent years, relations between Britain and the Kingdom of Saudi Arabia have flourished. Britain, amongst a number of other developed nations, has supplied a large number of skilled expatriate workers to assist the Kingdom in the implementation of its development plans. Many British companies have won substantial contracts in the Kingdom as the country's industrial and commercial base has expanded and consequently Britain has enjoyed an extremely favorable trade balance with the Kingdom.

Apart from industrial and commercial contracts, Britain has become a major supplier of military equipment, culminating in the sale of a number of Tornado fighter/bomber aircraft to meet the Kingdom's defense requirements. When the contract's provisions for maintenance and the supply of associated materials and services are taken into account, this sale, described by the British press as "the sale of the century", will almost certainly prove to be the largest single arms contract ever awarded.

On one subject, Britain and the Kingdom of Saudi Arabia have failed to see eye to eye. With the discovery and exploitation of North Sea oil, Britain became a major oil exporter in the 1980s. Despite this economic fact, the British government has persistently refused even to discuss the possibility of co-operating with the Organization of Petroleum Exporting Countries in stabilizing the oil price by adjusting the volume of oil production. While other countries (for example, Norway and the Soviet Union) have perceived the wisdom of at least trying to moderate wild market fluctuations which damage the economies of producers and consumers by turn, Britain has persisted in a "free market" philosophy, happily reaping the benefits of others' restraint in the early 1980s by selling as much oil as it could pump and still to this day refusing to co-operate in efforts to stabilize the oil price at a level which is fair to both producers and consumers. Such a short-term, commercial approach scarcely seems appropriate in the context of an essential and finite energy source.

In the next century, the real issue will be the question of how to manage a dwindling resource in the interests of a highly inter-dependent world economy. When Britain's own oil runs out and it rejoins the ranks of oil importers, there will, once again, be a "seller's market". At that time, the argument that producers and consumers should work together to establish a price that is fair to both will no doubt gain momentum in Britain. In this context, it is appropriate to quote from an article in the London *Times* (4th January 1990):

> There are hopes that the Opec policies of the 1990s [when non-OPEC oil

sources begin to dwindle] will be more realistic [than in the 1970s] and that the organization will realize the benefits of having a stable price so that more serious long-term economic planning can take place.

18.2.2 SAUDI ARABIAN RELATIONS WITH THE EUROPEAN COMMUNITY

Saudi Arabian relations with the European Community have both a political and an economic dimension.

On the political front, Saudi Arabian relations with the European Community, and the individual members of it, have been excellent, although, from the Saudi Arabian viewpoint, they have never entirely fulfilled their promise. In 1980, the European Economic Community pledged its support for the principle of Palestinian self-determination (the Venice declaration), but the Community has not converted this support in principle into effective diplomatic pressure. To some extent, this ineffectiveness has derived from a lack of political cohesion and determination amongst the member states of the European Community (the old rivalries between ex-colonial powers evidently dies hard). But, to be fair to the European Community, it has to be admitted that Europe's ability to influence Israel is modest in comparison with that of the United States of America, which holds the key to any peaceful solution to the Palestinian/Israeli problem.

At the same time, the Kingdom of Saudi Arabia is eager to maintain the best possible political relations with the European Community, for, in efforts to find a just settlement to the Palestinian/Israeli problem, it acts as a moderating influence on the overtly pro-Israeli stance of the United States of America.

In economic terms relations have, at least in one respect, been rather disappointing. Western European countries played a major role in helping to build the Kingdom's infrastructure, and thus much of the wealth generated by the Kingdom's oil sales returned to Europe. As part of the Kingdom's industrial diversification, Saudi Arabia developed and expanded its petrochemical production capacity, in the hope that, just as it had given the EC countries free (or almost free) access to its own markets, the EC countries would reciprocate when the Kingdom exported petrochemicals. The Gulf Co-operation Council (GCC) raised the issue of a free-trade agreement between itself and the European Community several years ago but it was not until mid-1987 that talks began in earnest, only to meet with vigorous opposition, particularly from Western Europe's petrochemical industry. As the *Independent* newspaper reported (25th June 1987):

> Pressure by the six Arab countries in the Gulf Co-operation Council for a comprehensive free-trade agreement with the European Community has been gently rebuffed by EC governments.

The main cause for this "gentle rebuff" was the demand by the European petrochemical industry for protection.

This particular issue aside, economic relations between the Kingdom of Saudi Arabia and the European Community have been of very great mutual benefit. Just as the Kingdom is able to supply the Community with much-needed oil, so the Kingdom has been able to call on the expertise and advanced technology of Europe to help it achieve its developmental goals. As the Kingdom's diversification program continues, and the agricultural and industrial base broadens, the economic relationship between the Kingdom of Saudi Arabia and the EC will alter, but, with the undoubted goodwill that exists on both sides, there is no reason why the necessary adjustments cannot be readily accommodated.

Table 18.3 shows the trade exchange between the Kingdom of Saudi Arabia and Western European countries from 1974 to 1986.

Table 18.3 *Trade exchange between the Kingdom and Western European countries 1974–86*

Year	Exports		Imports	
	Value *(000 SR)*	*Index* *1974 = 100*	*Value* *(000 SR)*	*Index* *1974 = 100*
1974	63,874,286	100.0	2,522,185	100.0
1975	45,345,655	71.0	4,538,045	179.9
1976	55,353,837	86.7	10,458,347	414.7
1977	60,515,501	94.7	18,897,880	749.3
1978	51,444,233	80.5	30,090,757	1193.0
1979	85,806,120	134.3	35,377,915	1402.7
1980	150,398,467	235.5	41,392,739	1641.1
1981	166,077,644	260.0	47,591,175	1886.9
1982	91,834,108	143.8	56,909,284	2256.3
1983	37,382,880	58.5	56,200,644	2228.3
1984	26,301,257	41.2	49,116,592	1947.8
1985	23,839,446	37.3	34,261,540	1358.4
1986	23,968,799	37.5	28,543,325	1131.7

Source: Central Department of Statistics (Foreign Trade Statistics)

18.3 Saudi Arabian relations with the United States of America

Saudi–American relations began in 1933 when the late King Abdul Aziz ibn Sa'ud gave an oil concession covering a large area in the eastern part of the country to the Standard Oil Company of California. We have recounted the development of Saudi Arabia's relationship with the American oil companies elsewhere in this book. It is sufficient to say here that, up to 1940, Saudi–American relations remained purely commercial, a fact which is largely attributable to America's policy of isolation and non-involvement in world affairs at that time. This isolationism reflected a deep-rooted doctrine in the foreign policy of the United States. The Second World War, however, changed this situation and the United States began to take a more active role in world affairs, especially in the post-war era.

During the first years of the war King Abdul Aziz remained neutral. By 1943, the United States decided that it needed to secure a strategic airbase in the Middle East to connect Cairo with Karachi, in order to strengthen the war effort against Japan. The United States' Joint Chiefs of Staff named Dhahran as their objective. After top-secret negotiations, King Abdul Aziz granted an airbase lease to the United States; and, in March 1945, he declared war on Germany.

From that year on, "what followed could be described as a multiple increase of diplomatic, military, technical, and economic contacts between the United States and Saudi Arabia" (Source: *The Middle East in World Affairs* by George Lenczowski).

In February 1945, on board an American warship in the Great Bitter Lake of Egypt, King Abdul Aziz, in his first journey abroad, had met with President Roosevelt. It was reported that their meeting was mutually profitable. By 1948, diplomatic representation between the United States and the Kingdom of Saudi Arabia was upgraded to the status of an embassy (an American legation had been established on a permanent basis in Jeddah in 1943). Co-operation between the two countries increased at all levels and in various fields through to 1953. (It is perhaps interesting to note that Britain and the United States were the only countries that had serious relations with King Abdul Aziz in the period from 1915 to 1953.)

In 1974, the growing Saudi–American interdependence in trade and commerce led to the signing of an agreement which created the "US–Saudi Arabian Joint Commission on Economic Co-operation". The Joint Commission was set up, as a government-to-government arrangement, with the primary purpose of facilitating the transfer of technology from the United States to the Kingdom of Saudi Arabia. The work of the Joint Commission is undertaken by the United States' Treasury Department and the Saudi Arabian Ministry of Finance and National Economy. Under the auspices of the Joint Commission many programs have been implemented in the agricultural, industrial and scientific fields, aiding the Kingdom in its pursuit of the most advanced methods of technical development.

Common interests, pre-eminently in the fields of oil and finance, have ensured that commercial ties between the United States of America and the Kingdom of Saudi Arabia have continued to flourish in the 1980s.

Because of the importance of the Saudi–American relationship, it may be helpful to examine that relationship on a rather broader canvas. Despite obvious cultural differences, there is a surprisingly large area of common ground between the United States of America and the Kingdom of Saudi Arabia.

At the most fundamental level, the majority of people in both the United States of America and the Kingdom of Saudi Arabia are united by a common morality, the basis of which is religious in nature. The shared belief in the dignity of the individual human being is a moral value common to the three great monotheistic religions, first propagated in the Middle East. The relevance of a shared system of moral values cannot be emphasized too greatly in an assessment of the relations between the two countries.

Perhaps the most obvious example of the shared value system is to be found in the common commitment of aid to nations which have not been blessed with material wealth.

Since 1974, the Kingdom of Saudi Arabia has been one of the largest donors of foreign aid, both in relative and in absolute terms. In relative terms (as measured by the percentage of GNP contributed in foreign aid), the top three positions are shared by Saudi Arabia, the UAE and Kuwait (7 per cent of GNP). In absolute terms, only the the United States of America surpasses Saudi Arabia. Saudi aid given to developing countries grew from $335 million in 1973 to more than $3,000 million in 1978. In addition to bilateral aid, Saudi Arabia is a major contributor to the Islamic Development Bank, the Arab Bank for African Development, the World Bank, the International Monetary Fund, the World Health Organization, the Red Crescent (the Muslim equivalent of the Red Cross), multilateral emergency funds, UNESCO and the World Food Program. Under the leadership of King Fahd, the Saudi aid program has been increasingly directed towards addressing the pressing economic and social problems of Africa.

In the world of politics we also find large areas of common ground. Saudi Arabia has, as a primary political objective, stability in the Middle East. For reasons which we shall come to later, the Middle East is a highly volatile region of the world. Both the United States and Saudi Arabia are opposed to those elements in the Middle East (political or religious) which are committed to destabilizing the region. As a major supplier of the West's energy and as a major purchaser of Western services, it is in the interests of both Saudi Arabia and the United States that the causes of tension should be reduced by diplomatic means whenever possible.

In terms of economic interdependence, the case is clear. Because the Kingdom holds 25 per cent of the world's oil reserves and because the Kingdom, in its determination to develop its economy for the benefit of its citizens, needs the expertise of the West, there is an economic interdependence which binds the two countries together. Saudi Arabia's oil supplies are crucial to the economies of the Western world. Equally, Saudi Arabia is a major customer for the Western world's expertise, goods and services. It is in the interests of both the United States and Saudi Arabia to maintain and strengthen these economic ties.

In the military field there is again a large area of common ground. Because of the political and economic community of interest between the United States of America and the Kingdom of Saudi Arabia, there are common military interests. When diplomacy fails, there may be a need for military action, and the enemies of one country are likely to be the enemies of the other.

The inter-relationship between oil supplies, military sales and the extensive banking activities between the two countries has served to cement our mutual interests over an extended period of time. The pages of this book show that, in the exploitation of the Kingdom's oil and in the development of the Kingdom's infrastructure and industry, Saudi Arabia has looked to the United States as a major supplier of advice, expertise and qualified manpower; and that, as the West has purchased the Kingdom's oil and as the Kingdom has purchased the West's skills and expertise, a mutually beneficial relationship has developed.

As we have seen, the development of the Kingdom's oil resources, in particular, laid a firm foundation for co-operation between the United States of America and the Kingdom of Saudi Arabia. The formation of the Arabian American Oil Company (ARAMCO), originally known as Caltex, brought Saudi Arabians and Americans together in the exploitation of the vast oil reserves of the Kingdom – and today co-operation between the Kingdom of Saudi Arabia and the major American oil companies is still a significant factor in the world's oil markets.

It would, however, be misleading to leave a consideration of Saudi–American relations without reference to the Palestinian/ Israeli problem – for this is an issue which has been, is and will be crucial to the past, present and future development of that relationship.

In pursuit of a resolution of the problem, the United States of America has initiated a "peace process", but there seems to be a major obstacle to any form of progress. Israel will not talk to the Palestine Liberation Organization (PLO) – and yet the Palestinians have made it clear that they regard the PLO as their sole legitimate representative. There can be no move towards peace if one side refuses even to talk to the other. How is it that Israel can adopt such an intransigent attitude on the issue of Palestinian rights? How can she sustain a posture that is immoral and, in the final analysis, impractical – immoral because Israel's treatment of the Palestinians is corrupting the moral standards of Israel itself; impractical because Israel is an island in an Arab sea? Why then is Israel so stubborn? Because she is convinced that America, the most powerful nation on earth, will continue to support her, whatever position she takes.

The consequences of failure to find a solution to this problem are many. First, the inability of the parties involved to find even a hope of peace ensures that the region remains in a permanently unstable condition. Spread through the Arab world are groups of refugees, with a clear national identity, who feel profoundly aggrieved and who long to repossess the land and the homes which were theirs. The magnitude of the injustice they have suffered remains obscure only to minds closed by prejudice. Secondly, the failure to move towards peace leads some into terrorism. Terrorism is inexcusable but, when there is no hope of finding justice by diplomatic or political means, there are always those who believe the only way to generate pressure is to attract the world's attention – by whatever means. (South Africa is a another instance where the denial of human rights has led some to adopt violence.) Thirdly, the failure of governments to make any progress in the search for peace over many years is a catalyst for fanaticism, which in the Middle East has manifested itself on this occasion as religious fanaticism.

It would, of course, be foolish to suggest that, if the Palestinian/Israeli problem could be solved, all problems in the Middle East would disappear. Nothing is that simple. But a major cause and a continuing stimulant to these and other problems would have been removed.

Because the Palestinian/Israeli problem is central to politics in the Middle East and because the United States of America plays a pivotal role there, it is necessary to consider Saudi–American relations in the context of America's policy towards the region.

There seems to be a fundamental ambivalence in America's Middle East policy. America presents herself an an honest broker between Israel and the Arab world. But it is also the case that America takes as her basic premise that Israel's interests take precedence over all other Middle East considerations.

As an obvious example, when an Arab country asks to buy weapons, even a country like Saudi Arabia which has shown itself to be tireless in seeking diplomatic solutions to the problems of the region and which is particularly concerned about its own security, America is quite likely to refuse, on the grounds that the government in Israel and AIPAC (American Israel Public Affairs Committee) in America fear the weapons could one day be used against Israel. But when Israel needs the most advanced technology to maintain military superiority against all possible foes, real or imagined, America is prepared to give (not sell, but give) her full assistance. (The refusal of the American Congress to supply arms to one of its best customers is puzzling to say the least. The belief seems to be that the United States of America is the world's sole supplier of military hardware and that any dislocations in the American economy inherent in the decision not to supply American arms to a good friend are of no consequence whatsoever. It would seem that the effect of such a decision on the US job market and trade deficit fades into insignificance when compared with the perceived need to pacify an extremely militant and disproportionately influential minority group in America.)

The consequences of America's partiality towards Israel are entirely predictable. The first and most immediate result is that America's Arab friends are forced to look elsewhere for arms – and for a less biased view of the Middle East and its problems. A second and far more serious consequence of America's bias towards Israel is that, politically, uncritical support for Israel precludes a fair and just settlement of the Palestinian/Israeli problem.

What can be done to produce a fairer view of the problem and to "give peace a chance"? The first step might be to ask America to examine where her true interests lie. We can assume that morally the United States of America would like to see peace in the Middle East, a peace based on justice for all parties involved. If that is so, it is time that the rights of the Palestinians were given due weight. But let us, for the moment, leave matters of morality to one side and focus on America's political and economic interests.

The Arab world consists of some 200 million people, populating a region from the Gulf in the east to the Atlantic in the west; from Syria and Iraq in the north to Sudan and Somalia in the south. There people form part of a Muslim population of

1,000 million. The Kingdom of Saudi Arabia alone occupies an area roughly the size of Western Europe and under its land lies a quarter of the world's proven oil reserves. The Arab countries in general, and in particular the Kingdom of Saudi Arabia, are major export markets for the United States of America and, as the economies of the region develop, will have the potential to become even more important in this respect.

If America abuses her friendship with friendly Arab governments by pursuing a pro-Israeli policy in the Middle East, she weakens the position of those governments in the fight against their enemies who argue that only by removing American influence from the region will it be possible for the Palestinians to attain even some of their goals.

While America guarantees Israel and while that guarantee appears to be unconditional, Israel, perhaps understandably, will see no need to make any concessions at all. Therefore no progress can be made towards solving the Palestinian/Israeli problem except on Israel's terms – and, therefore, no progress will be made. While Israel maintains a policy of obstructing all moves towards peace, the preconditions for the continuation of the problems of regional instability, terrorism and religious fanaticism will persist. And the injustice which the Palestinians suffer will continue.

Before concluding this section, we should take a brief look at the Middle East on a broader basis. (After all, the population of Israel is a mere 4 million, whereas the Arab world constitutes a population of 200 million. There is more to the politics of the Middle East than the Palestinian/Israeli conflict.)

One of the dominant powers in the region is Iran, which, under its present regime, is bitterly opposed to the United States of America. Iran has expressed ambitions to export its radical form of Islamic fundamentalism and, inevitably, its anti-American sentiments, to other Arab countries. Such ambitions add a further and serious threat to the stability of the region by attempting to foment insurrection in Arab countries – in particular, those which are considered "moderate" and which have maintained good relations with the United States. In recent years, the political scene in the Middle East has been dominated by the Iraq/Iran war – a war in which Iran attempted, by direct military means, to extend its control over the Islamic world. Iran has been frustrated in this attempt but that is most unlikely to end its expansionist aspirations. At the same time, Iraq's success in frustrating Iran's ambitions is having a substantial effect on the political map of the Middle East. With the ending of the Iraq/Iran war, the United States of America should recognize the changing reality of the situation and develop a new political strategy to deal with it.

As the United States of America considers how to proceed in the Middle East, it will be aware that there is now a unique opportunity to make real progress in the search for lasting peace in the region. Early in 1989, the Palestine Liberation Organization officially accepted the right of Israel to exist and disavowed terrorism. Israel has yet to accept the right of Palestine to exist but a major obstacle to peace talks has been removed.

Through its moral authority in the Islamic world and through its own financial power, the Kingdom of Saudi Arabia plays a pivotal role in the politics of the region. The Kingdom of Saudi Arabia is eager to use its authority and influence to find just solutions to all the problems which beset the region. The Middle East is too important a region to be left in a permanent state of instability. All sides in the Arab/Israeli conflict are better armed than ever before, and Israel is reported to be equipped with nuclear weapons.

If the root problem is left unresolved, there is a serious danger that, at some time in the future, there will be another conflict. The course and the consequences of such a conflict are so horrific to contemplate that it is to be hoped that statesmen in all countries concerned will endeavor to find a way towards peace and will not be deterred by pressure groups and lobbyists, whose vision is sometimes so narrow that they harm their own interests as well as endangering the safety of the world.

For there to be any real progress, the United States needs to persuade Israel that Israel's long-term interests lie in coming to terms with the Arab world – not by negotiating treaties or accords with individual Arab states, but by addressing the problem which created the hostility in the first place. It should be clear to all that, in the long run, the Israelis themselves will be safe only if those who have been wronged are justly treated.

The position of the Kingdom of Saudi Arabia on this and other related issues is self-evident. The Kingdom has been tireless in its diplomatic efforts to find just solutions to Middle East problems. In the Gulf, between Iraq and Iran and in the Palestinian/Israeli problem, the Kingdom of Saudi Arabia has always been ready to take a positive and constructive approach. And, in all its diplomatic initiatives, its purpose has been clear – to find peace with justice.

The Kingdom of Saudi Arabia has never attacked others, has never sought to extend its borders. As guardian of the Holy Places of Islam, it has done all in its power to facilitate the great pilgrimage, *Hajj*, for all who come from around the world to perform their devotions. Blessed with the wealth that comes from oil, it has consistently contributed massive funds to less fortunate countries in the Arab world, in the Islamic world and in the world at large. Its Five Year Plans demonstrate its commitment to the development of its land for the benefit of its people. In education, housing and health, there has probably never been, in the history of mankind, so great an investment in so short a time.

Finally, there is no doubt that it is in the interests of the USA to maintain good and close relations with a state that has proved, over many years, its international stature, its credibility, its rational principles and its direction. The Kingdom of Saudi Arabia has shown its commitment to peace, to justice and to freedom wherever it is sought. It recognizes and abides by international law and has worked towards its own nation's progress and comfort, just as it is one of the first nations to lend its support to international efforts in both the moral and humane fields.

Table 18.4   *Saudi–US Trade 1975–87*

Year	Saudi exports to US	Saudi imports from US	Trade balance
1975	2,624.6	1,501.8	+1,122.8
1976	5,212.9	2,774.1	+2,438.5
1977	6,358.5	3,575.0	+2,783.5
1978	5,307.1	4,370.0	+ 937.0
1979	7,983.4	4,875.0	+3,108.4
1980	12,598.8	5,768.5	+6,830.3
1981	14,391.3	7,327.4	+7,063.9
1982	7,860.2	9,026.0	−1,165.8
1983	3,840.3	7,903.3	−4,063.0
1984	4,008.9	5,564.4	−1,555.5
1985	2,026.8	4,474.2	−2,447.4
1986	4,054.3	3,448.8	+ 605.5
1987	4,886.5	3,057.4	+1,829.1

Source: US Department of Commerce, Bureau of the Census. Compiled by: Commercial Office of the Royal Embassy of Saudi Arabia in Washington, DC

Table 18.5   *Trade exchange between the Kingdom and North American countries 1974–86*

Year	Exports		Imports	
	Value (000 SR)	Index 1974 = 100	Value (000 SR)	Index 1974 = 100
1974	5,956,087	100.0	1,751,797	100.0
1975	5,383,774	90.4	2,573,253	146.9
1976	7,708,576	129.4	5,774,967	329.7
1977	16,792,651	281.9	9,751,045	556.6
1978	23,765,306	399.0	14,672,770	837.6
1979	40,754,376	684.2	16,699,133	953.3
1980	63,049,376	1058.6	20,542,047	1172.6
1981	60,658,752	1018.4	26,123,745	1491.3
1982	22,042,879	370.1	30,123,332	1719.6
1983	12,876,158	216.2	27,901,133	1592.7
1984	8,862,692	148.8	21,431,449	1223.4
1985	5,576,015	93.61	14,884,046	849.6
1986	12,658,492	212.5	12,785,204	729.8

Source: Central Department of Statistics (Foreign Trade Statistics)

18.3.1   TRADE EXCHANGES BETWEEN THE KINGDOM OF SAUDI ARABIA AND THE UNITED
STATES OF AMERICA

Tables 18.4 and 18.5 show the trade exchange between the Kingdom of Saudi
Arabia and the United States of America in US$ from 1975 to 1987 and in Saudi
Riyals from 1974 to 1986, respectively.

18.4   Saudi Arabian relations with the Communist Bloc

The Kingdom of Saudi Arabia, as a country founded upon the tenets of Islam and
whose head of state is the Guardian of the Holy Places of Islam, is implacably
opposed to the atheistic, materialistic philosophy of Marxist states. This antipathy
has extended into the political and economic spheres. Indeed, at present, the
Kingdom of Saudi Arabia does not even have full diplomatic relations with the
Soviet Union.

Nevertheless, with the more liberal policies introduced into the Soviet Union by
President Gorbachev and, in particular, following the withdrawal of Soviet troops
from Afghanistan, there has been a thawing in Saudi–Soviet relations. Where this
will lead depends largely on the progress the Soviet Union makes in its program of
liberalization and in particular on the attitude it adopts to its own large Muslim
population.

Table 18.6 *Trade exchange between the Kingdom and Eastern European
countries 1975–86*

Year	Exports		Imports	
	Value (000 SR)	Index 1975 = 100	Value (000 SR)	Index 1975 = 100
1975	65,845	100.0	117,467	100.0
1976	99,280	150.8	327,563	278.9
1977	530	0.8	431,916	367.7
1978	3,363	5.1	1,081,314	920.5
1979	1,039	1.6	1,260,361	1072.9
1980	181,319	275.4	1,515,863	1290.5
1981	1,213,933	1843.6	1,379,578	1174.4
1982	400,159	607.7	1,043,749	888.5
1983	311,823	473.6	1,083,537	922.4
1984	85,458	129.8	1,077,419	917.2
1985	72,145	109.6	724,503	616.8
1986	151,529	230.1	615,168	523.7

Source: Central Department of Statistics (Foreign Trade Statistics)

18.4.1   TRADE EXCHANGES BETWEEN THE KINGDOM OF SAUDI ARABIA AND EASTERN
         EUROPEAN COUNTRIES

Table 18.6 shows the trade exchange between the Kingdom of Saudi Arabia and Eastern European countries from 1975 to 1986. Trade with Eastern European countries has been and still is modest in comparison with trade with the West and Japan, but up to 1981 there was a significant growth in both imports and exports. The reduction in trade with Eastern Europe since 1981 is largely attributable to the fall in the Kingdom's oil revenues.

19

Saudi Arabian aid to the developing world

The Kingdom's oil wealth and its own ambitious development programs have received wide international publicity. Perhaps less widely recognized is its commitment to helping those materially less fortunate in the developing world. It is an obligation on all Muslims to ensure that the blessings of wealth are used to help those less well-endowed. The Kingdom of Saudi Arabia is a Muslim state and the obligations that fall upon individual Muslims have been willingly accepted by the government of the Kingdom.

This chapter sets out to indicate the magnitude of that commitment, a commitment which the Kingdom has continued to discharge, to the best of its ability, even when its own revenues have declined.

> Since the mid-1970s, Saudi Arabia has been a leading donor in terms of ODA (Overseas Development Aid) volume and ODA/GNP ratio.
>
> Disbursements from 1975 to 1987 amounted to US$ 48 billion, second only to the the United States of America. The ODA/GNP ratio averaged 4.2% over this period, well above the highest among DAC countries (the DAC average is 0.35%).
>
> Under pressure of sharply falling oil revenues, uncertainties regarding the future of the oil market and the regional security situation, Saudi Arabian ODA volume declined from a peak of US$ 5.5 billion in 1981 to US$ 2.6 billion in 1985, but recovered to US$ 3.5 billion in 1986. In 1987, it was about US$ 2.9 billion. As a proportion of the Kingdom's oil revenues, ODA has risen from 10% in 1983–85 to 15% in 1986–87, and Saudi Arabia's ratio of ODA to GNP has remained by far the highest among all donors. Saudi aid is untied, quick-disbursing, and highly concessional, with a grant element of 96% (1986).
>
> *Source:* The World Bank, August 1988

Throughout its own development, the Kingdom of Saudi Arabia has been mindful of its responsibilities in the community of nations, especially in the Arab world and amongst the less developed countries. Blessed with its vast reserves of oil and minerals, Saudi Arabia has willingly accepted the Muslim obligation to share its wealth with those less favoured. Although a relatively young country, Saudi Arabia has quickly understood the reality of the inter-dependence which exists between one nation and another. The Kingdom is, of course, particularly involved with the industrialized nations of the West, supplying much of these countries' energy requirements and importing much of the West's technology. But there is also an inter-dependence, both moral and economic, between rich nations and poor. As a result, Mohammad Aba Alkhail, the Minister of Finance and National Economy, has truly been able to say:

> Financial assistance from the Kingdom of Saudi Arabia has come to form a significant share of total development aid reaching Third World countries.

The purpose of this section is to give details of the magnitude of this contribution. For those who have no special interest in this subject, the lengthy catalogue of grants and loans that follows may prove tedious. It is nevertheless hoped that the reader will see beyond the statistics to the very real human benefits enjoyed by those who have benefited and are benefiting from the Kingdom's past and continuing generosity.

The following extracts, slightly edited, have been taken from a Saudi Arabian publication entitled *The Kingdom of Saudi Arabia's Economic and Development Aid to the Islamic World*, published in 1988.

19.1   The role played by the Kingdom of Saudi Arabia in the area of developmental co-operation with Islamic countries

19.1.1   BROAD SURVEY OF THE KINGDOM'S ROLE

The Kingdom of Saudi Arabia has played an increasingly important role in the past several years in the area of supporting economic and social development plans and programs in Third World countries in general and in Islamic developing countries in particular. The Kingdom allocates a major part of its annual national product to assisting developing countries implement their respective development programs. In some years of the past decade, this assistance has amounted to 6 per cent of GNP, whereas the industrial countries as a group fell short of achieving the modest rate of assistance flowing from developed to developing countries as called for by the United Nations, namely 0.7 per cent of gross national product.

The total non-reimbursable development assistance and concessional loans provided by the Kingdom during the past fifteen years to the developing countries that are members of the Islamic Conference Organization amounted to about 77,000 million riyals. These funds have contributed toward the implementation of economic and social development programs and projects in 35 sister Islamic nations.

The Kingdom of Saudi Arabia provides assistance to developing countries through various channels: it is a major contributor to a number of Arab regional and international development institutions, including the Islamic Bank for Development, the Arab Fund for Economic and Social Development, the Arab Monetary Fund, the OPEC Fund for International Development, the Arab Bank for Economic Development in Africa, the African Development Bank, the African Development Fund, the International Fund for Agricultural Development, the International Monetary Fund, the World Bank for Reconstruction and Development, the International Development Agency, the International Finance Corporation, the Arab Corporation for Investment Guarantee, the Arabian Gulf Program for Support of the UN Development Organization, the Arab Fund for Technical Assistance to African Countries, the Funds and Centers of the Islamic Conference Organization, the Program for Fighting Drought in the African Countries of Sahel, and the Program for Eradication of River Blindness in West Africa. Table 19.1 shows the Kingdom's contributions to these institutions.

In view of the difficulty of detailing the Kingdom's efforts in the area of developmental co-operation with sister Islamic nations through the various regional and international bodies and channels mentioned above, and due to the fact that the Saudi Fund for Development is the main channel through which the Kingdom provides concessional development assistance to various developing countries, we concentrate here on reviewing in some detail the role played by the Kingdom in this area through the Saudi Fund for Development.

The Saudi Fund for Development was established by Royal Decree in the month of Sha'ban 1394 AH (1974) and began its operations in the month of Safar 1395 AH (1975). At the time of its inception, the Fund's capital amounted to 10,000 million riyals; however, due to the developing countries' increasing need for assistance in order to implement development projects, the Fund's capital has been augmented twice, and now totals 25,000 million riyals. Despite the fact that the Fund has been operating for a short time, it has made great strides in the area of international development co-operation. The Fund now contributes to the financing of 276 projects in 61 countries.

Project priorities are determined by recipient countries in the context of their respective development programs. The transportation sector obtained the largest share of assistance and was allocated 6,097 million riyals (36 per cent of the total) due to the fact that this sector is largely underdeveloped in most of the Islamic Conference Organization's member countries. In addition, this sector plays an important part in smoothing the flow of goods and people within each country and in developing the economy. Moreover, it strengthens relations and inter-dependence among neighboring countries. The sector includes projects such as roads, railways, ports and airports.

Food is a vital element in the survival of human beings. Due to the need to

Table 19.1   *The Kingdom of Saudi Arabia's contributions to Arab regional and international development institutions*

Institution	Capital (US Dollars)	The Kingdom's contribution	Contribution as a percentage of the total capital
Islamic Bank for Development	2,118,800,000	536,440,000	25.3
Arab Fund for Economic and Social Development	2,415,900,000	553,100,000	22.9
Arab Monetary Fund	1,294,000,000	187,300,000	14.5
OPEC Fund for International Development	3,435,008,438	1,033,279,607*	30.1
Arab Bank for Economic Development in Africa	1,048,825,000	255,584,153	24.2
African Development Bank	5,931,468,000	14,279,460	0.25
World Bank	96,600,000,000	3,032,764,000	3.32
International Development Agency	40,927,000,000	1,665,700,000	3.5
International Finance Corporation	1,300,000,000	17,911,000	1.37
Mutual Investment Guarantee Agency	1,000,000,000	31,370,000	3.14
IMF	116,983,815,000	4,163,120,000	3.6
African Development Fund	3,499,930,000	116,524,973	3.4
International Fund for Agricultural Development	2,340,924,675	333,778,000	14.25
Arab Corporation For Investment Guarantee	25,025,000	3,750,000	15

Table 19.1– cont.

Institution	Capital (US Dollars)	The Kingdom's contribution	Contribution as a percentage of the total capital
Arab Gulf Program for Support of the UN Development Organization	197,000,000	150,000,000	76
Arab Fund for Technical Aid to Arab and African Countries	60,080,000	13,563,000	22.6
The Funds and Institutions Established in the Frame of the Organizations of the Islamic Conference		214,662,000	
Program for Curing River Blindness	299,000,000	25,000,000	8.36
Program for Combating Drought in the Sahel Countries	240,000,000	130,000,000	54

Source: "The Kingdom of Saudi Arabia's Economic and Social Development Aid to the Islamic World" published by the Ministry of Finance and National Economy, 1409 AH

increase food production in most Islamic countries in order to combat potential food shortage, the agricultural sector was allocated 4,202 million riyals, or 24.7 per cent of total assistance, for the support of various agricultural projects, including irrigation and soil reclamation, digging of wells and cultivation of some areas, production and processing of some vital crops, building agricultural dams, and fishing. The Kingdom hopes that by directing its assistance to agricultural projects it can play a major part in tackling some of the difficulties encountered by Islamic countries, namely:

- stopping the exodus from the rural to the urban areas, thus alleviating the resulting social and economic problems
- focusing attention on the role played by agricultural development in economic and social development strategies

– curtailing imports of agricultural goods and products, hence improving the balance of payments position

As far as the social infrastructure projects are concerned (education, health, drinking water, sewerage), they also obtain a large share of the assistance provided by the Kingdom. This sector has been allocated 2,498 million riyals, or 14.7 per cent of the total. Such projects serve the people who are the cornerstone in leading the development process toward the right path.

Energy projects also receive a major share of assistance amounting to 1,769 million riyals, or 10.4 per cent of the total. These funds have been channelled toward the funding of a number of energy projects such as the dams built for generating electricity, and thermal energy stations. Energy is very important for it provides the main thrust to the economy of developing countries; moreover, making it available to the domestic economy boosts production and hence improves the economic performance of a number of sectors.

The industry and mining sector received 1,730 million riyals (10.2 per cent of the total) for the purpose of developing basic industries, providing support for productive sectors such as fertilizer and chemical plants, cement plants, textile and sugar plants, and building industrial complexes and cities. 686 million riyals have been reserved for projects that have yet to be determined, representing 4 per cent of the total.

In addition to the assistance provided by the Kingdom in the area of financing economic and social development programs in sister Islamic nations, 236 million riyals were disbursed to a number of the Islamic Conference Organization's member countries in Africa through the Facilities Program for the Sub-Sahara Countries. The Kingdom also provided assistance to other Islamic countries for the financing of development projects and other non-reimbursable funds in support of balance of payments deficits, financing economic recovery programs, supplying primary commodities, and alleviating the effects of disasters, etc. The Kingdom has also recently decided to contribute to the IMF special program for the enhancement and support of structural reform in the least developed countries. The Kingdom will contribute about 750 thousand riyals to this program through the Saudi Fund for Development.

19.1.2   ASSISTANCE PROVIDED TO THE ISLAMIC CONFERENCE ORGANIZATION'S LEAST DEVELOPED COUNTRIES

The Islamic Conference Organization's least developed countries enjoyed a large share of the Kingdom's assistance to the member countries of this organization. Of a total of 17,216.18 million riyals, the least developed countries obtained 6,114.88 million riyals, or 35.5 per cent. Among 36 countries classified by the US as least developed, there are sixteen Muslim countries, twelve of which are African and four Asian.

The Kingdom allocated a large part of its assistance for the development and modernization of the transport and communications sector. 2,329.4 million riyals (39.4 per cent) were dedicated to the modernization of roads, railways, ports and airports. The agricultural sector ranked second, receiving 1,084.1 million riyals (18.2 per cent of the total) for expanding food and agricultural production as a whole. Basic and social infrastructure (education, health, housing, urban development, water and sewerage) in these countries received 562.9 million riyals (9.4 per cent). Six per cent of the total (328.02 million riyals) was dedicated to the development of waterfalls to generate hydro-electric energy, thus helping to overcome severe energy shortages without the high costs normally associated with the traditional enhancement of energy sources. 1,073.1 million riyals (18 per cent of the total) were also dedicated to the upgrading of basic industries that support the productive sectors and contribute to the growth of the basic infrastructure sector such as cement and fertilizer plants and agro-industries.

19.2   The Kingdom of Saudi Arabia's efforts in the area of relief

19.2.1   BROAD SURVEY OF THE KINGDOM'S ROLE

During the past few years a number of sister Islamic nations and developing countries in general have experienced unusual crises and natural disasters such as droughts and earthquakes, in addition to an influx of refugees. Due to their limited resources, these countries seek the support of the international community in such circumstances in order to overcome these crises and to alleviate the suffering of the injured and the afflicted. In addition, support is needed to establish preventive programs in order to forestall the recurrence of such disasters or to mitigate their effects.

Realizing the dimensions of such problems and their negative effects on the social and economic conditions of such countries, the government of the Custodian of the Two Holy Mosques has consistently come to the rescue of these ravaged countries in order to strengthen the ties of fraternity among Islamic countries, inspired by the precepts of Islam that call for co-operation and solidarity among mankind.

Amongst the many examples of such aid, there is the Kingdom's participation in the efforts of African countries in the area of combating drought and the genuine fraternal support provided by the Kingdom on the official and national level, namely in providing shelter for refugees and earthquake victims. The Kingdom is also concerned with the problems of refugees who have been the victims of wars, conflicts and natural disasters in Asia, namely Palestinian and Afghan refugees and other victims of natural disasters.

The Kingdom's concern with such problems is manifested by the allocation of its God-endowed resources for providing relief to the afflicted through direct bilateral channels or through support of the efforts of international programs concerned with this area.

19.2.2   RELIEF IN AFRICA

The African continent is rich in natural resources. In addition to its large population, it has 97 per cent of the world's reserves in chrome, 85 per cent in manganese, 25 per cent in uranium, 13 per cent of rubber production, one-third of the world's coffee production, and 50 per cent of palm production.

Despite such natural and human resources, Africa is still the least developed area in the world, and the sub-Saharan countries have been plagued since 1980 by a severe economic crisis due to several years of drought. As a consequence, agricultural production in these countries declined sharply at a time when population was increasing markedly, a situation that led to a sharp deterioration of economic performance and falling annual revenues in many of the African countries.

Food shortages are closely associated with the drought in this area of the world; the level of underground water has become dangerously depressed and the effects on population and livestock dependent on such water have been devastating. In addition, large areas in Africa have been hit by other natural disasters such as earthquakes, floods, hurricanes, and more; the African continent is also still suffering from political instability, which has resulted in an influx of large numbers of refugees from Sudan and Somalia seeking refuge and looking for ways to earn their living. For all these reasons, the Kingdom of Saudi Arabia has promptly endeavored to alleviate the suffering of this continent's diverse peoples in various ways.

19.2.2.1   *The Kingdom's role in the bilateral sphere*

Since the onset of the drought problem, the government and the people of Saudi Arabia have promptly come to the rescue of the afflicted African countries of the Sahel. Donations and grants were extended through bilateral channels for support of reform programs and economic and social plans so as to ensure immediate and beneficial relief for the African peoples.

19.2.2.2   *The Kingdom's efforts on the official level*

The problem of drought
a)   The Saudi program for the digging of wells and rural development in African countries
During the third Islamic Summit held in the Holy City of Makkah in 1984, the Kingdom of Saudi Arabia announced the allocation of 382 million riyals for the implementation of an emergency program to assist the following countries of the Sahel affected by the drought in Africa: Cape Verde, Guinea, Guinea Bissau,

Gambia, Mali, Mauritania, Niger, Senegal, Burkina Faso, and Chad. Fifteen per cent of this amount was allocated for the provision of large quantities of foodstuffs and their immediate distribution to the afflicted victims. The balance, amounting to 318,750,000 riyals, was allocated to a special program for digging wells and rural development in the ten countries of the Sahel.

The Kingdom also completed – with the support of God Almighty – an emergency food aid program through which it provided 25,000 tons of grain and 10,000 tons of edible oil at a cost of 63,750,000 riyals, representing the costs of securing these items from world markets, as well as their transportation and distribution among recipient countries.

The program for the digging of wells and rural development which the Kingdom completed encompassed the digging of 2,556 wells; the provision of the necessary equipment and pumps; the construction of fifteen dams of various sizes and a number of underground tanks with the required distribution networks; and the maintenance of a number of other wells existing in these countries. The wells were completed in most countries by 1986 and have been put to good use; in addition, the wells greatly assisted the local urban population in facing harsh conditions, thus discouraging migration.

In response to a call addressed by the fourth Islamic Summit held in Casablanca for increasing aid to the African countries of the Sahel as a result of persistent drought and scarce rainfall, the Kingdom of Saudi Arabia allocated an additional 112,500,000 riyals for expansion of the Saudi program for digging wells and rural development. Each country's share of this amount was determined and the program's second stage plan – currently implemented in most African countries of the Sahel – was approved.

b)   Additional Assistance to African Countries

Due to the persistent and worsening drought conditions in the African countries of the Sahel, extending to other African countries as well, the Kingdom of Saudi Arabia has provided assistance in money and in kind, including grains, foodstuffs, medical supplies, tents, blankets, ambulance cars and the digging of a large number of wells in order to provide water for the inhabitants and their livestock. Total assistance amounted to about 975 million riyals benefiting 17 African countries, namely: Senegal, Mali, Niger, Gambia, Chad, Mauritania, Guinea, Guinea Bissau, Somalia, Sudan , Morocco, Zambia, Ethiopia, Djibouti, Togo, Sierra Leone, and Burundi.

The problem of refugees in Africa

The Kingdom of Saudi Arabia has been greatly concerned with the problem of African refugees in Sudan and Somalia, and of the victims of conflicts in Chad. The assistance in money, foodstuffs, medical supplies, and shelter provided to refugees in these areas amounted to more than 170,000 million riyals. In addition, the Kingdom donated 122,500,000 riyals for the UN's first and second conferences for assistance to refugees in Africa.

Victims of other natural disasters

Some countries of the African continent have been hit by natural disasters such as the earthquakes in the Algerian city of Al-Shleif, the hurricanes in the Comaro Islands and Madagascar, and the ravaging floods in some African countries. The Kingdom has promptly come to the rescue of the victims of such disasters by providing assistance in money and in kind and by contributing to the reconstruction programs. The Kingdom provided a total of 618 million riyals to seven countries: Algeria, Tunisia, Somalia, the Comoro Islands, Madagascar and Nigeria.

At the end of 1408 AH (1988) Sudan was ravaged by unrelenting floods that made more than two million people homeless and destroyed more than 130,000 homes. In response, the Kingdom undertook an around-the-clock air-lift to carry relief materials such as tents, blankets, foodstuffs, water aspiration equipment, rescue vehicles and helicopters (the latter to distribute supplies to the victims and to spray afflicted areas with medical pesticides in order to prevent the spreading of diseases and epidemics). Large quantities of relief supplies were actually delivered by air and by sea and, up to 19 Muharran 1409 AH, 177 airplanes carried more than 20,000 tents; 20,000 cartons of food supplies; 40,000 blankets; 900,000 kilograms of flour; large quantities of sugar, milk, dates and cold meat; therapeutical and preventive medication; 100 small jeep cars; water aspiration equipment; electricity generators and lighting equipment; and five helicopters for the distribution of the relief materials.

19.2.2.3 *The Kingdom's efforts on the national scale*

Due to the persistence of the drought problem in a number of the African countries for several years, growing worse and spreading its ill effects, the Custodian of the Two Holy Mosques called upon the citizens of the Kingdom to extend aid to their brothers in Africa. Official and national committees were formed in each Saudi city under the auspices of a high ministerial committee to receive contributions in money and in kind from citizens and to ensure that they were promptly delivered to the afflicted African countries. The response of the Muslim people of Saudi Arabia was prompt and generous. Throughout 1408 AH (1988), assistance in money and in kind amounted to more than 325 million riyals, including more than 152,120 tons of grains and various foodstuffs, clothing, tents, blankets, ambulances, water trucks, and fuel. This benefited more than 3.5 million victims in Sudan, Somalia, Mauritanian, Mali, Niger, Djibouti, the Comoro Islands and Morocco. Donation collection centers are still receiving assistance in response to this generous call, reiterated by the Custodian of the Two Holy Mosques, following the violent floods that hit the brother country of Sudan in late 1408 AH (1988). The Custodian of the Two Holy Mosques promptly made a personal donation of 30 million riyals. Donations collected from the citizens for their brothers in Sudan amounted to more than 15 million riyals up to 16 Muharram 1409 AH. Moreover, the Saudi Central Relief Committee sent approximately 45,000 tons of flour to Sudan.

In order to ensure the delivery of such assistance to recipient countries and its distribution to the victims, the Saudi Red Crescent Association opened field centers in Sudan, Mali and Niger. More than 180 doctors, pharmacists, technical assistants and administrators work in these centers, including 80 Saudis working officially or voluntarily. Foodstuffs, medical supplies and fuel are being shipped by air and by sea to the ravaged areas.

These donations have had a considerable impact in assisting the needy in Africa and were favorably viewed at national and official levels throughout the continent. Several associations specializing in the distribution of such assistance have expressed their appreciation of the Saudi government and people's efforts and of the Kingdom's prompt assistance to the needy and afflicted brothers in African countries.

19.2.2.4   *The role played by the Kingdom on the international level*

In addition to the Kingdom's intensive efforts to assist the victims of drought and other natural disasters and to support the means of sheltering refugees through bilateral channels, the Kingdom has not overlooked the support of international efforts in this area and has responded to the call addressed by the third and fourth Islamic Summits held in Makkah and Casablanca respectively under the auspices of the Organization of the Islamic Conference to provide assistance to the African countries of the Sahel afflicted by drought. The Kingdom implemented the aforementioned special program for digging wells and rural development in African countries and contributed to several international programs in this field, such as the World Food Program, the World Program for Combating River Blindness, the Arab Gulf Program for the United Nations Development Organization, and the WB-IMF Programs for support of the structural adjustment of the African sub-Saharan countries as previously mentioned.

Below is a brief outline of the Kingdom's contributions through various regional and international channels.

The World Food Program

This program is concerned with providing food to the needy all over the world, food being a vital element to human survival. Due to this program's importance, the Kingdom has recently extended to this program donations in money and in kind totalling more than 1,245 million riyals up to 1988, at a rate of more than 100 million riyals per year.

Official statistics show that about 50 per cent of this program's resources has been allocated in previous years to the African continent because of the persistent drought in many of its countries.

The Arab Gulf Program for the United Nations Development Organization

At the beginning of 1981, the Kingdom and the sister Arab Gulf nations established the Arab Gulf Program for the purpose of supporting the UN humanitarian and development organizations. To this program, the Kingdom has contributed to date

550 million riyals, representing about 78 per cent of the program's resources. The program provides assistance to the poorest countries of the world, in particular African countries, through the UN humanitarian and development programs, and has allocated about 40 per cent of its resources to UNICEF. The World Health Organization, the World Food and Agriculture Organization, the World Labor Organization, the World Food Program, the Environment Program, UNESCO, the Program for the Handicapped, the UN Development Program, the High Commission for Refugee Affairs, the World Fund for Agricultural Development, and the Fund for Population Affairs have also benefited from the program.

These agencies and institutions implement a large number of mutual intra-country and regional programs in the least developed countries of the world and have received a sizeable share of the resources of the Arab Gulf Program for the United Nations development and humanitarian institutions.

The World Program for combating river blindness disease
This program is concerned with the attempt to eradicate river blindness disease and to prevent it from spreading to an area of about 1,100,000 square kilometers. This program was initiated by the IBRD and the World Health Organization, with the collaboration of the West African governments, namely: Ghana, Ivory Coast, Mali, Niger, Togo, Burkina Faso. Realizing the importance of such a program, the Kingdom has participated in the international meetings on the mobilization of financial and technical resources for the implementation of this program's three stages during the period 1974–89. The Kingdom's contribution to such stages amounted to 92 million riyals, representing 8.36 per cent of the total donations of contributing countries.

The UN High Commission for Refugee Affairs
The Commission was established for the purpose of sponsoring refugees' affairs all over the world. It assists refugees by developing programs aimed at reaching permanent solutions, such as voluntary return of refugees to their home countries, if possible, or their long-term settlement in the local community of the first refugee country, or repatriation to any other country. Assistance provided in the framework of public programs includes meeting emergency needs, help in creating job and education opportunities, training, establishment of rural settlements, provision of social and health care, and contributing to the costs of repatriation.

The Commission receives annual contributions from the countries of the world in support of its regular budget, as well as donations in support of emergency and special programs. In appreciation of the Commission's humanitarian role, the Kingdom of Saudi Arabia makes an annual contribution to its budget, dating back several years. The Kingdom also donated 105 million riyals at the first conference organized by the Commission in 1981 for the purpose of collecting donations to assist refugees in Africa. At the second conference, held in 1984, the Kingdom donated 17.5 million riyals, and in 1988, it donated through the Commission large quantities of flour to the refugees in Somalia, amounting to 20,000 tons valued at about 30 million riyals.

19.2.3   RELIEF EFFORTS IN ASIA

The Asian continent has several areas where tension and armed conflicts prevail; some of its countries have been so greatly affected that their resources have been drained and efforts at development impeded. The unjust Israeli occupation of Palestine and some Arab territories was one of the worst events, as well as the Soviet invasion of the Muslim country of Afghanistan, the Lebanese war, and the war between Iraq and Iran. These distressing events have brought about a number of problems paramount among which are the problems of Palestinian and Afghan refugees, and the victims of war. The persistence of these problems for many years has led to an increase in the number of refugees and to the worsening of their living conditions.

19.2.3.1   *The role played by the Kingdom on the bilateral level*

The Kingdom has consistently endeavored to support security and stability in the Middle East region and in the Islamic world by various means, while seeking to provide prompt relief to the victims of such events. The Kingdom provides assistance in cash and in kind, in addition to medical assistance to the afflicted and the needy everywhere. Following are the Kingdom's most prominent efforts in this area.

a)   Palestinian refugees

The Kingdom of Saudi Arabia has been greatly concerned with the Palestinian refugee problem since the unjust Israeli occupation and the expulsion of the Palestinians from their homeland. Donations in money and in kind were extended through various channels to the Palestinian people displaced all over the world, particularly to the PLO and the Jordano-Palestinian Committee for Support of Resistance in the Arab occupied territories in response to the resolution of the Arab summit. The PLO has received a total of 2,900 million riyals since 1978, and the Joint Committee a total of 850 million riyals. This is an addition to the support provided to the inhabitants of Palestinian camps in Lebanon and to the educational scholarships provided for Palestinians in the Kingdom and overseas.

In addition to the Kingdom of Saudi Arabia's concern with the Palestinian cause, Saudi citizens have also provided all possible support and have demonstrated their closeness to and constant collaboration with the Palestinian people. Since the uprising in the occupied territories (the *Intifada*), the response of the Saudi people has been overwhelming: more than 50 million riyals were collected in the first eight months of the uprising.

b)   Afghan refugees

Since the Islamic world was plagued by the Soviet invasion of Afghanistan, the Kingdom of Saudi Arabia has been at the forefront of the countries that provided support to the Muslim Afghan people in these dire circumstances. The Kingdom denounced this flagrant invasion, endorsed the Afghan peoples' demands in international forums, and supported the international peace drive, termination of the Soviet invasion and repatriation of Afghan refugees. At the same time, the Kingdom provided support for the sheltering of Afghan refugees in Pakistan as well as donations in cash and in kind, and medical supplies valued at 200 million riyals, 67 million riyals of which represent the cost of such supplies. About 80 million liters of kerosene were provided to the refugees and to the forces of the High Commissariat for Refugee Affairs for distribution. The Saudi Red Crescent provided its services to the refugees and established its headquarters in the area of Peshawar, the gathering place of the Afghan refugees, in addition to various affiliated offices in other areas where refugees are housed. The Saudi Red Crescent also provides medication as well as health and social care to students and orphanages and pays the cost of providing artificial limbs to some of the war victims. The association has also established a health institute to train 100 medical assistants and technicians a year. The Kingdom has to date contributed about 60 million riyals to the budget of the Saudi Red Crescent office in this area.

In addition to the Kingdom's support of the Afghan cause, the Saudi people showed great sympathy emanating from the ties of Islamic fraternity. The Saudi response to the call addressed by the Custodian of the Two Holy Mosques to the Saudi citizens to support their brother Afghan refugees whose social and health conditions were deteriorating due to the Soviet invasion was prompt and generous. Donations in cash and in kind were received in large amounts by the national relief committees established in each city and village, totalling more than 4,000 million riyals to date.

The Saudi Central Relief Committee provides large quantities of tents, clothing, footwear, quilts, socks, blankets, and foodstuffs, such as flour, rice, lentils, sugar, tea, oil and some medication and medical supplies distributed directly to refugees in the areas of Peshawar and Kwaitah. Mosques and schools were established for orphans and appropriate housing and food were provided. The Makkah Surgical Hospital in Kwaitah with 120 beds is to be operated and managed at the Kingdom's expense. A physical therapy clinic was built in the city of Peshawar as well as the Nasseer Bagh factory that provides paid employment for the handicapped, widows and orphans. The factory has a number of productive sections which include clothing, quilts, blankets, tents, blacksmithing and carpentry. The Committee is also active in the area of well digging and building shelters for refugees instead of placing them in tents.

The victims of natural disasters

Some Asian countries have been hit in recent years by natural disasters that made a large proportion of the population homeless. Many houses and buildings were destroyed. The most violent disaster was the earthquake that hit the area of Thamar in the Arab Republic of Yemen in 1982, resulting in a large number of casualties.

Three thousand people were killed, injured or lost. Many homes were demolished and many people became homeless. Inspired by the spirit of Arab and Islamic solidarity, the Saudi government and people came to the rescue of the victims of the earthquake; emergency supplies including relief materials, foodstuffs, medical supplies, tents and blankets were sent to shelter the homeless and alleviate their suffering. The Kingdom also co-operated with the Yemeni government in the reconstruction of the area that was hit by the earthquake, the implementation of social and urbanization projects, and the construction of vital utilities. The total assistance provided by the Kingdom in this area amounted to about 443 million riyals.

Other disasters include floods and hurricanes that hit some areas in Bangladesh, Jordan, South Yemen, Oman, Pakistan, Sri Lanka and India. In these harsh circumstances, the Kingdom provides assistance to the victims and their families, in honor of the principles of solidarity called for by Islam. Total assistance provided by the Kingdom in this area amounted to about 850 million riyals, which included cash, food and medical supplies, means of sheltering, and a contribution to the reconstruction of the ravaged areas. The Kingdom also provided donations to the victims of earthquakes in Turkey on various occasions, totalling about 87 million riyals.

19.2.3.2   *The Kingdom's role on the international scale*

In addition to the Kingdom's direct efforts in providing relief to the refugees in Asia and in supporting the means of sheltering them through bilateral channels, it has not overlooked the support of international efforts made in this area. The Kingdom contributes to the budget of the United Nations Relief and Works Agency for Palestine Refugees in the Near East (UNRWA) and supports the activities of the International Red Cross dedicated to the refugees and to the relief of victims of wars and natural disaster in Asia. In addition, the Kingdom contributes to specialized international and regional programs as mentioned, such as the World Food Program and the Arab Gulf Program for the United Nations Development Organization.

a)   The UNRWA:

This agency was established by the United Nations following the Israeli occupation of Palestine, and the expulsion of hundreds of thousands of Palestinians, for the purpose of sponsoring Palestinian refugee affairs and providing them with humanitarian and social services, as well as for training and creating job opportunities for those who are capable of working.

In appreciation of the role played by this agency and the humanitarian activities that it has provided for more than 2 million refugees, the Kingdom has contributed 4.5 million riyals to the agency's annual budget in addition to exceptional donations on various occasions amounting to about 225 million riyals dedicated for several purposes, including funding budget shortfalls, implementation of the programs for construction of refugee camps in Lebanon, and providing educational services as well as relief, food and medical supplies.

b) The International Committee of the Red Cross

This is an independent humanitarian foundation that works as a neutral mediator in cases of conflicts and disturbances to protect and assist the victims of world and civil wars, thus contributing to the settlement of peace in the world. The foundation provides assistance to prisoners, refugees and homeless families, as well as to Palestinian and Afghan refugees and victims of the Lebanese and the Iraq–Iran wars, etc.

In appreciation of the humanitarian role played by this foundation the Kingdom has contributed 750,000 riyals per year to its annual budget since 1976 in addition to exceptional donations in cases of emergency, totalling about 79 million riyals, to support the foundation's budget and to enable it to implement some of the projects and programs for Palestinian refugees in Lebanon and the victims of the armed conflicts in Lebanon and the Iraq–Iran war.

In the next chapter we will look at the image of the Kingdom of Saudi Arabia in the West, in particular in Britain and the United States of America. There will be little or no mention in that chapter of the massive contributions the Kingdom has made to the developing world, for the simple reason that those contributions do not constitute a significant element of the Kingdom's image in the West. Nevertheless, it is hoped that the criticisms levelled by the author at Western media treatment of the Kingdom will be seen not only in the political, economic and social context provided in the next chapter but also against the backdrop of the generous aid that Saudi Arabia has given and is still giving to countries less well-endowed and often desperate for help.

Chapter **20**

How others see us – concluding thoughts

In his earlier work, Saudi Arabia: A Case Study in Development, *the author drew attention to the poverty of coverage accorded to the Kingdom of Saudi Arabia in British and American news and current affairs publications. This criticism is no longer valid. In recent years, the Kingdom of Saudi Arabia has attracted very considerable coverage in both the quality and popular press in Britain and the United States of America. This chapter looks therefore at the nature of this greatly increased volume of coverage and examines the image of the Kingdom that this coverage projects.*

This chapter is concerned with the image of the "Arab world" in the Western media. It is not a treatise on communications theory or on the mechanics of Western journalism. But it is an attempt to express the Arab view on how the image of Arabs is projected in the Western media; to analyze specific aspects of this image; to trace the sources of Western media hostility; and to suggest ways in which matters might be improved.

The data on which these comments are based come mainly from the British and, to a lesser extent, from the American media but, in broad terms, in some degree, the analysis is relevant to the Western media as a whole.

Before embarking on this difficult topic, it is worth pointing out a major complication. It is common for the Western media, particularly in its more "popular" manifestations, to refer to the "Arab world" in its reports on Arab affairs. In one sense, the "Arab world" is a fiction. There are 23 Arab states, with a combined population of some 200 million people. In this list will be found monarchies and republics; free-enterprise systems and socialist systems; countries rich in natural resources, others less well-endowed: countries that have moved a long way down the road of development, others which remain under-developed. It should be obvious that to generalize about such diverse states entails very grave dangers. It is rather like generalizing about Europe (east and west).

Of course there are several other senses in which there is an "Arab world". First, there is a common religion, Islam, which binds these countries together; and secondly, there is the Arabic language. But even here, we must be careful. Islam itself has been divided historically into the Sunni and the Shi'ite branches of Islam and, even within these two major divisions, there are variant sects. The Arabic language is spoken throughout the Arabic world, but the dialects differ so greatly from one end of the "Arab world" to the other that oral communication between Arabs from different countries is not always easy.

There is a third sense, in which there is an "Arab world" – in the aspiration of the Arabs to achieve unity – to bring into existence, if you like, an "Arab world". But that, despite some progress in terms of increasing Arab solidarity, remains a goal rather than an achievement.

The reason for drawing attention to the ambiguity inherent in the term "Arab world" is simple. One of the features of Western media coverage is to treat Arab affairs as though they emanated from a single, unified entity. Because there is an emphasis on the negative aspects of Arab countries in news coverage, this results in a tendency to condemn all Arabs for the actions of a few. It is perhaps rather like condemning the "European world" for the actions of the Baader Meinhoff group.

The image of the Arab states at large and of the Kingdom of Saudi Arabia in particular in the Western media is then a vexed issue. Arabs feel that the treatment meted out to them by the Western media is generally negative, highly biased and often offensive.

What is the image of the Kingdom of Saudi Arabia/the "Arab world"? (Because of the tendency of the media to treat all Arabs as part of a united "Arab world", it is not easy to separate the image of one country from the image of them all. From now, where appropriate, we will use the expression "Saudi/Arab(s)" to reflect this blurring of distinction.) Taking Britain as our example, we find that there are, in fact, two images; one generated by the "popular" press; the other projected by the "quality" press and, to a lesser extent, by the broadcast media. These two images are not contradictory (there is a good deal of overlap), but the "quality" press and broadcast media project, as we would expect, a more complex and rounded picture.

On the assumption that the popular mind is reflected in or formed by the media, or both, it is reasonable to deduce the "popular" image of Saudi Arabia in Britain from the coverage of Saudi Arabia in the British "popular" press. From a study of every item published in the British national popular press which mentions Saudi Arabia between 1985 and mid-1989, we conclude that the salient characteristics (in alphabetical order) of the popular image of Saudi Arabia are these: it is extravagant, greedy, hostile, hypocritical, intolerant, puritanical, ruthless, uncivilized, undemocratic, unstable and violent.

In the quality press and the broadcast media, much of this "popular" stereotype is confirmed (in of course more restrained terms), but there are some additions. First, the Kingdom is portrayed as active on the diplomatic front, generally in a constructive way (in seeking peace with justice in the various inter-Arab and other Middle East conflict situations). Secondly, the Kingdom of Saudi Arabia is recognized as a major source of revenue (especially through arms purchases) for Britain.

Returning to the "popular" image, is it possible to explain how a country which has had generally friendly relations with Britain; which has provided Britain with major economic benefits; which, in many areas of foreign policy and in its general outlook, is supportive of the West; which, by any standard, has been outstandingly generous in its aid to the developing world (giving up to five times as much as the United States of America as a percentage of its gross national product); why such a country should be characterized in this negative fashion?

The answer lies, we believe, in a combination of factors (political, economic, social and religious) and we shall try to identify them. Many of the factors could be broadly categorized under the heading "cultural dissonance" – differences in culture which either genuinely provoke hostility or which simply lead to misunderstandings. But there is another factor, a political issue, which runs through and to some extent underlies all the other factors – the Palestinian/Israeli problem.

Before exploring the particular effect of the Palestinian/Israeli problem, let us consider each of the general factors which have helped to form the Saudi Arabian image in the West, trying to see how the negative stereotype we have described has arisen. We shall attempt this task by looking at four perspectives on Saudi Arabia, first from the point of view of the West, then from the Arab point of view.

20.1   The Western Viewpoint

20.1.1   The Political Perspective

The Middle East is perceived as a highly volatile and dangerous region of the world. Not only are there wars and major conflicts (the Iraq/Iran war; the civil war in Lebanon; the *Intifada*, the Palestinian uprising against the Israelis in the occupied territories), but there are also many extremists for whom, apparently, indiscriminate killing is a way of life. The region is then unstable and violent. Since the West has vital interests in the region, pre-eminently oil, this instability and violence are seen as a threat.

In as much as the Middle East is considered by some as the most likely venue for the start of a super-power confrontation, the Middle East can also be seen as a global threat to peace. Furthermore, many of the Arab countries in the Middle East are presented as undemocratic. They have not adopted Western forms of democratic representation and, since freedom and democracy are closely linked in the Western mind, it is concluded that they, or rather the people within those countries, are not "free".

20.1.2   The economic perspective

Media coverage of the Kingdom of Saudi Arabia in the context of economic affairs centers, not surprisingly, on oil. In the oil market, the Kingdom of Saudi Arabia is seen as the leading force in the Organization of Petroleum Exporting Countries which (as we have seen in Section 8.3.4 above), is widely portrayed as an "evil cartel". (Although Britain is a net exporter of oil, the British media have consistently promulgated the Western oil-importers' view of OPEC.)

The oil price rises in the 1970s, which had an impact not only on Western governments and industry but directly on motorists, are well remembered and the actions of OPEC in raising prices were, and still are, widely depicted as economic extortion.

20.1.3   The social perspective

From the point of view of media coverage, this is the most sensitive and vexed area of all.

The stereotype of the rich Saudi/Arab oil sheikh, absurdly extravagant, travelling abroad and squandering money on luxuries, buying property at grossly inflated prices, embarrassing shop and hotel staff with disproportionate gratuities and indulging in every conceivable worldly pleasure, is well-entrenched in the popular imagination and manifested with monotonous regularity in Western newspaper cartoons.

It would not be surprising if such a caricature, suggesting incalculable (and, it is assumed, unmerited) wealth, prompted some degree of envy. But envy alone is not enough to explain the general antipathy towards Saudi/Arabs. There are far more serious causes. There are genuine cultural differences which engender hostility.

First, the Kingdom of Saudi Arabia (and the Islamic world in general) is seen as repressive in its attitude to women. While Western women, through the feminist movement, have fought for a greater degree of independence and greater opportunities in the work-place, the attitude of Muslims to women, which tends to maintain the view that a woman's primary responsibility is to her family, has often been cited as a major example of irreconcilable differences between the two cultures.

Another supposed irreconcilable difference, already mentioned above, is the "undemocratic" nature of the Saudi Arabian and most other Arab governments. In this context, it is argued that personal freedom is given a low priority in the Arab world and that therefore the governments in those countries are repressive.

Thirdly, there is the question of the penal system. In the Kingdom of Saudi Arabia punishment for crime, based on the Holy *Qu'ran*, is seen by the West as harsh and is often construed as barbaric. Murderers and rapists are publicly executed. The penalty for proven adultery can be death. Amputations (of the hands of thieves) and public floggings also form part of the penal armory. Such punishments are greatly at variance with the current approach of the West to the sentencing of criminals. Furthermore, the Kingdom prohibits the production and consumption of alcohol. For the West, where the consumption of alcohol is so firmly interwoven into social life, and, in particular, for Westerners who have resided in the Kingdom, this divergence of attitude sometimes seems to be the most difficult of all differences in social attitude to accommodate.

20.1.4   The religious perspective

Here we need to look at the image of Islam as presented in the West. The coupling of the words "Islamic" and "Muslim" with the words "extremism" and "terrorism" is commonplace in the Western media. The result of such journalistic pairings is the creation of an image of Islam as a bloodthirsty religion in which the lives of innocents have little or no value.

In all racial caricature and stereotyping, there has to be a grain of truth. But the consistently negative interpretation of almost every aspect of Saudi/Arab life merits further analysis. We will now examine each of the perspectives identified above, but this time, from the Saudi/Arab viewpoint.

20.2   The Saudi/Arab Viewpoint

20.2.1   The political perspective

Of course, the Middle East is a highly volatile region, but that does not mean all states within it are violent or unstable. The Kingdom of Saudi Arabia has been a model of stability, with an uninterrupted organic development within the tenets of Islam since its inception.

Of course, the Kingdom of Saudi Arabia has not adopted the democratic institutions of the West, but it would be the height of cultural arrogance to argue that the combative bi- or multi-party system of the West is the only way to run a country for the benefit of its citizens – or indeed, that it is the only way to give the people a voice in how the country is run. It is arguable that the consensus politics of the Kingdom, with ready access for all citizens to senior government officers, including the Head of State, and the traditional Arab mechanisms for consultation at all levels of society on all issues, actually provides a more effective channel for democracy than a single vote cast for one monolithic political party every few years.

20.2.2   The economic perspective

Of course, oil is crucial to the needs of the developed world, but it is widely recognized by all those competent to judge that, within OPEC, the Kingdom of Saudi Arabia has consistently argued for moderation, trying, against considerable opposition on all sides, to strike a balance between the interests of producing and consuming nations.

20.2.3 The social perspective

In the area of social stereotyping, we must deal with a number of factors.

First, wealth. Some Arabs and some Saudi citizens enjoy great wealth and some of those have flaunted their wealth. But the same is true of every country in the world. There were, after all, some Americans in Britain after the Second World War, and some British in India during the Raj who, with vast relative wealth, showed little sensitivity to the relative poverty in Britain or the absolute poverty in India which surrounded them. But the Kingdom of Saudi Arabia should not need to deploy such an argument. The numbers of Saudi citizens who flaunt their wealth is a tiny minority and, in any case, the wealth this tiny minority squanders passes into and thus benefits the economy of the host countries as earned income from abroad.

On a more serious level, there is the question of the Islamic attitude to women. We have recounted elsewhere in this book (see Section 15.7) the advantages, in terms of financial security and financial independence, which women enjoy under Islam and, in the Kingdom of Saudi Arabia, there is a high level of educational opportunity (see Chapter 16). It is true that women are still restricted in career opportunities but even here the case is overstated. With at least some women holding leading positions in business and even in Aramco, the state oil company, the obstacles to advancement are clearly no longer insurmountable.

Nevertheless, there is a significant difference. The family is still considered the basic social unit under Islam and it is widely believed by Muslims that, for the family unit to be stable and to provide full opportunities for all its members, it is necessary for most women to find a major part of their fulfilment in accepting and discharging a primary obligation to the family.

Western society seems to have rejected this view (although in only relatively recent times) but it is at least arguable (and is indeed argued by many men and women in the West) that this shift in attitude has not been an unqualified success. It is never easy to be sure of the causative processes in social change, but it seems most unlikely that the increasing social instability, the increased crime rates, the increasing materialism and the erosion of moral values widely noted by social commentators in the West are entirely unconnected with the undermining of the family as society's basic unit. We hear that in many British and American cities many women and elderly people are "afraid to walk the streets at night". We read of single-parent families reliant on public or private social services, struggling against the odds to provide the security of a two-parent unit within an extended family. We are told that crimes of violence (on the street, in the home and, in Europe, even at football matches) occur with ever increasing frequency, despite determined government efforts to deal with the problem. None of this seems, to the Muslim mind, to be an obvious social advance.

We are not arguing that the West or the Western media should admit the error of their ways. It is perhaps possible that the social problems described above have nothing whatever to do with the weakening or dismantling of the conventional family unit which seems inevitably to accompany the "liberation" of women. But I am suggesting that only a very prejudiced mind would argue that the Muslim attitude towards women and their role within society is self-evidently socially "wrong".

Then, there is the Kingdom's Islamic penal system. This is not perhaps the place to enter into a detailed explanation of the religious and cultural basis for the punishment of criminals under the *Shari'ah* but it is worth pointing out that a penal system where the proscribed punishments are clear to all and, within the context of the values of that society, seem to be appropriate to the offence, has certain distinct social advantages in terms of strengthening the values of that society and deterring citizens from offending against its laws.

The Western media tend to focus on those aspects of the Islamic penal code which are most at variance with Western thinking, ignoring the subtlety and flexibility of the system. The punishment for adultery is a case in point. Adultery in the West is not considered a crime. Islam, on the other hand, mindful of the need for society to protect the family, condemns it – and the punishment is accordingly severe. But Islam is not unaware of human frailty. To prove adultery, it is necessary that four people should witness the act of adultery itself, assuredly a demanding requirement for the proof of guilt. Unless a couple wilfully flaunt their offence, thus openly challenging the authority of Islam, they are unlikely to face the proscribed punishment. In this way, society's need to condemn the offence is reconciled with an understanding of the weaknesses of human nature, without condoning them.

As we have said before, it is never easy to trace cause and effect in social phenomena, but it is fair to point out that the incidence of crime in the Kingdom of Saudi Arabia is extraordinarily low, compared with Britain or the United States of America. There may well be other factors which account for this difference but it is not impossible that a system of punishment that is clear and unambiguous, albeit tempered, when appropriate, with flexibility, understanding and compassion, makes a substantial contribution.

While on this subject, it is worthwhile commenting that some aspects of the Islamic code of punishment may well be more in line with popular opinion in the West than is generally supposed. For example, capital punishment for murder has been re-introduced in several states in America and every public opinion poll in Britain on the question of capital punishment has shown a substantial majority in favour of its re-introduction for certain offences. In cases of proven rape, the Islamic punishment would, at the least, seem to show more respect for the rights of women than the derisory sentences not infrequently passed on rapists in the West.

Finally, we should add that, as in the West, all criminal cases are dealt with under due process of law and that the sentence of the court is subject to a comprehensive appeals procedure.

Of course, the differences in attitude are real and should not be under-estimated. The penal code in the Kingdom of Saudi Arabia places much greater emphasis on the protection of the individual and society, and much less on exploring the motivations of the criminal. All we would argue here is that the Western media tend to distort the Islamic penal system, ignoring its merits and presenting only those aspects which are most at variance with the Western culture.

On the subject of alcohol, there is unlikely to be a meeting of minds, but this much can be said without fear of contradiction. Alcohol is a drug, legalized in the West, which is implicated in many thousands of instances of civil offences and criminal acts (eg violence in the home, civil disturbances, motoring offences, sexual offences) in every country which permits its sale. Taken in excess, it can lead to the destruction of families and careers and contributes to the hardships of poorer sections of the community by absorbing financial resources better spent on necessities. While it may be impractical for historical, cultural and social reasons for Western countries to prohibit alcohol, it is surely not unreasonable for those countries that can to ban it.

20.2.4 The religious perspective

Finally, there is the religious perspective, under which heading we noted the Western media's practice of coupling the words "Islamic" and "Moslem" with the words "extremism" and "terrorism".

Of course, such words as extremism and terrorism are relative and, in any case, involve a value judgement. One man's extremist is another man's moderate; one man's terrorist is another man's freedom-fighter. But leaving such niceties aside and accepting the need for compression in journalistic writing, we concede that such terms can be justified, when they are used to distinguish between Muslim extremists and either Muslim moderates or other extremists who are not Muslim; or between Muslim terrorists and either Muslims who are not terrorists or other terrorists who are not Muslim. That is not, however, the effect such couplings have had. They have tended to encourage the view, certainly in the popular mind, that all the followers of Islam are extremists and all Muslims are, actually or potentially, terrorists. (The same is true of the oft-used designation "Arab terrorists" where, again in the popular mind, "Arab" is not so much used as an identifier but more as a kind of racial eponym.)

This is the saddest distortion of all. Islam is a religion of justice, tempered with compassion. It has nothing to do with the indiscriminate slaughter of innocents, and terrorist outrages are condemned as widely and as energetically (and the perpetrators pursued as relentlessly) in the Muslim world as they are in the West.

There are approximately 1,000 million Muslims and 200 million Arabs, the vast majority of whom are law-abiding citizens. To stigmatize such a large proportion of the world's population because of the actions of a tiny minority is, of course, absurd, especially when it is remembered that it is largely the Arab countries which are threatened by acts of terrorism perpetrated by Arabs.

20.3   The Palestinian/Israeli problem

We have now looked, albeit briefly, at how the West (primarily Britain and the United States of America) sees the Kingdom of Saudi Arabia and the "Arab world", and how the Kingdom of Saudi Arabia and the "Arab world" react to Western perceptions.

It is clear that there are major cultural differences and it is entirely legitimate that such differences should generate some cultural friction and entirely predictable that the Western media should reflect this friction. But the cultural differences are not, in our view, sufficient to account for the consistently hostile attitude of much of the Western media to Arabs, certainly not when the areas of common interest and mutual benefit in political and economic terms are taken into account. This conclusion leads us inevitably to consider the effect of the Palestinian/Israeli problem on Arab/Western relations, and this time I will begin by expounding the Arab view of this contentious issue.

All readers of this book will be familiar with how the state of Israel was formed. Zionist agitation throughout the early decades of the twentieth century, given renewed impetus by the Nazi persecution of the Jews in Europe in the 1930s and throughout the Second World War, eventually led in 1948 to Ben Gurion's declaration of a new state – the state of Israel, thus fulfilling Jewish aspirations for their own homeland.

But what is seen in the West as a truly epic story, as the legitimate aspiration of a people to find a home, was and is seen in the Arab world as the ruthless and systematic persecution and dispossession of the Palestinians by an immigrant, if not a colonial, power. The land where Israel was founded was not a vacuum, waiting to be filled; it was Palestine, a land peopled by Palestinians for centuries. Thus, as one people found, or perhaps more accurately occupied, a home, another lost theirs. Throughout the Jewish agitation for a state in Palestine, the Zionists' plans were opposed by the Palestinians in particular and the Arab world in general. When the founder of the Kingdom of Saudi Arabia, the late King Abdul Aziz bin Sa'ud met President Roosevelt on the cruiser USS *Quincy* in February 1945, President Roosevelt gave a promise – or rather two promises – to the Saudi King:

> – he would never do anything which might prove hostile to the Arabs
> – the US government would make no change in its basic policy on Palestine without full and prior consultation with both Jews and Arabs

Immediately after Roosevelt's death, President Truman ignored these promises and, perhaps more concerned with popularity at home than justice abroad, worked tirelessly for the formation and recognition of the state of Israel – and thus for the dispossession of the Palestinians.

Whatever the reasons for President Truman's decision to ignore the undertakings of his predecessor, this much is certain. When the state of Israel was declared, the Arab world felt betrayed. And the seeds of several wars, the sufferings of millions of refugees and the grim situation we face today were sown.

Well, some say, that is all history. Israel and those who support her hope that, with time, the Palestinian problem will disappear; that the Palestinians will be absorbed by other countries; and that their aspirations for nationhood and for the land of their fathers will somehow disappear. This is an irrational and extremely dangerous notion. The Palestinians know they have been dispossessed. Those who remain under Israeli rule are deeply resentful. The *Intifada*, the Palestinian uprising in the occupied territories, in 1988/89, in which hundreds of Palestinians, armed only with sticks or stones, have been shot dead by Israeli troops, gives some indication of how deep that resentment runs. And the Palestinian refugees living in camps in other Arab countries will not forget the homes and the land which belonged to them.

To the Arabs, it seems (as indeed King Abdul Aziz bin Sa'ud explained to President Roosevelt) that with a twisted logic, in some way, the Palestinians are being made to expiate the crimes of the Nazis. And that, because of those Nazi crimes, the Israelis are somehow excused for whatever action they take against those whom they have dispossessed. If this is the case, it is time the West acknowledged that the crimes of one society cannot be expiated by allowing the victims of those crimes to perpetrate crimes against another. If all peoples have a right to self-determination, then the Palestinians must have that right. If it is wrong to expel and persecute those who seek basic human rights, then surely the Palestinians have been sorely wronged.

For obvious historical reasons, the West has great sympathy for Israel. The persecution of the Jews by the Nazis has led, understandably, to feelings of guilt both in the country of the erstwhile persecutors and amongst other Western countries who could have done more to save the Jews from that persecution. (An indication of how deep that guilt runs is to be found in the frequency with which television programs and films in Britain and the United States of America still feature the Nazi persecution of the Jews.) But Arabs cannot understand how justifiable sympathy for one persecuted people can somehow excuse the persecution of another. If it was wrong for the Nazis to deny the rights of citizenship to the Jews, it must surely be wrong for Israel to deny the rights of citizenship to the Palestinians; if it was wrong for the Nazis to use the military power of the state to oppress a people, it must be wrong for the Israelis to oppress the Palestinians. If it was wrong for the Nazis to arrest Jews without due process of law, it must be wrong for the Israelis to carry out mass arrests of Palestinians without due legal process.

Of course the parallel is not exact. But it is sufficiently close for any reasonable person to realize that similar issues of moral principle are involved. And yet the media retain their sympathy for Israel, even when Israel's conduct clearly offends against basic human rights. In 1989, as the Palestinian death toll in the Intifada rose inexorably, the Red Cross, after many months of fruitless remonstration with the

Israeli authorities, condemned Israel in the strongest of terms for its brutal treatment of the Palestinians in the occupied territories. Yet there were no front-page leader headlines in the British press publicizing this condemnation and still the main tenor of press editorial comment in Britain and the United States of America argued for sympathy and understanding for Israel as it continued to obstruct attempts to find a peaceful means of according the Palestinians the right to self-determination in a land of their own.

What has all this to do with Arab/Western relations and with the image of the Arabs in the Western media? The answer is, or so it seems to Arabs, obvious. The only "satisfactory" way to deny human rights to a people is to deny that people's humanity. If the Palestinians are viewed as decent human beings, to deny them basic human rights is clearly morally unacceptable. But if it can be shown that they and their supporters have forfeited their claim to belong to the world community of decent humanity – because they are, for example, extravagant, greedy, hostile, hypocritical, intolerant, puritanical, ruthless, uncivilized, undemocratic, unstable and violent – the moral dilemma is, at least, diminished.

In other words, to some (and probably to a large) extent, media hostility to the Arabs ensues from a Western commitment to Israel's cause, and the consequent need to de-humanize those who oppose Israel, in order to justify Israel's inhumane behavior. The mechanism whereby this process is accomplished is a continuing emphasis on those aspects of Arab society which differ from Western culture – and, of course, an equally persistent emphasis on those aspects of Israeli society which Israel shares with the West.

Thus, Israel, which effectively disenfranchizes its Palestinian population, is nevertheless routinely described by the Western media as "democratic", in contrast with the "un-democratic" Arabs. Israel's judiciary, despite the random arrest and imprisonment of Palestinians, is characterized as based on Western principles of justice, in contrast with the "barbarity" of the Islamic penal system. Even Israel's ruthless suppression of the *Intifada* is often presented as the response of the forces of law and order to the violence of dissidents and terrorists, despite the fact that the *Intifada* is taking place in land which Israel has occupied as a foreign army.

It is generally recognized that in the United States of America (and, to a lesser extent, in Britain) politicians and the media alienate the Zionist lobby at their peril. It has even been said that no one becomes the President of the United States without the support of the pro-Israeli pressure groups. Aware of the need to sustain support for Israel, the Zionists, through the American Israeli Public Affairs Committee (AIPAC) and its British counterpart (BIPAC) and through other pro-Israeli pressure groups, use their influence to maintain the image of Israel as part of the Western community and draw attention to any cultural difference which divides the West and the Arab world. They have their clearly defined objectives and they work effectively to fulfil them.

Thus two great communities, the Western industrialized societies and the "Arab world" are, despite mutual self-interest, kept apart, and it would seem that even between the West and the Kingdom of Saudi Arabia, one of the West's staunchest allies amongst all the Arab nations, a wedge is driven.

It is to be hoped that one day soon the rights of the Palestinians will be fully recognized by the West and by Israel. In 1989, the Palestine Liberation Organization accepted the right of Israel to exist, thus conceding part of the territory to which they had a legitimate claim. The conditions for a peaceful settlement of the issue now exist. Israel, before all, should be able to understand the aspirations of a people for a land of its own and full rights to self-determination. If Israel still remains obdurate, she will forfeit the sympathy she still retains in the West. When the Secretary of State of the United States of America, Israel's patron and guarantor, can say, in an address to the American-Israel Public Affairs Committee:

> Forswear annexation. Stop settlement activities. Allow schools to re-open. Reach out to the Palestinians as neighbors who deserve political rights.
>
> James Baker, US Secretary of States, 23rd May 1989

it must be clear to Israel that the goodwill and the patience of even the most pro-Zionist of all countries is not inexhaustible.

If the hopes for a just peace are fulfilled, we are confident that the friendship and trust that should exist between the West and the Arabs will, at last, be allowed to flourish once again, unhindered by distortion, to strengthen the political and economic ties which naturally bind us together.

Selected bibliography

Arabian Days, Sheikh Hafiz Wahba, Arthur Barker Limited, London, 1964

Arabian Fauna, John and Patricia Gasperetti, Middle East Economic Digest, 1981

Arabia Unified, A Portrait of Ibn Saud, Mohammed Almana, Hutchinson Benham Limited, London, 1980

The Cambridge Encyclopaedia of the Middle East and North Africa, Cambridge University Press, 1989

A Guide to Doing Business in the Kingdom of Saudi Arabia, Commercial Office, Royal Embassy of Saudi Arabia, Washington, DC

The Middle East and North Africa, 35th edition, Europa Publications Limited, London, 1989

OPEC Statute, Organization of Petroleum Exporting Countries, Vienna, 1986

OPEC Annual Report – 1987, the Organization of Petroleum Exporting Countries

OPEC at a Glance, Organization of Petroleum Exporting Countries, Vienna

Riyadh, The City of the Future, published by the King Saud University Press, Riyadh

Saudi Arabia: A Case Study in Development, Dr Fouad Al-Farsy, 4th edition, Kegan Paul International, London, 1986

Wild Flowers of central Saudi Arabia, Betty A Lipscombe Vincett, 1977

The World in 1989, The Economist, London

The statistical information in this book has been drawn primarily from Saudi Arabian government sources.

Extensive use has been made of the Kingdom's *Statistical Year Book* (1987 edition), published by the Central Department of Statistics, Ministry of Finance and National Economy, and of the many other documents, containing invaluable statistical data, published by that Ministry.

The sections on the planning process within the Kingdom use as their source the Development Plans published by the Ministry of Planning.

In addition, the author has obtained from the Kingdom's governmental and other institutions current information on their responsibilities, performance and plans.

Index